Social Work Supervision

Social Work Supervision

Classic Statements and Critical Issues

Edited by
Carlton E. Munson

THE FREE PRESS
A Division of Macmillan Publishing Co., Inc.
NEW YORK

Collier Macmillan Publishers
LONDON

The Free Press
A Division of Macmillan Publishing Co., Inc.
866 Third Avenue, New York, N.Y. 10022

Collier Macmillan Canada, Ltd.

Library of Congress Catalog Card Number: 78–72149

Printed in the United States of America

printing number

           6 7 8 9 10

Library of Congress Cataloging in Publication Data
Main entry under title:

Social work supervision.

    Includes bibliographical references and index.
    1. Supervision of social workers--Addresses, essays,
lectures. I. Munson, Carlton E.
HV41.S6615   658.3'02   78-72149
ISBN 0-02-922280-X

To Joan and Camellia

Contents

III. STRUCTURAL CHARACTERISTICS

IV. ORGANIZATIONAL AUTHORITY AND PROFESSIONAL AUTONOMY

V. RESEARCH

VI. FUTURE TRENDS

Preface and Acknowledgements

Supervision is generally considered an essential component of effective and efficient social work; yet there have been no attempts before now to provide an overview of the relevant literature systematically interrelating the representative articles that have appeared over the years. This book is designed to bring together readings that survey both the historical and the current conceptions of social work supervision. They are oriented to the supervision of practitioners in traditional settings. All the readings have been previously published, except for two papers delivered at conferences (Sharlin and Chaiklin, and Young), and two chapters of my own (25 and 29) written for this volume.

The thirty-one selections cover six major areas: (1) historical perspectives, (2) essential knowledge and skills, (3) structural characteristics, (4) organizational authority and professional autonomy, (5) research, and (6) future trends. The articles in each section are summarized and interrelated in an introduction. The general introduction serves as an overview for the six sections and provides a brief summary of the historical evolution of the literature.

The material on the historical aspects of supervision is especially important because it is the first published attempt to document its origins and early conceptions. The view presented here will be considered controversial by some, but the arguments are based on thorough and repeated reviews of the early literature as well as hours of stimulating discussion with former professors and colleagues. I hope that these views will generate more discussion and academic debate in this area.

The issues of structure and authority involved in supervision have been addressed in various jorunals, but no previous effort has been made to focus and unify this material. The idea of exercising authority over professionals has always been an underlying theme in supervision and is today receiving renewed and refocused attention in social work; it is my intention that the material on authority included in several sections of this text will contribute to systematic analysis.

The book is designed for use in graduate and undergraduate social work programs as a primary text or supplemental reader and for teaching supervision as a part of staff development and continuing education. Since the articles cover several different areas, educators and staff-development specialists can use the entire text, several sections selectively, or individual sections or articles, depending upon the needs of the group involved and the time available. The book can also serve as a ready reference for use in daily practice as problems and questions arise. For both new and experienced supervisors wanting information about how to exercise authority appropriately and how best to structure supervision, many of the articles describe practical applications and potential problems to be aware of at the outset. The book can serve as a helpful guide and source of ideas as an individual supervisor or an agency staff tries to reconceptualize or restructure supervision practices.

The bibliography at the end of the volume includes all the major materials on supervision I encountered in reviewing the literature, including many outstanding and relevant readings that are not reprinted here because of space restrictions. Decisions on inclusion were based on an article's representativeness of major historical and current issues in supervision practice.

The bibliography also includes citations on field instruction and psychiatric supervision, two important areas that are related to but distinct from professional social work supervision. Presumably many readers of this volume will also have an interest in the field-instruction literature. References on psychiatric supervision have been included because of the similarities in supervision of the two disciplines and because the psychiatric literature is much more research-oriented than has been the case in social work, and thus has much to offer in terms of models and methodological frameworks for conceptualizing research.

I have been reading, gathering materials, researching, discussing and debating, and teaching classes and workshops in supervision for more than ten years, since the idea for this book first occurred to me, and there is no way I can state my appreciation to all the people who have contributed to the process of making this book a reality.

However, there are a number of people without whose assistance I would probably not have achieved the knowledge necessary to take on such a project. I am indebted to Drs. Ruth Young, Daniel Thursz, Verl Lewis, Harris Chaiklin, Ernest Kahn, and David Lewis, who guided my initial research on supervision. All of these people provided help in numerous other ways as well, and I will remain appreciative of their professional generosity throughout my career. I want to thank Gladys Topkis, editor at The Free Press, who has provided assistance and support throughout this project, and Fred Sard at the Free Press for his diligence and help with the many details of preparing the final manuscript. I also appreciate the remarks and suggestions of the anonymous reviewer of the initial manuscript.

I am especially appreciative of the support and encouragement provided by my wife, Joan, who spent long hours struggling with the typewriter, the dictionary, and the footnotes to produce the final manuscript. If it had not been for her, this book would not have been attempted or completed.

I cannot name them all, but I want to express deep appreciation to all the agencies, workers, supervisors, students, and colleagues who over the years shared their ideas and experiences with me. These people gave their time and thoughts freely and responded in a way that has given added strength to my already strong commitment to the profession of social work.

CARLTON E. MUNSON

About the Contributors

PAUL ABELS, PhD, is Professor and Associate Dean, School of Applied Social Science, Case Western Reserve University, Cleveland, Ohio. Dr. Abels has published articles in *Social Work, Child Welfare*, and *Public Welfare*, and a book entitled *The New Practice of Supervision and Staff Development*. He has been a Fellow in Human Relations at Boston University and a Fulbright Lecturer in Turkey

LUCILLE N. AUSTIN was Professor of Social Work at the New York School of Social Work of Columbia University at the time her article was written.

FRED BERL, PhD, retired, formerly Director of Professional Services, Jewish Family and Children's Service, Baltimore, Maryland. Dr. Berl has published articles in *Social Work, Social Casework, Journal of Jewish Communal Service*, and *Journal of Casework Process*.

JEFFREY RICHARDSON BRACKETT, PhD (1860–1949), educator and author, taught social work courses at Johns Hopkins University, Harvard University, and Simmons College. He published several books and many articles on social work during his career.

HARRIS CHAIKLIN, PhD, is Professor, School of Social Work and Community Planning, University of Maryland at Baltimore. Dr. Chaiklin has published articles in *Orthopsychiatry, Social Work, Social Service Review, Child Welfare, Public Welfare, Journal of Sociology and Social Welfare, Health and Social Work*, and *Rehabilitation Literature*. He has published a book entitled *Marian Chase: Her Papers*. During 1976–1977 Dr. Chaiklin was a

Senior Fulbright Lecturer at Haifa University and during 1977–1978 a Visiting Professor at Morgan State University.

CARY CHERNISS, PhD, is Assistant Professor of Psychology, Department of Psychology, University of Michigan. Dr. Cherniss has published articles in *Community Mental Health Journal, American Journal of Community Psychology, Psychiatry, Professional Psychology, Social Work, Journal of Consulting and Clinical Psychology.*

EDWARD EGNATIOS, MSW, is Executive Director, Inter-faith Center for Racial Justice, Grosse Pointe, Michigan.

LAURA EPSTEIN, MSW, is Professor of Social Work, The School of Social Service Administration, University of Chicago. Professor Epstein has published articles in *Social Work* and *Child Welfare.* She has written two books with William J. Reid entitled, *Task-Centered Casework* and *Task-Centered Practice.*

YONATA FELDMAN, ACSW, was formerly Case Consultant for the Jewish Board of Guardians in New York City.

WILBUR A. FINCH, JR., DSW, is Associate Professor, School of Social Work, University of Southern California. Dr. Finch has published articles in *Social Work Education Reporter, Journal of Education for Social Work, Public Welfare, Social Work, and Social Work Papers.* In 1977 he received the Distinguished Faculty Award presented by Los Amigos de la Humanidad at the University of Southern California.

RUTH FIZDALE, ACSW, resides in New York City and was formerly Executive Director, A. Lehman Counseling Service, Newark, New Jersey. She has published articles in *Mental Hygiene, Social Casework, Journal of Jewish Communal Service*, and *Social Welfare Forum.* Ms. Fizdale has written a book entitled *Social Agency Structure and Accountability: The Arthur Lehman Counseling Service, A Case History.* She has served on the Board of Directors of the National Association of Social Workers, and in 1970 received the Social Worker of the Year award from the New York State Chapter.

LILLIAN HAWTHORNE, MSW, is Supervisor of Children's Services, Department of Public Social Services, Los Angeles, California.

DOROTHY HUTCHINSON (1905–1956), educator and author, taught social work at the School of Social Work, Columbia University, New York, New York.

ALFRED KADUSHIN, PhD, is Professor of Social Work, School of Social Work, University of Wisconsin (Madison). Dr. Kadushin has published articles in *Child Welfare, Social Work, Social Service Review,* and *Social Casework,* and his books include *Social Work Interview, Social Work Supervision, Social Work Consultation,* and *Child Welfare Services.*

CHARLES S. LEVY, DSW, is Professor, Wurzweiler School of Social Work, Yeshiva University. Dr. Levy has published articles in *Social Work, Social Service Review, Journal of Education for Social Work, Adult Leadership,* and *Journal of Jewish Communal Service.* His books include *Social Work Ethics, Justice, Justice Shalt Thou Pursue,* and *Education and Training for the Fundraising Function.* Dr. Levy is Chairman of the National Association of Social Workers' Task Force on Ethics.

BETTY REID MANDELL, MSW, is Associate Professor, Boston State College. Ms. Mandell has published articles in *Social Work, Journal of Education for Social Work,* and *Social Welfare in Appalachia.* Her books include *Where are the Children? A Class Analysis of Foster Care and Adoption* and *Welfare In America: Controlling the Dangerous Classes.* She has served on the editorial board of *Social Work.*

CARLTON E. MUNSON, DSW, is Assistant Professor of Social Work, Graduate School of Social Work, University of Houston. Dr. Munson has published articles in *Journal of Education for Social Work, Offender Rehabilitation, Arete, Social Work, Human Services in the Rural Environment, California Sociologist,* and *Journal of Sociology and Social Welfare.* In addition to this volume, he has published books entitled *Social Work Education and Practice* and *No Nonsense Research.*

MARY RICHMOND (1861–1928), practitioner, educator, and author, was General Secretary of the Baltimore and Philadelphia Charity Organization Societies, and faculty member of the New York School of Philanthropy. She wrote several books and many articles on social work during her career.

VERNON RICKERT, MSSW, is Clinical Social Worker and Student Supervisor, Family and Children's Agency, Louisville, Kentucky. Mr. Rickert has published articles in *Social Casework* and *Marriage and Family Living.* He also is coauthor of a chapter in the book, *Parenting,* edited by Paul F. Wilczak.

FRANCES H. SCHERZ, MSW (d. 1972); from 1950 until her death in 1972,

Ms. Scherz was Director of Casework, Jewish Family and Community Service, Chicago, Illinois.

W. RICHARD SCOTT, PhD, is Professor of Sociology, Department of Sociology, Stanford University. Dr. Scott has published articles in *Administrative Science Quarterly, Journal of Health and Social Behavior, Annual Review of Sociology,* and *Milbank Memorial Fund Quarterly.* His books include *Formal Organizations,* with P. M. Blau; *Medical Care,* with E. H. Volkart; and *Social Processes and Social Structures: Evaluation and the Exercise of Authority,* with S. M. Dornbusch.

SHLOMO A. SHARLIN, PhD, is Dean and Associate Professor of Social Work, The University of Haifa, Israel. Dr. Sharlin has published articles in *Child Welfare, American Journal of Orthopsychiatry, Educational Technology,* and *Social Casework.* He is coauthor of *Child Neglect: Understanding and Reaching the Parent.*

EVELYN STILES was Assistant Professor at the School of Applied Social Sciences, Western Reserve University, Cleveland, Ohio, at the time her article was written.

JOHN E. TURNER, MSSW, is in private practice of social work in Louisville, Kentucky, and is Assistant Adjunct Professor at the Raymond A. Kent School of Social Work, University of Louisville. He has published articles in *Social Casework.*

HARRY WASSERMAN, DSW, is Associate Professor, School of Social Welfare, University of California at Los Angeles. Dr. Wasserman has published articles in *Social Work, Public Welfare,* and *Smith College Studies in Social Work.*

JOHN H. WAX, MA, is Chief Social Worker, Veteran's Administration Hospital, Palo Alto, California.

RUTH YOUNG, DSW, is Dean and Professor, School of Social Work and Community Planning, University of Maryland at Baltimore. Dr. Young has published articles in *Public Welfare* and *Child Welfare* and a book entitled *The ABCD Project: An Assessment of a Black Adoption Project.*

ELIZABETH R. ZETZEL, MD, was consultant in the Veteran's Administration and on the staff of Massachusetts General Hospital at the time her article was written.

Introduction

Since the time social work was first identified as a profession, supervision has been considered an essential and important source of growth and competency in practice. Supervision has served as an arena where much of the knowledge about practice has evolved, and it has long been regarded as a process designed to promote effective and efficient delivery of service. Because of these aspects, teaching and administration traditionally have been considered the two basic functions of supervision. A third function of help or support was added later, when a therapeutic orientation to certain practice areas developed.

Over the years a number of books and articles have appeared that focus in some way on the teaching, administration, and/or helping functions of supervision. These writings generally suggest methods to best implement these functions or to address problems, issues, and dilemmas presented by the supervision of professionals who have a dubious degree of autonomy in practice. Authority is a theme that runs throughout the literature and cuts across all three of the supervisory functions. There has been no final resolution of the authority-versus-autonomy dilemma, and it will probably remain a problem for some time to come.

The earliest definitions of supervision dealt with managing agencies as helping institutions and efforts to promote social justice for individuals admitted to them. When training for social work emerged in the late 1800s and the concept of the professional social worker was established, individualized supervision developed around articulating roles and tasks of the supervisor and the worker. When the individual case method emerged at the turn of the century and emphasis shifted from supervising the case to supervising the caseworker, the concept of individual supervision became a part of the struggle over control; the agencies and the newly founded training schools for social work used the indoctrination provided to trainees in supervision to demonstrate the "best" means to educate workers for practice and to illustrate their respective philosophies regarding the worker's most suitable role and function. As the schools grew and agency training programs diminished, the schools increasingly drew on theory to prepare students for practice, and agency directors feared that this emphasis would be at the expense of practical knowledge.

The theory utilized by the schools to organize teaching was largely drawn from psychology; in fact, the educational leaders and writers of this era used supervision as a means of teaching psychological theory by applying it to the supervisees as much as to the clients. From this point on, supervision became associated heavily with training for the profession, which is essentially an indoctrination and controlling process. Psychological theory, mainly Freudian, dominated writing and teaching in supervision until the 1950s. The general emphasis was to use psychological theory to promote the growth of the supervisee, who was viewed as an immature person to be developed through identification with the supervisor. In the late 1950s, when social work became professionalized through the establishment of a broad-based professional organization, attention turned to defining and distinguishing between administration and teaching in supervision. The underlying focus of argument seemed to be autonomy versus control of professionally trained practitioners. At the same time, the literature from the 1950s to the present really reflects the culmination of a process that was taking place for quite some time before. Only through understanding these origins can we deal with and understand supervision as it currently exists.

Since the 1950s, the trend in supervision has been to shift from psychological to sociological theory. Modern writers have drawn on the work of Weber, Simmel, Merton, Goffman, Mead, Etzioni, Blau, Gouldner, and other sociologists to conceptualize supervision on the basis of roles, positions, statuses, and interactions within organizations rather than focus, as before, on individual occupants of positions. This new theoretical orientation has tended to crystallize the problem of autonomy within organizations. Although the frame of reference for analyzing supervision has gradually shifted, there is general agreement that supervision will play an important role in the professional lives of social workers for some time to come; and the image of the social worker functioning with the degree of autonomy characteristic of certain other professions is not a very realistic hope. Recent developments within the profession, such as licensing laws, emphasis on specialization in practice, differentiation in levels of practice, concern with lifelong learning, mandatory continuing-education requirements in certain positions, reconceptualization and restructuring of social work education, unionization and collective bargaining, and the involvement of social workers in professional-standards review organizations in some settings, all have implications for supervision. Some of these changes have more impact than others, and some are so new and unclarified that the nature of the impact is unknown.

It was with the historical development of supervision in mind—at the same time trying to address some of the positive potential and the prospective problems raised by emerging trends in the profession—that I decided to develop this book, sequentially organizing and interrelating representative writings. Much of the early literature is helpful in understanding the heritage of supervision that has evolved over the years. One aim of this book is to help overcome the misconception of many students and practitioners that professional social work somehow originated in the 1960s. With more accurate understanding will come, I hope, a more general appreciation for the extensive heritage of the social work profession. Some of the readings in this volume and the bibliographic citations may provide the stimulus to search further in the rich and abundant literature on the history of supervision and the profession.

Much of the previous literature specifies procedures and processes for conducting supervision that are relevant today and yet are largely ignored in practice. Selections from this literature have been included so that those concerned with supervision can organize their approaches efficiently and avoid reinventing the wheel, a redundancy a dynamic profession such as social work can ill afford in a complex, rapidly changing society.

PART I

Historical
Perspectives

INTRODUCTION

IN EXPLORING CONCEPTIONS of social work supervision, the early writings defined it as a broad institutional process which involved providing surveillance of all charitable and correctional institutions and recommending changes that would make them more efficient and economical in operation.[1] Supervision of public institutions was carried out by boards and associations under the sanction of the state legislatures.[2] Early private or voluntary charity was brought under similar administration and supervision in a single agency [3] with the development of the various charity organization societies (COS). Only later did the concept of individual supervision develop, when it became increasingly clear that effective case treatment could be achieved only by full-time workers with education, experience, and professional discipline.[4] This realization led to the development of training schools for social work.

By the early 1900s the concept of individual staff supervision was well defined. Its functions were to keep the work of the agency up to the standards it set for itself and to promote the professional development of the staff.[5] The first function of individual supervision is similar to the conception of institutional supervision in terms of regulation, control, and accountability. Institutional supervision cannot be equated with individual, but there seem to be similarities, parallels, and links between the two concepts historically that have remained unexplored. The first article in this section, by Jeffrey R. Brackett, helps shed light on the earliest conceptions of supervision at the institutional and individual level.

Control has always been an element in social work supervision. In the very earliest stages of dealing with social problems it took the form of controlling institutions. As various groups working in this area became involved directly in administering budgets and dispensing resources, control in the sense of the supervision of institutions became direct and complete. In this process the object of concern shifted from protecting the individual against inhumane practices to public accountability for expenditures.

With the emergence at the turn of the century of the individual case method and the concept of individual supervision, there occurred a subsequent growth of training schools for social work which came to use psychological theory in training caseworkers and supervisors, making a rather distorted use of the ideas of earlier leaders to build theories of supervision. The association of supervision with training for the profession became prevalent, and writing on and teaching of supervision was pervaded by psychological theory, largely Freudian. Recently, however, interest has begun to develop in supervision as an administrative process rather than one of personal growth, but most of the writing of this nature draws heavily upon the emerging theory of organizations, which also deals directly with authority and control.

Brackett, in a selection from his book *Supervision and Education in Charity,* published in 1903, surveys the events of the era related to supervision as the role of the individual worker was emerging. For him academic education was essential, but training was defined as a separate and important component in which the professional worker was guided by experienced practitioners. The value of this training was to be measured through judicious leadership governed by a scientific spirit. Brackett illustrated this view by describing Zelpha Smith's early effort at group supervision, more appropriately referred to as group consultation, and emphasized the need for the formalization of such programs. Through scientific application of standards, Brackett believed, better-educated people would be attracted to social work, and high-quality schools would be induced to establish social work programs. Brackett summarizes the events taking place at the turn of the century and explains how the educative function of supervision was established; he also gives a preliminary definition of individual supervision as experimental training through association with skilled workers as personal assistants.

The selections by Mary Richmond on "The Comparison of Material" and "Supervision and Review," originally published in 1917, discuss supervision in the context of diagnosis. She explored the role of the supervisor and emphasized the importance of recording as a vehicle through which the supervisor and worker can study case material. This discussion is refreshing in light of recent findings by Kadushin [6] that in spite of the increased availability and economy of electronic teaching devices, there is virtually no sharing of practice material in the supervisory relationship. Richmond also viewed the sharing of recorded case material as a means of discovering wider aspects of cases and detecting recurring problems so that they could be reported to those responsible for social reform. This description comes close to the modern conception of the supervisor as mediator, but research by Munson [7] reveals that few workers today so view their supervisors. Richmond was not concerned with control, emphasizing the supervisory relationship as a way of building knowledge for the profession. Her "Supervision and Review Questionnaire" has been included because it still has relevance today as a guide for evaluating performance.

The Milford Conference Report, published in 1929, demonstrates the same concern with building knowledge and the adequacy of training programs articulated by Richmond. Supervision is viewed as important because of the lack of good university-based educational programs. The participants focused on contracting between organizations and employees in matters of personnel and professional development. The administrative aspects of supervision are discussed in this context and combined with the teaching function, which was introduced in earlier writings. Richmond's conception of the wider aspects of supervision and documentation of common recurring problems are stated with more precision in the report's statement that the supervisor has a reciprocal responsibility to workers and that supervision should be conducted in an atmosphere of teamwork, which permits worker involvement in formulating policy. The function of supervision is defined as the promotion of standards of service and professional development, and the essential characteristics of the supervisory role are evaluation, accessibility, and recognition.

Hutchinson's article, published in 1935, demonstrates the impact of psychoanalytic theory on supervision. She places heavy emphasis on relationship and uses the principles of Freudian theory to compare the supervisor-worker relationship with that of the worker and client. The influence of psychoanalytic thinking is demonstrated in her contention that some problems encountered in supervision warrant the intervention of a psychiatrist. For Hutchinson, the concepts of authority, domination, control, and checking are distinguished from intervention into workers' personal problems through the supervisory relationship. However, as later articles reveal, this distinction was hard to maintain; eventually it blurred and became problematic.

The article by Zetzel illustrates the moderate shift away from emphasis on psychoanalytic principles in supervision that began in the 1950s as the modern concept of professional social work emerged. There is renewed emphasis on the educative aspect of supervision in which the role of the supervisee is equated with that of the learner in the child-rearing process. Supervision is portrayed as a maturation process, and Zetzel postulates that didactic and therapeutic situations are incompatible. Even though supervision is not therapy, the relationship need not be cold, formal, and uninvolved.

The evolution of social work supervision described in this section is based on an orientation of relationship and interaction which sets the stage for the remaining sections of this book, in which the roles of education, administration, and helping in supervision are discussed and explored in depth.

NOTES

1. Walter I. Trattner, *From Poor Law to Welfare State* (New York: The Free Press, 1974), p. 79.
2. *Ibid.*, p. 78.
3. *Ibid.*, p. 80.
4. *Ibid.*, p. 92.
5. Report of the Milford Conference, *Social Case Work: Generic and Specific* (New York: American Association of Social Workers, 1929; reprint ed., Washington, D.C.: National Association of Social Workers Classic Series, 1974), p. 55 [see Chapter 4 below, p. 33–34].
6. Alfred Kadushin, "Supervisor-Supervisee: A Survey," *Social Work* 19 (May 1974), p. 295 [Chapter 22 below, p. 254].
7. Carlton E. Munson, *The Uses of Structural Authority and Teaching Models in Social Work Supervision*, doctoral dissertation, University Microfilms, Ann Arbor, Mich., 1975, pp. 160–162.

1

Training for Work

Jeffrey R. Brackett

ACADEMIC WORK IS RARELY TRAINING, if a distinction, for the sake of convenience, may be made between teaching and training. Occasional inspection of institutions is of comparatively little value. The first thought, and most of the thought and time of college students, must be given to classwork, lectures, and reading. Above all, the essential element in training can seldom be found—the constant guidance in details of the person of experience, who knows of, and thinks constantly of, and believes in, the little things as well as the larger issues of philanthropic work.

Persons who take up philanthropic work as a calling or a leading interest, whether as paid officials or as volunteers, need to get as quickly and well as possible, with little waste to themselves and injury to others, the element which enters with instruction to make up education—experience. They should, if possible, give their best thought for a time to achieve observation and practice, under the guidance of persons of experience, who have learned how to focus with reasonable accuracy the objects before them, who really know somewhat of the needs and resources of the needy, or ill, or delinquent, or defective individuals for whom they care.

A first thought, very naturally, is that each institution or agency which does intelligent, thorough work must be, to some extent, a training school in its particular field of work. A few institutions do give specific teaching and training; notably some of the leading hospitals for the insane, as was pointed out to the national conference as early as 1887. It is interesting to note that the year-books of the Elmira reformatory,

From *Supervision and Education in Charity*, by Jeffrey Richardson Brackett (New York: Macmillan, 1903).

under Mr. Brockway, recorded a spirit of scientific inquiry there; that the resident chaplain of the San Quentin state prison, California, has written the result of his observation of prisoners; that Professor Henderson has issued, at the request of some of the prison wardens of the National prison congress [*sic*], an outline of study for officers of correctional institutions. But these are only indications for the future. So far, the number of institutions and agencies, strictly of charity and correction, whose officers would and could give training of much value, is very small.

At the International congress of charities in 1893, Mr. Homer Folks, secretary of the State charities aid association of New York, described the three types that have appeared in the development of the philanthropic worker. The first was the "good man" who had not proved his usefulness in any other work; the second was the man of good clerical ability to whom employment in a charitable agency is much the same as in a grain warehouse or a street-cleaning department, who has little, if any, real interest in the subject-matter. The third type, different from the other two, considers his work a profession, and takes it up as men of parts have taken up law or theology or medicine. This one, looking forward over the years of a lifetime, uses his work as no temporary makeshift, but for his own growth, for the welfare of society and the advancement of knowledge. Many of our institutions and agencies are still managed by persons of the first and second types.

The few that have officials of the third type are frequently sought to furnish leaders for new or reform work. The Associated charities and the Children's aid society of Boston are notable examples of agencies which aim to choose with care and to train with much pains their new officials—with the result that a number of their officials have been called away to lead similar work in other communities. The more we can get the right men and women at the head of our institutions, the more will these become training schools, as the master used to train his apprentice and the doctor his pupil. But training and instruction, worthy of the name, means a serious giving out of time and thought only to those persons who work with them with the aim of joining their staff, of adding to their own forces.

A very interesting beginning of a school for teaching and training as a preparation for institution life and work was begun in 1890 at the Burnham industrial farm, by Mr. W. M. F. Round, long the secretary of the New York prison association. From it grew "the Order of St. Christopher, a training for institutional service," in which several young men were prepared for and sent out to work. The order was essentially the creation of Mr. Round, and was given up for a time with his retirement owing to illness.

There are a number of schools for deaconesses and others who are to be aids of the clergy in missionary and parish work. Some of them give a knowledge of care of the sick, hygiene, preparation of foods, etc.; but as to work in charity and correction, few if any give any instruction whatever. Some of the graduates themselves are the best examples of the need of instruction and of reasonable training in it.

At the International congress in 1893, Mr. Robert A. Woods, head worker of Andover house, now South End house, Boston, presented a paper on university settlements as laboratories in social science. The basis of acquaintance and friendship, he said, upon which the neighborhood work of settlements stood, was not only a dictate of human feeling and common sense for the improvement of persons, but was equally a dictate of science for good social investigation. "Social science, if it is to be truly scientific, dealing with human beings, must use the most delicate human apparatus in the way of personal acquaintance and sympathy, in order to gain accurate and delicate results." The reproach which he brought against social science was that so far it had not "sought out and presented the elusive but distinctive quality and essence of human life!" The acquaintance which the settlement, as he saw it, should seek is not only with individuals but with the families and whole neighborhoods; and so the need of information would broaden into the field of social economics. And the settlement library, with its literature, both standard and current, would tell what other persons were doing in work and study in various parts of the world. In all such ways, "the university settlements stand as laboratories in the greatest of all sciences," contributing, among other things, "to develop skilled social workers, and to send them out, not merely into professional charity and philanthropy, but into every kind of human activity, in order that they may broaden every kind of human activity so as to make it a truly social function." The recently published bibliography of settlements gives the number of college, social, university, and church settlements in the United States as about one hundred. Its introduction says frankly that "the name 'settlement,' as well as the idea on which the movement is founded, have been and are increasingly abused. Unfortunately it has become the fashion for missions, schools, parish houses, institutions, and others to label themselves settlements." The name, as the words "charity organization," has been used blindly by many persons, as if a name was something to conjure by. Some of the so-called settlements know little of the lofty aim set and so well followed by the few leaders of the settlement movement.

Over a dozen settlements are affiliated with well-known institutions of learning. Three of them are called "college settlements," because chiefly controlled and supported by college women, under an organization formed in 1890. Other settlements, as Hull house, Chicago, or East Side house, New York, draw upon workers and friends more generally, from all directions in their communities. In one way, which sometimes is least noted, this movement has been of great educational value in opening more widely the eyes of patrons, of those who represent the prosperous, to the knowledge of the vital interdependence of all parts of a community. The students who have gone from their academic life to lead classes or clubs in settlements, for one or two evenings a week, have unquestionably supplemented in a valuable way the class instruction in charity, ethics, or economics. There are sixty to seventy-five Harvard students who each year lead one or more classes in Prospect union, with its 500 workingmen members, under an executive committee which was one year composed, we read, of "a professor, a painter, a poet, a political economist, a philosopher, a postman, a politician, a printer, a philanthropist, and a parson!" What one of these student teachers said of himself must have voiced many—that he was getting a deeper insight into life and was being trained into habits important to society. But the hours given to settlement work by students who do not live in settlements are few.

The College settlements association of women can make the admirable report that of 300 women who have been in residence in its three houses, for short or long periods, nearly a half are engaged, in various places, in some form of philanthropic work. From their settlement workers, twenty-three women have been appointed to positions as head workers outside their own organization. But the weakest point of settlement service, as a whole, is the too short period of residence. Experience shows that very few persons of promise can afford in means and time, or are free from home duties, to live in settlements for a sufficient time to get real training.

A few of the leading settlements have indeed done noteworthy work in instruction and training. The recent reports of the University settlement society of New York, for example, include results of local studies by two young men, one of whom is now the head of a new charity organization society in an important city of international note; the other is the chief paid official of the officers of public aid in an important New England city. But while paying full tribute to the leading settlements as strong forces for inspiring, and to some extent for instructing and training, a number of good charity workers, the reminder must be given that such training as is described by Mr. Woods cannot be had in many of them. Some of the residents, in their enthusiasm to right wrong conditions, have themselves failed to get into right perspective the various elements of usefulness on which the welfare of society depends. The educational value of the work done depends on the judicious leadership, governed by the scientific spirit.

The bibliography of settlements gives the publications on the settlement movement and books by the leaders in the movement. Of books, the most valuable, and very valuable they are, are "Hull house maps and papers," several articles on "Philanthropy and social progress," by Miss

Jane Addams and Mr. Woods, and "The city wilderness." The bulletins of South End house, Boston, and the year-books of the University settlement society of New York are examples of current literature of settlement work which is most educational.

If the opportunities for training offered by the best settlements are to be availed of, the establishment of scholarships and fellowships is most urgent. The University of Michigan christian association, for the past five years, has provided the means for several students from the university to live and study at Chicago commons. Two of them have been in residence for five months, and made investigations and reports, one on the ethical substitutes for the social function of the saloon, which was used by the Committee of fifty on the liquor problem, the other on juvenile delinquency and dependency in Chicago. These fellows are appointed by the university, and credits are given for the theses written as the result of original work. At the Northwestern university, Chicago, the undergraduates have recently provided a student fellowship at the university settlement, and the report of that settlement for 1900 contains the result of the inquiry of the first fellow into "the housing of the wage-earners of the sixteenth ward." At South End house, Boston, the residents have just been increased by three young men holding fellowships from Dartmouth, Harvard, and Amherst colleges. The first has been provided through the influence of President Tucker, as part of a plan for a new graduate school of economics and politics at Dartmouth; the others have been guaranteed for two years by groups of alumni in Boston. Appointments are made to all on account of distinction in sociological study; the fellows are under the direction of the departments of their respective faculties as well as of the chief residents of the house, and the time spent in work may count toward an advanced academic degree. All take an active part in the general settlement activities, but each has to follow some special investigation. One has been studying the workingman's standard of life, the habits, the likes and dislikes, and the ambitions which most strongly mold him; another, the problems of juvenile employment; the third, the causes of congestion of population in factory districts. I feel, writes the last, that I enjoy advantages which a student of social science should prize very highly. In the course of such an investigation as I am making, "many interesting facts present themselves which a theoretical student would hardly anticipate. In theoretical discussion one is inclined to single out certain particular facts from which to draw general conclusions, but in practice one is surprised to find how intimately correlated are the social problems, and to see how comprehensive a view of all social factors must be taken before one can arrive at a true conclusion upon even a small theme." Such recognition by leading institutions of learning of the value of these efforts to apply scientific methods to social work is hastening the taking up of philanthropic work as a calling by well-educated men.

At Harvard university there are two fellowships directly applicable to philanthropic work, one established nearly fifteen years ago, the Robert Treat Paine fellowship of $500 "to one or more graduates of any department of the university wishing to study either at home or abroad the ethical problems of society and the efforts of legislation, governmental administration, and private philanthropy, to ameliorate the lot of the masses of mankind"; the other, the Henry Bromfield Rogers fellowship of $450, "for the study of ethics in its relation to jurisprudence or sociology."

At the International congress of 1893, Miss Anna L. Dawes of Pittsfield, Mass., entered a plea for "training schools for a new profession." She had seen the difficulty of getting suitable men or women to be secretaries of societies for organizing charity, especially in small cities and towns. This difficulty, she said, must be overcome in some way, for "the whole question of the success or failure of charity organization depends upon the discovery of some individual who adds to knowledge wisdom, and combines with right theory some experience." She knew what the colleges were beginning to do in instruction, what the settlements were beginning to do in study of social problems, and that there were opportunities for training in methods of religious work, as for deaconesses; but the need she felt was not filled in any of those ways. She thought the time had come "when either through a course in some established institution, or in an institution by itself, or by the old-fashioned method never yet improved upon for actual development— the method of experimental training as the personal assistant of some skilled worker—it ought to be possible for those who would take up this work to find some place for studying it as a profession." She suggested some course of study whereby those who were already learned in the study of books could be taught "what is now the alphabet of charitable science—some knowledge of its underlying ideas, its tried and trusted methods, and some acquaintance with the various devices employed for the upbuilding of the needy, so that no philanthropic undertaking, from a model tenement house to a kindergarten or a sand heap, will be altogether strange." Some more immediately practical experience of the work likely to be required, some "laboratory practice," should be given also. But this proviso was added, that the course be so arranged and be made to cover so brief a period, "should be so superficial, if you choose, to say so," that it need not be unduly expensive, for a *sine qua non* of the new profession was the possibility of getting trained workers for a moderate salary. Miss Dawes urged her plea before the congress because she felt that the problem must be urgent in all localities.

In 1897, at the National conference of charities and correction, and also in an address to the civic clubs of Philadelphia, published in *The Charities Review* for June, Miss Mary E. Richmond, then general secretary of the Baltimore charity organization society, urged the need of a training school in applied philanthropy. She looked chiefly at the needs existing in large cities, not merely for officials of charity organization societies, but for many institutions and for offices of public aid. She felt that all such persons, to be properly equipped, should have a reasonably sympathetic and intimate acquaintance with various branches of charitable and reformatory work. She suggested, therefore, a school with a two years' course, in which the best specialists would lecture, theory and practice would go hand in hand, all students would take together the exercises on general principles, and specialization would follow. Above all, the school should be under the direction of a university trained man who had wide practice experience in educational charity work.

Miss Richmond repeated her plea at the annual meeting of the American academy of political and social science in 1898, at Philadelphia, when the teaching of sociology and its relation to philanthropy were discussed. She feared to have such a school as she suggested attached to a university lest the theoretical side should overshadow the technical, the practical work. Over that point there were differences of opinion. Miss Frances R. Morse, one of the leaders in Boston, had suggested in a letter to the National conference of 1897, that such practical work might stand a better chance of being in the end of the best quality if it were attached to a leading university. She feared lest in a separate school "we should get a somewhat academic and opinionated graduate— the young men and women who had gone through a two years' course would feel too much that they knew all that could be learned. This seems a frivolous objection, if they could really learn in such a school as the medical student learns in his school, and the sophomorical feeling would be soon outgrown; but the analogy of the medical school is not a true one. Philanthropy cannot be measured by such exact standards as can medicine." Miss Morse's suggestion was that persons wishing to enter philanthropic service might, under the direction of some representative advisory committee, seek to work, for periods of several months each, in a leading charity organization society, a leading children's aid society, and perhaps under other agencies, as an institution or office of public aid. The needs voiced by Miss Dawes and Miss Richmond have been felt more and more as charity organization societies, material relief agencies, child-saving societies, and public aid officials have come to see, not only how much wisdom, but how much knowledge and experience is required for the best treatment of needy families in their homes, for the best care of children, for the best use of institutions, and for the development of volunteer service, both in dealing with individuals and on boards of management.

The Boston associated charities began some years ago the requirement of a certain period of instruction and training by the general secretary and an experienced agent, for applicants for the positions of district agents. The agreement is that those in training drop out, after a reasonable time, if they prove to themselves or to the officials of the society to be lacking in characteristics essential to their own success and the welfare of the society and of the needy. The Boston society, also, will not give a hearty recommendation to any of its officials called elsewhere until they have been in its service sufficiently long to let its recommendation be based on reasonable surety of fitness for the details of charitable work. The Boston plan of training agents has been followed largely in Baltimore for several years, with the result already found in Boston, that a few months of practical work under skilled officials shows that even college graduates who have studied sociology, and women of apparent hard sense with some business experience, may or may not have that "fitness" which is absolutely necessary for the work. Such a result proves the success and even necessity of some such plan.

Conference courses and study classes have been tried in several cities, not so much to rouse interest as to help in the training of workers. For instance, a class for study of friendly visitors' work, arranged by the general secretary of the Brooklyn bureau of charities in 1891–1892, was composed of a representative from each of the fourteen district conferences of the bureau and of a few office workers and delegates from churches and King's daughters. It met for an hour weekly for twelve consecutive weeks; type-written copies of the topics to be considered with page references to books were distributed before each meeting; reviews were made by members of the class in order to enforce the conception of the relation of each topic to the general field of charitable work and to the specific uses of friendly visitors; questions and answers and suggestions were stimulated. An experienced agent spoke approvingly of this course at the National conference in 1892. Although the students, she said, were somewhat irregular in reporting to their conferences what they learned, yet there was a general improvement in the work of the friendly visitors. In a small New England city, a class made up of a half-dozen experienced charity workers and a half-dozen young women not long from school or college, has recently been reading Miss Richmond's "Friendly visiting," with kindred reading suggested and with discussion. "It is a simple beginning," says one, "but a very enthusiastic and satisfactory one."

Such classes as these, and several might be mentioned, have usually been occasional, have not formed part of any systematic course, and make more for stimulus and teaching than for training.

There is one means of training, not perfect, of course, but very valuable, which can be used in any community where there is one interested person who knows the standard literature of charity and who has done persistent personal work in the homes of the needy. It is a study class, like the one Miss Zilpha D. Smith, general secretary of the Boston associated charities, has led for three years. It should consist of not over a half-dozen persons. Those of some experience are preferred. No mere student or office worker would be received. It does not merely read—it studies certain books and papers. Experiences are compared, customs are probed, good ways are proved. A condition of membership is personal work for the uplift of a family in distress. Fourteen morning meetings are held at fortnightly intervals, lasting from one and a half to two and a half hours; each member is expected to give six to eight hours of study in the fortnight. The first thought is to get the right conception of the aim of the associated charities; the next is to see the social conditions within which it works; the rest of the time is given to study from various points of view of problems of charity and correction. Warner's "American charities" and much related reading is used, some of it not being usually included in the literature of philanthropy but yet very suggestive to a charity worker. Members of the class are urged to make notes and ask questions; the leader tries to learn the needs of each individual. Questions of social and economic causes and conditions are included. Turns are taken in reviewing what has been read; then the discussions are general. The attendance at the classes has been steady. The excellence of such classes as these lies in their being made up of a few persons who are really applying themselves to study and to personal service, under the direction of one who is well informed, well balanced, and has given years to educational charity work.

During the summer of 1894 a class in "practical sociology" was conducted for two months by Dr. P. W. Ayres, the general secretary of the Associated charities of Cincinnati. It was made up chiefly of graduates from several universities, a theological seminary, and a training school for teachers, some of whom had been interested in lectures on care of the poor in cities during the preceding winter. The class visited and studied somewhat the charitable and correctional institutions of the city and several industrial establishments; were made familiar with the principles and methods of the associated charities, each member having the opportunity of taking "some particular family in charge, over whom he or she was to have particular guardianship"; and undertook to make investigations and reports upon the sweating system and tenement houses in Cincinnati for the State bureau of labor, several members being commissioned as agents of the bureau.

The class was described in *The Charities Review* for December, 1894. Most of its members have since done good work; four of them took positions of responsibility in the associated charities of three cities. That one member attempted to do too much in a short time without proper preparation is shown by the crude views which he gave in print in *Lend-a-Hand* for June, 1895, "A life class in sociology." The attitude which beginners should take was well told by Miss Richmond in a lecture delivered before the social science club of the Woman's college, Baltimore, and published in *The Charities Review* for February, 1896, entitled "Criticism and reform in charity."

In 1894 the Hartford school of sociology was opened under the Society for education extension. The aim was to meet, by a three years' course, the growing demand for a broader and more complete course of instruction in sociology than any of the universities gave. The plan included lectures by many eminent specialists, and seminary work. Throughout the third year, under the direction of the general secretary of the Hartford charity organization society, who had been an instructor at Johns Hopkins university, there were to be conducted (1) a course in general economics as a foundation for the study of sociology, (2) a sociological conference weekly, (3) field-work for training in special investigations and visitation of institutions, (4) a special conference of friendly visitors for practical philanthropic work. Hartford was deemed an unusually helpful center for a school, owing to its varied population, large manufactories, and extensive charitable effort, wise and unwise. The school opened with a few representatives of several colleges, two being graduates from Johns Hopkins university and Chicago university. Five completed the full program for two years, when the school closed for lack of adequate support. The special work in philanthropy had not been reached, but a good deal had been done meantime in friendly visiting, at the social settlement, in visits to institutions, and discussions on current literature of charity.

In *The Charities Review* for May, 1898, the announcement was made of a training class, to be conducted under the Charity organization society of New York for six weeks during the summer approaching. A careful review of opinions on the need of a training school, and the reason for opening the class were added. The very modest claim was now put forward, that an opportunity for higher training should be given to the large number of persons who desire to labor in the field of charities and correction, "leaving to the future the question as to whether such a training may finally be regarded as an indispensable condition of appointment." Due consideration was given to the fact that officials of charity organization and children's aid societies, usually overworked by the demands of their immediate duties, could not be expected to undertake the training of persons for philanthropic work throughout the country. The proposed class was not expected to give a thorough training, and no diplomas were to be conferred or promises made about future employment. It was a move in the direction of some definite system of training, "an experimental contribution toward the end in view." The school was opened accordingly in June. Twenty-seven students representing fourteen colleges and universities and eleven states were registered in the class—more than were planned for. The completion of a college or university course or a year's experience in philanthropic work were required for admission, and a little over half the class had had some experience in such work. All but two of the members registered worked steadily to the close. Each one gave two weeks of actual service in the district offices of the society; some gave more, continuing after the class ended. Each one presented to the class two reports of inquiries into subjects connected with philanthropic work in New York. Visits were made to a number of institutions. Opportunities were offered to individuals to visit families in need, but few found time to do that. Talks were given the class by some thirty men and women, practical workers, many of them leading specialists of the land. Dr. P. W. Ayres, who was directly in charge of the class, summed up as follows the results which were seen immediately: "All the members have a clearer view of the value of work properly done, of the harm of work improperly done. Five of them who were not already at work, all but one university graduates, have secured positions in charitable work. Three or four others have discovered that they were not fitted or were not ready for such occupation, and several of them determined to take up volunteer work for a time."

This class, repeated in the summers following, has become the Summer school in philanthropic work. It is managed by a special committee of the New York charity organization society, with several representatives from societies in other cities and universities. During the first three summers seventy students from seventeen states in the Union have attended these courses. Of these, twenty-two have entered the paid service of charity organization societies in different cities, two of whom are general secretaries, one is an assistant general secretary; fifteen hold paid positions in the work of other societies and institutions; eight are residents in settlements, of whom three are head workers; two are in kindergarten work; two are in the paid service of churches; three have given courses of university lectures based upon the work of the school; and the remainder are serving as volunteers in their respective communities. The details of work in the school are given in the reports of the New York charity organization society and in current numbers of *Charities*. In 1900 three weeks were given to the subject of the care and treatment of needy families in their homes; one week to the care of destitute, neglected, and delinquent children; another week to neighborhood improvement, and another week was divided between medical charities and institutional care of adults. The method of the school is practical, the speakers are leaders in their lines of work, and some of them, spending several days with the members of the class, add the personal acquaintance and opportunities for informal talks.

The school now merely gives a bird's-eye view of the wide field of opportunities, with points of special interest carefully pointed out by those who know them well. The program is arranged by a very representative committee and carried out under a director with the cooperation of chosen representative workers, so the danger of having beginners attempt too much with insufficient direction is minimized as much as possible. One of the class of 1900, a college graduate, who had given several years to responsible work in one of our best associated charities, wrote at the close of the course: "It is intensely interesting. I am collecting the opinions and suggestions of different members of the class about the school. They all consider it of the greatest value, and speak of it as a rare opportunity."

In the brief period of six weeks, say the committee in charge, "it is not possible to train workers for paid positions in philanthropy. While it is true that some of the new workers who have taken the course have secured paid positions, it has usually been as agents in training with the societies employing them. At least one year of preliminary work is necessary in most instances before new workers can assume the full responsibility either of caring for families in distress or of administering the affairs of a charitable society or institution. The central council of the Charity organization society has approved a plan of giving longer training to selected students as soon as the necessary means can be secured for it, and will receive funds for this purpose."

An arrangement for scholarships, in sums sufficient to cover the cost of board in New York for the six weeks, has allowed a few persons to come to the classes. The establishment of fellowships for continued work is earnestly desired.

2

The Comparison of Material

Mary E. Richmond

"I AM ASTONISHED," says Dubois, "to see how many young physicians possessing all the working machinery of diagnosis do not know how to make a diagnosis. It is because the art of diagnosis does not consist merely in gathering together a great many facts, but in co-ordinating those that one has been able to collect, in order to reach a clear conception of the situation." [1] And we are told that the historian first collects his material, then collates it, and only after it has been collated attempts his final interpretation. He weighs his evidence, of course, as we do, item by item when it is gathered, but a reweighing of the total is necessary when all the items are in. "After a student has learned to open his eyes and sees," writes Dr. Richard Cabot of clinical teaching, "he must learn to shut them and think." [2] So must we. Nevertheless, this stage of assembling our material, of relating its parts and trying to bring it up into consciousness as a whole, will not be easy to illustrate, since it is the most neglected part of case work technique.

Speaking broadly, the social case worker of an earlier day did little visiting of anyone except his client and so observed only within those narrow limits. He was mentally sluggish, moreover, and guilty of much thoughtless prescribing. The case worker of today is more active physically—sometimes doing too much running around, one is tempted to believe—but his advance in usefulness over earlier workers would be greater if he would oftener "shut his eyes and think," if he would reduce the visible signs of his activity and assemble his forces in order the better to deliberate upon his next move before he makes it. Case records often show a well-made investigation and a plan formulated and carried

From *Social Diagnosis*, by Mary E. Richmond, pp. 347–352, © 1917 by Russell Sage Foundation, renewed 1944 by Russell Sage Foundation, New York.

out, but with no discoverable connection between them. Instead, at the right moment, of shutting his eyes and thinking, the worker seems to have shut his eyes and jumped. On the other hand, however carefully the inquiries are recorded and the diagnosis which grew out of them indicated, however carefully a plan of action is decided upon, etc., the processes by which the diagnosis is arrived at—what parts of the evidence have been accepted or rejected and why, what inferences have been drawn from these accepted items and how they have been tested—can none of them be revealed in a record.

Some case workers feel that their conscious assembling of material comes when they present a summary to the case committees of volunteers who assist them in making the diagnosis and the plan of treatment. This is especially true if any of the members of the committee have a social experience that has made them both critical and just in their valuing of testimony. One worker writes, "Repeatedly, flaws in my investigation have not occurred to me in reading over the record, but they have become only too evident at the moment of presenting the case to my committee. The standard in my mind of what the committee ought to know in order to make a fair decision has then suddenly revealed weaknesses to me before they were brought out in the discussion."

The same bracing influence comes from submitting findings at this stage to a case supervisor who is responsible for the work of a group of social case workers. Indeed, the process of comparison, in so far as it can be studied at all at present, is found at its best in the daily work of a few experienced supervisors. Unfortunately they are usually persons who are much overburdened. Although committees, at their worst, can be useless as critics, when well chosen they have an advantage over any one referee in that they bring not only less jaded minds but more varied experiences to bear upon each problem. Either supervisors or committees have the advantage over the worker who makes his analysis unaided, that they do not know the client or his story, and that consequently they are not already so impressed with any one part of the story as to be unable to grasp the client's history as a whole.*

1. SUGGESTIONS FOR SELF-SUPERVISION

In the absence of a competent supervisor or of a committee, the case worker will often have to take the place of both by consciously setting

---

* A case reader of wide experience suggests here that, in fields of work where no committee is possible and no supervisor is at hand, someone with a keen mind be introduced to case record reading and that current problems be "tried out on him." Even where there is a committee it is important that someone on the committee besides the case worker read the record before the case comes up for discussion.

aside some time in which he will strive to look at his own work as if he were a critical outsider.*

a) He can try to review each item of a case with all the others in mind. When each particular piece of evidence came to him, he judged it by what he then knew. How does he judge it now in the light of all the evidence?

Gross suggests another way of testing our material which is psychologically more difficult; namely, to consider a part of it with other material deliberately excluded.[3]

> This is what a probation officer had to do, probably, when a father lodged complaint against his boy for stubbornness and for thieving from his older brothers. The home seemed so satisfactory that she was inclined to seek the cause of the trouble in outside influences that would have led the lad to take first small sums and then much larger ones. When, however, the time came for planning, the explanation had not been found, and, having a mind that demanded specific data instead of falling back upon an unsupported theory, she began her search anew and excluding from her mind for the time being the favorable family appearances, found two court records of the arrest of the father, one for buying junk from minors and the other for peddling without a license. These may seem small offenses, but they were serious enough in the father of a boy who was also developing a tendency to lawlessness.

b) Sometimes, as Gross suggests also, the grounding of a fact has been so difficult, has taken so much time, that we slur over the task of establishing its logical connection with the whole, or do that part of our work "swiftly—and wrongly."[4] Or sometimes the slurring is due to the desire to make a definite report with promptness, as in the following case:

> A charity organization society was asked in August by the state's attorney to interest itself in a non-support case, in which the man of the family had been arrested for not making weekly payments to his wife on the separate support order of the court. A week later the society submitted

---

* Any detailed discussion of the worker's case records must be reserved for a separate book on that subject, though self-supervision might well include not only the case work but its recording. Charles Kingsley warned a young writer that he should never refer to anything as a "tree" if he could call it a "spruce" or a "pine." If that lesson had been impressed upon the present generation of case recorders, the task of writing this book would have been an easier one.

Among the general terms against which collectors of family histories for eugenic study are warned by the Cold Spring Harbor Eugenics Record Office (see Eugenics Record Office Bulletin No. 7, p. 91) are *abscess,* without cause or location; *accident, decline,* without naming the disease; *cancer,* without specifying organ first affected; *congestion,* without naming organ affected; *convulsions,* without details and period of life; *fever; heart trouble* and *heart failure; insanity,* without details; *kidney trouble; lung trouble; marasmus; stomach trouble.*

The social case worker's Index Expurgatorius would have to cover a much

a report of its inquiry upholding the wife. In October, however, when the man made application to have his children removed from the home, an exhaustive study of the case revealed bad conditions there. A critic of this case record writes, "Before your first report to the state's attorney was sent, contradictions in the evidence had developed that should have made it clear to you that further investigation was needed. The sources of information were at hand and the winter's rush was not upon you."

c) As was the case in the foregoing example, a review of our material will often reveal unsuspected contradictions in the evidence. Where these contradictions cannot be reconciled we may safely infer that further evidence is needed; where, though all the evidence points one way, no explanation of the difficulty or guide to its solution has been revealed, we must again look for additional facts.

d) The rhetorics tell us that the first and last paragraphs of an essay are the two that make the deepest impression upon the reader. It may be well to ask always, therefore, whether the story as told by the first person seen, or the first theory adopted by the worker has received undue consideration in shaping the final conclusion; or whether the last statement made has been allowed this advantage. Anyone who has had occasion to note the eagerness of each of two complainants to tell his grievance first will appreciate that we have an intuition that first impressions are lasting. Where there have been matters in dispute, however, the strategic position—second only in value to the first—is the last. In short, we must guard against the impression made by first and by last statements in an investigation. . . .

2. SUGGESTIONS FOR COMPARISONS MADE BY A SUPERVISOR

What should a supervisor look for in a case record in which the work has reached the stage of evidence gathered but not yet compared or interpreted? For convenience of reference the treatment of this topic has been reduced to questionnaire form [appears in Chapter 3, pp. 23–28, below]. . . . The questionnaire for supervisors summarizes material . . . under the heads of (a) the case worker's relations with client, (b) with client's family, (c) with outside sources, (d) the conduct of the inquiry as a whole, and (e) wider aspects of the inquiry.

Good supervision must include this consideration of wider aspects.

---

wider range of subjects; but some of the commonest substitutions are *relative* for the word expressing the exact degree of relationship; *Italian* or *Austrian* or *German* for the term descriptive of a native of the particular province or other political subdivision; *day laborer* or *salesman* or *clerk* for the particular occupation; and *bad, dull, unsanitary, shiftless, incompetent, unsatisfactory, good, bright, industrious, proud, refined,* and a host of such adjectives for the specific act or condition.

. . . [T]he habit of keeping in mind the bearing of each individual fact on general social conditions gives added significance to the statements in a record. This habit may also open broader avenues of usefulness. Every case worker has noticed how a certain juxtaposition of facts often reappears in record after record, and must have suspected that this recurring juxtaposition indicates a hidden relation of cause and effect. Or else he must have noted that some twist in the affairs of clients showed again and again a marked similarity of outline such as to suggest a common cause, though no rational explanation came to hand. It is here that the "notation of recurrence," as it is called, becomes a duty of supervisor and case worker. Not only should these repetitions be noted but they should be compared carefully. Some situations that seemed similar will be found upon examination to be different in essence, but the remainder, if they are likely to throw light on social conditions or on the characteristics of any disadvantaged group, should be submitted to those specialists in social reform who can make a critical and constructive use of them. The getting at knowledge that will make the case work of another generation more effective may be only a by-product of our own case work, but it is an important by-product.* . . .

NOTES

1. Dubois, Paul, The Psychic Treatment of Nervous Disorders (The Psychoneuroses and their Moral Treatment), translated and edited by S. E. Jelliffe and W. A. White (New York: Funk and Wagnalls Company, 1907), p. 277.
2. Cabot, Richard C., Case Teaching in Medicine (Boston: D. C. Heath and Company, 1969), p. vii.
3. Gross, Hans, Criminal Psychology: a manual for judges, practitioners, and students, translated from the fourth German edition by Horace M. Kallen (Boston: Little, Brown, and Company, 1911), p. 12.
4. Ibid., p. 143.

* Dr. Adolf Meyer, addressing a group of after-care committees for the insane, just after having read some of their records, says, "I had to put a big black cross in my mind over the town of Waterloo. There is a town which evidently contains centers of infection, which the community cannot afford to tolerate, and which can be attacked if one has sufficient material against them. . . . The authorities and the good and bad people may not pay much attention to remonstrations until sufficient material accumulates and is plunged at the right time, and then you may be able to do something. These are difficult tasks, I know, but there is no way of doing anything by keeping quiet or by making abstract complaints."—After-care and Prophylaxis, p. 16. Reprint of an article in the State Hospitals Bulletin, March, 1909, authorized by the State Commission in Lunacy, Albany, N.Y. Utica, N.Y, State Hospitals Press, 1909.

3

Supervision and Review

Mary E. Richmond

. . . THE QUESTIONNAIRE OF THIS CLOSING CHAPTER turns from disabilities, which are not always the most important consideration in social work, to the other diagnostic topics likely to be of service to a case work supervisor. When inquiry into a client's situation has reached the stage of evidence gathered but not yet compared or interpreted, and the record comes to a supervisor, or when, in the absence of supervision, the case worker must review the evidence without assistance, what are the things to look for? This final list of questions is an attempt to answer the query. Needless to say, it does not indicate a routine to be followed; some questions will apply to the given case but many will not. . . .

SUPERVISION AND REVIEW QUESTIONNAIRE

I Relations with Client

1. Does the record of the first interview indicate that the client has had a fair and patient hearing, and that a sympathetic understanding, or at least a good basis for further intercourse, was established at this early stage?

2. Are there indications that advice has been given prematurely, or that promises have? Or has the client been put off with such artificial reasons for delay or inaction as "my committee," "we never pay rent,"

From *Social Diagnosis,* by Mary E. Richmond, pp. 449–453, © 1917 by Russell Sage Foundation, renewed 1944 by Russell Sage Foundation, New York.

"this is contrary to the rules of the institution," etc.? Have there been too many ultimatums? Have "no-thoroughfare" situations developed between case worker and client due to these, due to failure to sift contradictions, etc.? Are there signs that the worker's lack of grasp of the situation has developed the scolding habit?

3. Were good clues to outside sources of insight and co-operation procured in the first interview? What clues, indicated as possible by the story, seem to have been neglected? Do these belong to a group which this case worker often finds it difficult to get, or usually overlooks?

4. Were the possible signs of physical or mental disease or breakdown noted early, and were medical examination and care procured immediately thereafter? If the assumption that the client was lazy, indifferent, or incorrigible was made, was it possibly due to neglect of these precautions?

5. Has the worker who has conducted the first interview and seen the client's family also seen the important outside sources, or were these parts of the inquiry entrusted to someone else? Does the information procured from outside sources suggest that the inquirer had a sense of the relation of the part to the whole?

6. Were any confessions, especially those that were damaging to the client who made them, accepted as necessarily true? Has the client been protected from misrepresentation of any kind?

II Relations with Client's Family

7. Does the record give its reader a sense of the main current of the lives of the people recorded, or does it detail unrelated episodes and incidents only?

8. Have the relations of the members of the family to one another been noted? Have any crises been noted that tested the family power of cohesion?

9. Does the record reveal whether the family has or has not shown good judgment, on the whole, in its economic choices? Have expenditures been the expression of an innate craving, have they been due to imitation, or are they indicative of little judgment?

10. Are characteristic disabilities belonging to the racial or economic group all charged against the individual family?

11. Have the children of the family, especially the growing children, been individualized? Is there any clear picture of both their home

and school life? If the problem is a family one, have the older children, those who are grown and at work, been consulted?

12. Has the man of the family been seen? Were he and his wife seen separately?

III Use of Outside Sources

13. Was the confidential exchange consulted promptly? Was the identifying information there procured promptly followed by consultations with the agencies named? Were any inquiries that had already been made by these agencies unnecessarily duplicated? Were the different agencies each consulted about the kind of fact that each was best able to give? Has any transfer of the case to another agency for treatment been preceded by sufficient inquiry to justify the reference?

14. If not all the clues to outside sources were followed up, does an intelligent choice seem to have been made? For example, were *some* relatives on both sides of the house seen, some former employers, etc.? Was the order in which the sources were consulted wisely chosen? Were any of the sources consulted found through supplementary clues—clues revealed casually, that is?

15. Have statements been sought, as far as possible, at first hand and not through intermediaries—from doctors, for example, rather than from patients, where medical facts were in question, etc? Or has hearsay evidence been accepted without challenge? In evaluating the testimony of witnesses, has their personal bias been allowed for?

16. Has the worker expressed opinions, in the letters attached to the record or elsewhere, on matters about which he is not informed? Have the outside sources been consulted about possible plans of action, or have they merely been persuaded to agree to plans proposed by the case worker?

17. In first contacts with relatives, have questions of the material assistance procurable from them obscured more important matters?

18. Are the medical diagnoses from which social inferences have been drawn up-to-date? Has discrimination been shown in seeking medical advice, and has the needless multiplication of medical advisers been avoided?

19. Are the school reports quoted merely formal ones, or have the individualized observations of teachers been sought?

20. Have the work records been entered perfunctorily, or do they cover the points that would be of value in procuring new work, reinstate-

ment, or advancement? Has underpaid or unwholesome work that
tended to disintegrate the family life (such as the twelve hour shift,
supplementary earning by the homemaker away from home, sweat-
shop work, or premature withdrawal of children from school) been
noted?

21. Is any inexactness in the data at hand due to failure to consult
    original documents of birth, marriage, baptism, death, property,
    immigration, or court proceedings? Or to failure to consult out-of-
    town directories? Or newspaper files?

22. Were interviews with present neighbors limited quite strictly to
    procuring needed court evidence? Have the characteristics of the
    neighborhood been kept in mind, and have experienced neighborhood
    social workers been consulted about them?

IV Conduct of the Inquiry as a Whole

23. Have all the assets for reconstruction revealed by the client's history
    been carefully and sympathetically noted? Have they been summed
    up in black and white? Or are there signs, on the other hand, of
    a tendency to overemphasize the discouraging things?

24. What indications are there of the case worker's habits as a questioner?
    Have leading questions been asked with full knowledge of their
    danger, and with good reason for taking the risk? Have any marked
    personal prejudices of the case worker's been allowed to warp the
    account?

25. Is there evidence of a tendency to substitute such formulæ as
    "maladjustment," "underfeeding," "chronic laziness," "hopelessly shift-
    less," "drink the sole cause," "large family," "insufficient wages," for
    the specific fact or facts? Are there indications that the worker is
    hampered by some professional habit useful under other conditions
    but not here? Are there signs of automatism, of following a routine
    unthinkingly?

26. Has the worker been careful to clear up unfavorable items of evidence
    instead of leaving them neither proved nor disproved?

27. Has the worker been hurried into hasty and ill considered action
    by a tendency to cross bridges before they are reached, to regard
    situations as "emergent" that are not really so? Has some picturesque
    minor incident of the story demoralized the inquiry?

28. Is there a tendency to "make out a case" at all hazards by over-
    emphasizing one side? Has the worker "held a brief" for or against

or has he dealt even? Are first theories promptly abandoned when the facts tend to disprove them?

29. What hypotheses and inferences of the worker and of others have been accepted without the necessary testing? Have any popular explanations of things been accepted without challenge?

30. With regard to the record itself, does it develop an individual and colorful picture, or are the main issues obscured by repetition and by unverified impressions? Does it show skill in what is omitted? Is the present situation, for example, described in such detail as to throw the more permanent aspects of the story out of perspective? Are the words used as specific as they might be? Are general terms avoided? Are acts described instead of qualities? Are the statements of the record merely added or are they weighed? Are there brief entries that help the supervisor to understand the relation of an unknown witness to the matter about which he is quoted and to measure, in some degree, his disinterestedness and his personal characteristics?

31. Are there signs of wasting time, of doing relatively unimportant things under the impression that there is no time for the important ones? Does the investigation center round and round some one point in the story, or does it lose itself in aimless visits, many times repeated, to the client or his family? Are there, on the other hand, signs of "economy of means," of achieving results, that is, with the fewest possible motions and the smallest possible friction?

32. Has the inquiry, as it has developed, supplied a reasonable explanation for the present situation? Does the investigation, that is, lay bare the personalities of the chief actors plus the factors external to themselves that have brought them to their present pass? Does it look back to their highest achievement in the past, and give any sense of their possible resources in the joint task of reinstatement or development which is still ahead? How far does the inquiry suggest not only the diagnosis of the difficulty, but plans for its constructive treatment?

33. If needed evidence has not been procurable, and only partial or temporary diagnosis can be made, what modifications in treatment could be devised in order that a part of its necessary services might become also a means of pushing the investigation forward?

V Wider Aspects of the Inquiry

34. Is the record one in which this case worker has tried to make an especially thorough and skilful inquiry? If not, are there any such records?

35. Does it contain an instance of effort to push further into an unsolved problem by presenting it, in this concrete form, to specialists in the national social reform associations or elsewhere who might be able to suggest a solution? (Examples: the possible relations between occupation and disease in a given case; the problem of the energetic boy who wishes to sell papers out of school hours; the chances of recovery for tuberculous patients returned to their own country—when, for instance, a case committee suggests sending back such a one to Messina, etc.)

36. If there is no adequate provision for the feeble-minded, or no legal redress when housing conditions threaten health (to give only two instances), what attitude does the record reveal toward these evils? Is the situation accepted, or is a disposition manifest to push hard in some helpful direction? Is the evidence bearing upon the matter accurately enough stated in the record to make it part of the data needed for community action?

37. Are there any hopeful signs of breaking through routine, of getting a result by new or unusual methods? What new outside sources, for example, have been brought to light? Have any such new methods been noted and placed at the service of other case workers?

38. If anyone has made an inquiry, supplied information, or aided at this stage of the case in any way—if a teacher has shown interest, for example—will that interest be remembered and will it be strengthened? Has any note been made, looking to that end, to report later upon the further developments of the case, especially upon any really significant ones?

4

Personnel

A Report of the Milford Conference

EFFICIENCY IN THE MANAGEMENT of personnel will characterize the competent agency in social case work. For some reasons the dependence of professional standards upon qualified personnel presents greater difficulties to social work than to other professions. As compared with medicine, the ministry, law and probably teaching, social work is much less well-equipped with programs for professional education, with professional organization and technical literature. Professional education, professional organization and technical literature are powerful reinforcements of the stability of any profession. Except for the native ability of the practitioner, they together constitute the most important single medium for the development of professional standards. Lacking anything like adequate resources on these three points, the reliance of social case work for high standards in practice must be upon the two factors of organization and personnel. The efficiency of each of these factors depends largely upon the personnel practices of social case work agencies. The success of the agency in meeting its obligations to its public is in the hands of its staff. The professional development of social case workers which, in the long run, determines the standards of social case work, is largely influenced by the administrative setting provided for them by social case work agencies.

Personnel management has within recent years become a matter of close study. Social case work is one form of activity which has contributed, along with industry and other fields, to the understanding of the problem. Here, again, however we approach a problem of social case work for which our awareness is much more nearly adequate than our understanding. We suggest, nevertheless, that the experience of social case workers in the management of personnel has proved the validity of some important principles.

These, we believe, can be divided into three categories, involving:

1. Aspects of the relationship between agency and employee which should be matters of contract.
2. Aspects of the relationship between agency and employee which have a basis in professional ethics and are of the nature of professional privileges to be accorded the employee and of professional obligation on the part of the employee to the organization beyond those things which should be embodied in a contract.
3. Methods of conducting staff relationships so as to insure the efficiency of the organization through the safeguarding of the privileges and obligations discussed under No. 2.

ITEMS OF CONTRACT BETWEEN THE WORKER AND THE AGENCY

We are assuming that an agency has a definite routine for the selection of employees which gives it an adequate basis for judging the qualifications of candidates. Every employee of a social case work agency should have a written statement which defines the duties of the position to which he is appointed as precisely as possible, the length of the period for which he is employed, the salary he is to receive, the hours during which he is expected to be on duty and the length of his annual vacation. It has been found desirable by many agencies to include as a condition of engagement that employees submit to regular physical examination, usually not less often than once a year. There is also a growing interest in the possibility of including in the contractual relationship between agency and employee provision for a pension or other allowance upon retirement.

Positions in social case work under public auspices are usually covered by civil service regulations which are in the nature of a contract between the government and its employees. The complete set of regulations covering any one position or any type of position in the public service being fixed by legislation is ordinarily less flexible than the contractual practices of a private agency need be. Nevertheless we believe that all of the items which we have suggested as desirable in the contract between the private agency and its employees should be included in the civil service arrangements for positions in social case work under governmental auspices.

The termination of the contractual relationship between a competent agency and its employees involves obligations on both sides. An agency which wishes to terminate this relationship is under obligation to give its employee adequate notice. At the termination of the relationship on the initiative of an agency, a social case worker is entitled to receive from the agency, confidentially if he desires it, an exact statement of the reasons for the termination. When the relationship is terminated on the initiative of a worker, the obligation to give the agency ample notice is exactly the same as that which rests upon the agency when it takes the initiative.

THE PROFESSIONAL PRIVILEGES OF THE SOCIAL CASE WORKER IN AN AGENCY

Definiteness in the terms of a contract between worker and agency insures an indispensable feeling of security on the part of both in regard to the social case worker's tenure in the agency. No contract, however, can reflect the full professional obligation of the agency to its staff. As we have already pointed out, the maintenance of high standards of social case work practice is dependent preeminently upon professional growth in the personnel of social case work. This professional growth is a natural by-product of the daily experience of the social case worker in the field. Daily experience in the field, however, needs to be supplemented by other professional experiences if anything like maximum professional development is to be achieved by social case workers. Many such experiences can be made possible for social case workers only with the co-operation of the agency.

Among the more obvious ones which are completely within the control of the agency and which will contribute directly to its efficiency are such opportunities as are afforded by individual projects for study with time allowed by the agency for the purpose, an equitable policy regarding promotion both in salary and responsibility, participation in study groups within the agency.

A privilege which is possible only with the co-operation of the agency is leave of absence for study, on some occasions with salary and even with the agency defraying, in addition, a part of the expense. Attendance at national and state conferences with some regularity is also indispensable to sound professional development. The sabbatical year has not yet become common in social case work, although it has been adopted to a limited extent. It is also due to the social case worker that he have the freest possible access to opportunities offering new positions in other agencies. Since one of the problems in social case work is to define ways of lengthening the tenure of social case workers as social case workers, the principle of staff development involved in these privileges should be recognized as part of agency policies.

PROFESSIONAL OBLIGATIONS OF THE CASE WORKER TO HIS ORGANIZATION

Since social case work is carried on almost exclusively through the medium of organizations, it is obvious that the standing of social case work agencies is the concern not merely of boards of directors but, in an equally vital sense, of members of the profession. It seems clear, therefore, that a contractual agreement between the social case worker and his agency can no more define the full obligation of the worker to the agency than it can define the full obligation of the agency to the worker. The most obvious obligation of a social case worker to his organization would seem to be to give the best that he has of professional skill to his work, and this should mean continuous effort by the social case worker to use every resource which is open to him professionally to increase his efficiency. In view of the almost universal overloading of social case workers by agencies, we hesitate to suggest that overtime is inevitable. Nevertheless it seems to be in practically every field of activity which is professional in character. The present excess of overtime in social case work could be materially reduced by an increase in the resources of agencies, which is primarily the responsibility of the board of directors, and it could be still further reduced by better organization of time and existing resources which is partly the responsibility of social case workers themselves.

A second obligation of the social case worker is that of loyalty to the policies and regulations of the organization. We believe and shall reiterate the belief later that the members of the staff of an agency for social case work should have an opportunity to participate in the formulation of policies. At times disagreement by the individual worker with the policies of his organization is inevitable. The staff of a social case work agency, however, represent a group which, with respect to many of its important activities, must act as a group. It must be assumed that policies once adopted by an agency are binding upon its entire personnel, including members of the board, members of the staff and members of the volunteer force. Good teamwork requires willingness to abide by group decisions. The social case worker who finds himself in revolt against the policy of his organization has only three courses open to him. He may restrain his tendency to revolt and abide by the decisions of the organization; he may do this and also exert his influence fairly within the organization for a change in policy; or he may resign. Any person who chooses to ally himself with a group sacrifices some measure of freedom. The physician in private practice, the artist, and the reformer may be as markedly individualistic as they choose to be. The contribution of the social case worker, however, to progressive social welfare can at the present time be made only through organizations and for many years to come there is not likely to be any considerable development of free-lance social case work. Under these circumstances, organization loyalty would seem to be a prime responsibility of the case worker, not merely in the interests of his agency but in his own interests as well, not to speak of those of the community at large.

Another question of organization loyalty arises when the work of the organization is judged in the community by the conduct of the staff. We believe that an organization has no right to concern itself with the private affairs of its employees, unless their private affairs reflect disadvantageously upon the organization. The pursuit of this argument leads quickly into areas where one can hardly tread surefootedly. Freedom of speech and other phases of individual liberty, one likes to think, are part of the bill of rights of mankind. No social worker loses all his rights as a citizen and an individual because he becomes part of an organization. Nevertheless, regardless of any philosophy of individual liberty, social case workers whose professional standing makes them assets to an organization inevitably represent that organization in many relationships outside the boundaries of their immediate professional duties. A social worker whose high professional attainments may be an asset to his organization may become a liability if, because of his personal conduct, he alienates from the organization a measure of the community's moral support which, in the interests of general social welfare, it ought not to lose.

STAFF RELATIONSHIPS

In the preceding discussion of the contractual and ethical obligations of the agency in regard to the professional development of the social case worker we have suggested some of the staff relationships which would tend to promote the morale of a competent agency for social case work. We believe in general that the supervision of a staff should be conceived of as having two functions: first, to keep the work of the agency up to the standard it has set for itself; and second, to promote the professional development of the staff. Supervision which is based upon democratic organization of staff relationships will be more conducive to the development of morale than supervision which is autocratic in character. One of the most important implications in a democratic organization of staff relationships is that it will give the entire professional staff an opportunity to participate in formulating the policies of the agency. It is also indispensable to a democratic organization that there be sufficiently frequent conferences of the members of the staff to insure their vital participation in general discussions of the work of the agency.

A sound procedure of supervision will include methods of appraising the work of every member of the staff. It will also include such a routine of staff contacts as will give to the staff members the feeling of easy access to all the members of the supervisory force from the general executive down. Every social case worker is entitled also to a periodical survey of his work and progress in consultation with a supervisor. Moreover, recognition of achievement by social case workers should be given whenever the occasion arises. Such recognition is to a large extent indicated by promotion and increase in salary but it should not be left to be taken for granted. Few human beings fail to derive security and stimulus to sustained effort from appreciation on the part of those under whom they work. This is as true of supervisors in relationship to general executives and of general executives in relationship to boards of directors as it is of workers holding subordinate positions. Assuming it to be true, recognition by supervisors of achievement on the part of social case workers would seem to be an easy and telling method of contributing to staff morale. We should like to add that in our judgment the value of this practice is not in the least sentimental but wholly practical.

We realize that agencies for social case work vary greatly in size and resources. Some of the suggestions made in this chapter are obviously beyond the possibility of achievement in many agencies with high standards of competency. These suggestions, however, have rather more than the force of illustrations. We believe that none of them is wholly fanciful for every one is in effect somewhere in the social case work field. Moreover they are presented here more as indications of tendencies in the management of personnel than as forming collectively a comprehensive discussion of this problem. There are many aspects of personnel management, particularly in specific social case work which we have not covered. We have attempted to do no more than to suggest the spirit in which the problem should be approached by the administration of an agency and to present some concrete illustrations of ways in which particular agencies have infused this spirit into the mechanics of their personnel relationships.

5

Supervision
in Social Case Work

Dorothy Hutchinson

THE WORD "TECHNIQUE" as applied to supervision in social case work has a dull and rigid sound. The word "art" is more stimulating, if we can release ourselves from a certain shop-worn feeling in its presence. But supervision in its performance and in its demands is neither dull nor shop-worn: It emerges as a living concern to those who practice it. Its quality has the power to determine self-development and, indirectly, the kind of service secured to our communities. Despite its importance, there is a feeling abroad that we know rather little about it. As a teaching process it has grown up out of common practice. There is no library to turn to nor a school of social work to tell us just how to become supervisors. The following reflections on the subject are offered merely to bring out some leading thoughts with the hope that they be used as a basis for future discussion.

What makes a supervisor? How do we become supervisors? Was it a matter of chance with us or an opportunity that came to us? Did our own drive enter in or was it because we had certain qualities that we became supervisors?

It seems fairly obvious that some of the reasons we have for choosing social work as a profession will have to do with the kind of supervisors we are today and our potentials for growth as future supervisors. The temptation to dominate may create an inhibiting supervision. The need to protect may be an effective means for retardation of growth—of both worker and supervisor. Perhaps few of us are skilful enough to unravel the intricate combination of reasons that contribute to our being in

From *The Family* (Family Service Association of America), April 1935, pp. 44–47.

supervisory positions. There is the clement of chance, the natural growth of the social agency, leadership ability as shown with clients, one's need for recognition, one's prodding financial reality, and sometimes, prosaically, knowing the right people.

Have I a right to supervise if, quite frankly, I was timidly insecure in my own family and therefore have a pressing need to protect others? Should I practice social work if, quite frankly, I feel a drive to attain prestige or a need to dominate others? The human thing in answer to such questions is to classify various reasons as positive or negative for ourselves, forgetting that the crux of the matter lies not in whether we have needs or not (and who has not?) but in the use we make of our personal drives and our awareness of them. If they obstruct our functioning in relation to workers, if we have no awareness as to how our personal drives may harm others, the vibrating results will be felt in the morale of our office and in the caliber of the case work we succeed in having our workers do.

The gravitation from case work to supervision will depend on many intermingling factors. Growth of a worker does not always mean that she becomes a supervisor. On the other hand the worker who changes from a job in which she assumes leadership of clients to one in which she assumes leadership of personnel has always great opportunity for growth—if she has capacity for it.

In the actual, day-by-day process of supervision probably the greatest and most important factor for us is the kind of relationship we create between our workers and ourselves. We have heard a good deal about the worker-client relationship—of the client's right and freedom to keep his own problem rather than having it taken out of his hand, and of his right to participate. The philosophy behind this represents an advance over the old one in which we as case workers took full responsibility for our clients and assumed we had all the answers to life. The relationship between supervisor and worker has perhaps shown the same trend. We, as supervisors, used to take full responsibility for our workers and for their case work. We were not clear about anything except that the responsibility fell heavily upon our shoulders. Many of us still feel this responsibility and because it becomes such a weight we are not free to give what we have of other and more essential qualities—such as teaching ability, leadership, and increased knowledge.

What is this relationship between supervisor and worker? What is the supervisor's responsibility for her worker? It would seem that the most important and outstanding factor is responsibility for the worker's growth. Of course some workers will never grow. They carry on their jobs in a routine way, even performing some part of it efficiently; but they never will make any creative contribution—with or without supervisors. Perhaps this class of workers will disappear as we become more skilled in selecting staff members and as the community in general becomes more aware of the value of training in social work.

The supervisor-worker relationship should be a growing, dynamic one in which each is free. The supervisor is essentially a leader and a teacher of workers and does not impose herself or her ideas on the worker. She assumes responsibility for the worker in that it is her job to know and find out what is going on in the worker's mind, what the worker really thinks and feels. It is her responsibility to understand the worker well enough to know why she does certain things and why she is blocked on others.

How do we supervisors get to know our workers? Certainly, in the first place, by taking time to know them. If our conference times are hectic, constantly interrupted affairs in which we appear pressed and burdened, our workers will catch this atmosphere from us and will consequently bring to us only such routine things as can be hastily answered. Second, by creating an atmosphere in which the worker herself feels free. If our worker senses that she cannot tell us the things that are going well, if she fears our disapproval or, more important, must watch for our approval, she is not free. This is not to imply that supervisors do not criticize workers. If a worker feels free with a supervisor she desires her criticism for her own interest and growth. Finally, by showing interest in our workers and what they are doing. By this is not meant a routine matter-of-fact concern but a sincere interest because, as supervisors, we really are interested. There is nothing that will encourage and stimulate a worker more than this.

If we are successful in building up a free, untrammeled relationship between worker and supervisor, soon one will raise the question as to whether this means that as supervisor we leave the worker so free that we assume no responsibility for her case work. Perhaps we are approaching the day when all workers will be so skilled that this can be done. Many supervisors, however, will hesitate at this: they believe in the first place that workers are not really skilled enough, and second that they, as supervisors, represent the agency and have a responsibility to the community for its case work.

Is there not, however, a fine distinction between taking a personal responsibility for everything our workers do and sharing responsibility with workers who feel free? In the first case we take the burden from the shoulders of the workers entirely; in the second, we share the responsibility with them. In the first place the chief emphasis lies on case work; in the second, on the worker. If we put the emphasis on the worker and her growth, I believe we need not worry about case work.

But what about the immature worker who will, through inexperience and lack of knowledge, do overt things in her case work that we, as supervisors, know are harmful? We reason with ourselves that, if we watch her case work closely, we can prevent these things from happening. This is true certainly, but if we "watch" her to the degree of taking away her initiative and independence of thought, we may succeed in keeping her immature. Most workers grow more from their mistakes than from their successes. It is a healthy experience for a young worker to make blunders which she herself recognizes and profits by. If she can take these to a supervisor who will in an understanding way help her evaluate them, she is not likely to repeat them. But suppose this same young worker, by rushing in, unwittingly harms her clients? Should her supervisor not prevent her from doing this? Yes, theoretically, but is there not such a thing as a supervisor who protects her clients too much and by protecting them from her workers defeats her own goal, that of growth of the worker and service to the client?

If we assume responsibility for a worker's growth we automatically assume a teaching responsibility toward her. And this function is closely allied with and built upon a free relationship with the worker. Being teachers implies that we know more than those we are teaching and also that we have a capacity to impart what we know.

Our teaching of workers is achieved largely through association. By this is not meant a personal identification or association but that simply through a wider knowledge and enlarged experience the worker learns to think and feel about clients, for instance, as the supervisor does. The worker may begin with a confined and narrow perspective in social case work. From association with the thinking and feeling of the supervisor her perspectives are enlarged. She begins, often, with a judgmental attitude toward people; she grows into an attitude of understanding. This is a big responsibility for supervisors. It means that, despite pressures, we need to find time to read, to think, to take courses, and to discuss problems among ourselves. Supervisors need to grow even more than their workers and herein, it would seem, lies their greatest responsibility.

Many supervisors feel limited in their teaching function because of a traditional check-up function. Supervisors are only human. Some "Billy" does not get his tonsils out and some "Mrs. Jones" does not have a clinic examination unless some supervisor checks up on some worker. If such omissions slip by, supervisors are frequently reminded of them by their executive or a member of the community. They, therefore, turn to "checking" with renewed vigor. If supervisors are treated often enough along this line, it is easy to let supervision become a stereotyped checking affair, with the function of teaching and leadership taking subordinate places.

The philosophy behind checking is usually fear on the part of supervisors and a realization that all workers are vulnerable. It is not the place here to say that there is no place for this kind of function in the technique of supervising, but perhaps it can be suggested that "checking" as such has lost status and that, when the relationship between supervisor and worker is free, checking has an infrequent and subordinate place. Supervisors who take responsibility for the growth of their workers enable them to check their own work.

Again this suggests the question, Is there any place, then, for discipline in the techniques of supervising? Where is there a worker so skilled, so mature, and so well organized that she does not need to be "reminded" now and then? Probably a majority of workers under supervision today are unable to measure up to this but supervisors are not usually bothered deeply for, within a frank and free relationship, both supervisor and worker equally discipline one another. They act in an open, matter-of-fact, professional way behind which is the philosophy of understanding each the other, of both being human and of both being busy.

But what of discipline when the supervisor has an upstart, an individualist, and a non-conformist on her staff? Supervisors have all had experience with workers who have a chip-on-the-shoulder attitude, who like to bedevil their supervisors, and who show other manifestations of infantile behavior. These workers are often immature, still bound by childhood relationships in which the supervisor becomes identified with some member of their families.

Just how much supervisors should go into the personal lives of their workers is a question for discussion. Just how much they can keep from doing this is another. Just how much they are equipped to do so is still another. Any kind of an exhaustive research into these questions is impossible here but a few factors seem clear enough to bring out now, as possible bases for future discussions:

1. The problems of some workers (and some supervisors) are so deep-seated that only a psychiatrist (an analyst) can and should help.
2. A supervisor's justification for entering into the personal life of a worker should arise only as the worker's problems prevent her from functioning at her job in the agency, and as they openly offend the social workers of the community in which the agency is located.
3. Within a free and frank supervisor-worker relationship, a certain amount of personal information regarding the lives and personalities of workers has a natural place.

4. No supervisor has a right to indulge herself in the personal problems of her workers.

There are other kinds of discipline in supervision: There is the discipline of an authoritative supervisor who needs to be authoritative; there is the discipline that a worker demands of herself on her own authority; and there is the discipline that is the result of the group morale of an agency. And certainly there is always a place for self-discipline, for both worker and supervisor.

Within the supervisor-worker relationship there are two particular dangers for supervisors: the danger of over-protection, and the danger of authority. Protection of workers is largely protection of ourselves as supervisors. We may have, in our own experience of being supervised, unhappy memories that tend to make us over-identify with our workers and shield them from too painful reality. Sometimes we protect our workers from clients and sometimes our clients from workers; in either case we lose our balance and our perspective. The danger of authority is the danger of the use of authority. It grows out of a supervisor's need to punish and usually shows itself in a sadistic attitude toward workers. Suffice it to say at this point that domination as a form of supervision is out of date.

Supervision cannot be made a stereotyped affair applicable to all supervisors and all workers. It will change with the pressures and demands of various kinds of social agencies. It will, in the last analysis, always be an individual adjustment between one certain supervisor and one certain worker. It may be labeled a "technique" or an "art." It may, with some, be a cramped form of checking. It may take the nature of a systematized piece of machinery. It may be growth for both worker and supervisor but, whatever its character and expression, it holds a place of high importance as a function in the field of social case work. Supervision, finally, is the fine use of power—whose misuse is evident not only in the field of case work: we see its depleting effects today in a chaotic world of politics, in business, and in individualism. Supervision as a use of power is a use of men. As such its requirements are sobering.

6

The Dynamic Basis
of Supervision

Elizabeth R. Zetzel

SUPERVISION IS A TEACHING SITUATION of a very special kind. Because of the nature of the material being studied and also because of special features of the interpersonal relationship between teachers and students, dynamic factors with both positive and negative potentialities are always present. Broadly speaking, these factors are emotional; the emotions concerned are both conscious and unconscious or in more everyday language both explicit and implicit. These emotional factors, moreover, are not unilateral. They are concerned not only with the student's emotions toward the supervisor but with the supervisor's toward the student. The purpose of supervision may be regarded as primarily and basically didactic. Obviously, however, dynamic or emotional factors, since they are ubiquitous, play a large role in the career of the social worker during training, and in casework practice, teaching, and supervision. Various emotional reactions may be anticipated in students or workers in relation to supervisors, and vice versa.

HISTORICAL PERSPECTIVE

It may be helpful to take a historical point of view and to relate developments in supervision to the development of dynamic concepts, not only in psychiatry proper, but also in progressive education, particularly in the training and the bringing up of children. Social work, in the early days, was not influenced by psychoanalytic thought but devel-

From *Social Casework* 34 (April 1953), pp. 143–149. Reprinted by permission of the Family Service Association of America.

oped as an independent discipline in the setting of the educational and social attitudes of the period. Professional training in social work, however, grew up during the period when dynamic psychiatry was making its first impact on professional thought, not only in relation to specific psychiatric problems but also to education and concepts of child training. Before this impact, the approach, particularly in relation to pedagogic problems, was predominantly intellectual and didactic. The teacher or parent, that is to say, was expected, out of his superior education and experience, to impart the fruits of his knowledge to the student or child. The latter, in contrast, was expected to accept the authority of teacher or parent, and to absorb the knowledge and advice offered to him.

It is unnecessary to emphasize how radically the point of view has been changed as a result of infusion of dynamic concepts into the field of education. The recognition that emotional factors not only may, but inevitably do, play a leading role in developing capacities for performance as well as in the acquisition of intellectual knowledge, is now widespread. It is not appropriate in this article to discuss the role of emotional factors in the learning process itself. Learning difficulties of a general intellectual nature, I believe, do not present a serious problem in the education of professional social workers.

The experiences of progressive education, however, may have some parallels in the development of social work training. In progressive education dynamic psychology has also played an important role. The emergence of dynamic concepts—and I am not referring here specifically to Freudian psychoanalytic thought—closely paralleled the development of progressive education. On the premise that emotional difficulties and learning problems were partly the result of the formal educational procedures of the period, the early progressive schools tended to throw discipline and formality overboard. As further developments of dynamic psychology revealed the complexity of intellectual and emotional development, and also that, for very real and cogent reasons, children need the support of some sort of disciplined framework, the progressive schools have modified their procedures. The importance of the emotional factors, however, has not been in any way minimized. Progressive education now recognizes that the child develops and learns best if given a satisfactory and secure framework, that is, one that provides sufficient outlet for emotional expression and free play of fantasy and, at the same time, makes certain educational demands on him. The emotional basis for furthering such satisfactory development is on the whole implicit rather than explicit. In other words the setting, including teaching personnel, is carefully planned in the light of modern knowledge, with a view to providing the child with experiences that help him progress toward maturity, not only in his emotional and interpersonal relationships, but also in the important task of acquiring knowledge and the tools he will need for further training. Where, for any reason, the emotional problems of any individual child interfere with his satisfactory development, individual treatment measures are advised. On the whole, serious problems are not anticipated and the main educational task of the school proceeds within a secure framework with adequate emotional outlets.

The development of progressive education has analogies in many other fields, including psychoanalysis itself. From a dynamic point of view, two aspects may be distinguished. First, we see here the tendency —which itself has obvious dynamic implications—of converts to respond, after conversion, with what might be called a total reaction. The striking emotional response to new scientific discoveries is a relevant example. Psychoanalysis, like the theory of evolution, had its passionate foes and its equally passionate adherents. It is characteristic of converts to invest their new belief with so much emotion or cathexis that their sense of reality or everyday common sense tends to be somewhat impaired for a time. There is some evidence to suggest that the impact of psychoanalysis on the field of social work roused to some extent this type of emotional response which, for a time at least, led to relative overemphasis on various dynamic concepts. The therapeutic implications of transference reactions, both as they appeared in practice and as they manifested themselves in the supervisory situation, perhaps received some such overemphasis.

We must also consider the development of these two professions in their correct setting, that is, in relation to dynamic psychology itself. The early period of psychiatry, too, was characterized by therapeutic hopes that were not always fulfilled. Its adherents were swept up on the tide of the exciting impact of Freud's earliest discoveries about the nature and content of the unconscious mind and its significance in early personality development. Gradually, however, the emphasis has shifted, partly as a result of increased clinical experience which has added much to our understanding of the complexity and difficulty of many transference reactions, but also, and even more, as a result of further investigation into the development of the ego and the various defense mechanisms. Briefly, we have learned that the understanding and elucidation of mental content revealed in the transference situation is therapeutically effective only when it is combined with understanding of individual modes of defense. This understanding has brought about definite changes, not only in therapeutic procedures but also in many general educational applications of psychoanalytic findings.

It is the primary aim of this paper to discuss in some detail the specific dynamic features characteristic of the supervisory situation in general. In view of their obvious importance, however, the emotional reactions of students in training will first be considered.

SPECIAL FEATURES OF THE
LEARNING SITUATION

The student caseworker will inevitably respond to the emotional impact of his first clinical experience. The handling of these unavoidable emotional reactions at the beginning of training raises special problems for the supervisor. In the first place, the need to enable the student to experience and utilize these emotions as a positive factor in emotional growth is of paramount importance. In supervision, we are dealing with the whole problem of emotional growth which inevitably demands the mastery of disturbing emotional experiences. The student reactions, however, will frequently come with startling suddenness because the student is emotionally unprepared for the experiences. The experiences, however, do not differ in any essential qualitative way from other decisive experiences that the growing immature individual must face along the path toward emotional maturity.

The special and important aspects of these potentially maturing experiences lie in their occurrence in the somewhat artificial setting of professional training instead of in the natural course of the individual's personal development. The student is faced with a double task. He must deal with whatever personally disturbing emotions and shocks are produced by his sudden recognition of what we might broadly call some facts of life; at the same time, and without at first much time for assimilation, he must use this new knowledge in the framework of his professional training. There is, moreover, the added complication that his theoretical knowledge at the time of this experience is probably just enough to make him feel disturbed by the psychopathological implications of his reactions, yet not sufficient for him to recognize that these reactions may in fact be perfectly normal.

To digress a little, Bertha C. Reynolds,[1] in her advice on the handling of these early upsets, seems to me to be entirely sensible in her practical suggestions. She suggests, for example, emphasis on practical points that can be taught, such as policy, administration, and so on, and recommends that the student's reports should be concise and factual. In other words, she suggests that the student should be permitted to work through for himself, as far as possible, the anxieties roused by new emotional experiences, but that the supervisor, at the same time, should provide a framework of security and certainty within which the student can master these anxieties. This concept closely resembles contemporary psychological orientation toward certain childhood fears and anxieties that are universally experienced by all children at some stage of development. The enlightened parent tries to provide security, warmth, and affection, that is, a framework of safety in which the child can master his own anxieties. The similarity is obvious; it is unnecessary to emphasize the fact that the relationship of supervisor to student inevitably parallels in certain respects the relationship of parent to child.

In short, the task of the supervisor, at times of initial and repeated anxieties roused in the student by the emotional impact of the work, is to observe, to stand by, and to offer security and reassurance by placing emphasis on certain practical tasks until the student appears ready for further responsibilities based on emotional growth.

SPECIAL FEATURES IN INDIVIDUAL STUDENT REACTIONS

Just as the wise parent or teacher, who provides a framework of security and affection, must recognize when a child's anxiety becomes excessive or pathological, so must the wise supervisor provide a similar framework and also recognize anxieties or other pathological reactions that suggest either that the student is fundamentally unsuited for professional social work or that he is in need of psychiatric help if he is to master his emotional difficulties. It is probably extremely difficult, even for the most experienced supervisor, to come to definite decisions during this initial period during which many allowances must be made for immature or excessive reactions, in the hope that the student may be able to find his own path to professional maturity. This period, however, should offer valuable pointers as to the student's future potentialities. Experienced supervisors can and often do recognize both hopeful and ominous features in the students' reactions to the initial period of training. Just as, for example, the experienced army psychiatrist could learn to evaluate the inevitable reactions of young soldiers during their initial period of training, or as, in England, the officer selection boards learned a great deal by observing officer candidates in a fairly well-controlled stress situation, experienced supervisors in social work will probably be able to distinguish between the anxiety and transient symptoms displayed by the essentially sound but inevitably immature student, and the more ominous defenses and character reactions demonstrated by more disturbed individuals.

So much then for the special features of the learning situation, which the new student will meet in his first contact with case material, be it medical or be it psychiatric, and which will inevitably continue to a greater or less extent, not only during the period of training, but throughout the worker's professional career.

PROFESSIONAL TRAINING
IN SUPERVISION

I should like next to consider the development of training in professional social work with particular emphasis on the question of supervision. I shall not attempt to discuss the development of casework or the frequently debated question on differences between casework and psychotherapy. Much of what I am going to say, however, has indirect, if not direct, bearing on the important questions so often raised about the significance and the techniques of handling the transference situation in casework.

Professional social work today has progressed a long way from its origins in the charity organizations of the past. Corresponding to the period when orthodox education prevailed, social work, as well as psychiatry, was unaware of the importance of dynamic factors, not only in causing the social, economic, and psychiatric difficulties with which it was concerned, but also in influencing the degree to which clients profited by the help, whether financial or admonitory. Gradually, however, experience and knowledge led to greater understanding of these factors, resulting, on the one hand, in an emphasis in social work on helping the client to help himself—an emphasis similar to that of modern progressive education—and, on the other, in the recognition of the emotional factors in the interpersonal relationship between client and worker which could help or hinder the work. For a time, however, or so it seems to me in retrospect, there was a tendency to give so much weight to these emotional factors as to lead at times to an apparent under-emphasis on the *reality* of social and economic factors. Greater knowledge and experience have largely overcome these early difficulties.

How do these considerations apply to the problem of supervision? The answer to this question is not altogether simple, although the points I have been making have application here too. Supervision can be compared with both educational and therapeutic processes. In the first place, supervision is primarily didactic in purpose and therefore it is comparable to other educational processes. Supervision, however, involves a special type of interpersonal human relationship, in which the emotional factors concerned bear certain important resemblances to (and equally important differences from) the client-worker or patient-doctor relationship. We therefore must consider not only both these aspects of the supervisory situation but also the relationship between them. The didactic purpose, as I have already said, is primary. Important and essential as the emotional factors in the learning process are, the main purpose of education is to educate. The task of supervision, therefore, is to provide a method and a setting which, by taking into account the action of emotional factors, permit both intellectual and emotional growth to proceed freely.

We come now to the vitally important question of the interpersonal relationship between supervisor and worker. I have been deeply impressed by the careful and intelligent attention given to this question in the social work literature. At the same time, I have formed the impression that some writers, particularly during the 30's and early 40's, showed a tendency to treat this relationship as something excessively fragile and vulnerable. This tendency resembles not only the earlier writings of many psychoanalysts, but also the attitude of almost every candidate in training for the practice of psychoanalysis toward the transference situation. The inexperienced analyst, in his handling of the transference situation, tends to feel and to act as though he were treading on egg shells. He fears that every remark and interpretation he makes may have some dire effect on the progress of the analysis. Gradually, however, as he makes mistakes—which he inevitably does—he comes to recognize that far from being excessively vulnerable, a good transference situation can withstand many knocks and bruises. The emphasis here, of course, must be on the word *good*. The parallel, in the supervisor-worker relationship, is that it too must be a good one.

Supervision, as I understand it, began as a purely didactic relationship with relatively little emphasis on the personal relationship between those concerned. The experience in social work of endeavoring to understand the reasons for frequent difficulties in the relationship—with particular reference to the importance of transference phenomena—coincided with the impact of dynamic psychology on the field. These findings brought about a shift of emphasis, until—at least in some of the literature—the emphasis appears to be *mainly* on the interpersonal relationship, with some tendency to turn away from a didactic purpose to one at least implicitly therapeutic.

Let me amplify this point by comparing for a moment the supervisor-worker relationship with another, and in many ways comparable, didactic relationship—that of the candidate in psychoanalytic training with his control analyst. The candidate begins his training by undergoing his training, or didactic, analysis. After a variable period of time, depending on the progress of his analysis, he begins the more didactic part of his training—first attending theoretical, then clinical, courses and finally undertaking the analysis, under supervision or control, of several patients. By the time he reaches this part of his training, the student will have had more than two years' personal analysis. Sometimes his analysis will have been completed. His supervisor, moreover, is always a very experienced training analyst with many years' experience in handling transference situations. The analytic candidate, unlike the student social worker who is relatively unfamiliar with the kind of material he is handling, is always an experienced psychiatrist, and usually an experienced psychotherapist. It might be assumed, therefore, that here is, if anywhere, a teacher-pupil relationship in which the emotional or transference features should be minimal if not absent. Moreover, it would be anticipated that any emotional reactions on either side could be handled in the light of the personal insight—self-knowledge and awareness—of the individuals concerned. In the early days of formal psychoanalytic training, this was the general anticipation. Unfortunately, it has proved far from being the fact.

I cannot, of course, go into a detailed discussion of this subject, which is of extreme complexity, but nevertheless wish to emphasize the fact that even in this very controlled situation there is often a tendency for this didactic situation to develop into a therapeutic one. Where the candidate is still in personal analysis it is obvious that such a development is undesirable, and that any such problem should be referred back to the analytic situation. Where the candidate has finished his personal analysis, and the problems arising are not of a serious nature, it might seem permissible, if not desirable, for these problems to be handled in the control situation. In general, however, it has been discovered that even in this highly controlled and special situation, personal therapy of the student is incompatible with a sound teaching situation.

The two points relevant to our topic which emerge here are, first, that even in this most controlled situation where emotional factors have been dealt with as fully as possible, transference phenomena with potential therapeutic implications arise; second, that in the considered opinion of most experienced teachers in this field, a direct approach to these phenomena is incompatible with a sound didactic situation. In short, the control analyst will anticipate and recognize transference phenomena in the students he supervises. In the vast majority of cases, however, he will allow these phenomena to maintain a subterranean existence, that is, to be implicit, rather than explicit. Only if and when either the transference phenomena are of a nature to interfere with the didactic work, or there is other definite evidence of unresolved emotional problems for which further therapy is indicated, will the control analyst, himself, refer to the personal difficulties of the candidate.

It is obvious that this attitude and point of view are not related to any incapacity of the control analyst to handle transference situations, but rather to the conviction, based on long experience and supported by theoretical knowledge, that didactic and therapeutic situations are mutually incompatible. My conviction—that supervisory situations in social work should aim toward maintaining a sound didactic situation and avoid therapeutic implications—is based on the same reasoning.

The similarities between the supervisory and the analytic training situations are obvious. I believe that the basic dynamics in a good interpersonal relationship between teacher and pupil are identical in the two situations. There are, however, differences that may make the task of the supervisor more difficult and complex than that of the control analyst. In the first place, the analytic candidate is either still in analysis or can relatively easily be advised to have more analysis. He is aware of the nature of unconscious conflicts and recognizes that solution of these conflicts is indispensable for his successful professional development. The student social worker, on the other hand, is very seldom in analysis, and at this stage of his career, might find the idea of considering psychotherapy an extremely difficult and disturbing one. This advice, therefore, is nothing to which the supervisor can resort with any ease. Moreover, the candidate's difficulties are not related as a rule to any obvious, new feature in the material he is handling. The student social worker, in contrast, is receiving many new impressions with very great emotional significance; it is easy to understand the difficulty of entirely avoiding the development of more or less overt transference phenomena with possible therapeutic implications. In my opinion, the crucial point, and the most difficult one, is the assessment and handling of these phenomena with the basic aim of furthering good teaching.

DIFFERENCES BETWEEN DIDACTIC AND THERAPEUTIC SITUATIONS

Finally, we must consider, in dynamic terms, some of the important differences between a good didactic and a good therapeutic situation. We must take it for granted that transference phenomena will inevitably occur in both. The differences must therefore lie in our attitude toward, and our handling of, the phenomena. First of all, we must not allow the fact that we give the emotional reactions of student to teacher and vice versa a technical name (I have not considered in this paper, except by implication, the importance of counter-transference reactions which inevitably occur both in therapy and in teaching) to rob the relationship of its realistic, common-sense meaning. The fact, however, that the purpose of a relationship is didactic does not mean that it must be cold and impersonal. Nor does it imply that the teacher must maintain a distant, objective attitude toward the student at all times, or that he should not be willing on occasion to allow the student to discuss some personal problem. We must not allow our recognition of the unescapable fact that most, if not all, of our emotional reactions have far-reaching, unconscious dynamic implications to blind us to common sense. We must not, in short, allow the unconscious to displace the conscious any more than we can let the symbol displace reality.

I should also like to stress again my earlier remarks about the stability and strength of a good transference situation. In therapy, transference is usually the manifestation with which we work to obtain therapeutic results, aiming as a rule to alter or at least modify the individual's basic defenses and conflicts. In analysis, of course, we handle the transference by interpretation rather than by any manipulative process. In other methods of therapy our handling of the transference shows considerable variations. Although we recognize and utilize it for therapeutic purposes we may allow its existence, from the patient's point of view, to remain more or less implicit. In education, creation and maintenance of a good relationship are an important aim of the teacher. Its main value, however, does not rest on the potentialities it offers for bringing about fundamental alterations in the personality or private emotional life of the student, but on the creation of a stable and secure setting in which he can work out his own problems and progress as smoothly as possible toward the development of a stable and mature professional self. Obviously, it is a matter of extreme delicacy to maintain a warm and interested human relationship, on the one hand, and, on the other, not to respond to the therapeutic needs that the student may reveal either directly, by the development of symptoms, or indirectly, in his handling of his case material.

Perhaps the dividing line—admittedly indefinite and difficult to delineate—for the supervisor to draw, in his attitude toward the emotional reactions of his students, is between what is conscious and what is genuinely unconscious. It seems relatively safe to respond to the conscious emotional reactions of students, both to the material under discussion and also to the supervisor himself. Whether, and to what extent, these matters need to be discussed is another question which obviously depends on the individual case. This does not mean that the supervisor, particularly one with an analytic orientation, will not often have a very good idea of the unconscious implications of the conscious reactions, and that this knowledge may not help very considerably in the evaluation of the student. I do not, however, feel that the supervisor can cross this dividing line without serious risk of turning a teaching situation into a therapeutic one.

SUMMARY

I have tried to bring the problems of supervision into a particular historical perspective with reference to the development of dynamic psychology, with particular reference to the therapeutic handling of the transference situation. I have suggested that in social work, as in progressive education, the first impact of dynamic thought gave rise for a time to overemphasis on and somewhat anxious attention to certain psychological phenomena and, as in psychoanalysis itself, to what many of us today would consider undue optimism about its therapeutic potentials. Greater knowledge and experience have increasingly enabled these disciplines to combine the new understanding of underlying meanings with many sound dynamic premises which, in the pre-dynamic era, went under the name of plain common sense.

I shall conclude, therefore, with a very common-sense remark which, I hope, is also based on sound, if recognized, dynamic thought. I do not believe that the well-trained and experienced supervisor who genuinely feels and believes his task to be didactic runs much real risk of getting into a therapeutic situation, however much he may recognize the deeper implications of some of the reactions evinced on the part of his students. He will, in short, understand the complex factors he is facing but will utilize this knowledge to create for the student, who must in the process of learning recapitulate to a greater or less extent some of his earlier emotional problems, a framework of security in which to develop and learn. This framework is similar, dynamically, to that which is essential to the infant and child in the decisive years of earlier development. The student who cannot develop and learn in such a situation is probably either basically unsuited for professional social work or in need of active psychiatric treatment.

NOTES

1. *Learning and Teaching in the Practice of Social Work*, Rinehart and Company, New York, 1942.

PART II

Essential Knowledge and Skills

INTRODUCTION

IN THE 1950s, as the formal professionalization of social work evolved, supervision received renewed attention with a broader focus than that of the psychoanalytic/personal-growth model of the past. Teaching was the first role of the supervisor, and later the helping and administrative functions were added. The articles in this section, written in the 1950s and 1960s, reflect the efforts to clarify, consolidate, and coordinate these functions. Much of the conceptualization of supervision during this era is the basis of strategy in many agencies today, and the skills and techniques identified and explored still have much relevance for dealing with problems and issues in practice.

The article by Austin reflects the gradual transition from a purely psychoanalytic model of supervision. Earlier writings based on the traditional psychoanalytic model explored supervision primarily in terms of the personalities of the worker and the supervisor. Austin's article, however, emphasizes the components of the *role* of supervisor, which she views primarily as teaching and secondarily as administration. She talks of laws of learning, job descriptions, principles, techniques, and elements of supervision. She revives, and adds depth to, the view of supervision as an organizationally sanctioned position, which was outlined by the Milford Report. Austin does not move completely away from the psychoanalytic model but rather integrates it with the more objective role-performance model that was emerging at the time. Thus psychoanalytic principles are related to learning theory and the educational component of supervision. Emphasis is placed on the tutorial method, which is based on relationship; and although little distinction is made between student and practitioner supervision, a clear distinction is made between supervision and consultation: two terms that still occasion much confusion and debate in the profession. The discussion of educational diagnosis and evaluation in relation to the degree of independence in supervision has much relevance for current practices.

Scherz's article also illustrates the movement away from psychoanalytic orientation, emphasizing administration as the essence of supervision. This article is an attempt to use a logical, rational approach based on the premise that the worker must accept responsibility for his or her own practice. Scherz questions the assumption of a correlation between the worker's growth and development and direct, close supervision. The supervisor's responsibility is explored from the perspective that his or her role is to facilitate the work of the practitioner, and the responsibility of the worker is discussed in connection with self-motivated learning and growth. Within this context there is a valuable discussion of the use of feedback and evaluation techniques in supervision. Scherz sees relationship as based on a positive recognition of job responsibility, and she distinguishes between control and authority.

Stiles relates the administrative functions of supervision discussed by Austin and Scherz to communication, to promote effective internal functioning of the agency and to better external relationships with the larger community. From this perspective, emphasis is again placed on the role of the supervisor as mediator and "enabler" as applied to the three primary social work methods—casework, group work, and community organization. A distinction is made between student and staff supervision, and the role of the supervisor in using qualitative rather than quantitative methods to avoid dependency is explained. Building on Scherz's definition of job responsibility, Stiles develops the concept "implicit contract" and assesses the quality of supervision in content, method, and goals.

The article by Berl attempts to provide a comprehensive view by identifying four operational components of supervision. The institutional component deals with the tension that results from organizational versus professional views of supervision; the methodological matches learning and administrative goals; the educational moves the practitioner-learner through various stages of development; and the psychological confronts the complementarity in role expectations of practitioner and supervisor. Berl's operational components provide a unified perspective on the articles by Austin, Scherz, and Stiles.

The articles in this section illustrate the shift in the analytic focus of supervision from personality to organizationally sanctioned role positions and job responsibilities. The selections reflect a gradual reorientation of the relative emphasis placed on teaching, administration, and helping. In many ways these articles are a continuation of the historical development of supervision theory explored in Part I, as well as a basic compilation of the skills and techniques essential to sound supervisory practice to the present day. Many of the practices and principles discussed here become points of discussion again in the sections on authority, autonomy, and trends in supervision as the profession has developed new concerns in these areas.

7

Basic Principles of Supervision

Lucille N. Austin

SUPERVISION, AS IT HAS BEEN DEVELOPED in social work, is commanding respect in other professions as well as in social work education and training. Because in supervision the basic laws of learning have been applied in new and meaningful combinations, it is making a distinctive contribution to education methods. It has synthesized knowledge about intellectual processes, derived from the educational field, with knowledge about the emotional and social components in learning, derived from both psychoanalytic psychology and social work practice.

What are the elements that go into supervision? A review of job descriptions of supervisory positions would reveal a variety of assignments. Increasingly, supervisors are devoting some time to practice; they also carry certain administrative responsibilities. The central responsibility of the supervisor, however, is teaching, that is, participating in the professional education of students and in the professional development of agency staff members. The supervisor's contribution to administration is rooted in his competence to ensure service to clients, and in his ability to increase the effectiveness of staff performance and to make judgments about the promotion, reassignment, or dismissal of staff members. Supervision is to be distinguished from consultation, which is based on voluntary interrelationships and does not carry the same evaluative responsibility.

Mastery of professional practice in social work requires a continuous period of learning and doing. The supervision of students and of staff members, therefore, differs only in the point at which learning is taking place, and not in the application of a different set of principles and

From *Social Casework* 33 (December 1952), pp. 411–419. Reprinted by permission of the Family Service Association of America.

techniques. As learning in one area is achieved, the student or worker is expected to assume responsibility for independent functioning in that area, whether he is in his first year of school training or a worker in his third year of practice. The recognition of continuity in the process of professional development is in itself important; it gives supervisors perspective on the nature of a particular individual's ability to progress and provides clues to repetitive learning problems. It places on schools and agencies the responsibility for outlining their expectations at different points of professional development.

In educational terms, supervision utilizes the tutorial method. In social work, the teaching situation is affected by the supervisor's parallel administrative responsibilities for evaluating the worker's performance and for ensuring adequate service to clients. The use of the tutorial method results in an intensity in the teacher-student relationship which is recognizable at the outset. This method creates a closer relationship than can prevail in even a small classroom situation. The relationship elements, therefore, are in the foreground. The management of them is intermingled with teaching techniques and with responsibility for service to clients.

In social work, the learning is vitalized by the subject matter. The discussions deal with living situations—with the welfare of human beings who will be affected by the actions taken. Because social work deals intimately with personal conflict, pathology, and lack of adjustment, which may have parallels in the supervisee's own life experience, the content itself stimulates introspection and subjective reactions. Hence, learning about people, in order to help them, is a highly charged emotional experience. Learning is made usable, largely, through the support of a positive supervisory relationship which leads the worker to new insights about people, including himself.

Before we go further in identifying the skills in supervisory teaching, it may be helpful to review principles of learning from both the psychoanalytic and educational fields.

PSYCHOANALYTIC PRINCIPLES

Social work has drawn on psychoanalytic psychology in developing its learning theory. The contributions of Freud and his followers to the understanding of mental life and emotional development have been incorporated into social work teaching, as well as into its practice. It is true that the psychoanalytic group has not presented a formal learning theory, but learning principles are implicit in the theory of personality development and in the studies of children and adults who encounter difficulties in learning and in social functioning.

Let us look at some of the psychoanalytic principles already in use in social work practice and education.

1. Learning patterns follow the same principles that apply to other kinds of behavior. The science of learning is a part of the science of personality. Among these basic psychological assumptions about behavior which social work has accepted are: an individual cannot be understood except in relation to his experiences and background; an individual's behavior or activity cannot be understood apart from some view of his personality as a whole; and unconscious motivations color the nature of conscious thought and action and must be taken into account in appropriate ways.

2. Learning takes place either as a result of direct experience or through a relationship with another who imparts knowledge and the benefit of his experience. Because learning everything through direct experience is wasteful and impractical, a large part of knowledge must be mastered through acceptance of the tested experience of others. Such acceptance is furthered by a positive relationship between the learner and teacher.

3. The ability to form and utilize relationships is dependent on the maturity of the personality which, to a great extent, is dependent on a relatively successful resolution of the infantile psychosexual conflicts, and the formation of a kindly superego. Energy is released and the motivation to engage in adult pursuits is strengthened when the ego gains mastery over these childhood conflicts. The resolution of these conflicts is a continuous process. Freud says "the processes necessary for bringing about a normal outcome are not for the most part either completely present, or completely absent. They are, as a rule, partially present, so that the final result remains dependent upon quantitative relations." [1] The child learns to relate to other persons and, under favorable conditions, this capacity can be extended and deepened.

4. The higher mental processes of logical thought—the ability to discriminate and to generalize—may be impeded by emotional conflicts that absorb the individual in unconscious fantasies and lead to an excessive use of regressive defenses and symptoms.

5. The physical and socio-cultural conditions provided by the structure of a society are also involved in learning. The opportunity to go to school to engage in social experiences, to be in contact with other minds and new subject material are all essentials.

Examination of these assumptions will explain why, in teaching and supervision, personality considerations of the teachers as well as the pupils are inevitably involved. With improved methods of selection of candidates for admission to the schools of social work, it is possible that, in the future, the schools can count on a larger percentage of students with positive learning patterns, whose energy is free and not restricted by crippling neurotic conflict. Even currently, the schools get a fair share of such students. The nature of social work, however, attracts persons who are motivated by altruism. Because social work is a profession that aims to help, it can provide a channel for true sublimation, but it can also serve as a defense against underlying destructive wishes. Fortunately, reactive traits and defenses can sometimes be reinforced to approximate sublimation or, more constructively, anxiety can be reduced so that old defenses give way and permit sublimation.

EDUCATIONAL PRINCIPLES

Social work has also drawn on educational principles in supervision, but not fully or in a disciplined manner. What are some of these educational principles that apply to the supervisory process?

It is noteworthy that educational method also stresses individualization. Dewey says, "Teaching carries with it the responsibility for understanding the needs and capacities of the individuals who are learning at a given time. It is not enough that certain materials and methods have proved effective with other individuals at other times. It is important to pay attention to what is educative with particular individuals at particular times. . . . There is no such thing as educational value in the abstract." [2]

If teaching is to be effective, the subject matter to be learned and the student's way of learning must be related to each other. The ability to impart knowledge is dependent on possession of knowledge. A good bedside manner, on the part of a physician, is not a substitute for proficiency, nor is a good personal approach, on the part of a social worker or a teacher, a substitute for knowledge. A clear conception of what is to be taught is the first requisite of a good teacher. [3] On the other hand, students always learn best from a teacher who not only knows his subject and knows how to teach, but who likes and is liked by the students.

The subject matter of social work training, unquestionably, needs further study and elaboration, both in terms of knowledge to be acquired and technical methods to be mastered. The content of student field work and of advanced practice does not lend itself easily to classification and to orderly sequences. The "case" determines the knowledge that must be applied. In case assignments, it is possible, within limits, to proceed from the simple to the complex, that is, to move from the better known and more objective problems of social need with the related normal reactions to ones of personal breakdown and complicated psychological reactions.

When the focus of field teaching is on professional methodology, the teaching content can also be unified to a certain degree. Fact finding (social study), diagnosis (social planning), and treatment (implementation) underlie casework, group work, and community organization. Teaching a student how to explore a problem, how to understand it, and how to work on solutions provides the groundwork for teaching him these basic processes. Mastery of these processes equips the student to move into independent work.

The student, in his field work, must be helped to meet the demands of a particular situation, and then move from the specific to the general. Classroom teachers and field work supervisors teach both principles and their application.[4] Experienced workers and supervisors have a special responsibility to develop and articulate new principles and methods.[5]

SELECTION OF TEACHING METHOD

Experience in supervision confirms Dewey's statement that there is no such thing as educational value in the abstract. What appears to be a simple step—to impart knowledge—is conditioned by the variety of teaching and learning patterns that grow out of the personality characteristics and needs of teacher and student. An essential skill in supervision, therefore, is the selection of a teaching method based on an individualized educational diagnosis. This educational diagnosis includes an evaluation of the worker's performance in person-to-person and group relationships which inevitably is conditioned by his personality attributes as well as his intellectual abilities. Evaluation outlines include such points as: ability to form relationships with individuals and groups in such a way as to be of service; ability to work with people with needs and personalities different from the worker's; ability to translate theory into practice; capacity for sufficient self-awareness to be able to help others.

The formulation of an educational diagnosis starts with an evaluative process, sorting out what the worker is able to do and how effectively he is doing it. It then moves to a diagnostic phase, to determine why he is able or unable to achieve certain objectives. Such an appraisal is based on norms of performance and on clinical evaluation of the supervisee's ways of learning and doing, not as isolated responses but as reflections of his personality. This diagnostic process contains some of the elements that go into making a psychosocial diagnosis in casework. This kind of diagnosis, based largely on an appraisal of one's functioning on a job, differs from a psychoanalytic diagnosis, which is based on exploration of symptoms and personality development, including an understanding of the etiology and interconnections of unconscious mechanisms. The educational goal, although utilizing some of the same understanding of personality, must be differentiated from both analytic and casework goals. The focus in the supervisory situation is on learning and performance.

What factors must be considered in constructing an educational diagnosis? The student's work as revealed in his records, and his contacts with supervisors and others, will indicate his capacities and areas of difficulty. The appraisal of his performance leads to the next step of evaluating the nature and degree of his anxiety and the capacity of the ego to master anxiety and to engage in creative learning.

As in all emotionally charged new experiences, a degree of anxiety is inherent in the training situation. Charlotte Towle has described the anxiety that is aroused in the training experience when demands are made on the ego for the integration of new knowledge.[6] The special anxieties of the experienced worker coming to school for training have also received attention.[7] In general, these reactions to new and difficult problems of adaptation might be termed "situational anxiety." In addition to this general anxiety, social work training often precipitates a deeper and more threatening anxiety, the roots of which lie in personality organization; a peripheral or central unsolved personal problem is touched off by the close contact with other human beings in trouble, or by the demands of professional training. Such personal involvements are present in most students in varying degrees; the involvement may be manifested in the inability to work with parents or with children, to deal with money, to work with hostile clients, to help the mentally ill, to succeed with an interracial group program, or to amalgamate groups with conflicting ideas in a community organization assignment.[8]

The supervisor, by noting the worker's defenses as they are mobilized to cope with demands of the learning situation, can come to understand the strength and weakness of the worker in helping others and also the degree of stress he feels in the process. Defenses—their character as well as their fluidity—offer important clues for a preliminary educational diagnosis.

It is also important, in working with students and staff, to identify character traits and neurotic or psychotic manifestations when they are present. Psychological knowledge must be used with discrimination; like all knowledge, it can be used to hurt. In the hands of the disciplined and trained supervisor, however, it can be used to help the student or worker gain the guidance or treatment he needs.

What other data besides the appraisal of students' performance are necessary to formulate an educational diagnosis? References give some information about the student or worker. If the reports are read with a diagnostic eye, they give facts about intelligence, interests, and accomplishments.

The autobiographical material submitted to the schools is useful even though the student is usually guarded in his statements or may feel uncertain about how much or how little to tell. Admission and pre-employment interviews also yield important material about the individual's motivations in choosing social work as a career, and about his expectations of himself and the profession.

The superivsor may later elicit further facts in the medium of the understanding supervisor-worker relationship, usually in connection with a specific case or work assignment. The main principle that should govern the supervisor in engaging in such personal inquiries is the relevance of a particular attitude to job performance. The content of the worker's life history sometimes holds the clue to the blocking in his learning or activity. The connection must be conveyed to the worker if he is not already aware of it, which he often is. He may—or may not—wish to discuss the details of his personal life with the supervisor, and the supervisor may also wish to place limits on personal revelations. Usually the supervisor, on the basis of a generalized awareness of the kinds of experiences that cause particular problems, can point up the possible connections that the worker should consider. Current problems that interfere with work by draining away energy may also be appropriately discussed.

Observation of the worker's bearing and appearance provides another source of data. The impressions he makes on the supervisor, staff, and community groups often reveal ease or insecurity. The worker's responses to the supervisor and his ways of using supervision provide concrete examples of his attitudes toward authority and about dependency. In his discussion of his clients or in his handling of the supervisory conference his manner, facial expressions, and tone of voice connote varying degrees of frankness or evasion, of organization or disorganization, and of depression or overt hostility. These reactions must be related to other facts, but it should be remembered that persons usually do not act "out of character" even when under especially strong stimuli.

PATTERNS OF LEARNING AND DOING

Patterns of learning and doing begin to emerge as the various pieces of behavior are related to each other.[9] Only a few common patterns will be mentioned.

One familiar pattern is marked by the following manifestations: The worker uses theory intellectually, rather than as a tool to help him understand a problem at hand; he engages the supervisor in a constant battle of wits; he is supercilious toward other students or staff members; he tends to be logical to the point of literalness with his clients; he holds rigidly to high standards for himself and others and resorts to a variety of protective and controlling actions.

Another pattern has the following characteristics: The worker, in subtle ways, conveys the idea that he has special talents; his interviews, such few as he has had time to dictate, may show special sensitivity to client feeling, but he does not meet the requirements of dictation and office reports, or carry heavy work responsibilities. This type of worker often attempts to lure the supervisor into accepting his own self-evaluation—that he is "gifted" and should not have to meet "ordinary" requirements. If he is reasonably successful in this maneuver, he may soon be promoted to a supervisory position—where he will not have to dictate. Unless he is fortunate enough in the beginning to have a supervisor who understands his defensive behavior, he will remain undisciplined and may never fully develop the gifts he possesses. More seriously, if the worker does not have the talents he has laid claim to, his clients and later the workers he supervises will be "short changed" because of his limitations.

The student who looks and acts younger than his years also is often utilizing defensive mechanisms. He usually manifests eagerness for supervision and relates to his superiors in an admiring, but essentially dependent, way. He is unable to set limitations firmly and supportively, either in contact with clients or as the leader of a group. Unless he can be helped to resolve some of his adolescent conflicts, he will remain a person of limited usefulness.

Other patterns, of course, are characterized by comparatively open relationships, absence of handicapping ambivalence, relatively straightforward ability to help others, and real intellectual curiosity. Although persons with such qualities may have had their share of anxiety, their life experiences, on the whole, have promoted trust rather than resentment. As a result, they are able to empathize with suffering but also have a realistic optimism and faith that human beings, given the opportunity, can surmount obstacles. Their progress, too, has ups and downs but the prognosis is highly favorable.

Because considerable range and variation in ability to learn and to modify attitudes exist within any pattern of behavior, a differential diagnosis is important. The findings on which diagnosis is based emerge naturally from the training and work situation, accumulating from the worker's professional performance. The supervisor's understanding of interconnections between various pieces of evidence leads to a rounded picture of the worker's personality and aptitudes. I should like to stress, again, that the findings for arriving at an educational diagnosis emerge from the teaching situation itself. Supervisors can learn to recognize evidence at hand and see new meaning in it; it is not always necessary to open new avenues of exploration. The use made of an educational diagnosis is bounded by the nature of the supervisory responsibility—which is to *teach*. The responsibility does not include manipulating or "bossing" the worker on the one hand, or, on the other, "treatment" of his personality problems.

It should be noted, also, that students and workers are able to appraise their supervisors. The "grapevine" is a remarkable source of information. Workers also are able to observe. Often they are intuitive even before they are knowledgeable. They may not formulate their diagnosis in sophisticated terms but it is frequently clearer and more telling than one clothed in technical language.

Human beings always pass judgment on one another. Workers must appraise their supervisors in order to understand and sort out their own reactions. If supervisors are not fearful themselves, they can let workers tell them what helps them and what bothers them in their supervisors' temperaments and ways of working. What is sauce for the goose is sauce for the gander.

USE OF THE EDUCATIONAL DIAGNOSIS

How does the supervisor use an educational diagnosis to further the supervisee's professional development? Supervision, naturally, is directed toward helping the student learn the content of social work and the methods of practice. It aims to promote intellectual learning, which is dependent on the integration of appropriate feelings. From the beginning, the student is guided into gaining some self-awareness of his attitudes and reactions. Psychotherapy has contributed to social work knowledge about ways of furthering such self-awareness, which, technically, might be described as "secondary insight"; it is not primary insight in the psychoanalytic sense. The goal in supervision is to help the student gain some awareness about what he does—and why. Such understanding provides a basis for effecting changes in thinking and acting. The difference between education and personal therapy should be kept clearly in mind, but their similarities should not be overlooked.[10]

Many students and young staff workers, as they gain knowledge, become aware themselves of the influence of their life problems on their current feelings. This is true especially of the relatively normal persons whose problems are residual, rather than extensive and neurotic. Recognition of these interactions is often spontaneous and results in considerable relief and increased learning ability. The neurotic person, however; needs more help; he is able to reveal himself only if the supervisor is sensitive and skilled in identifying his problems and in making them discussable.

The flexible use of a range of teaching methods is essential if the supervisor individualizes the student's learning problems. A method that is helpful to one student may be useless to another. A supervisory plan that encourages a high degree of independent action may be right for one student and crippling for another. A supervisor has his own preferred ways of teaching, and whenever possible it is educationally sound to assign him students who learn best from his way of teaching. But supervisors, like workers, must be adaptable. They must utilize their capacity, which they learned in practice, to work with a wide variety of people.

Supervisory teaching is centered on the teaching of a "case." * Leading case discussions calls for supervisory competence in diagnosis and treatment. The supervisor, at the same time, must know the worker and sense what kind of help the worker needs to enable him to help the client. Teaching must proceed in a way that will extend and integrate the worker's knowledge, and also enrich and deepen his perceptions and feelings. In many instances, the worker uses the discussion of the case not only for the purpose of deepening his understanding of the client but also for self-understanding. The discussion of the client can be a vehicle by which the supervisor communicates ideas and understanding to the worker. "Double talk" is an effective technique in many human relationships.

The case discussion method, when based on interviewing and diagnostic skill, is a potent educational instrument. The supervisor can detect and handle the ways in which the worker's conflicts block the acceptance of certain ideas and the nature of his resistance to them.

By evaluating the particular response in the light of the whole, the supervisor can determine the appropriate time to inject new ideas. Before focusing directly on the worker's problems, even those based on lack of knowledge and experience,[11] the supervisor waits until the worker has built up success in some areas. As the supervisor becomes familiar with the worker's ways of learning and performing, he may discover both areas of clarity on the part of the worker and blind spots. Blind spots— the points of non-comprehension that continue after logical teaching has taken place—are often the result of personal involvements. Such involvements lead to over-identification with or rejection of the client and the use of the relationship to gain hidden gratifications. These personal involvements show themselves in partisan attitudes, false reassurances, an inability to let the client bring out his real feelings, cutting off the client's line of thought, or in control of the client, sometimes, even to the point of punitive action.

If the worker perceives what he is doing and opens up his reactions for discussion, the conference is one step ahead. If the supervisor must raise questions, the worker frequently responds to them with projection or hostile argument. If the supervisor has the ability to identify the defenses and assess the anxiety, he will know how to proceed. He may

---

* "Case" is used here to mean a unit of work with an individual, a group, or a community organization project.

drop the point for the time being and pick it up in another conference when the point will be better illustrated. Or he may hold to his point, standing the "gaff" of the hostility until the worker, aided by the firmness and consistency of the supervisor's conviction, comes to terms with his problem.

If the worker's difficulties reflect deep personal involvements, the supervisor is alerted to the need for careful evaluation. He will, as he does with all students, observe, but not disturb, the worker's defenses. If the worker approaches things intellectually, the supervisor will respect this; if he emphasizes his independence and shows fear of being controlled, the supervisor will give him leeway. The supervisor will give him what assistance he can use in such a way as not to humiliate him. Gradually he may learn that his fears are unjustified and that he can do better thinking if he does not try to do it alone.

Some anxiety in the worker is bound to be aroused by self-examination. In such a period, the supervisory relationship becomes intensified and techniques of psychological support must be employed. The supervisory relationship together with the skilful use of therapeutically oriented teaching techniques usually make it possible for the worker to relax sufficiently to gain some self-awareness and to shift his handling of his clients.[12]

HANDLING TRANSFERENCE REACTIONS

The supervisor must be adept at creating a worker-supervisor relationship in which positive feeling is in the foreground. The appearance of certain negative aspects from time to time is inevitable. The supervisor, by error or because of the demands of the job, may place too great a burden on a worker, thus provoking legitimate anger. Obviously, such provocations should be kept at a minimum. But, in addition, the learning and work situation precipitates transference responses.

The understanding and handling of transference and countertransference reactions are as important in teaching and administration as in direct treatment situations. These displacements of feeling elude rational measures designed to create smooth relationships with clients and colleagues. They account, sometimes, for the "dependency" of experienced staff members who cling to supervision rather than move into leadership positions; for the exaggerated distrust of workers for their supervisors, seeing them as persons determined to stand in the way of the workers' progress; for the "acting out" of workers who, by stirring up hostilities in others, break down student and staff morale; and also for illness, unfinished work, and dictation problems.

Transference reactions must be recognized by the supervisor and reduced, either by discussion or by shifts in the teaching approach. Neurotic hostility, of course, must be distinguished from justified anger. The distinction is more difficult to make if poor supervision, inadequate channels for staff expression, and closed opportunities for advancement are actually major issues. Good administrative practices provide the necessary base for good supervision.

EVALUATIONS

The responsibility for formal evaluation of the student's or worker's performance is lodged in the supervisor. The evaluation is based on criteria of learning and performance norms at different levels of development. The process of evaluation includes mutual discussion in conferences, after the worker and supervisor have both reviewed and re-examined selected records and other data. The worker is free to express disagreement and to give his evidence and point of view.

The supervisor's responsibility to point up limitations has many difficult aspects. Negative points that have been talked over piecemeal often seem more serious when brought together in a unit. The failure of a worker to meet certain performance requirements must be carefully evaluated in order to establish a prognosis. Negative evaluations are handled most constructively when the worker has had a fair chance to learn, and when the supervisor has not met hostility with hostility. If the worker comes to terms with his set limitations he can then survey kinds of work he can undertake and set his goals realistically.

The matter of promotions also deserves attention. Judgment about the worker's readiness for them must be based on evidence of competence, which should include an evaluation of the worker's psychological ability to undertake greater responsibility; there should be evidence that the worker's competitive drives and negative reactions to authority are under reasonable control. Psychological knowledge about the hazards of being in authority—who can assume it, whom it will unnerve, and who will misuse it—underlies such an evaluation. These problems of dependency and authority are closely related to the degree to which the early childhood rivalries with parents and siblings have been resolved. In psychosocial terms, the resolution of the oedipal conflict determines the individual's psychological ability to be a parent, literally or figuratively, and to assume other adult responsibilities, of which work is one. The ability to work with pleasure and without undue anxiety, the ability to use authority constructively, and the qualities of generosity and tolerance all grow out of positive identifications with parents and other adults. People whose early life experiences have been too damaging and who have not had subsequent corrective experiences will be vulnerable in these areas and may not make good social workers.[13,14]

References, like evaluations, should be shared with workers. The content should point up work problems as well as strengths so that repetitive problems can be identified. The supervisor can be a resource for guiding the worker in his vocational planning within the field of social work. The supervisor's ability to spot interest and talent and to suggest opportunities to the worker in the light of needs in the agency and the field is a service to the individual as well as to the profession.

SUMMARY

To acquire supervisory skills, of course, is as difficult as to learn to be a skilful worker. Training for supervision has not received adequate professional attention. Planning for more adequate training in the future is an essential—not a luxury. Learning new methods from the educational field, adapting casework principles to education, moving into positions that currently are identified with status and authority, are challenges that must be met by the field. Learning to supervise under supervision is the most effective way of gaining the requisite skills.

NOTES

1. Sigmund Freud, *An Outline of Psychoanalysis,* W. W. Norton & Company, New York, 1949, p. 31.

2. John Dewey, *Experience and Education,* Macmillan, New York, 1938, pp. 45–46.

3. Yonata Feldman, "The Teaching Aspect of Casework Supervision," *Social Casework,* Vol. XXXI, No. 4 (1950), pp. 156–161.

4. Charlotte Towle, "The Classroom Teacher as Practitioner," *Social Work as Human Relations,* Columbia University Press, New York, 1949, pp. 140–157.

5. Lucille Nickel Austin, "Supervision of the Experienced Case Worker," *The Family,* Vol. XXII, No. 9 (1942), pp. 314–320.

6. Charlotte Towle, "The Emotional Element in Learning in Professional Education for Social Work," American Association of Schools of Social Work, New York, January, 1948. Also Charlotte Towle, "The Distinctive Attributes of Education for Social Work," *Social Work Journal,* Vol. XXIII, No. 2 (1952), pp. 63–72, 94.

7. Rhoda Gerard Sarnat, "Supervision of the Experienced Student," *Social Casework,* Vol. XXXIII, No. 4 (1952), pp. 147–152.

8. Florence Hollis, "Emotional Growth of the Worker Through Supervision,"

Proceedings of the National Conference of Social Work: 1936, University of Chicago Press, Chicago, 1963, pp. 167–168.

9. Eleanor Neustaedter, "The Field Supervisor as Educator," *Social Work as Human Relations,* Columbia University Press, New York, 1949, p. 135.

10. John Dollard and Neal E. Miller, *Personality and Psychotherapy; An Analysis in Terms of Learning, Thinking, and Culture,* McGraw-Hill, New York, 1950.

11. Margaret Williamson, *Supervision—Principles and Methods,* Woman's Press, New York, 1950, p. 95.

12. Mary C. Hester, "Educational Process in Supervision," *Social Casework,* Vol. XXXII, No. 6 (1951), pp. 242–250.

13. Sidney Berengarten, "Pilot Study: Criteria in Selection for Social Work," *Social Work as Human Relations,* Columbia University Press, New York, 1949, pp. 170–194.

14. Henry W. Brosin, M.D., "Psychiatry Experiments with Selection," *Social Work as Human Relations,* Columbia University Press, New York, 1949, pp. 158–169.

8

A Concept of Supervision
Based on Definitions
of Job Responsibility

Frances H. Scherz

THE POINT OF VIEW expressed in this paper is that the job of case-work supervisor is, in essence, an administrative job. Both of the major components of casework supervision—teaching and management—are administrative functions. I should like to discuss in some detail the job responsibilities of a supervisor and a caseworker, the specific performance requirements of each of these jobs, and the effects of the differences between the job responsibilities of these two positions on the content of supervision and on the supervisor-caseworker relationship.

The following suggested definitions of job responsibility are based on two specific premises. First, the caseworker, whose job assignment is the giving of direct service to clients, must assume the primary responsibility for his own work and for his own continued professional development. Second, the supervisor, by nature of his job assignment, has the primary responsibility for facilitating the work of the casework staff. Both the caseworker and the supervisor are responsible for implementing the purpose and function of the agency, although their job assignments are different. The point at which these two jobs meet is in the mutual concern for giving effective service.

The executive staff of the Jewish Family and Community Service of Chicago presented to the supervisory staff the following propositions: (1) that the core of the supervisor's job is administrative leadership; (2) that the caseworker bears the major responsibility for his own work. Meeting together as a group, the executive and supervisory staffs were asked to examine job content and supervisory practice in the light of these propositions. The willingness of the staff members to be freely

From *Social Casework* 39 (October 1958), pp. 435–443. Reprinted by permission of the Family Service Association of America.

critical of the agency's established practices and procedures created an atmosphere in which everyone could react, consider, and work together on these propositions. The group is continuing to examine the formulations presented in this paper, their applicability to supervisory practice, and the traditional professional attitudes that further or impede their implementation.

Although the point of view that supervision is inherently an administrative function is a departure from the usual concept that supervision has two distinct components, teaching and administration, the two specific premises are neither new nor startling. The literature is replete with discussion of the roles of the supervisor in teaching and management. The long history of attempts to interpret and implement these roles is one of trial and error. A great deal of both positive and negative emotion has been associated with these efforts.

BASIC ASSUMPTIONS

Basic to the considerations presented in this paper is the assumption that every professionally trained staff member has some measure of competence. By this is meant that, upon completion of training in a school of social work, a caseworker is presumed to be able to meet the requirements for the position of Caseworker I, as described in many agency classification plans and in such statements as *A Guide to Classification of Professional Positions and Evaluation Outlines in a Family Agency*.[1] Moreover, a caseworker who has had work experience is hired on the basis of his presumed ability to meet designated job classification requirements. The agency is responsible for delineating in relation to the worker's level of experience the job assignment in regard to such specific matters as the nature of the caseload, qualitative and quantitative standards of practice, explicit recording requirements, routines, evaluation procedures, and the agency resources available for help in carrying out the job. Supervision is one of these resources. Within this framework, the agency assumes that the caseworker will use his knowledge and capacity to the best of his ability and that he will use all of the available professional resources in the interest of continuing to increase his capacity for giving effective service.

These assumptions about competence and self-responsibility have been neither clearly understood nor wholeheartedly accepted. For example, although schools of social work state that the new graduate has some ability to perform in a job, they, as well as agencies, have stressed the need for the recent graduate to have "very close supervision" for the first several years of practice. Relatively little emphasis has been placed on the beginning caseworker's ability to perform and to take responsibility for further developing his capacities. Rather, emphasis has been placed on the quality and quantity of supervision, as if the caseworker's development proceeds in direct ratio to the kind and extent of supervision. This concept is highly questionable. We know that the most effective learning is learning that is self-motivated. It is stimulated by normal impulses toward growth and reaches its highest level when associated with self-responsibility for achievement. Even in the instance of an externship, it is unsound to have the achievement of the educational goals largely dependent on supervision as the main medium for learning.

The new graduate does not entirely accept the fact that he has the ability to perform on a job. His doubts are revealed in his anxiety to be given "good supervision." Nor is this anxiety confined to the worker who is seeking his first casework job. Much of it stems from the wish to be helpful to people, but some of it is related to the inordinate value falsely placed on supervision as a means of learning and of assuring good service.

RESPONSIBILITIES OF THE SUPERVISOR

Essentially, supervision is a job of administrative leadership. The agency is responsible for designating the job responsibilities and requirements for supervisors at various levels of experience. Since schools of social work cannot provide specific training in supervision within the Master's curriculum, the agency has to establish an in-service training program for the beginning supervisor. In hiring a supervisor with experience, the agency assumes that (1) he has the degree of competence in casework practice that is required to facilitate the work of casework staff; (2) he is able to transmit knowledge effectively; (3) he is capable of assessing the performance and the professional developmental needs of casework staff; (4) he has a body of knowledge about differential supervisory methods which he can apply discriminatingly; and (5) he understands authority and uses it appropriately.

The agency expects the supervisor to continue to develop his skills in casework and supervisory practice. He is not necessarily expected to be the most skilled practitioner in the agency. He is expected, however, to re-examine casework concepts, to acquire new knowledge about human behavior as it emerges, and to encourage the casework staff to examine and experiment with new concepts and techniques. He is expected to use the resources both within and outside the agency to enhance his casework knowledge and supervisory practice.

The supervisor is not expected to have achieved mastery in all the areas of casework knowledge. His lack of knowledge in certain areas may make him unable to be of assistance to casework staff in dealing with some cases. Both the supervisor and the administrative personnel to whom he is accountable should accept the fact that he has both strengths and limitations and that he may have "blind spots" in respect to certain cases and in his supervisory methodology. Such acceptance should make it possible for the supervisor to handle these variations in his knowledge comfortably, and should free him and the staff to use other helpful resources appropriately. The supervisor is not expected to work with all members of the casework staff with equal ability or ease, but he is responsible for using his reactions to different staff members and their ways of working in a disciplined fashion.

Certain responsibilities that by tradition have been attached to the supervisor's job no longer seem valid. The supervisor has been held accountable for the specific service given in a case, for knowing the total caseload, and for promoting the competence of casework staff. In the wish to provide good service, agencies have fostered the idea that the supervisor is responsible for the service given in a case by calling him, not the caseworker, to account when the community complains. Not only has this concept increased the worker's unwholesome dependence on the supervisor and the supervisor's over-control of the worker, but it also has served to place the supervisor in the untenable position of a buffer or protector between caseworkers and other administrative personnel. At times it is necessary for the supervisor to be specific and direct about what must be done in a particular case in order to avoid serious consequences. This is clearly an appropriate use of supervisory authority, but it should not be thought of as sharing with the caseworker the responsibility for the case. The supervisor is not responsible for, and cannot share responsibility with, the caseworker for either the kind or the quality of service given in a case.

The supervisor cannot know the total caseload to the extent that he can control the quality of service or prevent errors, nor should he attempt to do so, since the management of cases is the caseworker's responsibility. Similarly, the supervisor cannot make caseworkers competent by injecting knowledge into them. The quality of casework service in an agency depends upon the quality of casework staff. The latter, in turn, is highly influenced by the caseworker's motivations for giving the best service of which he is capable. The supervisor can and should serve as a vital resource in the caseworker's own achievement efforts. Indeed, the supervisor is responsible for providing leadership in this area.

Another traditional concept of the supervisor's role that requires re-examination is that the supervisor's primary job responsibility is teaching. A nod is given to the so-called "administrative" aspects of supervision, which are considered less important and somewhat distasteful. As a teacher, the supervisor has been in conflict about discharging various administrative duties; including evaluation of workers, since these seem to intrude like a foreign body into the benign teacher-learner relationship.

The teaching component in the supervisor's job has been stressed because he has been held responsible for the casework service given and for the level of competence of the casework staff. The evaluation of his own supervisory competence has often been related to the success or failure of his supervisees. If, as has been stated here, the caseworker is responsible for his own work and is largely responsible for his own continuing development, and if the supervisor's job is one of administrative facilitation, it becomes manifestly impossible to separate the teaching and management components of supervision. They are fused together and form an integrated unit.

SPECIFIC JOB RESPONSIBILITIES

Within the framework described above, the specific job responsibilities of the supervisor may be described as follows:

1. The supervisor is responsible for (a) knowing how effective the caseworker's service is, (b) assisting the caseworker to give service according to the standards of the agency, and (c) assisting the caseworker to develop further skill in giving effective service. Beyond this, he is responsible for developing ideas and content which will influence the standards of casework practice in the agency.

The supervisor learns how effective the caseworker's service is and how he may assist the worker in implementing and enhancing the service by evaluating the worker's request for supervision. In preparing for a discussion with the worker, the supervisor needs to assess the purpose and validity of the request in terms of its appropriateness to the case and to the worker's level of skill and experience. Although it is not possible, in this paper, to describe the specific supervisory methodology to be used in a variety of situations, one important principle can be noted: the supervisor should teach the concepts relevant to the handling of a case rather than the specifics of what the worker should do. The basis for conceptual teaching is the educational principle that a person can learn to apply his knowledge to a variety of situations more rapidly, more effectively, and more creatively when his learning is based on general theories and ideas than when it is based on specific knowledge gained in one case which he attempts to apply to another. In following this principle, the supervisor does not teach the specifics of practice in a given case but teaches, instead, the various possibilities, both theoretical and practical, that might affect the nature of service. Although these possibilities can be thought through in the supervisory conference, the caseworker is left with the responsibility of deciding what particular concepts or techniques are best suited to the management of the case and how and when they are to be applied. This is not to say that there may not be an occasion when a caseworker requests and uses supervision that is specific in regard to what and how to do something, but such an occasion should be considered special and unusual.

Basing his judgment on the caseworker's level of experience and skill, the supervisor has to decide when to offer assistance, when to leave the problem with the caseworker, and when to suggest the use of other agency resources in the interests of the case. Conceptual teaching requires of the supervisor a greater degree of casework knowledge and more self-discipline than the teaching of specifics case by case. For example, the supervisor should consider with the caseworker the problems that are impeding service rather than teach all the dynamics in the case or how the case is to be handled. Should a further supervisory conference seem advisable, it is the supervisor's responsibility to set the purpose and time for it. When action in a case is imperative, however, the supervisor must use his authority to see that it is carried out.

The supervisor can also estimate how effectively service is being given by frequently reading a sample of the caseloads of his supervisees for the purpose of observing trends in quality of service, the workers' areas of competence, and problem areas that require supervisory consideration. Reading for the purpose of observing trends should enable the supervisor to assess areas of competence and limitations. The worker should be told of both kinds of observation. I should like to stress the value of letting the caseworker know about his successes since so frequently the supervisor is inclined to stress the failures. When problems are noted, the supervisor should assess whether they are due to the worker's lack of sufficient data, to his lack of understanding of psychological concepts or techniques, to his difficulties in understanding or responding to manifest or concealed meanings in the material, to his lack of awareness of his reactions to people, or to his inability to tolerate or manage the variety of emotions expressed. Are his problems related to working with the different phases of a case—intake, social study, evaluation, and treatment—as well as to his differing abilities in dealing with various problems and personalities? Trends in the quantity of his production are equally important to note.

It is obvious that the supervisor's reading to discover trends cannot be effective unless the agency sets recording requirements that are clear, specific, and feasible. The casework staff needs to understand the purpose that recording serves in relation to the supervisor's responsibility for facilitating service. The supervisor is responsible for orienting the caseworker to the agency's recording requirements and for dealing actively with the worker if there are problems in meeting recording requirements.

Knowledge derived from a continuous examination of trends through case reading, as well as from requests for supervision by the caseworker, enables the supervisor to understand the caseworker's characteristic ways of working and learning and his level of ability to give service. It enables the supervisor to formulate differential supervisory plans related both to service needs and to the caseworker's ability to meet these needs according to the job expectations for his position classification.

In thinking through a possible supervisory plan or in making a decision that no supervisory intervention is required, certain questions must be answered by the supervisor. Do the trends in performance appear to be within normal expectations for the caseworker's level of experience, and, if so, are certain problem areas best left untouched while the caseworker accumulates knowledge and experience or can development be facilitated by supervision? Are there special areas of difficulty in groups of cases that can be singled out for consideration with the caseworker? How serious are particular difficulties as they affect service in a single case or a group of cases?

The supervisor is responsible for taking action when the need for such is indicated by general trends or by the developments in a specific case. Such action requires self-discipline on the part of the supervisor. He must judge how important the problem areas are in relation to service to the client and also to the worker's job requirements. He must permit the worker some freedom in making errors and should contain his concern until he knows their consequences in terms of service. A supervisory plan should be specific and should be discussed with the caseworker, so that there is mutual understanding as to the specific areas to be worked on and the time to be devoted to this purpose.

The supervisor should plan, in relation to each of his supervisees, the particular supervisory methodology and the learning resources to be used. How does the caseworker learn best? What are the indications for limiting his teaching to a circumscribed area or for extending it beyond what the caseworker recognizes or asks for? What should be handled by didactic teaching? Which learning blocks does the caseworker need to become aware of; which are best left untouched? What other resources in the agency does the supervisor need to call upon in working with the caseworker?

A third way in which the supervisor can facilitate or enhance service is by using the knowledge gained from an examination of trends to determine when individual supervision is most useful and when a group process is preferable. Although it is not possible within the limitations of this paper to describe in detail the various uses of groups, I should like to emphasize the supervisor's responsibility for leadership in assessing the need for a particular type of group and for bringing this need to the attention of the appropriate administrative personnel.

2. The supervisor is also responsible for facilitating the work of the casework staff through using agency procedures and routines in such a way that a smooth flow of service is assured. He orients the casework staff to the management aspects of the job. He takes leadership in initiating staff discussions of management operations and in implementing agency policies. He conveys to the executive staff his observations in regard to the casework program, the quality of practice, the developmental needs of staff, and so forth. He encourages casework staff to bring questions and ideas concerning program, practice, and operations to appropriate personnel in the agency.

3. The supervisor is responsible for evaluating the casework staff in accordance with agency classification requirements and for making appropriate recommendations in relation to salary changes, promotions, separations, and so on. In many agencies, evaluations are expected to serve two main purposes: (a) the assessment of performance as a basis for salary changes, and (b) the assessment of the worker's progress and his future developmental needs. When used in this way, the periodic evaluation serves an educational as well as a practical purpose. The caseworker often shares in the evaluation process, and the written document shows the results of joint consideration between caseworker and supervisor. Material about the caseworker-supervisor relationship is frequently included. Using the evaluation process as an educational device is highly questionable.

The written periodic evaluation is an *administrative* document to be prepared only for the purpose of making judgments about changes in salary or job assignment and about reclassification or separation from the agency. Hence, the written evaluation is a statement concerned specifically with the performance of the caseworker in accordance with the requirements of the job. It is not concerned with describing the difficulties the worker has overcome or the areas that he will be expected to work on in the future. It is not concerned with how the caseworker learns or the nature of the supervisor-caseworker relationship. If the supervisor and worker have engaged in continuing evaluation for any length of time, the written document should contain no surprises for the caseworker. It may vary in length from a very brief statement indicating that the caseworker has met agency requirements to a full assessment at a point of reclassification or marked change in performance.

The evaluation that represents an administrative judgment is written by the supervisor without prior discussion with the caseworker. It is objective insofar as it is based on accepted criteria for performance; it is subjective insofar as it represents a judgment. Whenever possible, the judgments of the supervisor and of appropriate administrative personnel should be pooled to ensure objectivity, but the supervisor has primary responsibility for collecting the data and making the assessment. The significant data on which an assessment is based are the trends in performance judged in relation to the designated requirements of the job. The written evaluation may well be used as the basis for discussion between caseworker and supervisor of the worker's present performance and his developmental needs. The caseworker should discuss with appropriate personnel his questions about or disagreements with the written evaluation.

In summary, since supervision is essentially an administrative job, the functions of teaching, management, and evaluation cannot be separated from each other nor can they be assigned to different persons within the agency. Individual supervision should remain as one part of an agency's staff development program. Groups may serve certain training purposes or may be used to implement certain aspects of the agency's work. The core of the supervisor's job is giving administrative leadership to the casework program.

THE CASEWORKER

The caseworker has the primary responsibility for giving direct service to clients to the best of his ability and within the job requirements for his level of experience. He must assume the major responsibility for his own performance and for continuing to acquire knowledge and skill. The new or beginning staff member should be given orientation to the agency, to the specifics of its program, policies, and resources. But he also needs to be granted freedom to take responsibility for his own work—freedom to use his capacities and to discern and work on those areas in which he needs to develop further.

1. The caseworker is responsible for identifying his areas of competence, of partial ability, or of limitation. This includes identifying gaps in his theoretical knowledge or in the application of theory to practice, his special skills or problems in psychosocial evaluation and treatment, his special abilities or limitations in dealing with various problems or personalities, and his acknowledgment of personal reactions that enhance or interfere with his service. Making these identifications takes time; it can be accomplished only through his continuous experience in integrating theory and practice. The caseworker should use the supervisor as an aid in this process, but the latter cannot share responsibility with him for the quality of his casework or for the service he gives. Freedom to perform means taking responsibility for success, for failure, and for errors, seeking assistance in the interests of effective service, and deciding both the specific help he needs and which of the available resources he will use. He may choose to use the supervisor or other personnel the agency provides.

The caseworker has not been clear about his responsibility for his casework practice. As indicated previously, he has been confused because he has thought of case management as a responsibility shared with the supervisor. He has become resentful because he has felt that the supervisor was really directing his cases. Moreover, he has felt guilty over withholding from the supervisor difficult or "pet" cases. He has not felt the need to think through as clearly as possible the specific aspects of a case that are puzzling him and that may require supervisory consideration. He has tended to ask for help in general terms, with the result that the sheer mass of supervisory teaching has made him feel dependent and out of control in the management of the case.

The caseworker learns to recognize his skills and his gaps in knowledge not only by day-to-day work on cases, but by formulating concepts derived from an examination of groups of his cases. Such examination is the base for increasing his knowledge of his areas of mastery and the areas for continuing professional development.

As the caseworker gains experience in noting and assessing the trends in his work, he should be able to work skilfully and securely in the areas of his competence and to accept his limitations without loss of self-esteem. When the caseworker and supervisor work together appropriately, the caseworker is free to use supervision at any level of experience without the burden of dependence, hostility, or guilt. He is thus comfortable about seeking assistance in cases in which his limitations might seriously interfere with giving service. He can also use the supervisor's help in considering parts of a case, or a group of cases, for the purpose of conceptualizing his techniques, re-evaluating certain casework concepts, or experimenting with new or different concepts or techniques.

From the outset of his employment in the agency, the caseworker, whether beginning or experienced, should know that he will be held accountable for his work—for formulating his own thinking about a case prior to seeking supervisory assistance, for deciding what specific areas in which cases require supervisory consideration, and for examining the trends in his work. His purposeful use of supervision is more important than the frequency with which he seeks it.

2. The caseworker is responsible for his own continuing professional development. In a work situation, learning is not a specific goal in itself, but is related to the goal of increasing one's ability to provide effective service. Personal growth cannot be set as a job requirement, nor is it an appropriate area for supervision. As the caseworker identifies his own developmental needs, he should decide where and how these are to be met—how much reading he needs to do, what institutes or classes he might attend, and when to use supervisory help or other resources in the agency. Initially, the supervisor may encourage the caseworker to use a variety of resources; with experience, he should gain assurance and skill

in choosing appropriate resources without necessarily channeling his requests through his immediate supervisor.

Accepting this concept will mean making changes in supervisory methodology. Making an assessment of the worker's educational needs has long been considered an important part of the supervisor's job. Supervising the new or beginning worker closely has been justified on the basis of helping him to develop his capacities. Thus, emphasis has been placed on the caseworker as "learner" rather than as "doer," and the worker has viewed himself as a learner for an unspecified number of years. Once it is clear that the caseworker has complete responsibility for doing his job and for developing his own skills, the supervisor should observe how the worker performs and learns before making a specific plan for supervising him.

This confusion about the caseworker as learner, or worker, has resulted in considering the more experienced worker an "independent worker" who may ask for "consultation" rather than for supervision or who may use the supervisor for guidance in certain questions of agency policy. When the caseworker is held responsible for his own work, there should be no question of dependence or independence, supervision or consultation at any level of experience. Rather, there should be a differential use of resources based on the complexities of the case material and on the caseworker's demonstrated abilities in relation to job expectations.

Viewing the supervisor as the major, and in some instances the sole, medium of continuing professional development has hampered the worker's achievement of professional maturity. His feelings of dependency and hostility have been stimulated, and he has reacted by "flight or fight." The supervisor has tended to become over-controlling and protective. Under the plan suggested here, there is no reason to fear organizational confusion or the undermining of what has been in the past a rigid and hierarchical agency structure. The caseworker should be able to judge when the supervisor's knowledge will be useful to him and when consultation with other personnel will be appropriate. Being able to use the agency resources freely should enhance his ability to render good service.

3. The caseworker is responsible for managing his job assignment—handling his caseload in such a way as to serve as many people as possible, organizing his time so that he can meet production standards, assembling statistics, and so on. Case recording is an integral part of giving direct casework service. The case record is a working tool designed for the caseworker's use, a means by which he pulls together his data and thoughts about a case in order to formulate plans, check or recheck his assessment, evaluate the effectiveness of his service, and plan for the future of the case. From his case records the worker should, with super-

visory assistance, be able to identify the trends in his practice and the areas in which he needs to develop greater skill.

In summary, the caseworker's job requires that he be responsible for the quality of his casework service to clients, for the maximum development of his capacities, for the management of his job in the interests of giving as much service as possible, and for using the resources the agency provides to implement and enhance his service.

THE SUPERVISOR–CASEWORKER RELATIONSHIP

The supervisor-caseworker relationship should be a positive one, based on knowledge and respect for each other's competence and job responsibilities. Clarity about these responsibilities should do much to minimize such problems as dependence, hostility, independence, and so forth. Dependence is not in and of itself evil, but the unwholesome, childish dependence which is stimulated when job responsibilities are ill-defined and ill-used has created problems in both casework and supervisory practice. Mature interdependence, which results from the appropriate use of the strengths of others without loss of self-identity, is highly desirable in the complicated process of serving people through casework. Control by the supervisor when confused with authority also creates problems. Administrative leadership requires the use of one kind of authority; casework practice requires another.

Much has been written and said about the anxiety created in the supervisor-caseworker relationship. Certainly, when the supervisor controls or protects the worker and removes the responsibility that belongs to him, the latter responds with conflicted emotions that are often expressed as anxiety, feelings of pressure, resentment, and the like. Normal anxiety is desirable in a work situation. The wish to succeed, the concern about meeting job requirements, the desire to give good service, concern about a new setting or agency, the feeling that a case is not going well—all are useful anxieties in stimulating self-motivation for meeting responsibilities. Normal resistance to change, which is always present in learning and doing, and periods of regression under particular stress or under the impact of trying to integrate new material, are familiar behavioral manifestations in both caseworkers and supervisors and need not cause concern. The intensity and persistence of these phenomena offer clues to the need for intervention and assistance. Some dependence, frustration, and displacement of feelings will always exist in working relationships but are of concern only when they become predominant or persistent.

Problems in these areas are exacerbated when the caseworker's performance or characteristic ways of behaving are assessed in personal or clinical terms rather than in relation to his job responsibility and the agency's requirements. Again it must be emphasized that it is the supervisor's responsibility to use supervision in the interests of facilitating service and to assess the individual only in relation to his work.

If the concepts outlined in this paper are to be implemented, the executive staff of an agency must take leadership in defining job responsibilities and requirements. It must also facilitate a different type of supervisory practice.

The staff of the Jewish Family and Community Service of Chicago has begun to test these formulations in practice. Thus far, the caseworkers have expressed satisfaction with the clearer definitions of job responsibility and a feeling of relief that evaluations are used solely for administrative implementation of salary scales. The supervisors have said that they know more about a caseworker's abilities in a shorter time than previously and, therefore, are better equipped to plan for differential supervision. They are keeping track of the various uses of supervisory time made by casework staff in the hope that this information will clarify the areas in which supervision can be useful and also the appropriate nature and size of a supervisory load.

The process of learning new ways, unlearning old ways, and combining what was useful in the past with what is done in the present is painful but exciting. Specific applications of these formulations must be tested, and new applications must be developed. It is to be hoped that the continued development and testing of new concepts will add to the growing body of knowledge of the practice of supervision. It is a practice that utilizes special methods and processes and that requires specific abilities and training.

NOTES

1. Family Service Association of America, New York, 1957.

9

Supervision in Perspective

Evelyn Stiles

ONE OF THE HALLMARKS of a profession is its willingness and ability to examine time-honored professional practices and, on the basis of the examination, to affirm, alter, or discard them. The social work profession, in its persistent search for sounder concepts and better techniques, has focused special attention on supervision, for the supervisor has always occupied a central position in social work education and practice. During the past few years, the profession has subjected the supervisor's functions to special scrutiny—attempting to analyze the purpose, the components, the techniques, and the effectiveness of supervision.

A controversy arose several years ago about the use of supervision in staff development. Major criticisms have been that supervision is endless, that it has no specific aims, and that it fosters the dependency of workers and inhibits their professional development. In a recent publication Harriett Bartlett stated:

> Staff supervision is a part of administration, with responsibility for getting the job done as effectively as possible. Social work has always emphasized the educational aspects of supervision, which aims to further the growth of the worker. Presently the profession is reviewing its supervisory activities and trying to answer the question of whether social workers are being held under supervision too long and thus remaining dependent. Although social agencies and social service departments are generally considered to be responsible for staff development through supervision, professional meetings, and similar activities, greater emphasis is now being placed upon the individual social worker's responsibility for furthering his own professional growth.[1]

From *Social Casework* 44 (January 1963), pp. 19–25. Reprinted by permission of the Family Service Association of America.

If it is true that present-day staff supervision fosters dependency in the worker both as regards his day-to-day practice and as regards his long-range professional growth, then the profession has the responsibility to give these criticisms full consideration before recommending radical changes.

To gain a clearer view of supervision, it may be useful to consider recent definitions, its historical development, and certain aspects of current practice. This discussion deals primarily with supervision in casework although the definition applies to all three social work methods.

SOME RECENT DEFINITIONS OF SUPERVISION

The recognition reflected in Bartlett's definition of staff supervision quoted above—that staff supervision is a component of administration—has taken time to develop, although staff supervision has been a part of the structure of casework agencies almost from their beginnings. The administrative aspects of supervision were rarely discussed in the professional literature until the late 1940's. Then the profession began to formulate a definition of staff supervision. In the analysis of supervisory practice, two major functions—teaching [2] and administration [3]—were identified. A little later, Lucille Austin posed the possibility that the administrative and the teaching functions might be separated, and that no one person should be expected to carry out these seemingly conflicting sets of tasks.[4] In 1958, however, Frances Scherz wrote:

> . . . the job of the casework supervisor is, in essence, an administrative job. Both of the major components of casework supervision—teaching and management—are administrative functions. . . .
>   . . . the point of view that supervision is inherently an administrative function is a departure from the usual concept that supervision has two distinct components, teaching and administration. . . .[5]

THE ROLE OF THE SUPERVISOR

In further consideration of this definition, the function of administration has to be examined—which in any setting is to carry out as effectively as possible the purposes for which the organization was established. In a social agency the purpose is the provision of services to its clientele. In terms of this particular purpose, agency operation involves a relationship to the total community; a program; and specific services, which may be many or few, of high quality or low.

What part does staff supervision play in this process?

As an arm of administration, supervision affords a rich medium for the communication and staff interaction at all levels that are essential to the effective functioning of an agency. Though the administrator should make provision for the staff to use many channels for communication—staff meetings, committees, workshops, and so on—the existence of these forms of communication does not obviate the need for supervision.

The workers' daily practice is an important source of information about the relationship of the agency to the total community. This information is readily accessible to the administrator as a result of the supervisor's regular contact with workers and his over-all familiarity with their caseloads. Through him the administrator is ensured a steady flow of data about the changing needs of the community, the attitudes of the community toward the agency, and interagency relations. The data can then be used in molding the agency's program and in formulating its policy.

An equally important role performed by the supervisor is the communication of information to the worker about the purpose of the program. Even an experienced staff may interpret a policy in a number of ways, with the result that its implementation within the agency may not be uniform. Because his knowledge of cases is broader than the workers', the supervisor is able to detect variations in procedure and to assist the workers in developing a consistent, yet flexible, application of agency policy. The supervisor also promotes the creative participation of the workers in the administrative process: he encourages them to examine the effects of policy on their daily practice, to contribute their ideas about revisions, and to help bring about changes that are needed.

In connection with services per se, a careful apportionment of the agency's workload is imperative; quantity must be controlled in the interest of quality. Here the role of the supervisor is obvious. He is in a focal position from which to evaluate workloads and to make appropriate adjustments between the needs of the agency and the capacity of each worker to manage a caseload. When work pressures mount, the supervisor helps the worker plan his work so that he can do his job as adequately as possible. In addition, the supervisor can provide the executive with comprehensive information about the quantitative demands placed on the agency and the resources available to meet them.

Giving service of high quality always has been a governing principle of the social agency, and the supervisor has carried the administrative responsibility for seeing that this is done. Often this facet of supervision has been considered a teaching function geared to the professional development of workers. The supervisor's primary obligation, however, is not to the worker but to the maintenance of an acceptable standard of agency practice. Staff supervision is not analogous to student supervision. Student supervision is an educational activity that includes the teaching of administrative responsibility; staff supervision is an administrative activity, one aspect of which is staff development through teaching. In staff supervision, the professional growth of the worker is not an end but a means to an end; it is a "by-product and not the purpose of supervision." [6]

It is true that inherent in the agency's basic obligation to provide the best quality of service for its clients is an obligation to contribute to the professional development of the agency's staff—though it is essential that each worker take ultimate responsibility for his own continued professional education. The transmission and advancement of a profession's knowledge and skill are difficult and lengthy tasks, not to be undervalued. To deal with the intimate problems of human beings requires knowledge, patience, dedication, and self-understanding. A variety of methods of staff development can impart theoretical information and emotional support to workers; individual supervision, however, makes a special contribution. The supervisor's careful review of cases hastens the time when the worker can translate his knowledge of theory into practice. The opportunity for a private exchange of ideas also enables the supervisor to gain intimate knowledge of the worker's responses to his clients. Both activities are necessary for improving the social worker's performance.

A supervisor affects the quality of service in ways other than through the direct teaching of staff. Because he knows the abilities of each worker, he is able to make assignments that ensure the best use of the staff's interests and skills. Periodic evaluations help to clarify the supervisor's understanding of the workers' progress and their emerging talents or changing interests, and help him to determine their future responsibilities. On the basis of his special knowledge, the supervisor is able to make recommendations to the agency executive about promotions or other personnel changes and about the general needs of the agency in the area of staff development.

HISTORICAL DEVELOPMENT

Almost from the beginning, supervision has been an important part of the functioning of the casework agency. Advances in casework techniques have been paralleled so closely by advances in supervisory practice that it is impossible to describe the development of supervision without referring to the development of casework. Some historians date the beginning of family casework to 1869 when the London Charity Organisation Society was established in England to consolidate the existing relief agencies into one organization. This was the first agency to work with families "of the poor" on an individual basis. The COS movement quickly spread to the United States. In 1877, the Buffalo Charity Organization Society was established; fifteen years later there were eighty-four such societies in the United States.[7] The staffs of these agencies consisted of volunteers, with one person, the secretary, responsible for ordering the work of the society. The secretary soon became a full-time, paid staff member, known as the agent. For many years the secretary or agent and volunteer visitors carried on the activities of the organizations.

The COS movement was founded on certain beliefs that provided a new approach to meeting human needs. These beliefs, which became the underpinning of social work philosophy and practice, stressed the following: a planned method of giving charity, an individualized interest in the unfortunate person, a sincere respect for human nature, an understanding of the causes of social ills in order to remove them, broad reforms to alleviate social and economic distress, and the training of philanthropic agents. The leaders in this movement were convinced that wholesale relief did not help the poor and that it was possible to use a systematic approach to charity, that a science of charity was possible in which action was to be based on facts.

In working with individuals the aim of the COS movement was to foster the development of personal resources within families by giving them sympathetic attention. The plan was to assign to each family a friendly visitor who would offer kindly, courteous service rather than alms. From the start the agency provided staff training to ensure a uniformity of method and a high quality of performance: "scientific charity called for knowledge and skill as well as good intentions." [8] Octavia Hill of the London Charity Organisation Society "stressed the need for organizing the visitors, for training and oversight and advice along the way so that their efforts might be strengthened and directed and inevitable periods of discouragement overcome." [9] Emphasis was placed on a studied and consistent handling of problems, an understanding of the client, the delineation of appropriate behavior for the visitor, and the support of the visitor in his contacts with the families.

A number of educational devices were used for training purposes. Excellent reading material—books, brochures, reprints—were accumulated quickly, and most societies soon formed libraries. Training manuals were prepared about local facilities, statutes, marketing, food preparation, and other items related to family affairs. The manuals contained outlines of the proper conduct for visitors, and recommendations were made that they behave with "delicacy, tact, respect, and sympathy . . . get acquainted with all members of a family, . . . look at life from their point of view, not . . . act until they understood what was needed." [10] Many agencies organized groups for staff development. Agents met to discuss the training of new workers and to gain guidance and support from each other. Agents and visitors discussed specific situations in case committees; they advised one another about ways of helping a family, and they speculated about the reasons for success or failure in a case.

Planned individual supervision was an essential part of staff development. In 1891 the Boston COS started five training programs each year for new agents; they worked under the supervision of experienced workers, participated in teaching sessions led by the general secretary, and were responsible for completing reading assignments. The supervising agents and the general secretary met regularly to exchange ideas about the method and content of teaching. Other agencies followed this pattern.

Because the training ventures of the societies were too varied and too limited, the need for a charity training school began to be discussed. In 1898 the Training Class in Philanthropy, which became the Summer School in Philanthropic Work, was established by the New York COS. When this summer course was expanded to a one-year course in 1904, the institution became the New York School of Philanthropy.[11] The program included didactic teaching and agency practice under expert individual supervision. Four other schools were organized by 1908, but even so the number of graduates available was so small that the practice of training staff members in agencies continued for many years. Child welfare services and medical social work also adopted plans for staff development similar to those in the charity organization societies. During this period, social workers began to be used in psychiatric facilities. At first they were trained by psychiatrists, but in 1914 an apprenticeship program for psychiatric social workers was instituted at the Boston Psychopathic Hospital, with courses in social work and psychiatry and with supervision in agencies.

During the early part of the twentieth century casework made rapid strides in developing a body of knowledge, and supervision continued to play a significant part in this development. Two books by Mary Richmond, *Social Diagnosis* in 1917 and *What Is Social Case Work?* in 1922, represent the culmination of this period. Miss Richmond's definition of casework and her outline of the casework method are generally accepted as the best formulations made during this time. The method she described offered a systematic means by which help can be given to individuals and families. There is a strong emphasis in her work on the value of extensive history-taking. It was assumed that if the worker collected enough facts, correct inferences could be made and a proper plan of treatment could be instituted. Treatment entailed mainly the use of community resources.

Miss Richmond described some of the difficulties encountered in the practice of casework, and she stressed the remedial importance of supervision: workers often assembled complete data, but they missed their significance in making a diagnosis and formulating a treatment plan;

at other times, despite an extensive history, workers took action before they had analyzed the meaning of the information. Supervisors helped the workers learn the techniques of obtaining data; they pointed out gaps and discrepancies in the case histories assembled, and they helped the workers to take all of the data into account in an attempt to reach a sound diagnosis. Miss Richmond commented that this process of analyzing material ". . . in so far as it can be studied at all at present, is found at its best in the daily work of a few experienced supervisors." [12]

By 1920, social work was emerging as a profession rather than continuing a part-time, philanthropic endeavor. Casework agencies, whenever possible, were employing full-time, trained personnel, but supervisors were still in short supply and most of them had limited professional experience. The number of casework graduates remained far below the demand for them, and they were appointed to supervisory positions as soon as they finished their training. For example, in psychiatric social work ". . . a candidate fresh from a school of social work, often inexperienced, was left to work out unaided the complicated problems of adapting her own experience, education and 'point of view' to an uncharted job." [13] Despite these limitations social workers were beginning to increase their understanding of the supervisory process. Psychoanalytic concepts were beginning to affect supervision as well as casework. As social workers became aware of the emotional component in learning and the importance of the teacher-student relationship, they expressed a need for more knowledge about this process. In 1929, the Milford Conference stressed the need for developing sound supervisory methods as part of social work's responsibility for defining and advancing all aspects of its practice.

Before the developments of the 1920's could be fully integrated within casework and supervision, the profession felt the impact of the depression of the 1930's and of World War II in the 1940's. The depression produced a large clientele with serious social problems. Public welfare agencies were rapidly expanded, and an insufficient number of qualified workers was available to staff them. An increase in the number of untrained workers and volunteers, heavy caseloads, inadequate funds, and limited supervisory personnel made the achievement of high quality difficult. Despite extreme time pressures many agencies considered it imperative to have staff development programs if they were to provide the kind of assistance their clients needed so desperately: orientation, in-service training, and supervision continued to be significant aspects of these programs. World War II brought additional stresses with the expansion of casework services in community agencies, in the armed services, in psychiatric facilities—with no abatement in the shortage of trained workers and supervisors.

From 1930 to the latter part of the 1940's supervisory practices continued to be refined, but external pressures made action take precedence over education. The next decade saw an increase in the number of schools of social work and graduates, so that there were more supervisors with more experience than there had been previously. New workers had a chance to be supervised before assuming administrative responsibilities. In addition, there was relative stability in casework, and for the first time there was an opportunity to consolidate the knowledge about supervision, to examine its method, and to make improvements. This situation is reflected clearly in the literature of the late 1940's and the 1950's. Yet by 1956 some social workers were beginning to question the value of supervision and were making suggestions about alternative teaching devices.

In reviewing the history of supervision, it is impressive to observe the seriousness with which those in the casework field recognized, from the time of its origin, the value of staff development and the essential role of the supervisor. A basic tenet of the charity organization movement was the training of agency personnel. Supervision was one means of transmitting knowledge in order to attain and maintain quality of service. When casework began to evolve a definite method, supervision became an important means of enabling workers to refine their practice. From the outset supervision was viewed as a specific process to be performed with deliberation, and an abundance of knowledge about supervisory techniques has been amassed. Social work has been a leader among the professions in formulating theory and improving practice techniques in the field of supervision. Emphasis on conceptualizing the process of supervision, however, has come only in the past fifteen years; consequently the opportunity to integrate these ideas and test their validity has been relatively brief.

CURRENT SUPERVISORY PRACTICE

What is the current practice of supervision in social work agencies? Do social workers know the extent to which supervision is used in the field, the average duration of supervision for workers, how it is used, or how it is done? The profession may have certain impressions about these matters, perhaps correct ones, but until verifiable data are available, social workers will have difficulty in evaluating supervision accurately.

As was mentioned earlier, a major criticism of supervision is its interminable duration. Some social workers claim that continued supervision tends to inhibit the professional growth of the supervisee. This criticism may be valid. However, an over-emphasis on this point has led members of the profession to neglect another important issue—the quality of supervision. In discussing the possible deleterious effects of supervision, it is essential to distinguish between good supervision and poor supervision. Is it the ineffectiveness of supervision or the ineffectual use of supervision with which the profession should be concerned? The belief that supervision in itself fosters dependency seems contrary to social work concepts about dependency. The elements of dependency that exist in any significant relationship do not necessarily impair a person's functioning. When dependence is met appropriately, the result can be an increase in a person's independence. Thus, a good supervisor can help a worker increase his knowledge, productivity, and creativity. He is set free rather than bound by this kind of supervision.

A crucial question, therefore, is the quality of supervision. Any supervisory relationship contains an implicit contract: the worker is responsible for attempting to maximize his performance and for continuing his professional development; the supervisor is responsible for helping him achieve these goals. A competent supervisor effectuates this contract, and the worker becomes increasingly independent in the performance of his role. If workers are not making full use of their potential abilities, it may be that the cause is a lag in supervisory practice. The wide knowledge about supervision that has been revealed in the professional literature may not yet have been integrated with practice.

There are several significant aspects to be considered in assessing the quality of supervision. The first aspect is the *content* of the supervision. To what extent are supervisory conferences used to clarify and extend social work knowledge and skill? Is the conference devoted to a superficial review of recent events in several cases or to a thoughtful, creative analysis of one case? Does the supervisor challenge the supervisee to use his intellectual capacity? Does he present the worker with new knowledge and suggest possible new directions he can take in his subsequent work with clients?

The second aspect is the supervisory *method*. To what extent is the supervisor an enabler rather than an overseer? Are conferences held regularly and without interruption? What is their length? Is there mutual preparation? Has each participant read the case record carefully and formulated his thinking about the problem, its determinants, and the treatment approach? Is there mutual participation in conferences? Is the worker free to express his ideas and feelings about the client, the supervisor, the agency, the community, and the profession? Does the worker become aware of his own reactions in the treatment process? How is this awareness achieved? Does the supervisor enable the supervisee to evaluate his own performance realistically, to recognize his own abilities, and to spot the gaps in his knowledge and skills?

The third aspect is the setting of *goals*. To what extent does the supervisor have a working educational diagnosis of the worker? Do the supervisor and worker both have a clear idea of the goals of their work together? Do the goals change as the worker progresses?

Skillful supervisors use other measures in addition to direct teaching to ensure the growing professional competence of workers as well as the vigorous operation of the agency. They involve new workers in tasks in which they are directly accountable for specific aspects of the administrative process. When appropriate, the worker is asked to deliver speeches, to participate in agency committee work, and to represent the administration in interagency deliberations. As the worker advances, increasingly complex demands are made on him—he is assigned selected cases requiring special ability, supervisory or teaching responsibilities, or permanent administrative duties. It is essential that workers continue to grow and develop their potential capacity. When the worker assumes supervisory responsibilities, the content of supervisory conferences changes; his work as a supervisor becomes a part of his discussions with his own supervisor so that he can use their meetings to acquire new knowledge and learn new techniques. Finally, the supervisor encourages him to take a responsible role in the affairs of the profession and the community.

CONCLUSION

Although an integral part of social work from its beginnings, the practice of supervision has been limited in scope and technique. Certain aspects must be examined before the future course of supervision is determined. More information about current practice is needed. There has also to be an assessment of the intrinsic value of supervision through a careful delineation of its purpose and the extent to which this purpose can be fulfilled.

Systematic data are required. Despite the plea of the 1929 Milford Conference, almost no studies on social work supervision have yet been undertaken. There are many subjects for investigation in this area. Is supervision indispensable? What is the effect of supervision on agency operation? Are staff recruitment and staff turnover related to the availability of skillful supervision? To determine the effect of supervision on the professional development of workers, trained workers who received competent supervision could be followed up. The profession would then learn the extent to which these workers subsequently assumed increased professional responsibility in supervision, consultation, administration, and teaching. Social workers tend to be timid about undertaking research efforts, but projects need not be pretentious in design, execution, and cost to yield useful facts.[14]

Supervision is said to be an expensive and time-consuming activity.

Mediocre agency operation and mediocre social work practice, which yield a poor return on the community's investment in services, are even more expensive and time-consuming.

NOTES

1. Harriett M. Bartlett, *Analyzing Social Work Practice by Fields*. National Association of Social Workers, New York, 1961, p. 62.

2. Yonata Feldman, "The Teaching Aspect of Casework Supervision." *Social Casework*, Vol. XXXI, April 1950, pp. 156–61.

3. Sidney J. Berkowitz, "The Administrative Process in Casework Supervision." *Social Casework*, Vol. XXXIII, December 1952, pp. 419–23.

4. Lucille N. Austin, "An Evaluation of Supervision." *Social Casework*, Vol. XXXVII, October 1956, pp. 375–82.

5. Frances H. Scherz, "A Concept of Supervision Based on Definitions of Job Responsibility." *Social Casework*, Vol. XXXIX, October 1958, p. 435 [Chapter 8 above, pp. 70–71].

6. Sidney S. Eisenberg, "Supervision as an Agency Need." *Social Casework*, Vol. XXXVII, May 1956, p. 237.

7. Margaret E. Rich, *A Belief in People*. Family Service Association of America, New York, 1956, pp. 3–10.

8. *Ibid.*, p. 37.

9. *Ibid.*, p. 32.

10. *Ibid.*, pp. 37–38.

11. Elizabeth G. Meier, *A History of the New York School of Social Work*. Columbia University Press, New York, 1954, pp. 8–9.

12. Mary E. Richmond, *Social Diagnosis*. Russell Sage Foundation, New York, 1917, p. 348 [Chapter 2 above, pp. 18–19].

13. Lois Meredith French, *Psychiatric Social Work*. Commonwealth Fund, New York, 1940, p. 251.

14. An excellent example is the study by the Western New York Chapter, National Association of Social Workers, Committee on Social Work Practice, reported in "Opinions on Supervision: A Chapter Study." *Social Work*, Vol. III, January 1958, pp. 18–25.

10

An Attempt to Construct a Conceptual Framework for Supervision

Fred Berl

ALTHOUGH MUCH HAS BEEN WRITTEN about supervision in social work, the emphasis in such articles is usually on one or two aspects of the subject. Both the educational and the administrative elements have received considerable attention, with some writers viewing these functions as antithetical to each other and others believing that they can be harmoniously combined. Attention has also been given to methodological aspects, usually in the context of a particular setting or helping method.

In the seminar * on which this article is based the members noted that little attempt has been made to analyze supervision as a generic social work operation or to construct a conceptual framework that would have application to all settings, regardless of the methods used. The need for such a framework was recognized and the group, therefore, assigned itself the task of constructing a model. The framework presented here should be regarded as the attempt of one group to relate the basic elements of supervision to each other. It is hoped that this attempt will underline the need for a conceptual framework and will stimulate further efforts to construct one.

In the seminar we first undertook to identify the components that are essential to an understanding of the operational practice called

* There were eight members in the seminar, representing various fields and methods of social work practice. The members were: Rev. John Bicsey, Mrs. Stephany Keyser, Marta Korwin, Robert Lanigan, Hortense Lilly, Mrs. Grace Llewellyn, Genevieve O'Leary, and Dr. Daniel Thursz [doctoral seminar on supervision led by Dr. Berl, Spring 1958, at the National Catholic School of Social Service, Catholic University of America, Washington, D.C.–ED.]

From *Social Casework* 41 (July 1960), pp. 339–346. Reprinted by permission of the Family Service Association of America.

supervision. We identified four components: (1) the institutional, (2) the methodological, (3) the educational, and (4) the psychological. This paper will present a discussion of these components and of the interaction between them.

THE INSTITUTIONAL COMPONENT

Social workers have a tendency to define supervision as a professional, rather than an institutional, operation. As a professional operation, supervision has certain defined norms and values, but these do not exist in vacuum; they are an intrinsic part of the norms and values of our society. It is true that a profession has an identity of its own, within the larger society, but it is not divorced from the larger entity. Supervision, therefore, should be viewed as an institutional, as well as a professional, operation. A social agency has responsibility to provide certain services to eligible clients in the interest of the welfare of the community as a whole. The staff members of an agency therefore have a special responsibility—one that goes beyond the responsibility of citizenship and community membership—to perform certain services and to develop methods appropriate to the purpose of the services.

An agency, in establishing methods of control, has two major purposes: the first is to make services available and the second to set standards for these services. The methods of control tend to become institutionalized in the structures and processes of the agency. Supervision plays a specific role in the institutional control of both the availability and the standards of service.

What is this role? Supervision itself is not a means of creating services or of determining standards. The services and standards of an agency are influenced by many other factors, such as professional methods and professional values (to which agency personnel contribute), social norms and values, and the social reality. The latter is subject to change as social needs and social attitudes change. The institutional component of supervision, therefore, encompasses those aspects that are concerned with the control of service and standards. Such "control" does not imply a mechanistic function but, rather, an integrative one. The control stems from the supervisor's understanding of the social forces and processes that have an influence on the agency's program.

In carrying responsibility for integrating and controlling the various institutional elements, the supervisor is subject to certain characteristic tensions. These tensions are related to (1) the supervisory function, (2) the supervisory role, and (3) the supervisory process.

1. *Tension related to the supervisory function:* Each agency and each community must attempt to establish an equation between traditional

operations on the one hand and new values and goals on the other. An agency that is future-oriented may still have deep roots in the past, even though it is working toward change. It must utilize various processes of communication to establish a balance between the two forces. An agency cannot follow its vision of the future exclusively, but must also take present-day realities into account. The latter are related to hard facts of community need, budget limitations, availability of staff, and so forth. If an agency refuses to deal with certain realities on the ground that doing so would impede the attainment of new goals or the establishment of desired professional standards, it stands on a weak social base. Such refusals obviously are not likely to be helpful in attaining the new standards. If we understand the real meaning of a social institution, we shall also understand that tension is a necessary part of its very functioning. One might describe the tension as a conflict between the ideal and the reality.

2. *Tension related to the supervisory role:* The supervisory role, which prescribes both equality and inequality between professional colleagues, invites tension. The role of supervisor is one of equality in relation to such essentials as client service, community welfare, and the advancement of professional knowledge. The same role prescribes inequality in relation to job responsibilities, authority, and status. The supervisor, therefore, has the task of handling this dual requirement in a way that does not nullify either aspect. There is the danger that a supervisor may place so much emphasis on the authoritative elements that the equality of purpose will be lost; at the other extreme, he may minimize the authoritative elements to the extent of failing to discharge his essential institutional responsibilities.

Various psychological and sociological patterns for reducing the tension inherent in the dual task suggest themselves. One is the *primus inter pares* model, that is, the pattern in which a person is accepted by other members as the superior of his group. A supervisor may be in the fortunate position of being accepted as a leader, not only because of his status but because staff members have placed him psychologically in a superior position, recognizing his competence and professional helpfulness. Another model is that of *esprit de corps* which emphasizes the unity and common purpose of the group; the differentiations in status and authority are minimized, and leadership often comes to be viewed as that of the group's own choosing. Still another model is the one of the "boss," with a division of labor; the emphasis here is on the value and importance of everyone's job in the total undertaking. In order to function as the "boss," the person must live up to certain rules and norms in relation to fairness, competence, and so forth. It would seem that these, as well as other models, may be used in social agencies in discharging supervisory requirements and achieving effective group functioning.

3. *Tension related to the supervisory process:* The supervisor's conception of supervision and his actual experience in the process are not always identical. There may be differences between his concept and that of his supervisee's in relation to expectation, responsibilities, purposes, and so forth. Also, the supervisor's role and responsibilities are defined by the norms and structure of the agency. The experience of the individual supervisor, however, does not always conform with these institutional expectations. It is a mistake to consider the institutional norms and ideals as characteristic of the individual experience. It is also a mistake to consider an individual experience as a basis for defining norms. In order to understand certain tensions that are involved in supervision, it is necessary to understand the degree of discrepancy that may exist between the institutional norms and the individual's own experience. A certain degree of tension is to be expected. Obviously, the way to reduce the tension growing out of such differences is by attempting to reduce the gap between the institutional demands and the individual's demands. Both the agency and the individual may need to make modifications in their concepts and requirements. Such modifications often result in the establishment of new norms for the agency and for the profession.

The above discussion of supervision as an institutional operation may suggest that the seminar group supported a relativistic philosophy. But this was not the case. Our reasoning was as follows: The chief aim of supervision is to help workers gain the capacity to perform adequately. It seemed to us that a clearer understanding by social workers of the institutional elements in supervision would help sharpen the understanding of the professional elements. There has been a tendency in social work to emphasize the professional elements and to neglect the institutional ones, with the implication that the latter are "unprofessional." It is true that certain relativistic standards are used in the practice of supervision, but these standards are not necessarily dominant. However, institutional elements, such as the functions of the agency, community needs, the agency's resources, and the training of the staff, enter into supervisory practice with its goal of helping workers to perform adequately. Institutional standards obviously must be related to professional standards. Although standards of "adequate performance" may vary considerably among agencies, professional standards, and the values forming them, have a high degree of homogeneity.

THE METHODOLOGICAL COMPONENT

Method is essential to social work practice. It represents an attempt at conscious professional control of the multiple factors that enter into an agency's program. Traditionally, this control has been exercised through the interplay between board members, administrators, supervisors, and practitioners. Each of these segments of an agency may play a part in determining standards of supervision.

In most analyses of the responsibilities of the supervisor, two functions have been singled out—the administrative and the teaching. There has been disagreement about the respective weight that should be given to each, with some persons placing greater emphasis on the administrative aspects and others urging that supervisors be freed from the burden of carrying the administrative ballast.

Conceptually, both the administrative and the teaching responsibilities are essential elements of supervisory practice in a social agency. Since an agency is responsible for the results of its services, it must set up administrative controls to assure that standards of practice are maintained and it must devise methods for evaluating the service given. The very need of agencies to maintain standards of service is the major motive for developing educational programs—both within and outside the agency. The seminar group believed that, ideologically, the administrative and teaching functions of supervision are not divisible. This assumption seemed valid because of the common frame of reference for both these functions. Teaching, as well as administration, is a method for focusing, limiting, and enhancing service. The responsibility for determining, through administrative methods, the usefulness of a worker in a particular field—or in the total professional field—influences the nature and form of the teaching methods used. Vice versa, the availability of teaching opportunities, as well as the results achieved, influence administrative decisions about providing certain services.

Essentially, the administrative goal of an agency is to square the responsibility for meeting community needs with the availability of agency resources, which include staff able to maintain professional standards of service. In supervision, the administrative processes are formulated empirically. The variation in agency programs and in community conditions makes it necessary to rely on empirical methods. Such realities as client needs, community pressures, and limitations of resources are determining factors in establishing administrative processes and methods. In the endeavor to understand supervisory practice, it is necessary to be aware of this empirical element in administrative methods.

The teaching function of supervision, on the other hand, is more clearly conceptualized by the profession and has a firmer scientific underpinning. Because developmental goals for staff members are defined, teaching tends to be systematic; it can subordinate irrelevant variables. A systematic teaching approach in supervision can bring cohesion to elements in practice that are unstable, such as variations in agency policy, changes in programs, and so forth. The major enemy, so to speak, of systematic teaching is the frequent change in community conditions and administrative policy. This unpredictable element of change, with which the board and the administrator are constantly struggling, creates an obstacle for the supervisor. Teaching requires a certain degree of stability.

It seemed to the seminar group, in view of the points discussed above, that supervisory practice should combine administrative and teaching functions. Three supervisory stages might be used to facilitate the worker's development. The first would aim at individualization of the worker's unique potentials, with the aim of helping him carrying responsibility for service. The second aim, through the medium of teaching, would enable the worker to move toward independent functioning. In the third stage, the aim would be to clarify learning goals for the worker and to motivate his self-advancement.

At its best, the supervisory method can provide necessary agency controls and at the same time further sound professional development of staff members. When the supervisor has conflict between the two roles, the integration of the administrative and teaching functions is not achieved. The supervisor may then resort to efforts to control and manipulate staff members and to rationalize about deficiencies in the agency.

Much has been said in recent years about the undesirable features in supervisory practice. It seems likely that a clearer understanding of its diverse elements may help to improve methods and reduce dissatisfactions. One test of the adequacy of a supervisory method might be the extent to which it achieves the goal of individualizing the worker and of enabling him to function on a higher level. This goal transcends the purely professional goal, since it encompasses basic values of our society. Another test of a supervisory method might be the effectiveness of the work of staff members. Greater objectification is needed in all parts of social work practice, including supervision. Such testing, however, should take place under optimal conditions because of the many variables in supervision and the high degree of subjectivity about it.

THE EDUCATIONAL COMPONENT

Some learning is implicit in the performance of any professional service. In a social agency, the learning becomes particularized because of the standards set for the performance of various services. Although supervisory operations have an essential place in fostering the learning of staff members, these operations are only a part of the total educational framework. Staff members draw on many other sources, both within and without the agency, for knowledge and enhancement of skill. In any consideration of staff development, one must be aware of the total framework of educational resources and processes.

In analyzing the supervisory operations, we agreed upon an approach that seems central to the learning needs of staff. This approach consists of a constant and a number of variables. The constant may be defined as the process by which staff members are helped to move from less to greater adequacy in knowledge and skill. Such progression is the common aim of all educational endeavors. Also, in the educational process there are recognized stages of moving from less to more adequate performance.

Within this constant, we identified certain differential characteristics in social work learning. The major differential is in the subject matter itself. The complex content and the requirements of the helping process place unusually heavy demands on the learner. Mastery of content is closely allied to mastery of skills. It is difficult to determine whether this close relationship is necessitated by the character of social work learning or whether it stems from tradition.

Another differential in this process is that it involves the learner in a "living experience." It is true that all learning demands some personal involvement, but the involvement in social work learning is particularly intense. It requires a correlation of intellectual grasp and emotional development.

In social work one needs to learn in order to perform and to perform in order to learn. In the beginning stage, the learner has feelings of inadequacy and a need to rely on someone with superior knowledge; he also gains security from the stability of an organizational structure and its processes. He then moves into the stage of mastering the subject matter and of establishing a pattern of functioning. In this stage he must make many shifts and readjustments in his patterns of thinking and acting. As a result, he tends to be critical of external power, whether it is represented by the supervisor or someone else. Later, he has less need for dependence and develops greater ability to function as part of an established structure and to carry the demands of the job.

In addition to the constant and its differential characteristics, a number of variables in social work learning were identified by the seminar group. One variable is the *situational* element, that is, the functions, services, policies, philosophy, and morale of a particular agency. Another variable is the *technical* nature of the assignments given and the responsibilities expected from the learner. A third variable is the nature of the *relationship* between the learner and the supervisor, that is, the elements in their interaction that foster or impede learning.

It is as important to be aware of the variables in the learning process as of the constant. These variables may create problems in teaching but they are the "very stuff" with which the supervisor must deal in furthering the learner's development. The type of assignment, and the level of skill required, help to particularize learning. The specifics are the means of feeding into the learning process the elements that are needed at various points in the worker's development. Supervisors have developed much technical know-how about utilizing agency structure, policies, services, and so forth to advance the competence of staff members.

In utilizing these variables for generic learning, the supervisor should be aware of two major requirements. One is that he adapt the demands of the assignment to the stage of the worker's learning. The other is that he be aware of the interplay between the relationship elements and the total learning process of the worker. The relationship can be a catalyst for speeding up, or slowing down, the learning process. The relationship is the base for learning, since it helps the learner assimilate and integrate all other aspects.

THE PSYCHOLOGICAL COMPONENT

The application of psychological principles is essential in the provision of services for which the social agency exists. The supervisor, therefore, needs to have a sound grasp of psychological theory, not only to assure that adequate services are given, but also to handle the supervisor-worker relationship. An important aspect of learning in social work is the opportunity provided in the supervisory relationship for the worker to experience psychological processes similar to those required of him in giving adequate service to clients.

One psychological factor in supervision is the degree of harmony between the supervisor's personality and the role he must assume. By definition, this role carries a strong element of authority. The authority delegated to him may initially provide a sufficient base for him to perform effectively for a time. His effectiveness will not continue, however, unless he earns the right to the authority by demonstrating his competence in relation to various aspects of his job. Persons who have difficulty in carrying an authoritative role are likely to have difficulty in meeting the role expectations of the supervisory position. Able and competent persons sometimes have conflict about carrying this role and their uneasiness is reflected in negative reactions on the part of the persons they supervise.

Ability to carry a particular social role requires a certain degree of maturational development. If we apply this principle to the supervisory role in the social agency, the question of maturational standards arises. Considerable study will be necessary to determine what psychological qualifications are needed by persons who are expected to meet the role requirements of the position.

Another psychological factor in the supervisory relationship is the complementarity of roles. Complementarity is implicit in the very nature of the social agency and its organizational structure. The supervisor and the worker are necessarily dependent on each other in order for each to discharge his functions. The worker's dependence on the supervisor is generally recognized as well as the risks involved in the dependence. To a large degree, such dependence is institutionalized and cannot be changed by decision on the part of either the worker or the supervisor. The institutional nature of the supervisory relationship places some limitations on the worker's independence and, in reverse, some responsibility on the supervisor to handle the dependence. A point that is often overlooked, however, is that there is also a mutuality of dependence; that is, the supervisor also depends on the worker. In order to make his own job a reality and in order to function effectively, the supervisor must rely on the participation of the worker.

In the teaching process, too, there is complementarity. The content of the worker's learning is largely the social data he has gathered and the problems with which he is attempting to deal. The supervisor, in attempting to understand the data, learns from the worker in much the same way as the worker learns from the client. Each must be able "to listen" in order to be of help. The participation of superivsor and worker is based on a mutuality of interests and an acceptance of their complementary roles. Such mutuality and complementarity do not conflict with their specific roles or with the definition of their respective responsibilities. Helping, learning, and teaching are linked together in one interacting psychological process.

Transference and countertransference phenomena can be expected to occur in the supervisory relationship, as they do in other relationships. In the supervisory situation, however, the reactions are heightened by such factors as the power and control of the supervisor, the dependence and insecurity of the learner, and the closeness of the relationship. These factors may tend to stimulate anxiety and hostility on the part of both participants. Special note should be made of the authoritative element. The worker may react to the supervisor's authority with fear and defeat his own learning by becoming overly independent or rebellious. The supervisor, in reaction, may then assert undue authority, thereby setting up a vicious circle.

In the course of gaining greater independence, the learner will experience certain transference phenomena that are similar to those characteristic of the maturational process. The process of separation and of establishing independence will be accompanied by anxiety and projection. The supervisor, as well as the learner, is involved in the process and will have subjective reactions.

INTERACTION

It is evident in the foregoing discussion that the components that enter into supervisory practice form an interlocking process. No one of the four—the institutional, the methodological, the educational, and the psychological—is paramount.

The social agency itself is a complex structure, often made up of many organizational units and staffed by persons discharging various functions. The clients, too, must be considered part of the total configuration, since the agency exists for the purpose of extending help to them in meeting social problems. The concept we wish to suggest here is that the field of transaction in an agency includes both the social problem to be dealt with and the helping methods.

Any problem experienced by the client group is the result of a chain of interrelated forces and events—psychological, interpersonal, and social. Social work is moving away from the former tendency to view the "problem" in terms of the individual client, with emphasis on his psychological difficulties. The trend is toward broadening the theoretical base and toward developing new technical methods for working within the broader framework. The current literature reflects this trend.[1] A similar trend toward enlarging the theoretical and operational base has been taking place in the psychiatric field.[2]

The wider field of transaction in social work suggests the need for a re-evaluation of supervisory practice. Supervision in many instances is still geared to the methods developed at an earlier period when the focus of the helping services was more limited. Supervision, in a sense, has been isolated from the main stream of technical developments. Much of the current criticism of supervision may stem from the fact that the emphasis in supervision is still on helping the worker acquire skill in a single operation, with little effort to have him participate in other processes and in the wider responsibilities of the agency. Supervisory practice should be related to the agency's total operation and to forces and events that shape its program and the helping methods.

This broader concept of supervision does not imply that standards of performance should be lowered. The agency's expectation of types of performance must still be made specific. However, greater individualization of responsibilities for particular workers may be indicated as an agency program becomes more diverse and relies less on a single helping method.

In our seminar discussions of the components of supervision, we made reference to a number of areas of tension. We agreed that tension is inherent in the supervisory task, which involves the integration of many, and sometimes conflicting, elements. As mentioned earlier, the supervisor must function in roles that prescribe both equality and inequality. He must deal with both future-oriented values and reality limitations of the present. He must weigh his own individual experience in teaching against the agency's patterns and methods. In addition, he must develop a pattern for bringing these interacting elements into some sort of harmony so that the services of the agency are effectively rendered. Such interactional transactions always create tension but the degree depends on the supervisor's ability to integrate the various components. Tension should reduce with successful experience. In relation to workers, supervision also has certain tension-producing elements, such as the anxiety involved in learning and in working under authority. However, it also has some tension-reducing elements. Tension tends to diminish as the worker gains mastery of the subject matter and as he finds a balance between the interacting forces that affect his performance.

Despite the fact that tension for both supervisor and worker is a reducible factor, it should be recognized that a certain degree of tension is inevitable. Overemphasis on the tension, with attempts to short-cut or eliminate the supervisory process, would tend to undermine client service, staff learning, and the advancement of professional knowledge. Denial of the tension, however, might lead to the same undesirable ends, since such denial would result in ritualistic enactment of roles on the part of both supervisor and worker.

The major problem in supervisory practice is the need for the participants to find and maintain a balance between the tension-provoking elements inherent in the process. This problem, in a sense, is the problem faced by all individuals in the process of daily living. It comes into sharper focus in a professional operation because of the specific demands made on both supervisor and worker to render a community service, to maintain and advance standards of service, and to observe professional ethics.

Supervision has been blamed for the existence of many problems, including the creation of disabling anxiety in the practitioner group. Supervision has also been lauded as a valuable educational device, one that provides the practitioner with needed emotional support while he is mastering content and skills. Our seminar group recognized that objective standards for evaluating the shortcomings and values of the process would be difficult to establish. Our appraisal was that the values outweigh the shortcomings. The important values lie in the maintenance of client service, in the improvement of performance on the part of the practitioner, and in the provision of a framework through which he can find a balance between the interacting processes that are part of professional performance in a social agency setting.

NOTES

1. As illustrations, see:

Nathan W. Ackerman, M.D., *Psychodynamics of Family Life*, Basic Books, New York, 1958.

John P. Spiegel, M.D., "The Resolution of Role Conflict within the Family," *Psychiatry*, Vol. XX, No. 1 (1957), pp. 1–16.

Seymour Fisher, Ph.D., and David Mendell, M.D., "The Communication of Neurotic Patterns over Two and Three Generations," *Psychiatry*, Vol. XIX, No. 1 (1956), pp. 41–46; "The Spread of Psychotherapeutic Effects from the Patient to His Family Group," *Psychiatry*, Vol. XXI, No. 2 (1958), pp. 133–140; "Approach to Neurotic Behavior in Terms of a Three-Generation Model," *Journal of Nervous and Mental Diseases*, Vol. CXXIII, No. 2 (1956), pp. 171–180; "A Multi-Generation Approach to the Treatment of Psychopathology," *Journal of Nervous and Mental Diseases*, Vol. CXXVI, No. 6 (1958), pp. 523–529.

Viola W. Weiss and Russell R. Monroe, M.D., "A Framework for Understanding Family Dynamics," Parts I and II, *Social Casework*, Vol. XL, Nos. 1 and 2 (1959), pp. 3–9, 80–87.

Gardner Murphy, Ph.D., "New Knowledge about Family Dynamics," *Social Casework*, Vol. XL, No. 7 (1959), pp. 363–370.

Frances H. Scherz, "What Is Family-Centered Casework?" *Social Casework*, Vol. XXXIV, No. 8 (1953), pp. 343–349.

M. Robert Gomberg, "Family-Oriented Treatment of Marital Problems," *Social Casework*, Vol. XXXVII, No. 1 (1956), pp. 3–10.

2. Alfred H. Stanton and Morris S. Schwartz, *The Mental Hospital*, Basic Books, New York, 1954.

August B. Hollingshead and Frederick C. Redlich, *Social Class and Mental Illness: A Community Study*, John Wiley and Sons, New York, 1958.

Otto Pollak, *Integrating Sociological and Psychoanalytic Concepts: An Exploration in Child Psychotherapy*, Russell Sage Foundation, New York, 1956; "Relationships between Social Science and Child Guidance Practice," *American Sociological Review*, Vol. XVI, No. 1 (1951), p. 63.

Maxwell S. Jones, and others, *The Therapeutic Community: A New Treatment Method in Psychiatry*, Basic Books, New York, 1953.

PART III

Structural
Characteristics

INTRODUCTION

HISTORICALLY, supervision has evolved as an individual, one-to-one, tutorial arrangement, which has never been questioned seriously until recent times; even now alternative models are frequently viewed as supplemental to the traditional one.

Discussion of the structure of supervision has involved promoting autonomy for workers. It is difficult to separate structure and authority, and little distinction has been made between the two concepts. There have been increasing demands for worker autonomy, and group supervision has recently been seen as an alternative structure to promote it. In spite of the claims advanced for group supervision, however, research has demonstrated that it has not been implemented on a broad basis; and where it has been used, it has not answered the question of autonomy *ipso facto*. The failure to develop group approaches to supervision is most likely related to supervisors' feelings of lack of skill in group methods and their fear of loss of control.

Beyond group supervision, independent models have not been developed systematically by the profession. Workers who have a great deal of independence frequently complain that this is due to default rather than design. Providing for independent supervision means more than just leaving the worker alone, as Wax explains in his article. Also, the role of the agency in advancing or impeding development of alternative structures has not been explored thoroughly; this is discussed in the article by Fizdale.

Wax believes that the traditional model should be limited to two years at most and terminated at a planned point in favor of an independent model. The latter should be based on accountability through periodic administrative review and an adequate staff-development program which fosters the application of knowledge as well as the ability to impart knowledge to others. The process of supervision involves three objectives: (1) socialization of the worker to agency and community, (2) development of skills, and (3) development of professional judgment. The model is based on the premise that because of the increased emphasis on professional education, the worker has basic knowledge which the supervisor must take into account. The time-limited process of supervision is explored through the concepts of sophistication, versatility, taxing limits of intellectual and professional resources, and expansion of the professional self, which result in a professional maturity that should signal the end of traditional supervision.

Fizdale discusses an independent model of supervision which must be created in the agency when traditional supervision has been virtually eliminated for experienced workers. This article deals with the basic question of how to structure supervision once it is recognized that the practitioner is ultimately responsible for his or her own practice. To make the supervisor responsible for evaluating the practitioner's performance sets up a functional barrier to the latter's use of his or her resources to develop self-awareness and self-assessment. In this model the supervisee is free to draw on consultants from other disciplines to deal with troublesome material. Both Wax and Fizdale indirectly separate administrative supervision and clinical consultation, which becomes the basis for the emerging model of supervision discussed by Munson in Part 6.

Abels' article is characteristic of the way in which the theory of group dynamics has been applied to group supervision. He begins with a general explanation of group dynamics and applies the concepts specifically to supervision. The function of groups is portrayed as mediation of the relationship between society and its members, which presents three basic problems: (1) means of carrying out group tasks, (2) provision for group maintenance, and (3) coming to terms with the system of which the group is a part. With these problems in mind, the group supervisory transactions are defined and explained through the concepts of encountering, contracting, reconnaissance, and autonomous learning.

Abels' approach to supervision is more traditional than Wax's and Fizdale's in that he takes a more conservative stance toward authority and the teaching role of the supervisor in the group setting. His approach is better suited to inexperienced practitioners, whereas Wax's and Fizdale's views are more appropriate for experienced workers. Abels' article can serve as background for the expanded ideas on group supervision discussed by Young in Part 6.

Epstein's article links the discussion in this section with the material in the next, inasmuch as it interrelates the models of structure currently in use and deals with the question of authority and the degree of autonomy granted workers who function primarily within organizational settings. She defines various supervision models—growth model, quasi-autonomous model, group model, and autonomous practice—and explores the exercise of autonomy in relation to each model and combination of models within organizational constraints. The author explains her belief that qualified autonomous practice is possible if authority is decentralized and the teaching role is de-emphasized in supervision, since there is now more emphasis on professional educational programs.

Rickert and Turner use supervision of neophyte family therapists in a family agency to describe a model of "live supervision." It is their belief that this method is more compatible with the shift in practice from the "art" to the "science" of treatment. They offer contrasts between the live model and traditional forms of supervision, and they suggest specific techniques for use of the telephone as a supervision device. This article is a good aid for the supervisor who is planning to use new technological devices.

The article by Sharlin and Chaiklin also discusses new technology, in this case videotape equipment, to take supervision to remote areas. This article is based on a project conducted in Israel by the authors, the main objective of which was to take knowledge generated in the university to workers in remote areas of the country rather than to use the predominant and more expensive pattern of bringing the workers into the university. This paper—which has relevance for training and supervision in countries with substantial rural populations, including the United States—is the first in the literature to offer a model for supervision of the rural practitioner.

11

Time-Limited Supervision

John Wax

THE THESIS OF THIS ARTICLE is that under proper conditions individual supervision can and should be terminated by the end of two years.* By "proper conditions" is meant that (1) the supervisee is a graduate of an accredited school of social work and has the incentive, capacity, and opportunity to be a competent professional; (2) the supervisor has sufficient command of supervisory skills to be able to complete the task in two years; and (3) the agency has confidence in the competence of its practitioners and supervisors, is prepared to have administrative personnel shoulder the administrative aspects of the supervisory job, and is prepared to provide a planned staff development program to meet the ongoing developmental needs of staff.

To the extent that supervision is educational it should, like other educational endeavors, be planned sequentially with individualized but defined educational goals tied to defined stages or steps in the educational process. Like other educational processes, it should have an end point or graduation. Too often supervision just peters out when worker and supervisor realize that the sessions are more ceremonial than productive. Worker and/or supervisor become too busy to keep supervisory appointments. The worker functions with greater independence, but both parties are anxious and guilty about their evasion of the agency's

* The writer is mindful of the fact that the certification requirement of the National Association of Social Workers may have the effect of institutionalizing the two-year period of supervision and wishes to make clear that he does not rest his case on the certification requirement, although in agreement with the assumptions upon which it is based. While the Academy of Certified Social Workers contemplates two years as a minimum, the writer thinks of this as a maximum.

intention that the worker be supervised. The supervisor feels bad about not having had more to give to the worker and the worker feels bad because he has been denied the satisfying experience of having his professional coming of age legitimized with appropriate ceremony.

The three major objectives of supervision are (1) socializing the worker to agency and community, (2) developing his service skills, (3) developing his professional judgment. It is the writer's conviction, after five years' experience with time-limited supervision, that these objectives can be accomplished within two years (they may, in fact, be accomplished in as few as four months for an experienced and competent worker who needs only to learn the setting, or from eighteen months to two years for a worker with no professional experience) and then sustained, extended, and enriched by a comprehensive staff development program.

SOCIALIZATION TO AGENCY AND COMMUNITY

Work on this objective tends to be concentrated in the first six to nine months of the two-year period, with additional spurts of growth and consolidation continuing through the entire period of the worker's stay with the agency.

The supervisor helps the worker to an understanding of, and professional-emotional commitment to, the agency theory of human nature and philosophy of service. Upon this foundation rests the task of helping the worker understand, accept, and apply the various agency policies dealing with eligibility, program emphasis, deployment of agency resources, and the agency's place in the social organization of the community.

The new worker quite properly tends to be highly client-centered. He must be helped to understand and respect the fact that the agency has multiple commitments. In addition to the commitment to the client, the agency has commitments to the body, governmental or private, which provides its mandate and monies; to the social, economic, cultural, political, and welfare organizations of the community; to the professional and administrative requirements of its staff; and to its institutionalized forms, traditions, and goals.

The worker is helped to see and use the regulations and procedures of the agency in a way which comes to terms with their restrictiveness, but emphasizes their usefulness in meeting client needs. He is trained to use the other resources of agency and community, ranging from the dictating machine through the psychiatric consultant to the community welfare council. He learns to meet administrative requirements of the agency, such as keeping statistics and records, and develops an ability to capitalize on some of these procedures, to accept some and merely to tolerate others, all the while developing a growing understanding of the rationale behind these administrative demands.

Socialization of the worker also involves his learning a large repertoire of behaviors appropriate to specialized relationships with clients, colleagues in his own and other disciplines, supervisory and administrative personnel, secretaries, board members, and so on. In a small family agency the number and variety of relationships may be fairly limited. In a large hospital, in which there are numerous professional groups with overlapping functions, the socialization process is vastly more complex and may be a primary focus of supervision for months.

During this period the supervisee will be struggling to learn about his place in the power structure and communication network of the agency. He will learn to distinguish between the formal and informal life of the organization. He will learn about the agency's decision-making processes and how he can get his thinking and experience into those processes. He will learn how statuses are assigned and how roles are prescribed and developed. And he will make his own place in the system.

DEVELOPMENT OF SERVICE SKILLS

The second major objective of supervision has to do with the mastery of the service skills required by the agency and its clientele, and it receives sustained attention through the entire two-year supervisory period. Extremely important here is that the supervisor and worker recognize explicitly that the new worker is a novice to the agency, but not to the profession. The worker, having completed two years of graduate training, including two years of supervised field work, comes to his first job with a substantial body of knowledge and skill. Supervision does not start from scratch. It starts with an assessment of the foundation of competence that the worker brings and proceeds systematically to build on that competence.

The two-year period of developing service skills is characterized by two types of progression, the first having to do with sophistication, the second with versatility. By *sophistication* is meant that with the passage of time and the acquisition of additional skill, the worker approaches a given task with a greater range and depth of diagnostic perceptions and a broader and sharper repertoire of treatment techniques. For example, a worker in a mental hospital will be doing casework with delusional patients. He might, very early in his practice, encourage the patient to discuss his delusions. He soon progresses to a recognition that discussion of delusional material is not an effective way of helping the patient deal with reality problems. He moves from helping the patient to talk to helping him talk about reality problems, such as using hospital treatment or returning to the community.

At the end of six months the worker has several techniques available to him for moving patients from delusional material to problem-solving material. However, his timing is still occasionally off and his shifts of focus are sometimes too abrupt and sometimes insufficiently firm. By the end of a year he is relatively skillful and comfortable with the management of most delusional material, and he is helped to see that certain types of delusional material can be understood as a special type of communication and employed in the solution of reality problems.

Through all this the worker becomes steadily less oriented toward the *single* correct technique or the *one* correct diagnostic formulation. He views a steadily widening range of diagnostic possibilities compounded of psychological and social dynamics. He has available to him an expanding range of alternatives based on an expanding knowledge of communication theory and learning theory, as well as casework, role, and psychoanalytic theory. He has developed excellent mastery of the simple casework techniques, such as support and clarification, and is developing mastery of the more difficult techniques, such as reality confrontation, patterning, parenting, and dynamic interpretation. In short, sophistication refers to qualitative improvement in the execution of specific responsibilities.

The second type of progression, *versatility*, refers to quantitative increase in skills and responsibilities. Again using the mental hospital as an example, the worker starts with individual casework. Initially, the stress is on casework tasks that are fairly simple, as, for instance, helping a motivated patient plan for discharge. By the end of six months the worker is handling more difficult casework tasks, such as helping an institutionalized patient accept the hospital requirement that he return to the community, and helping patients and relatives understand and alter dysfunctional family interactions. Close to the end of his two years, the worker should be ready for an admission service, where he will be expected to work with highly resistive committed patients to help them make constructive use of the enforced hospital experience. He will also be expected to do a comprehensive and penetrating social diagnosis.

While casework skills are developing, other new responsibilities are worked in. After his first few months in the hospital the worker is introduced to multiple interviewing wherein he and one or several other staff members meet with a patient or relative, or patients and relatives together. Within the first six months he takes on a group with clearly defined social work goals, such as discharge planning, orientation to the hospital, or social skill re-education. Within the first year he is doing some family therapy, and by the end of two years he may be leading community therapy meetings or be the staff person working with patient government.

As the worker's skills expand and his reputation grows, he is called upon to help select student cases on his ward, to participate in the orientation of new personnel on the ward, to have a student social worker, psychologist, or nurse as an observer-learner in his group. Other members of the ward team begin to use him as a consultant and he learns how to help members of other professions use their knowledge and frame of reference to apply the information, insight, or perspective that he, as a social worker, offers. He is also increasingly expected to serve on staff committees, to contribute his thinking at case conferences, to participate in the decision-making activities of the department, and to interest himself in the National Association of Social Workers and community activities.

Obviously, the progressions will vary greatly from specialty to specialty and setting to setting, but the principle remains the same. Expectations and goals associated with the mastery of skills can be arranged sequentially and pursued systematically.

PROFESSIONAL JUDGMENT

The third major objective of supervision is to develop the worker's professional judgment. Certainly professional judgment is subsumed under the two objectives of supervision described above. However, with this third objective, which is concentrated in the last six months of supervision, there is a sharp focus on helping the worker assume responsibility for making his own professional decisions. He is trained to take responsibility for the quality of his service to clients and for his own professional development.[1]

Having a time limit changes the character of the supervisory relationship from the beginning. Although the worker's initial anxiety and dependency needs are considered and handled (he has virtually unlimited access to the supervisor in the first three months), the supervisor uses two strategies to prepare him for progressive self-responsibility. The first is *to tax consistently his intellectual and professional resources to the limit*. In discussing a problem he is required to list and examine the range of formulations or behaviors available to him. When he has exhausted his own knowledge and experience the supervisor begins to teach by suggesting additional alternatives and helping him examine these. He is trained to look to his own knowledge, skill, and experience as his first recourse, and to make the fullest possible use of his professional self.

The second strategy is to help the worker *expand his professional self* by giving him ready access, not only to the supervisor's skill and wisdom, but to all the intellectual resources of the setting. Instead of trying to centralize all his learning in the supervisor, as though the supervisor were omniscient and omnicompetent, he is encouraged to go to others on the staff who have greater technical competence in the problem area than has the supervisor.

For example, the supervisor who is a highly skillful caseworker will exert his teaching ability in this area, but will encourage the worker to go to another social worker or perhaps a psychologist for more expert help with a group therapy problem. With increasing frequency during the two-year period the supervisor steers the worker toward other social workers or other task-competent people in medicine, psychology, admissions, the business office, and so on. In so doing the supervisor does three things with the supervisee: (1) He helps him formulate and define the problem in workable terms. (2) He helps him decide where to go for help. (3) Last, and most important, he helps him incorporate the assistance he receives into the social work plan and integrate the new knowledge into his expanding professional identity as a social worker.

The supervisor also forcefully conveys to the worker the agency philosophy that a worker's adequacy is measured not by his appearing so independent that he never needs help, but rather by his appropriate, effective, and timely use of help. The worker retains major responsibility for the quality of service he gives. He uses consultation or other forms of help as a way of meeting his responsibility, not as a way of delegating or abdicating responsibility. Workers understand that they are evaluated on the dimension of how well they take advantage of the helping resources available.

In summary, professional judgment revolves around the worker's ability to make, and take responsibility for, sound professional decisions. These decisions involve the use of himself in the agency social system and his use of treatment and other service skills. In larger measure, professional judgment revolves around his reaction to both subjective and objective signals which indicate that the best possible service to the client requires that he add an increment of information, skill, or perspective which can be provided by another helping person. It is as the worker learns when and why he needs help, where to find it, how to ask for it, and how to apply it, that he develops professional judgment.

PROFESSIONAL COMING OF AGE

When worker, supervisor, and administrator agree that the three objectives of individual supervision have been substantially achieved, supervision is terminated. This professional coming of age is accompanied by

an appropriate change in title, status, and income, i.e., promotion from
junior grade to senior grade.

Although no longer supervised, the worker remains accountable for
the quality and quantity of his work. The administrative official to whom
the worker is directly responsible may be the former supervisor, a section or unit chief, an assistant chief in charge of a program area, or the
agency executive. The administrator remains knowledgeable about the
worker's performance by using combinations of the following devices:
(1) review of correspondence, summaries, reports, and other materials
of record; (2) review of statistics; (3) direct observation of the worker
in those situations in which he uses the administrator as a helping person; (4) regularly scheduled (usually monthly) briefing sessions in
which the worker informs the administrator about program developments,
trends in practice, case load management, staff relationships, special
cases and situations, and so on; (5) direct observation of worker's performance in multiple interviews, case conferences, community therapy
meetings, staff meetings, seminars, group consultations, interagency meetings, community and NASW activities; (6) knowledge of his professional
reputation among his colleagues.

This last point is worthy of special comment. The writer is convinced
that a worker's concern for his professional reputation provides the most
mature, healthy, and effective motivation for high-quality practice. At the
Veterans Administration Hospital workers are encouraged to be reputa-
tion-conscious, and staff life has been organized in such a way as to
establish high standards of professional performance to which workers
subscribe, and which they, in large measure, enforce. The hospital attempts to make the worker's professional performance as socially visible
as possible. In a variety of group situations, taped interviews are played,
cases are presented, and other professional behaviors are examined and
commented upon. Social pressures from the colleague group replace the
pressure of the parent surrogate supervisor.[2] In repeated instances it has
been observed that workers who are either tacitly or militantly resistive
to supervision respond to the social pressure provided by their professionally respected colleagues.

STAFF DEVELOPMENT

It will be recalled that one of the requisites for termination of individual supervision is the presence of an adequate staff development program. Agency resources that have been invested in supervision can be
diverted into other forms of staff development. The scope and quality of
the staff development program will vary with agency philosophy, budget,
personnel, location, function, and so forth. The obvious devices of bring-

ing in consultants and lecturers or sending staff to university, NASW or community-sponsored courses, workshops, and the like at agency expense hardly require comment. Staff meetings, committee projects, and other frequently used staff development devices are readily available. The real challenge in staff development is the imaginative use of agency staff in such a way as to develop not only expert practitioners, but leaders, teachers, and consultants as well. For example, the use of unlimited colleague consultation alluded to in the discussion on developing professional judgment makes it possible for a worker with a technical problem to go to that staff member who has the reputation for being the most expert in the problem area. Not only does the worker with the problem get help, but the worker who helps enjoys the recognition and is encouraged to expand his expertness in his area of special interest.[3]

The recognition provided by the worker's colleagues is only half the encouragement. The other half comes from the agency, which also recognizes the worker's special competence and underwrites the cost of additional training in order to expand his competence and leadership potential.

The mandate to the agency for staff development goes beyond supporting the growing expertness of its workers. There must also be a systematic effort to help workers become skillful in imparting their knowledge. Worker-consultants must be trained to be more than troubleshooters. They must learn to move from the case to the concept and the other skills involved in being a good consultant and/or teacher. A program of individual and/or group consultation gets work problems solved, expands the expertise of the consultee and consultant, and facilitates the emergence of professional leaders for the agency in particular and for the profession in general. It opens new vistas and opportunities for practitioners, giving them added status and recognition, making it less necessary for them to leave the practitioner ranks.

The agency responsibility for staff development obligates it to make available a broad range of learning possibilities. To make this meaningful, the agency must also provide a climate which genuinely encourages workers to avail themselves of these opportunities. The agency that has a fine staff development program on paper, but assigns case loads which make it impossible for workers to participate in staff development activities, will not fool its staff for very long.

Once the agency has made opportunities available it falls to the worker to make good use of these opportunities. One opportunity for examining the effectiveness of this program is the annual career planning conference which, for the experienced worker, replaces the traditional annual evaluation. In this conference worker and administrator sit down to discuss the worker's long- and short-range professional goals. These are examined from two perspectives, first, as to whether the worker is doing everything in his power to achieve his professional objectives, be these maximum job satisfaction today or an administrative position five years hence. This discussion has many evaluative implications, of course, as worker and administrator review the worker's progress in relation to his aspirations. The administrator is then able to suggest reading, academic work, and other ways in which the worker can move more effectively toward his goals.

The burden, however, is not entirely on the worker. The second stage of the discussion revolves around what the agency can do to help him reach his objectives, e.g., changing work assignments in order to provide a variety of experiences, underwriting the costs of training outside the agency, bringing certain types of consultants to the agency, altering administrative practices so that workers have the maximum time and energy available for professional purposes. In short, the worker and the administrator become partners in the worker's professional progress, an arrangement from which both profit.

It has been found that, although this type of annual discussion has some evaluative implications, it is not approached with anything like the same amount of anxiety as the traditional evaluation. In a sense, the agency is being evaluated, as well as the worker. The status and power disparity between the participants is not nearly as great as it is in a traditional evaluation.

CONCLUSIONS

Confronted with the realization that they do not have a lifetime of supervision in which to get the job done, worker and supervisor must think clearly and specifically about learning needs and goals. Agency expectations must be formulated and articulated. Focus and pace become crucial issues.

In many respects the task is more demanding for reasons which by now must be obvious. However, in this time-limited supervisory program the supervisor's burden is greatly eased because he is no longer expected to be the repository of all wisdom. The fact that the worker is learning from a variety of people makes it possible for the supervisor to concentrate his teaching time and energy on the things he is best equipped to do, namely, to teach those skills in which he has the greatest proficiency and also—and more important—to help the worker integrate varied information, skills, and attitudes into a coherent and consistent social work identity.

Workers find the system more comfortable because their use of a wide variety of learning resources dilutes their dependency on the supervisor, a fact which has extensive emotional and intellectual ramifications.[4] They also enjoy, take pride in, and live up to the vote of confidence which the agency has accorded them.

The writer's experience with this supervisory program has been most rewarding. Morale and effectiveness have been found to be high and turnover remarkably low. The eagerness of workers to be treated as responsible professionals is reflected in the large numbers of applications received by the hospital. Also, the status of the social worker in the hospital has been found to be immeasurably higher, since he has taken his place in the ward team with the same support from his service as the psychiatrist and psychologist have long enjoyed.

It is a sociological axiom that professionalism and bureaucracy (the word is here used in the sociological rather than pejorative sense) are inherently antagonistic. The professional derives his authority less from agency delegation than from his own education and technical competence. The more self-consciously professional he is the more likely he is to resist bureaucratic forms and practices that restrict his professional decision-making.

This fact has tremendous implications for the future of social work. In recent years there has been marked improvement in the quality of social work education and practice. At the same time NASW has been conspicuously successful in its efforts to formalize, codify, and articulate the professional culture of social work. It is not mere coincidence that this intensification of professionalism has been associated with the phenomenal growth of private practice.

In conversations with social workers in private practice the writer has, of course, heard talk of money and status. But the theme which recurs with most frequency and feeling is the desire for greater responsibility and autonomy. Those who are charged to recruit and retain competent staff are in a difficult position. They would not, if they could, arrest or delay the further development of social work as a profession. They should not, if they could, prevent their colleagues from moving into work situations which afford them maximum opportunity for responsibility, creativeness, and autonomy.

Agency executives have but one course. If the profession wants to keep its professionals, it must treat them as professionals. Lifelong supervision is a vestige of the subprofessional past. Social workers do come of age. They can be proud of their training and confident of their skill. They must be accorded the respect, responsibility, and autonomy to which the professional is entitled.[5]

NOTES

1. Frances Scherz, "A Concept of Supervision Based on Definitions of Job Responsibility," *Social Casework*, Vol. 39, No. 8 (October 1958), p. 435 [Chapter 8 above, p. 70].

2. John Wax, "The Pros and Cons of Group Supervision," *Social Casework,* Vol. 40, No. 6 (June 1959).

3. John J. Appleby, Virginia C. Berkman, Robert T. Blazejack, and Vicki S. Gorter, "A Group Method of Supervision," *Social Work,* Vol. 3, No. 3 (July 1958), pp. 18–22.

4. Charlotte Babcock, "Social Work as Work," *Social Casework,* Vol. 34, No. 10 (December 1953).

5. Lucille Austin, "The Changing Role of the Supervisor," *Smith College Studies in Social Work,* Vol. 31 (June 1961).

12

Peer-Group Supervision

Ruth Fizdale

SUPERVISION, WHICH is an integral part of education for the field of social work and of the administration of social services, has been subjected to much questioning in recent years. Social workers seem to agree that supervision has proved its value in helping the student and the beginning worker to integrate theory and practice and to develop social attitudes that are essential for work in our field. Our opinions about supervision are mixed, however, when we consider its purpose and function beyond the beginning years of practice. We are reluctant to say that workers can function independently, yet we chafe under the never-ending quality of supervision. We regard the long continuance of the worker-supervisor relationship as potentially detrimental to the professional maturation of the worker. We are concerned over the costliness of supervision. In all these discussions our aim is to gain some clarity about the values derived from supervision which we want to retain.

In the social work profession, supervision has carried more than training responsibilities. It has been the medium through which the experience of an agency has been made available to the administration in the development of standards and policies. Supervision has also led to increased professional competence through the identification of those areas of practice that require study and experimentation. Consequently, a continuance of a relationship between worker and supervisor was essential, even though the worker might have achieved sufficient skill to work independently in serving his clients. Many agencies are concerned with how to preserve the values of a supervisory structure which serves as the medium for review and improvement of an agency's practice, while

---

From *Social Casework* 39 (October 1958), pp. 443–450. Reprinted by permission of the Family Service Association of America.

permitting the caseworker gradually to assume more responsibility for his own practice. The Arthur Lehman Counseling Service is one such agency. Owing to circumstances derived from its basic purpose, the ALCS has been able to experiment in developing a structure for caseworkers able to assume full responsibility for the quality of their practice.

THE AGENCY STRUCTURE

First, I should like to describe the agency and its objectives briefly, since these influence the structure we have set up. I shall then describe a process the agency has evolved for helping the individual practitioner (as well as the agency) advance the quality of his service to clients. What I shall describe is not, in my opinion, "peer-group supervision," as this paper is entitled. To me, supervision implies responsibility for the training and teaching of others as well as the sharing of responsibility for the service given clients by the worker. In our process we share a mutual interest in serving clients and in deriving benefits from each other, but each person is responsible for his own learning and practice. Some social workers, however, will find that the process described here falls within their definition of supervision. The name we give the process does not seem important. What is important is whether this as yet unnamed process does enable workers to mature professionally and to be more productive, and whether it does have values for advanced workers that individual supervision does not have.

The ALCS is a nonsectarian agency. It was established as a result of the concern expressed by certain lay and professional leaders in the community that persons in the middle and upper income groups did not avail themselves, to any appreciable degree, of casework counseling help provided through the social agencies. Since it was clear that the problems brought to these agencies were not confined to persons in any one economic group, it was considered essential—in the interests of those who need help and the future of the social work profession—that the barriers be further broken down and that these groups be reached. The ALCS was set up as a demonstration unit whose purpose it would be to discover and test (1) the circumstances under which these persons would use casework counseling services, (2) the structure that would be needed, and (3) the extent to which such a service could be self-maintaining, yet have as its primary objective provision of the highest possible quality of service. It was hoped that, as experience and knowledge were accumulated in these areas, social agencies throughout the country would be encouraged to set up similar services and would do so with more confidence as a result of the ALCS experience.

To achieve these objectives it was decided to offer a casework counseling service identical with that offered by family agencies (without such complementary services as homemakers, and so on), to invite persons serving on the boards of other social agencies to serve on ours, and to have an advisory committee of professional leaders. The close relationships between the ALCS and other agencies that have been established through the board and advisory committee have encouraged the free exchange of material, experience, and questions. The ALCS experience is readily available to other agencies, and the ALCS has benefited from their reactions to its work.

The ALCS is supported by client fees ($12.50 an interview) and by the Adele and Arthur Lehman Foundation. No funds are sought from other sources. Persons are invited to serve on the board because of their conviction about the value of the social work profession, their interest in the purpose of the agency, and their belief that the ALCS experience may prove valuable in the future planning of other agencies. A technical advisory committee (composed of the director of the Family Service Association of America and the executives of five of the major family agencies in New York) helps the ALCS plan its program so that the results of its experience may have value to the profession as a whole. The ALCS was set up, then, as a pilot demonstration project with responsibility for extending casework counseling to that portion of the community that had not been sufficiently reached—the upper and middle income groups—and for answering certain professional questions related to quality of practice and costs.

The ALCS considered it essential to stabilize the factor of staff competence if its findings were to have validity. Staff members were to be casework practitioners who had demonstrated their capacity to carry full professional responsibility for their work. The criteria for a competent staff member included: (1) sufficient knowledge and skill to enable the practitioner to offer help in the majority of situations with which he would be called upon to work; (2) sufficient self-awareness and professional integrity to know when he needed consultation, how to seek it appropriately, and how to be able to integrate the help given into his practice; (3) the ability to grasp the purpose and goals of the agency and to participate, on a mature level, in their achievement.

The present professional staff consists of four full-time caseworkers and the administrator.* All the caseworkers have had over ten years' experience in the field. They were considered by their last employers to be capable of "independent" practice. All have had successful experiences as supervisors, but prefer direct counseling service. All have also taken advanced training, either in a third year, or a doctoral, program at a school of social work or in one of the several analytically oriented

---

* In addition there are five part-time caseworkers engaged in an evening program who are not included in this discussion.

training centers in New York City. In addition to the caseworkers and administrator, there are three clerical workers and two part-time staff members who serve as consultants in research and publicity. There is also a consultant in psychiatry who is a practicing analyst with considerable experience in working co-operatively with caseworkers. The medical consultant is a practicing internist who has served as a consultant in other social agencies.

Partly as a result of the quality of the staff and partly because of the agency's commitment to a joint research approach to matters related to professional standards, it was felt that the traditional relationship between the workers and the administrator would be inappropriate in the ALCS setting and would not be conducive to the atmosphere essential for research on such matters as production. The structure evolved in the three and one-half years since the agency was established bears many resemblances to group practice. Group practice is carried on by several persons of equal caliber who are able to carry full responsibility for their own professional service and are united by a common bond of interest and a willingness to work together toward the objectives set. At ALCS the common bond of interest is the over-all concern with giving a high caliber of service to clients and the desire to answer, through demonstration and research, questions that may have value to the profession's future. The framework of the agency was devised for independent functioning and for joint work toward the agency's objectives.

THE WORKER'S RESPONSIBILITY

Each caseworker carries full responsibility for his casework practice. As he sees clients in intake, he himself decides whether a case is appropriate for the agency's service or should be referred elsewhere. He carries full responsibility for the method and techniques he uses.

Each worker carries full responsibility for knowing when he needs consultation, whether in determining the appropriateness of a case for the ALCS service or in his work with a family he is seeing regularly. He is responsible for periodic review of his own work, through review of closed cases and of agency statistics, through participation in group meetings, and so on. He is responsible for identifying the area of his difficulty, should one exist, and for bringing to the group questions he wants to discuss. *There is no casework supervisor or consultant. There are no regular individual conferences between the administrator and other staff members.* All matters pertaining to casework practice are dealt with in two weekly staff conferences. At one, only the casework staff and administrator are present; at the other, the consulting psychiatrist is also present. Workers are free to request time for discussing any problems they have concerning their work in either group conference. A staff member may also wish to bring to the attention of the rest of the staff an interesting case that seems to have some special significance as far as the ALCS practice is concerned or that suggests a new professional question.

Recently, it was agreed that staff members would present to the group cases that probably would be of long-term duration. Such a case will be presented when the staff member has made a tentative diagnostic appraisal and has set his objectives. In addition to case discussions, a worker may bring to a staff meeting any question he may have about some general trend he has noted in his work. For example, in a review of her own closed cases, one worker became concerned over the fact that a number of her clients had terminated contact with the agency earlier than she had expected. These were clients who seemed to the worker to be poorly motivated, but whose motivations she had believed could be strengthened. As she reviewed these cases, she was not certain whether she had missed some diagnostic clues and therefore had been overoptimistic or whether it was difficult for her to sustain her interest in these clients. Another staff member once asked the group's help in understanding an inconsistency she had noted in the amount of time and effort she put into referring clients to other agencies.

Questions about the appropriateness of continuing to work with a particular client or family may be discussed in either group meeting. However, when the worker has a question about the clinical diagnosis or the potential risks involved in working with a client, the case is discussed at the group meeting with the agency's consulting psychiatrist. In these meetings his professional opinion is an important, but not the deciding, factor in reaching a solution. Occasionally he has felt that the ALCS could continue working with a client, but the caseworkers have felt that the kind of help needed was outside the realm of casework. The staff members, however, do follow his thinking when his clinical diagnosis indicates that it is inadvisable for them to work with the client. At the meeting with the psychiatrist, the staff also discusses cases in which the worker is unclear about the dynamics of the personality or would like consultation about the risks involved in opening certain areas for discussion with the client. It has been found that the consultation often results in obtaining more than the contribution of the psychiatrist and incorporates the joint thinking of all the staff on the needs of a particular client or family. Individual case consultations with the psychiatrist are not scheduled except in emergencies.

In addition to the group meetings there are individual consultations between the workers themselves. These are scheduled as needed. Caseworkers who are working with different members of the same family may arrange conferences with each other to co-ordinate treatment plans. Individual staff members may be experimenting with a particular problem or have a special skill. When another worker believes that it would be help-ful to discuss a particular client's case with the person who has a special skill or is doing special work, a conference is arranged. For example, one staff member has done considerable interviewing of both partners to-gether in marital counseling cases. She has developed, therefore, a special skill in the handling of these "joint" interviews, and has special knowl-edge about when they can be productive. It is quite usual for any staff member to consult with her about the value of a joint interview in a particular case or to get her help in preparing for such an interview or in reviewing the results. Finally, if a worker finds himself in need of immediate consultation on a case and cannot wait for the group meeting, he can avail himself of the help of anyone who is free at that time.

The ALCS is also able to purchase the services of a psychologist and consultation from psychiatrists whose special knowledge in a particular area—for example, treatment of children or group treatment of family members—would be useful to the agency. The caseworker arranges such consultations as the need arises.

THE ROLE OF THE ADMINISTRATOR

I should like to comment on the role and function of the administra-tor. In the group meetings I carry no special responsibility *insofar as the discussion of the cases is concerned;* I am merely one of the participants. I do, however, carry a special role in relation to the group—a role that may be related to the fact that we have all had to learn how to work in new relationships to each other. I observe the group process and indi-cate what it is that apparently hampers our full use of each other's help or where we are holding on to former relationships and attitudes. Perhaps the following will clarify what I mean.

In the beginning, the workers tended, in case discussions, to with-hold any comment about a colleague's own problem in helping a client. They seemed to feel that this was my responsibility. When I brought this to the attention of the group, they agreed that this was a carry-over from previous agency experiences where responsibility for such help was solely that of the colleague's supervisor. They agreed that, if I were to assume this role, I would again be in a supervisory position, and our objective of functioning as a group of independent practitioners would be lost. It was agreed that in our setting no one person would carry such a responsibility, but rather it would fall to any one of us who might first see the source of the difficulty in the case being presented for discussion. As might be expected, what happened next was that each staff member, in an attempt to fulfil his new responsibilities, acted as if he were the other person's supervisor. Friction ensued. Again I brought this fact to the attention of the group. As a result, a series of discussions was held in which we clarified our responsibilities to each other. We saw that it was essential for each staff member to contribute to a case discussion whatever he felt might result in more helpful service to a client. However, what the caseworker whose case it was *did* with our contribution was his responsibility.

The group then became aware that it was not possible to feel divorced from the quality of a colleague's practice as long as we were working in an agency setting. They felt that the reputation of all was dependent upon the quality of work done by each. The concern for clients which each of us felt could not be delegated to someone else, since no supervisor existed. Hence, one could not just sit by and watch a colleague fail to see his difficulty in serving a client. In a traditional social agency the responsibility for a colleague's work lies with the supervisor or administrator; although a worker may have doubts about another colleague's practice, he has no direct responsibility to his colleague. In fact, assuming such responsibility is discouraged. In our structure, the workers felt that they were directly affected by each other's practice, and we thus had to define what would enable each of us to permit the others freedom to practice as they saw fit. We realized that, aside from the staff qualifications we had established, it was essential for us to feel that each staff member sincerely wanted to improve his practice and was a learning person, not so content with the current level of his skill that he had no desire to advance his professional knowledge. These discussions have resulted in each worker's having a genuine investment in helping and trusting that the colleague whose case it is will be able to integrate into his practice whatever has been helpful in the discussion. As these new staff relationships have developed, I have become but one of the participants. No special emphasis is given to my contribution. It is as often accepted, modified, or rejected as the contribution of anyone else.

I have also carried responsibility for observing what resources the experienced worker seems to need in order to sustain his level of competence or to increase his skill. After discussion with the group, I assume the responsibility for providing the resources needed. For example, in regard to psychiatric consultation, we began with the traditional concept of a consultant in psychiatry, a competent analyst who would give individual consultations on cases as required. As we moved along, we noted that our need for consultation was less than anticipated, but that the stimulation of other points of view to challenge our thinking and to enrich our understanding was extremely important. We also saw the need for specialized consultations—for example, in our work with children or work with clients in certain diagnostic categories. We anticipated that problems of counter-transference might occur and that we would be ill-advised to use either the group or our consultant for help with these.

When these needs were clarified, it was my responsibility to inform the board and the technical advisory committee and to work out with them how funds could be provided for these purposes.

GENERAL COMMENTS

A few comments on our experience may be in order. Perhaps it is already obvious that the crux of the agency's structure is the selection of staff. I hope at some future time to present a paper on the process of staff selection that the ALCS has evolved. We have succeeded in securing persons with the kind of skill desired, but we need to consider whether our selection process is too costly in time and money, and too difficult for the applicant, and also whether our standards need be as high as they are at the moment. I should like, however, to make one comment on a special problem I have encountered in the hiring process.

The success of our structure depends upon the ability of the group members to respect each other's practice, to have faith in each other's professional integrity and desire to advance one's skills. Aside from staff participation in the selection of new staff members, it is equally important that the applicant consciously and frankly face the question of whether he can be identified with the purpose and philosophy of the agency, can respect the other workers as peers, and can see some professional rewards in such an association. Most applicants approach an agency with the feeling that they are being selected and, although secretly eying the agency to see if they want to work in it, they feel that there is no real opportunity for them to share equally in the selecting. To help an applicant freely and openly to consider the suitability of the job for him, to assess his own readiness for such an experience, his interest in it, its potential values for him, has brought new challenges to the administrator in the hiring process.

Our profession has come a long way in training persons for independent practice. Judging from our own experience, I can state that the social work profession produces excellent technicians, with skills, great integrity, and the ability to function within the structure of an agency setting. By this I mean that the average worker unconsciously relies on the structure of the agency—the existence of the supervisor and administrator, the yearly evaluation, the periodic review of production, and so on—for calling to his attention questions about his practice. Caseworkers have all learned to detect, in direct work with individual clients, their need for consultation and help. However, they rely upon the annual evaluation or the supervisor to call to their attention problems that may not be apparent in the case-by-case work or discussion and that only become apparent as one attempts to gain some over-all picture of one's practice. At ALCS we have agreed that, in order to develop true self-awareness, the worker must also periodically review his own work (closed cases, statistics, and so on) for the purpose of discovering his general problems and assets. This process requires a new type of self-discipline and new work habits.

In social work practice, in general, a worker's relationship to a colleague is colored by the fact that the colleague is responsible to a supervisor or administrator. Hence, in group discussions workers have absorbed and retained beyond the point of need the pattern of withholding certain comments about a colleague's work lest it interfere with the process between the colleague and his supervisor. This is wise when the person is learning and needs to have a relationship with one person who is aware of his pace of learning and his learning problem. As the profession accepts its objective of the development of professional persons who can function independently, it will need to develop a method for achieving this objective, including the development of work habits and attitudes consistent with the eventual goal.

The ALCS staff members all report that carrying full responsibility for one's casework practice is a maturing experience. It helps the worker face up to his own evaluation of his capacity to help, forces him to develop a philosophy of practice and to define his responsibility to clients. As he does these things, he finds it necessary to test his thinking with colleagues, to hear and weigh other points of view, to read, and to experiment with ideas that hold potential value for clients. As I make this comment, I am fully aware of the fact that I am simply reporting an "experience" of several people and have no proof of a factual nature to substantiate this statement. However, it has been of interest to observe that each new staff member who has come to the agency has gone through a similar process of taking in more thoroughly the meaning of the agency structure and discovering that he *was* responsible for his practice. Each person has commented on his surprise at this experience. Each has said that he was never before aware of the degree to which he had relied on supervisor, administrator, or agency structure to help him maintain the quality of his practice.

To me, the most exciting part of the ALCS experience has been to watch the development of constructive exchange among the staff members, as previously described. They have worked out the nature of their responsibilities toward each other and have clarified what are the essential qualities in each one that permit mutual respect and trust. The result has been an interesting process of what I shall call "cross fertilization."

One staff member, on coming to ALCS, expressed concern over a tendency in the agency to schedule the initial intake interview in marital cases with both the husband and wife together. She felt that this was unsound for professional reasons, that it created unnecessary problems for the clients in being able to relate to the worker, to feel free to discuss the problem as they saw it or to discuss confidential matters. Her conviction was that she could not conduct such an interview helpfully. Although several of us had other convictions, we felt no need to have her change her way of work. When clients specifically asked to be seen together, the case was assigned to someone else. If no such request was made, the case was assigned to her. It was inevitable that in group discussions, cases in which joint interviews had occurred were discussed. Her questions came forth naturally and were part of the general case discussion. Sometime later she asked for a special consultation with the staff member who had done considerable work with such interviews. Shortly thereafter she decided that such an interview might be helpful in a case she was carrying. After a time she used "joint" interviews as frequently as the rest of the staff, understood their potential value; she has contributed as much as anyone else to the group's clarification of their use.

Another staff member, who had come from a child guidance clinic, expressed discomfort with her work with children at ALCS. She had been accustomed to having, in advance of seeing a child, a psychiatric and psychological evaluation. The group challenged her, not on her concept of how work with children should begin, but on the fact that she had tried to work contrary to her convictions. Her response that no one else here worked this way was not accepted as valid. She knew there was no fixed policy on this, and arranging psychiatric and psychological examinations and consultations was her prerogative with no need for prior clearing. Actually, this worker had begun to re-evaluate her former approach and was asking the group for their opinion and help. Such an exchange results in enrichment of everyone's practice.

Such discussion brings into play a free exchange of knowledge and of conviction that stem from one's own experience. Since several types of experience are represented among the staff members—some have done more work in children's agencies, some have had the bulk of their experience in a hospital setting or a family agency—each one can bring to the discussion a wealth of information that can only be accumulated in a specialized setting. If the atmosphere is such that no one feels the need to accept the views of others or to force acceptance of his own views, the exchange can be enriching. Skilled practitioners, although functioning in accordance with the same general principles, do develop an individual "style." In the course of staff exchange these individual approaches, which may be unique to the persons present, are revealed. Often, as a result, one caseworker is able to borrow a bit from the "style" of another when he feels it will be helpful to a particular client.

Another value in a group discussion by persons of equal competence and status is that their professional problems are likely to be similar, and therefore discussion on such problems can proceed more smoothly and can be more productive than is possible when the group is mixed in experience and skill.

I hope that these comments have conveyed some of the flavor of our staff's method of working together. We feel that we are increasingly clear about what we are doing, but we still need further experience and the continuing evaluation of it. To me, the process has been of special interest because I have developed through this experience a conviction that the structure of our profession—as well as of social agencies—is somewhat antiquated. Our professional structure was developed when we were still not professional workers, but were apprentices. Now that we have developed the characteristics and the knowledge that mark a profession, it is essential for us to reconsider many aspects of our traditional structures. Our concept of supervision is but one of these many aspects.

13

On the Nature of Supervision: The Medium Is the Group

Paul A. Abels

THE QUEST FOR METHODS of helping staff learn how to be of service to the client is a major concern of supervisors. This paper describes the applicability of one method, the use of the group, as a medium for education through supervision.

What we seek in supervision are opportunities that: (1) introduce the learner to some of the problem-solving techniques and skills that he will be called on to use in his work; (2) help him generalize his learning experiences; and (3) develop the attitudes and understanding necessary to be a helping person.

The traditional method of supervision, like field teaching in social work education, has been modeled after the one-to-one tutorial, related primarily to the learner's contacts with the client as processed into the case record and taught by the field teacher. Shannon writes:

> In the tutorial method characteristic of field instruction, the individual conference with the student is the basic vehicle for teaching. The individual conference (after the field instructor has read the student's process recording of his cases) enables the instructor to understand the student's particular learning needs and problems, the quality of his thinking and feeling, and his potentiality for becoming a caseworker.[1]

The individual conferences are augmented by other experiences such as attendance at staff meetings, staffings, and board meetings.[2] There is room for a number of approaches, ranging from the time-proved "one-to-one" supervisory conferences to the use of the work group as

From *Child Welfare* 49 (June 1970), pp. 304–311. Copyright © 1970 by Child Welfare League of America. Reprinted by permission of the publisher.

cosupporter of the educational process. The teacher must be ready to examine and utilize a number of techniques.

OPPORTUNITIES TO TRY A GROUP APPROACH

Groups have been used successfully as a medium for learning in staffings, staff meetings, orientation, and training; but the use of the learning group as a major tool for supervision and teaching has had slower acceptance by agencies and field teachers. Supervision in groups has some historical roots in the social work field [3] and has recently had increased use in agencies and schools of social work. The development of field work units under the direction of a faculty field work instructor has provided an opportunity for group supervision (the terms "supervision" and "teaching" are here used interchangeably). This development, combined with increased recognition of the potential of the group as helper in the change process, has spurred the use of group supervision.

In group supervision, the major supervisory tasks (teaching, administration, and enabling) are carried on in and with the group.[4] Supportive teaching opportunities such as individual evaluations, staff meetings, and individual conferences are essential. The responsibilities for teaching and content become those of all the instructional group members, and not only the formal supervisor. The latter's authority comes from the institution and his competence; the learner's authority to teach comes primarily from the instructional group, but also from his formal supervisor.

THE SMALL GROUP AS EDUCATIVE SYSTEM

The nature of the small group as both an educative and socializing force has been documented by writers in the fields of social work, education, and social psychology.[5] It suffices to say that the group offers its members opportunities to achieve goals that may be more difficult or impossible for them to achieve alone. People affiliate with groups for several reasons. Generally, the group offers satisfaction and security. People also may feel that the members of a particular group can help find solutions to problems they face. The quest is for the solution of a problem, although often the motivation might be unknown, e.g., "autonomy" and "self-actualization." [6]

The small group offers a natural setting in which this quest can be carried out. For the social worker the quest is for a professional identity in common with other staff and with the help of a supervisor-teacher. Together they share responsibility for this quest, each according to his function and what he has to offer. Each member will assess the group with the view of his own potential needs. He ". . . will attempt to explore the group and to establish a network of relationships which will optimize the gratification of his needs." [7]

A major task of the supervisor is enabling the group to develop working relationships among the members that expedite the learning situation: "Failure to establish relationships consistent with the nature of these learning tasks leads to a decline in motivation and a reluctance to participate in the affairs of the group." [8]

Any effective work carried out by an individual in the group can be terminated by the type of climate that forces the individual to defend himself, rather than cope with the situation. Bruner, in discussing this, points out: "Defending is a strategy whose objective is avoiding or escaping from problems for which we believe there is no solution that does not violate our integrity of functioning." [9]

The same sensitivity and concern for the individual, or what Towle calls "individualization," must be practiced by the supervisor in group supervision as in individual supervision. Although the increased inter-action and opportunities may at times seem to make this more difficult, it must be noted that other group workers also practice this same concern and, under therapeutic conditions, maintain the "helping climate."

THE GROUP AS A MUTUAL AID SYSTEM

The function of the group is to serve as a mediator between the members and society. In so doing, every group faces three major problems: (1) carrying out the task it has set for itself; (2) maintaining itself as a group long enough to achieve its goals; and (3) coming to terms with the environment or systems of which it is a part.

The goals of the supervisor and of the members are brought into focus for the group members. The needs of both are taken into account and the resulting transaction becomes the working agreement. Out of the common concerns of the individuals emerges an acceptable "group goal," which becomes an ". . . interdependent need system which arouses, maintains, and directs group behavior." [10]

One of the first assignments for the group is to determine what its task is to be. Although the group members may come with their own goals in mind and their own views of what the group can offer, there needs to be a "common goal." When this common goal is linked to dis-cussion of agreed-upon ways of achieving individual goals, there is a "group contract." [11]

Factors in the motivation to achieve both the individual and group goals are: (1) the involvement of the individual in the interaction process or "life" of the group; (2) his own individual need system, and his understanding of the link between his need fulfillment and the group's achievement; (3) the ability of the individual to find both security and satisfaction in the group; and (4) the enabling ability of the supervisor.

To achieve their goals, the members assume roles based on their own need system and what the group requires in order to carry out its tasks. The group is the instrument by which the group members are able to achieve the goal that brought them together. For a number of reasons, which may be related to the abstract nature of the goal, imposition of goals from the outside, the inability of the members to function with each other, or the hostility of the environment, groups do not always achieve their goals. Often groups have sought the advice or leadership of nonmembers, who attempt to affect the group process so that goals can be achieved. The supervisor or teacher is one such nonmember.

THE SYSTEM WITH SUPERVISOR

In addition to provision of educational resources, the major tasks for the instructor in the learning group are: (1) to help create the conditions under which learning can take place; (2) to help the worker to focus and integrate some of the learning experiences that are vital to the professional role; and (3) to help the staff make the best use of the group learning situation.

As with all groups and learning processes, certain obstacles to learning are likely to appear, and it becomes the function of the supervisor to help staff discern the nature of these obstacles and find ways to deal with them. These obstacles may include: (1) the inability to look at one's own or fellow student's practice in an objective manner; (2) the manner in which one presents or interprets material; or (3) inability to work on a problem that has a "loaded" meaning to the learner.[12] The supervisor must be able to help the group deal with blocks to its learning.

It is the supervisor's responsibility to keep the group focused on the material to be learned. The responsiility for working on the learning problems, however, lies primarily with the group members, just as in a one-to-one supervisory conference the responsibility to work at learning is the student's.

The learner-teacher transaction, whether "one-to-one" or in group, calls for a commitment by both parties and a sharing of responsibilities. The roles of each actor must be explicated as clearly as possible and the working agreement or contract clearly stated,[13] connoting that each has something important to contribute.

The decision-making procedures in this give-and-take relationship between members and teachers and among members will depend to a great extent on the manner in which the supervisor-teacher wishes to exercise his authority. The relationship creates problems for the student and the supervisor as well. Jenkins, in discussing the leadership conflict in the classroom, suggests ways of minimizing it, and points up some required teacher actions.

(1) The teacher accepts his power and authority. (2) He develops a working understanding with the class about areas of authority—which ones he retains and which he gives the class—and behaves consistently. (3) He sets behavioral limits. (4) He permits class members to suffer the consequences of their decisions. On rare occasions, he will interfere, and explain why he does so. (5) He works in a context of stated educational goals. (6) He respects the aspirations, wishes, and needs of students and expects the same consideration in return. (7) He is willing to be influenced by students in the same manner he expects them to be influenced by him.[14]

PHASES IN THE TEACHER–LEARNER TRANSACTION

Practitioners and researchers concerned with small groups have noted that there appears to be a natural progression in the development of a group's life. This progression is generally marked by the following phases: (1) initial group formation; (2) a period of testing of the group and its limits; (3) a period of productive accomplishments by the group; and (4) a phase generally seen as the termination, or change in the purpose or activity of the group.

The stages in the supervisory transaction can also be perceived in this manner. They call for different action patterns on the part of the group members and discrete action responses from the supervisor.

1. *The Encounter:* At this stage in the life or prelife of the group, the nature of the supervisory relationship is brought to the attention of the group members. This may be through: (a) a brochure that describes the nature of the agency or supervision; (b) contact with social workers or discussions with other staff; and (c) contact in some way with the agency. In essence, this exposure is an advance signal that something unusual may transpire in this learning situation.

Contacts with agency staff prior to the arrival of new staff may be required.

2. *Contracting:* The initial contact between learner and supervisor is the beginning of a relationship in which the initial goals of the transaction are worked out and the means of achieving them are discussed.

Reasons for using the group method of teaching in the field should be pointed out and the value of the participation of the members emphasized. The building of trust to enhance learning must start immediately; the nature of the early relationship has an important bearing on the subsequent frame of reference of both learner and teacher.

The supervisor interprets and clarifies the nature of the group. He helps define the goals, sets forth the expectations of both members and supervisor, and discusses the individual learning assignments and the responsibilities inherent in a supervisor-learner situation. The supervisor may also discuss the teaching techniques to be used. Guidelines for admissible types of concerns are discussed.

With new staff, the supervisor points out common learning needs and sketches the type of cases that the staff are likely to have, as well as anticipated problem areas. Discussion should follow on the role of supervisor in group and individual conferences. The matter of confidentiality of material also should be discussed; the supervisor should point out his responsibility to use the material brought up in the group with both the agency and the school.

The expectations and responsibilities of each group member should be discussed. The initial contract is the first in a series that establishes rules of the game with the group, but also seeks to gain "credit" from the group while members learn to trust both the group and the supervisor.

3. *The Reconnaissance:* This refers to the "scouting" period in which group members get to know each other and the supervisor, and the supervisor gets to know them. There is a general testing of members, limits, and the supervisor.

The group member is uncertain of what is expected of him in the agency and the group, and often is dependent on the supervisor and other members for direction. This is "normal," but efforts to utilize the supervisor as expert and to negate the value of the group should be discouraged.

At first there may be few attempts at risking of self, but as the group starts to be helpful and supportive of the member, the risk of self increases.

The supervisor must assume some initial responsibility for bringing to the group material of immediate and common concern, such as intake, recording of material, discussion of agency policies and clientele, and so forth. He immediately begins to make demands on the group to work on these problem areas, using the contributions of group members in the problem-solving process. The nature of the material required to make an adequate assessment of client need is a subject that lends itself to this type of discussion.

The supervisor helps the group members bring out learning needs that they, as beginners, feel are urgent in order to start working with a client; these concerns become significant parts of the group's agenda. He permits differences of opinion, even with him, and helps the group see that it can handle differences and still function productively. Toward the end of this phase group members are able freely to bring in practice for discussion in front of the group.

4. *Autonomous Learning:* As the trust in both the group and the supervisor develops, the ability of the group members to risk themselves increases. They are able to deal with more significant material. The supervisor encourages this, acting as a mediator if the material gets too threatening to any one individual, scapegoating occurs, and the group is not able to work. The supervisor begins to demand increased work from the students, and often brings in material from a student record. This should be discussed with the student beforehand if it is material he might not want to share in public.

As the material is fed into the group, the supervisor and the members share in the solving of the problem. The supervisor points out implications of action that might have been overlooked, helping the group to focus on the practice being discussed, although at times the group might help with a problem that is not necessarily a common one to the group, but is related to a particular member's learning experience.

INDIVIDUAL CONFERENCES

Although the group is the medium that the supervisor has selected for teaching, there are times when individual conferences are in order.

1. *Initial Encounters with the Agency and Supervisor:* In addition to the group orientation sessions, individual sessions may be held at which the worker can discuss at his own pace some of his concerns with the experience that he is about to enter.

2. *Evaluations:* The periodic evaluations aimed at assessing staff's growth and problems should be done individually. This becomes a private matter in which the individual's strengths and weaknesses, his performance with the client, and his total learning experiences are discussed. Needless to say, the group as a group must also have periodic assessments of its own development and ability to work on problems.

3. *Requests for Individual Conferences:* When the worker makes a specific request of the supervisor for a discussion of material that he feels cannot be discussed in the group, an individual conference should be arranged. Afterward, the supervisor may ask the worker to bring the matter up in the group. If this type of request from the worker is repeated too often, the reasons for this have to be examined.

4. *At Supervisor's Discretion:* At times the supervisor may feel that individual conferences are needed because the student is not making

progress in the group, or is not able to use the group as the medium. The supervisor can then help the worker on an individual conference basis. He should still be expected to work and learn in the group.

THE CONTRACT WITH THE GROUP

The basic contract is that the group is a work unit, and that both the supervisor and staff are there to work. The goal of the group is to increase skills as professional social workers. In this agreement, the supervisor is expected to bring his advanced knowledge, educational skills, and understanding of behavior; the worker brings his time, interest, knowledge, and the desire to participate in the work of the group. This goal is achieved not only through work with the clients in the field, but through work in the supervisory group, and by contributing examples, questions, concerns, insights, and differing views.

Just as in individual supervision, the ability to give of oneself in group supervision develops as one feels he can trust the experience and the people he is involved with. Konopka, in discussing the role of the worker, points out, "Nothing significant can happen until the members have learned to trust him." Just as the supervisor in individual sessions cannot expect trust to develop on initial contact, this does not happen immediately in group sessions.

There is a possibility, however, that the involvement of a worker in a situation with his peers, with common goals and concerns, helps create a climate of trust. The members gain strength to share their concerns, from the group and from the knowledge that this is a group expectation. There is less concern with authority and control as the group shares with the teacher the authority for teaching and control. The control rests in the problem to be solved and in the combined efforts of the members. The members become dependent on each other, not only on the teacher. The group will demand that members carry a fair share of the work. They, as well as the supervisor, will confront the student who is not able to share his experiences or contribute to the analysis of the material under discussion. They will point out the overdependence of a novice on the group or teacher, and wrestle with similar concerns within themselves.

CONCLUSION

Staff workers bring different backgrounds and abilities to the group. Some have more social welfare experience than others. New workers may add their own brand of inquisitiveness. If they have come directly from a school or inner-city community, they can contribute the latest theoretical concepts or neighborhood views. The supervisor's task here is to help them find a common ground, so that they recognize the contributions and responsibilities of each that are necessary in the group experience.

If one goal of the teacher-learner transaction is to help develop an autonomous professional, the supervisor, too, must be autonomous. He must be ready to attempt new ideas, and experiment with teaching techniques. As a professional he should be able to influence the agency and the profession.

When not certain of an answer, he can say, "We will explore and find the way together." The group has a way of maintaining honesty; the supervisor shares power with the group members, and they add their power to his. One result can be a lessening of the threat of the conference held behind closed doors. The teaching and the learning, the risk and the rewards are in the open, and all must come to terms with the situation. This is the power of the group—it helps determine the function of the leader; it can give or withhold, and these dynamics are of grave importance to the teacher. The group will demand honesty, work, and risk from the supervisor, just as he demands them from the group.

This give and take makes group supervision a complex process requiring a high degree of understanding of both individual and group behavior. It calls for teaching skills that enable members to make use of each other as well as the supervisor. It requires supervisors who can create the climate in which learning can take place, and in which the concerns with control and authority are minimized. Although the demands on the supervisor and the members are high, the rewards can be well worth the effort. There are an excitement and a sense of urgency in the work group that perceives the fruits of its struggle. As the members experience self-learning and teaching, and their goals come into sight, there is a thrust to inquire more, to learn more, to accomplish more, to be more. This is the human quest that education really is.

NOTES

1. Ruth Shannon, "Developing a Framework for Field Work Instruction in a Public Assistance Agency," *Social Casework*, XLIII, No. 7 (1962), 355.
2. Minna Green Duncan, "An Experiment in Applying New Methods in Field Work," *Social Casework*, XLIV, No. 4 (1963).
3. Leah Feder, "The Group Conference as a Method of Supervision," *The Family* (March 1932).
4. Charlotte Towle sees supervision as consisting of three major functions. To educative and administrative she has added "enabling"; see *Learner in Education for the Professions* (Chicago: University of Chicago Press, 1954).

5. See, Nelson B. Henry, *The Dynamics of Instructional Groups* (Chicago: University of Chicago Press, 1960); Herbert A. Thelen, *Dynamics of Groups at Work* (Chicago: University of Chicago Press, 1954); and Eileen Blackey, *Group Leadership in Staff Training* (Washington: Department of Health, Education, and Welfare, 1957).

6. For discussion of self-actualization as the essential and basic drive, see Kurt Goldstein, *Human Nature in the Light of Psychopathology* (New York: Shocker Books, 1963); and Robert W. White, *Psychological Review*, LXVI, No. 5 (1959).

7. Gale Jensen, "The Sociopsychological Structure of the Instructional Group," in Nelson B. Henry, ed., *The Dynamics of Instructional Groups* (Chicago: University of Chicago, 1960), 84.

8. *Ibid.*, 96.

9. Jerome S. Bruner, *Toward a Theory of Instruction* (Cambridge: Harvard University Press, 1966), 129.

10. Jack R. Gibb, "Sociopsychological Processes of Group Instruction," in *The Dynamics of Instructional Groups*, 127.

11. Paul Abels, *The Social Work Contract: Playing It Straight*, mimeo, 1967.

12. See Bernard Bandler, "Ego-Centered Teaching," *Smith College Studies in Social Work*, XXX, No. 2 (1960); and the discussion by Jerome Bruner, "Perceptive Metaphors," in *Toward a Theory of Instruction*, 134–138.

13. See Leland P. Bradford, "The Teaching-Learning Transaction," in Warren G. Bennis, Kenneth D. Benne, and Robert Chin, eds., *The Planning of Change* (New York: Holt and Rinehart, 1961), 493.

14. David H. Jenkins, "Characteristics and Functions of Leadership in Instructional Groups," in *The Dynamics of Instructional Groups*, 183.

14

Is Autonomous
Practice Possible?

Laura Epstein

SOLUTIONS TO THE OLD PROBLEM of oversupervision in social work have slowly evolved over the years. However, the process may be speeded up by the following contemporary factors: (1) The nationwide program of the National Association of Social Workers to certify social workers who are qualified to practice independently may loosen the bonds of close tutorial supervision.[1] (2) The kinds of social work being practiced and workers' educational levels are becoming increasingly diverse. (3) The traditional roles of professionally trained practitioners are shifting to ones that require higher levels of skill as workers with undergraduate degrees receive more recognition.[2] (4) There is increasing evidence that more professionally trained workers are going into private practice.[3] (5) Increasing numbers of professionals are urging that the purpose of graduate training should be to prepare students for self-regulated practice.

In this article, the author traces the historical development of social work supervision and describes the specific model of supervision that is associated with each phase. In addition, she points out that the theoretical justifications for supervisory practice are not in accord with empirical findings and discusses the ways in which current supervisory practice inhibits the autonomy of professionally trained workers and thus decreases their productivity.

REVIEW OF RESEARCH

Toren, in her 1969 review of research, concluded that it is lack of autonomy in performing professional functions, not bureaucratic authority, which creates tension between supervisor and practitioner. What social workers "resent and resist [is] the teaching function of the supervisor, which is perceived as encroaching upon their professional judgment, responsibility and competence." [4] This attitude is prevalent among workers despite the high value accorded the educational component in social work supervision.[5]

Most social work organizations have supervisory units, or "work groups," consisting of four or more workers who are responsible to a supervisor on a one-to-one basis. Although laboratory and field studies yield inconsistent findings, they generally suggest that group structure, climate, and interactions are paramount in determining the outcome of work. Supervisors who differentiate their role, take the initiative in planning next steps and structuring activities, are flexible in delegating authority, and are supportive and considerate of staff and minimize "checking up" on them induce in their workers less frustration, less overt and covert aggression (including withholding of work), and better performance.[6]

Some information is also available on the relative merits of different kinds of group characteristics related to work behavior. Groups appear to be superior when the needed action is of a problem-solving variety. However, if hierarchical differentiations within the group are apparent, effective problem-solving is curtailed. Thus supervisors who minimize hierarchical status distinctions tend to obtain better performance from workers than do supervisors who depend on power.[7]

Evidence indicates that team supervision is superior to traditional one-to-one supervision.[8] Team supervision, a variant of group supervision, takes advantage of the sense of equality that characterizes group supervision. Teams are capable of a division of labor that enhances productivity.

Runden found that executives of twenty private child welfare agencies in a large metropolitan area believed that the beginning professional's self-reliance should be maximized.[9] However, they doubted whether early dilution of standard supervisory controls was appropriate. Most of them were critical of field instruction in graduate school and of prolonged agency supervision of the beginning caseworker because they believed that supervision tended to create dependency. But they were ambivalent about implementing autonomous practice at the start of a social worker's career. Runden did not offer reasons for the executives' ambivalence, nor did he suggest any alternatives.

Wasserman found that professional social workers in a public welfare bureaucracy condemned outright the supervisory practices to which they were exposed.[10] These workers perceived their supervisors as incompetent, unhelpful, unprofessional, and weak. This study suggests that some supervisory practices clearly fail to achieve their assumed objective of worker support and education.

THEORETICAL IMPLICATIONS

Professional objectives make client service the central purpose of a social agency. Yet practitioners have legitimate expectations of personal rewards and satisfactions. Thus although practitioners and agencies agree in principle that service to clients is paramount, their interests do not necessarily coincide.

Supervision is a process of exercising leadership to facilitate the objectives of the practitioner *and* the agency. This dual function is the source of the dissonance perceived in the supervisory role. In social work the dominant mode for managing the duality has been to emphasize the psychological state of supervisees and, to some extent, supervisors.

The author believes this emphasis is an historical error. It fails to take into proper consideration the fact that the structure and processes of an organization such as a social agency decisively determine the work climate in terms of aims, quality of practice, distribution of power and authority, and behavior of staff and clients. The individual's aims and practices and the character of his interpersonal transactions with peers and superiors are determined by the organizational context, not the other way around, although each individual constructs his own role within an organization to an extent. Nevertheless, organizational structure and process are so powerful that supervisory practice must focus its major attention on them. An emphasis on differentiated bits of individual performance and interpersonal transactions results in tense interpersonal relations between supervisor and practitioner. By ignoring basic structural needs, supervision fails to attend to problems within the organization that must be solved if client service is to be achieved.

Eisenberg's well-known formulation of the social work supervisor's role illuminates this reversal of priorities as follows:

> It is the supervisor's task to rescue from oblivion the contribution of the caseworker. . . . What one caseworker can demonstrate, learn, or experiment with may, through the perception of the supervisor, be taught to others, or may be proposed as policy and utilized in many ways. If the caseworker always knew when he did something new, was aware that his particular skills were illuminating an unsolved agency problem, or could develop broad concepts from his own experience and was aggressive enough to bring them to the attention of administration, perhaps a supervisor would not be needed.[11]

Dealing psychologically with practitioners' responses to this appraisal adds insult to injury. To fail to make the necessary inferences about the kind of hierarchical constraints that give rise to such a presumptuous claim to superiority denies the respect that a professional worker's integrity deserves.

Etzioni, in his analysis of professional work, states that knowledge and creativity are basically individual characteristics and can be ordered and coordinated by a superior only to a limited degree:

> Students of the professions have pointed out that the autonomy granted to professionals who are basically responsible to their consciences, though they may be censured by their peers and in extreme cases by the courts, is necessary for effective professional work. Only if immune from ordinary social pressures and free to innovate, to experiment, to take risks without the usual social repercussions of failure, can a professional carry out his work effectively. It is this highly individualized principle which is diametrically opposed to the very essence of the organizational principle of administrative authority. In other words, the ultimate justification for a professional act is that it is, to the best of the professional's knowledge, the right act. He might consult his colleagues before he acts but the decision is his. If he errs, he still will be defended by his peers. The ultimate justification of an administrative act, however, is that it is in line with the organization's rules and regulations, and that it has been approved—directly or by implication—by a superior rank.[12]

Virtually all the theory and principles of supervision in social work originated from casework practice. Miller suggests that group workers experience greater autonomy than caseworkers because group work demands a "willingness to retain less control over the helping process than is in fact enjoyed in one-to-one helping."[13] The community worker's partnership with his constituents and the researcher's commitment to inquiry necessitate a boldness and independence that are the sine qua non of effective practice. In many respects, group work, community work, and research are highly visible; i.e., they are subject to public appraisal. Casework is private, and casework supervisors rely on conferences and written reports to replicate casework events. (The potential of audio-visual equipment for reducing the obscurity of casework practice is as yet unrealized.)

MODELS FOR SUPERVISION

Current supervisory practice can be viewed in terms of four models: the growth model, the quasi-autonomous model, group supervision, and autonomous practice. In the main, these models set forth ideals for practice, but none of them offers much help in guiding actions in specific situations. The beleaguered supervisor who wants to know how to make a staff member fill out statistical reports, keep appointments on time, change his way of relating to clients, or adopt a certain treatment ideology will search in vain for specific techniques. He will have to consult experienced colleagues or invent techniques on the spot.

Model 1. Growth Emphasis

This model postulates a three-part process: help, administration, and teaching. The supervisor's job is to help the practitioner develop self-awareness about his own inputs and responses to his work with clients, the community, and the agency. The supervisor manages the content and flow of the work and delegates various portions to the practitioner. He teaches the practitioner what he does not know—and, alas, overteaches the practitioner things he already knows or misteaches him.

The aims of Model 1 are to facilitate client service by enhancing the practitioner's use of self; mediate divergent interests of client and agency; and construct a practitioner-supervisor relationship that is open, flexible, and self-actualizing. The major method of controlling the worker's behavior is the regularly scheduled individual conference, which usually produces an intimate and introspective narrative evaluation. A controlled degree of intimacy between practitioner and supervisor is also sought. Therefore, attempts are made to define the line between "education" and "therapy."

The highest priority implied in this model appears to be education: i.e., the supervisor, acting as educator, tries to enhance the worker's capacity to serve clients, whether the worker is a professional or a student. This is where the model founders, because the learning posture of the professional practitioner is different from that of the student. An agency and a school are different social systems, and the failure to discriminate between them is the primary cause of dissonance between supervisor and supervisee. This dissonance leads to dysfunctions in service delivery, inhibition of the practitioner's personal responsibility ("Will my supervisor take a negative attitude toward this act?"), restraint of effort ("Why should I take risks that will be misinterpreted to my disadvantage?"), pretentious postures ("Keep cool under duress so I will avoid invasion of my privacy."), and so forth. These responses, which are typical of supervisees, promote self-protective devices in the interests of personal integrity and become a barrier to desirable performance. The growth model often fails to achieve its objectives because of these internal contradictions.

Model 1 arouses conflicts in supervisees who normally tend to emphasize independence in their work, regardless of ordinary residues of dependence. This conflict has been theoretically explained as reflecting an authority-dependency conflict that is universally experienced in personality development. However, it is implausible to define work behavior in terms of authority-dependency mechanisms within the personality. Although the developers of this model obviously intended no such interpretation, they could not anticipate the problems that would arise in applying it.[14]

Model 2. Quasi-Autonomous Emphasis

This model was ushered in by the famous analyses by Babcock and Schour, who urged that social work be conceived of as work, rather than an anxious personal experience.[15] But neither these authors nor those who followed their lead in developing reforms in social work practice envisaged sharp departures in the format of supervision. They still thought in terms of tinkering with the well-established system to make it fulfill its ideals.

In Model 2 the centrality of the idea of help is dropped from the definition of the supervisory role. The diffuse influence of interpersonal support (conceived of as help in Model 1) becomes an attribute, used selectively and somewhat sparingly, of the general supervisory climate. Supervision is viewed as administration and teaching, and it opts for locating these two functions in different persons. Latitude is provided for a variety of supervisory styles, which are adapted to the individual practitioner's needs, talents, and interests. Practitioners are often allowed to choose among available experts for advice and to use supervision sparingly and at their own initiative.

The objective of client service in Model 2 is achieved by facilitating the work of staff, providing service through supervisor-practitioner collaboration, developing resources for optimum staff functioning, and supervising differentially to free staff members' unique talents. Professional development is the practitioner's responsibility; the supervisor's responsibility is to facilitate this development. Breathing room for individual style, specialization, interest, and talent is legitimate. Differences and weaknesses should be tolerated.[16]

In Model 2 the importance of the individual conference is diminished in favor of group learning through seminars, consultations, and the like. The attempt is to make evaluation criteria more objective and focused on performance specifications, even though these remain difficult to pin down. Line practitioners, who sometimes earn as much as supervisors, undertake roles that include traditional supervisory duties, such as supervising new staff and students, research projects, community projects, innovations, and so forth. Administrative supervisors, if they wish, can enhance their managerial and planning skills. Teaching supervisors can develop expertise in education.

When the quasi-autonomous model is introduced in an agency accustomed to the growth model, administrators and supervisors immediately feel that they no longer know what is going on. Their habitual modes of obtaining information are curtailed or cease altogether, and more sophisticated means of gathering information and analyzing data must be developed.

Model 2 programs have a tendency to falter when anxiety about what is going on becomes a problem. The usual solution is to reestablish the tighter controls of Model 1. This is why some organizations that use Model 2 superimpose regular weekly conferences on staff in-service meetings, consultations, administrative review conferences, and so forth. What emerges is a mixed model, which is more time consuming and less conducive to autonomous practice than Model 2.

Although the mixed model combines the assumed values of both models, the mixture inevitably complicates agency life by combining the defects of both models. For example, a practitioner who is encouraged by the climate of Model 2 to exercise his autonomy may be unable to obey the message that he is both autonomous and dependent. To be sure, there are sensitive and capable practitioners and supervisors who can develop productive working arrangements within the mixed model, despite the unclear and risky areas.

Model 3. Group Supervision

Model 3 is a conglomerate of diverse experiences born of changing conditions in the field. It takes many forms, and it developed only partially as a means of reforming supervision. The need to modernize or rationalize existing methods of service delivery and manpower utilization were also important thrusts in its development.[17]

Group supervision is in a fluid stage and fortunately lacks rigid specifications that could deter its development. It is generally characterized by a diluted hierarchy and places substantial responsibility for service production on a specific work group. Some of these groups differentiate their members, not by the nature of their caseloads, but by function of work segments. Some child welfare teams carry all cases jointly, with individual practitioners taking on segments. Thus a worker who is particularly talented in working with certain types of children may see one child in a family while someone else works with the entire family. This model tends to generate innovations, such as various combinations of subgroups responsible for cases and functions and new treatment interventions.

In Model 3 the supervisor's role is perceived in several ways. Sometimes he is the leader-administrator. Sometimes he is not a supervisor at all in the usual sense; i.e., monitoring, review, coordination, and education are assigned to a supervisor outside the group.

Although some groups are composed entirely of MAs and MSWs, most are likely to contain diverse levels of staff, such as BAs, indigenous paraprofessionals, volunteers, and clerical workers. When a group uses staff differentially, it is usually called a team. The traditional child guidance and residential teams utilize varying levels of staff in working with specific cases. The newer type of team, now found frequently in foster care and child protection services, is different from the traditional team because it deliberately attempts to minimize status differences among its members. In other words, differences are attributable to a practitioner's actions in relation to clients, not to formal professional prerogatives, and roles change, depending on the case.

Group supervision and its team variants put into practice the findings referred to earlier, which suggest that groups are superior for problem-solving, and dilution of hierarchical power and status is an incentive for innovation and responsibility.[18]

Because it tends to open up elaborate and complex lines of intrastaff communication, group supervision markedly increases and legitimates consultation among peers and the use of many levels of administrative, supervisory, and consultation staff for subgroup and individual conferences.[19] It also promotes informal relationships among staff. Scattered reports indicate that group supervision promotes higher productivity and quality of work than the more traditional models.[20] However, groups also produce considerable conflict, which is often productive for solving difficult problems. However, group conflict can be excessive under adverse conditions. For instance, group cohesion serves to develop considerable concentrations of power. Although such power can be useful in efforts to get a difficult job done, self-serving power blocs can seriously disrupt a group's efforts. Excessive conflict is especially likely when prerogatives of status and hierarchy are strongly held by some members: for example, when a psychiatrist is in charge of the team and wields the power of his status, or when MA or MSW social workers have the highest status in a team composed primarily of BAs and paraprofessionals.

The primary structure of Model 3 is the work group session (usually called the team meeting), augmented by seminars and informal sessions to deal with specific problems and content. Because the group cannot avoid evaluating itself and its members, individuals tend to feel protected against supervisory bias. On the other hand, groups can be unfair and merciless to a scapegoated member. Professional development practices, of necessity, are highly differential. Teams, as a variant of group supervision, make administrative monitoring and coordination and in-service education all urgent necessities.

Model 4. Autonomous Practice

Conducting autonomous professional practice means exercising the right and power to practice without outside controls, within the context of appropriate social sanctions. Physicians, for example, practice autonomously, and their sanctions for doing so are custom, legal license, and professional surveillance by peers. Social work is gaining the sanctions of custom and licensing, and professional surveillance is now being introduced by the National Association of Social Workers.

Social work has been developing its own forms of autonomous practice within agencies. Fifteen years ago, Leader offered an exemplary formulation of supervisory levels and types that is still of contemporary interest. He was convinced that

> . . . the experienced, mature worker, if he is freed from a system of regular supervision, will become a stronger and more self-directing person, responsible for improving his own practice and for implementing policies or facilitating their modification.[21]

Runden devised a model for beginning practitioners that proposes administrative supervision only by the employing agency.[22] Group supervision for professional development would be conducted by leading practitioners from outside the agency on a fee-for-service basis.

There are practitioners (the number is unknown and hard to estimate) who are, in Etzioni's words, "answerable to their own consciences." [23] Some are young practitioners who are employed by new agencies or special projects that have spun off traditional agencies.[24] They may work under the auspices of organizations directed by professionals from another field, such as education or psychiatry. For one reason or another, the bureaucratic structures that contain this type of social work practice (as in community psychiatry) exercise diluted controls. The bureaucratic "home" may be geographically distant, chiefs may not be habituated to the social work supervision ethos, the work may be so new that no one yet knows how to control it, and thus premature controls are avoided to spur innovation and initiative. Experienced practitioners seek such positions to be released from the constraints of traditional supervision and modes of practice.

Experienced practitioners, to some extent, have also found ways of carving autonomous niches for themselves in traditional agencies by winning sufficient confidence from their superiors to be "cut loose." For example, one attraction of becoming a field work instructor is the benefits of collegial relations among faculty. The idea of academic freedom adheres to some extent. Some practitioners in time become "unsupervisable" and are assigned an independent role, which may be limited, but at least gives them the opportunity to conduct their own affairs and relieves the supervisor from having to engage in unproductive activities. Some experienced practitioners undertake private practice.

What is important about Model 4 is that it was never formalized. It developed with little theory or specific program planning. It has emerged as a natural solution to a difficult problem. It is a meritorious solution whose time has almost come, but it needs serious study and must be developed into a full-fledged model that can guide practitioners and agencies in planning careers and utilizing manpower.

CONCLUSION

Is autonomous practice possible in social work? The answer is a qualified yes! Institutional control cannot be eradicated entirely in any profession that operates within a bureaucracy. Organizations can become less rigid and reduce the number of hierarchical layers.

Increased opportunities for autonomous practice in the future will depend on two changes: (1) decentralization of bureaucratic authority and responsibility and (2) abandonment of the obligatory teaching-learning posture as the major means of controlling professional behavior. Decentralization is a matter of organizational policy and design. A strong tendency toward decentralization, with flexible, changing staff coalitions that are responsive to emerging issues, is evident today in many organizations.[25] Not only is ongoing professional education the individual practitioner's responsibility, it is the only way that such education can occur under any conditions. However, for practitioners to avail themselves of continuing education, the opportunities must be available, accessible, attractive, and divorced from mandatory tutorial education.

But if definite progress is to be achieved, many more agencies and their staffs must alter conditions to support autonomous practice. They should systematically monitor, appraise, and publish their results so that unrealistic expectations and myths about supervision may be laid to rest. What works best and under what circumstances needs to be identified in practice tests without reference to idealistic rubrics that are supported mainly by tradition and introspective appraisal.

NOTES

1. *See* Committee on the Study of Competence, *Guidelines for the Assessment of Professional Practice in Social Work* (New York: National Association of Social Workers, 1968).

2. Arnulf Pins, "Changes in Social Work Education and Their Implications for Practice," *Social Work*, 16 (April 1971), pp. 5–15; and W. E. Henry,

J. H. Sims, and S. L. Spray, *The Fifth Profession* (San Francisco, Calif.: Jossey-Bass, 1971).

3. *See,* for example, Virginia Franks, *The Autonomous Social Worker* (Madison: University of Wisconsin School of Social Work, 1967).

4. Nina Toren, "Semi-Professionalism and Social Work: A Theoretical Perspective," in Amitai Etzioni, ed., *The Semi-Professions and Their Organization* (New York: Free Press, 1969), p. 183.

5. W. R. Scott, "Relations to Supervision in a Heteronomous Professional Organization," in Phillip Fellin, Tony Tripodi, and Henry Meyer, eds., *Exemplars of Social Research* (Itasca, Ill.: F. E. Peacock, 1969), pp. 225–238 [Chapter 23 below].

6. Dorwin Cartwright and Alvin Zander, *Group Dynamics: Research and Theory* (3rd ed.; New York: Harper & Row, 1968), pp. 301–317.

7. P. M. Blau and W. R. Scott, *Formal Organizations* (San Francisco, Calif.: Chandler Publishing Co., 1962), pp. 116–134.

8. Edward E. Schwartz and William C. Sample, *The Midway Office: An Experiment in the Organization of Work Groups* (New York: National Association of Social Workers, 1971); and K. W. Watson, "The Manpower Team in a Child Welfare Setting," *Child Welfare,* 47 (October 1968), pp. 446–454.

9. L. K. Runden, "Research Toward a New Model of Supervision for Beginning Workers in Child Welfare." Unpublished manuscript, Walther Memorial Hospital, Chicago, Illinois, undated.

10. Harry Wasserman, "The Professional Social Worker in a Bureaucracy." *Social Work,* 16 (January 1971), pp. 89–95 [Chapter 19 below].

11. S. S. Eisenberg, "Supervision as Agency Need," *Social Casework,* 37 (May 1956), pp. 233–237.

12. Amitai Etzioni, in preface to Etzioni, ed., *The Semi-Professions and Their Organizations,* pp. x–xi.

13. Irving Miller, "Supervision in Social Work," in *Encyclopedia of Social Work,* Vol. 2 (New York: National Association of Social Workers, 1971), p. 1498.

14. Bertha C. Reynolds, *Learning and Teaching in the Practice of Social Work* (New York: Farrar & Rinehart, 1942); and Charlotte Towle, *The Learner in Education for the Professions* (Chicago: University of Chicago Press, 1954).

15. Charlotte G. Babcock, "Social Work as Work," and Esther Schour, "Helping Social Workers Handle Stresses," *Social Casework,* 34 (December 1953), pp. 415–422 and 423–427, respectively.

16. Lucille N. Austin, "The Changing Role of the Supervisor," in Howard J. Parad, and R. R. Miller, eds., *Ego-Oriented Casework: Problems and Perspectives* (New York: Family Service Association of America, 1963); and Frances H. Scherz, "A Concept of Supervision Based on Definitions of Job Responsibility," *Social Casework,* 39 (October 1958), pp. 435–442 [Chapter 8 above].

17. Donald A. Brieland et al., *Differential Use of Manpower: A Team Model For Foster Care* (New York: Child Welfare League of America, 1968); Laura Epstein, "Differential Use of Staff: A Method to Expand Social Services," *Social Work*, 7 (October 1962), pp. 66–72; D. G. Gil, "Social Work Teams," *Child Welfare*, 44 (October 1965), pp. 442–446; and Schwartz and Sample, op. cit.

18. G. S. Getzel, J. R. Goldberg, and Robert Salmon, "Supervising in Groups as a Model for Today," *Social Casework*, 52 (February 1971), pp. 154–163.

19. Ruth Fizdale, "Peer-Group Supervision," *Social Casework*, 39 (October 1958), pp. 443–449 [Chapter 12 below]; and John Wax, "The Pros and Cons of Group Supervision," *Social Casework*, 40 (June 1959), pp. 307–313.

20. Schwartz and Sample, op. cit., and Watson, op. cit.

21. A. L. Leader, "New Directions in Supervision," *Social Casework*, 38 (November 1957), p. 467.

22. Op. cit.

23. Etzioni, op.cit.

24. Franks, op. cit.

25. Carl Martin, "Beyond Bureaucracy," *Child Welfare*, 50 (July 1971), pp. 384–388.

15

Through the Looking Glass: Supervision in Family Therapy

Vernon C. Rickert and John E. Turner

First, there is the room you can see through the glass—only the things go the other way.

Lewis Carroll, *Through the Looking Glass*

ONCE ALICE WENT THROUGH THE LOOKING GLASS and discovered that a hill was a valley, she became disoriented, much as does any novice therapist who must remain sequestered in the looking-glass house of the therapy session.

This article discusses the beginning of a new training model in a family agency. Although the agency has offered a field placement experience for three to six trainees for several years, this training has always been done in the traditional model, that is, weekly individual and group supervision sessions in which trainees report their case activities. More recently, the trainees have had sporadic live supervision.

As the program's practice and philosophy were increasingly influenced by the structural approach to family therapy and by short-term strategic therapy, the authors' attitudes toward the efficiency, effectiveness, and quality of training also came under scrutiny. The new training format was developed which involved one supervisor and two trainees, with interviews observed and coached through a one-way mirror and a telephone. The trainees participating in the initial effort were from a graduate school of social work on a block placement of four months. The authors were not attempting to train finished family therapists, but were offering neophyte therapists beginning tools for bringing about change in family systems. The supervisor had minimal experience in supervision and, thus, came to this event without having to unlearn the traditional methods of supervision. The training approach taken is not new, but it does provide some interesting contrasts in approaches to training in family service agencies.[1]

The movement back to live supervision is indicative of a change in

From *Social Casework* 59 (March 1978), pp. 131–137. Reprinted by permission of the Family Service Association of America.

philosophical emphasis toward the "science" of therapy rather than the "art" of therapy. This model is based on the idea that much of therapy must be experienced to be learned. There is an obvious enriching dimension in maximizing the opportunity for a therapist in training to experience the correct way to bring about change and to enjoy a greater quantity of successful interventions. Jay Haley points out that this method was once more commonly used:

> Although it may appear modern to have the supervisor watch the actual therapy of a student, this is an old-fashioned procedure. In the nineteenth century, when therapists were commonly using hypnosis, they were trained by someone who watched them work. It would have been thought absurd to think the hypnotist could learn his art by reading about it and—never having watched anyone being hypnotized—go off alone into a room and hypnotize someone and return to tell his teacher how he felt about the experience.[2]

CONVENTIONAL SUPERVISION

Some generalizations about conventional supervisory styles sharpen the contrast with the new model. Conventional supervision has been characterized by "talking about" the trainee's therapy experience. Usually, a supervisor and the trainee meet for an hour each week to discuss the trainee's difficulties of the past week. The supervisor's focus is on helping the trainee understand the dilemma he is facing with a particular family. This focus is rooted in the supervisor's belief that understanding leads to change.[3]

"Talking-about" supervision has many difficulties. One difficulty is that the supervision is based on the trainee's self-report. Self-report has inherent weaknesses because of the trainee's efforts to please his supervisor, to avoid unpleasant material, or to be kinder because of the foibles of human memory. Haley notes that, lacking other observable data, the supervisor naturally attempts to use the material that is presented to determine what actually happened in the session.[4] Braulio Montalvo assumes a significant gap between the self-report of a case and what actually happened.[5] Additionally, the trainee's necessary condensation of the session in his report to the supervisor adds to the distortion. Delays between the supervisory session and therapy session also impede learning. If the learning of therapy does not occur with the practice of therapy, then the trainee learns little. Larry L. Constantine and the trainers at Boston Family Institute take a similar position.[6]

In "talking-about" supervision, the discussion gravitates toward dynamics rather than toward the therapist's involvement in the session. In such discussions, the family is often characterized as being difficult and highly resistant because the supervision is an uncomfortable relationship which supervisor and trainee "handle" with collusion against the family. This creates coziness in the supervisory session but does little to change the family. Collecting diagnostic information further encourages this triangulation. Thus, the trainee does not learn precisely about treatment techniques, intervention, and process, but rather learns a great deal of "gossip" about the family which, at best, is only marginally useful in his training. This problem becomes exacerbated with the beginning therapist as he has only an inkling of how to be helpful to a family. The neophyte needs the motivating force of early successes, very much as families need the hope lent to them by experienced, competent therapists.

LIVE SUPERVISION MODEL

Live supervision definitely contrasts with "talking-about" supervision. Live supervision employs a one-way mirror and a telephone to give immediate supervision to the trainee. Typical live supervision involves a session with one student interviewing and another present with the supervisor behind a one-way mirror. The supervisor has three alternatives for directing a trainee: telephoning, convening a brief conference outside the training interview, or entering the training interview. Before and after the training interview, there are brief teaching and planning sessions.

The model is hierarchical—the supervisor has the ultimate responsibility for the successful treatment of the family and the responsibility for the trainee's movement toward competency. This situation forces the supervisor to be extremely directive with the trainee. The supervisor must consider not only what the trainee needs to accomplish with the family, but also how to motivate and guide the trainee to carry out that instruction competently and effectively. The supervisor must be attuned to each trainee's range of interview behavior. For example, a trainee who was young, passive, and married, with no children, was having difficulty directing a mother to deal with her son in a firm and consistent manner— specifically, to make her son remain seated. Repeated telephone directives from the supervisor were unsuccessful in helping the trainee to motivate the mother to become firm with her son. This illustrates the triadic relationship of supervisor, trainee, and family. The supervisor faced the problem of convincing the trainee that firm parenting is therapeutic, because the trainee was certain to encounter this issue in many forthcoming interviews. In the planning and teaching session after the interview, the supervisor told some stories of similar but successful outcomes. This, however, had only minor impact. Later, when the trainee had observed another therapist trainee successfully direct a mother to be stern with her son and experienced the son's calm and secure response, the trainee accepted the therapeutic value of motivating a parent to exhibit firmness.

In the live supervision model, there is no possibility of the therapist trainee distorting the session, and the supervisor can directly observe the trainee's interaction with the family. Because the supervision is live, the supervisor can focus more easily on the trainee's relationship with the family and is less likely to collude with the trainee against the family. In addition, the supervisor and trainee do not waste time in repeating "diagnostic information," because the supervisor has the same access to the therapeutic session. More time can be devoted to the trainee's effect on the family. With the observation of the family's reaction and the supervisor's feedback, the trainee has a good chance for success in a particular therapy session, and there is no delay in the transfer of learning, because training and therapy are concurrent.

SUPERVISORY ISSUES

Experience with the live supervision model highlights a number of concerns.

Trainee Selection

The screening and selection of trainees is of primary importance. The supervisor, along with the agency's director of professional services, carries the major responsibility for screening the trainees, looking especially at the trainee's ability to work in a hierarchical model. Those trainees with previous experience and training in a different model may have difficulty adjusting to live supervision. Furthermore, a supervisor should be concerned that he select students with whom he can establish rapport. Of course, this is a concern every supervisor must have; however, it seems more critical in a live supervision model, which necessitates an intense working relationship between the trainee and the supervisor.

Case Screening

Case screening is only a minimal concern, because the supervisor is present for each interview. It is important for the beginning trainee to have some early success, and the supervisor may want to screen out those cases which could present extreme difficulties. For example, in the authors' experience, a child-abuse case brings undue complications for beginning trainees. Such a case involves a great deal of network communication and usually cannot be terminated during the brief training period. Thus far, this is the only kind of case automatically screened out. Haley has gone so far as to suggest tailoring case selection to the particular needs of the trainee.[7] In this setting it is impractical, because selecting a case would involve unproductive waiting time before training could begin.

Scheduling

Supervisors using this training model must maintain flexible schedules in order to be available for observation of trainee interviews. Initial plans were for the supervisor to carry a half-time case load; however, scheduling conflicts made this almost impossible. It is probably best that the supervisor concentrate strictly on his trainee's cases so as to avoid scheduling conflicts later. One advantage of the supervisor's continuing to carry some clinical cases, however, is the opportunity for the students to observe him early in the placement. From a procedural viewpoint, it is particularly useful for trainees to observe the supervisor, especially in an initial interview, as a model for explaining the observation room, the videotape, and the basic stages of an interview.

THE NATURE OF THE DIRECTIVE

Telephone Directives

The use of the telephone and the nature of the telephoned directives are very important and will vary according to the style of the supervisor. Reluctance to use the telephone can occur if the supervisor is not really committed to the model or is too sensitive to the trainee's feelings regarding his input. Such reluctance can be detrimental to the management of the case. For example, in one situation a trainee was reluctant to interrupt a client's monologue. The supervisor saw this reluctance "through the looking glass," and, as a result, struggled with interrupting the trainee, who was having difficulty interrupting the client. Until the supervisor managed to overcome his reluctance, very little was accomplished for the family, and very little learning occurred for the trainee.

On the other hand, the supervisor can be too intrusive with the telephoned directives. On several occasions, a student's transaction with a family was interrupted when the supervisor could well have sat down and watched the student get there on his own, perhaps not as quickly, but as competently. For example, the supervisor was concerned that the trainee move more rapidly toward including a peripheral father in a discussion with the family. Before the supervisor could call, the trainee moved his chair next to the father and began to engage him. Thus, whether and when to telephone is crucial. Allowing the student to engage the father on his own permitted the supervisor more opportunity to support the trainee's competence and motivated the trainee to experiment autonomously. However, the supervisor must judge that such behavior is within the trainee's grasp, because too much waiting may result in the trainee's conducting the therapy onto an unproductive course.

The supervisor's effect on the trainee should be monitored continually for too much or too little intrusion. Montalvo's contract between the supervisor and trainee facilitates this monitoring. If a trainee disagrees with a directive, then the trainee has the freedom to leave the session and attempt to convince the supervisor of a more appropriate directive or one that is equally good. If the trainee convinces the supervisor, then the trainee can carry out his own ideas. The supervisor, however, always has the right to say the trainee *must* carry out a directive if it is critical for the outcome of the case.[8]

The supervisor has the task of deciding not only when to give a directive, but also what content the directive should have. The directive should include only what is necessary for the trainee to carry it out. When the supervisor wants his exact words to be stated, the directive could begin with, "Say to the mother, 'Your son's behavior is disrespectful to you.'" When the supervisor wants the trainee to use his own words, the supervisor could say, "See if you can get the mother to control her son."

Telephoning permits only a succinct one-way conversation from the supervisor to trainee, usually only a sentence; a lengthy directive may confuse the trainee. The supervisor must decide what content the directive should have *prior* to calling.

The supervisor who tends to use the telephone frequently has to guard against encouraging excessive dependence on the supervision. The trainee may also begin to concentrate on the telephone rather than on the therapy. On one occasion, immediately following a series of instructions, the supervisor decided to sit back, not use the telephone, and see how a student would conduct the session. Instead of concentrating fully on the family, the trainee became puzzled at why the telephone was not buzzing, because he felt the supervisor could not be approving of all that he was doing.

Brief Conferences Outside the Interview

There are occasions when lengthy directives have their purpose, especially when the supervisor must help a trainee with the summation at the end of an interview. In such cases, the supervisor should hold a conference outside the interview room rather than telephone. For example:

> In a conference, a trainee was instructed to give the following lengthy directive to a family in which a daughter had been acting out but was now staying home in order to remain out of trouble.
>
> (*To the parents*) "Your daughter is unable to say no to her friends. She needs to be able to do this in order to grow and become a mature young woman. She cannot do this when she remains at home."
>
> (*To daughter*) "I want you to go out with a friend who has been in trouble with you. You need to demonstrate to your parents that you are older and can say no. Upon your return, I want you to meet with your parents, tell them about your outing, and at least one incident when you said no to your friend."

In short conferences outside the interview, the supervisor can provide some rationale for the directives. Montalvo opposes giving rationale to the trainee; however, a trainee can implement a directive with more conviction when the rationale is known.[9]

Entering the Training Interview

If the supervisor cannot be brief with a telephoned directive, he may choose the alternative of entering the training interview. An added benefit of the supervisor's entry is the theatrical effect on the case. For example:

> A student was having difficulty activating a mother and father to join together in a firm stance with their teenage daughter. After wrestling with this difficulty via directives over the telephone, the supervisor decided to enter the room and introduce himself. He had the daughter stand on a chair and, pointing at the daughter, stated very harshly to the parents that they were treating her as if she were a queen in their family. Then he promptly left the room. The intervention had a powerful effect on the family and upon the trainee, and it was a major event in the therapy. Later, the trainee stated that he was aghast as he experienced this intervention and fully expected the family to be alienated. He was relieved, however, when he saw a marked change in the parents' behavior with their daughter during the remainder of the interview.

This example illustrates the ability of the supervisor to extricate himself quickly from the training interview. It is always best to remain in the interview only long enough to solve the trainee's difficulty. Remaining longer than necessary is intrusive.

TRAINEE BEHAVIOR IN THE SUPERVISORY SESSION

At the first interview, the trainees are extremely anxious about how they will perform and the supervisor can alleviate much of this anxiety. It is very helpful to tell trainees that they will frequently fail (which they will), because they are more concerned about how they will look to the supervisor than about how to conduct the session. Such a comment is often a freeing experience for the trainee.

Because this particular live supervision model involves two trainees, competition between them is inevitable. It is important to limit criticism by one trainee toward another, as it engenders a situation ripe for side-taking by the supervisor. The supervisor has full responsibility for the supervision; therefore, it is best for the discussion after a training interview to take place primarily between the supervisor and the working trainee. After this is completed, comments or questions can be invited from the observing trainee.

The supervisor should be wary of too much discussion with the observing trainee while the other trainee is working with the family on the other side of the mirror. Focus should remain primarily on the working therapist. It is possible, however, to explain a directive briefly when necessary, or to have a short conversation about some aspects of the session. The likelihood of too much discussion behind the glass seems to increase with the number of persons observing the interview. Behavior behind the mirror should always reflect the tone and nature of the family session in the next room; that is, comments or behaviors of the trainees in the observation room should be congruent with what the trainee is doing in the interview room.

LEAVING THE SUPERVISORY NEST

Because of the intensive nature of the model, the supervisor should be concerned that he build independence as the supervisory process lengthens. Early in the placement, trainees have a great deal of information to receive, and therefore the supervisor must be extremely directive and involved with his trainees. As the placement lengthens, the need for this involvement lessens. This is important developmentally for the trainees, because they need to feel competent as the placement continues, as does a family as therapy continues. On the other hand, the supervisor must be careful not to release a trainee before he has the ability to work more independently. In this example, the choice of working without direct supervision was premature.

A trainee had seen a mother and her son, who had a presenting problem of a school phobia. The second appointment was arranged in the
evening so that the father could attend. This interview was videotaped and conducted without the supervisor. In viewing the videotape,
the supervisor observed that the trainee almost alienated the father,
who was essential in obtaining a successful outcome.

Independence can be built into the supervisory process in a number of
ways, for example, by using videotape. With certain cases, a student can
videotape a session when the supervisor is unable to be present. The
supervisor then schedules a time to review the tapes and makes plans
with the trainee for the next therapeutic session. Still another way to
build independence is to select a case which can be observed by the
supervisor for the first few sessions and then supervised by videotape
or by periodic live observations.

Videotape allows the supervisor to teach more general issues of the
therapeutic style and family interaction. Although time consuming, it is
very advantageous to videotape the live supervision. After the training
interview, the videotape can be scrutinized in the planning session, then
the general issues of therapeutic style and the specific issues of how to
change the family are integrated. If videotape is employed in lieu of
live observation, the disadvantage is that the supervisor's directives cannot be carried out until the next interview—thus slowing down treatment.

Another way, as yet untested, to build independence into the supervisory process is in the content of the directive. Early in the placement,
directives over the telephone could tend to be more direct and explicit
requests of the trainee: "Interrupt mother and have dad talk to the son
about an outing together." Later in the placement the telephoned suggestions could be raised more in the form of questions or observations:
"How can you get dad and son to have a positive experience?"

CLIENT AND TRAINEE ACCEPTANCE

At this point, it may be helpful to discuss client reaction to supervisory interruptions during the sessions. Only a few families have any
significant reactions to these procedures, as long as they are treated as
"normal" procedures by the trainee. Occasionally, some families will request not to be observed and, much more rarely, will be bothered
significantly by the occasional buzzing of the telephone. If requested,
a private interview room is provided. Also, once the supervisor goes into
a session, the immediate question which most trainees have is, "How can
I be reestablished as the primary therapist?" The authors have not observed any occasion where the family began to make the transfer of
therapist from trainee to supervisor. This, of course, is highly dependent

on the nature of the supervisor's behavior in the room and his ability to extricate himself quickly. Once the trainee experiences no change in the family's acceptance of him, then his worries about "losing face" are assuaged.

CONCLUSION

Training "through the looking glass" is exciting. Only after experiencing the model does one fully appreciate the inadequacy of training therapists or learning therapy in the conventional way.

Administratively, the model has these advantages:

1. Competent staff are involved more directly in the delivery of service than they are in many settings in which supervisors have no direct client contact.
2. Clients receive better service from trainees, as evidenced in the reduced number of "lost cases" after the first interview; malpractice is less a concern.
3. Trainees approach competency quickly.

Paul Watzalwick, John H. Weakland, and Richard Fisch make the point that often a family's solution to their problem becomes the problem. The family is engulfed in a "game without end" or first-order change. The therapist, being meta or beyond the family's dilemma, must invoke the next level of change, second-order change—a change of change—to be successful.[10] Similarly, in training "through the looking glass," the supervisor can be meta to the trainee's efforts in bringing forth change in a family. If Watzalwick, Weakland, and Fisch are correct, this suggests a boon of greater treatment success from the "looking glass," in addition to its advantages as a training model.

NOTES

1. Jay Haley, *Problem-Solving Therapy: New Strategies for Effective Family Therapy* (San Francisco: Jossey-Bass, 1976). The development of the authors' model has been strongly influenced by the Philadelphia Child Guidance Clinic and personal contacts through workshops there. Haley's chapter on "Problems in Training Therapists," in *Problem-Solving Therapy*, pp. 169–94, details the basic model and many of the specific techniques the authors have employed.
2. Haley, *Problem-Solving Therapy*, p. 178.
3. Ibid., p. 174.
4. Ibid., p. 177.

5. Braulio Montalvo, "Aspects of Live Supervision," *Family Process* 12 (December 1973): 343–59.

6. Larry L. Constantine, "Designed Experience: A Multiple Goal-Directed Training Program in Family Therapy," *Family Process* 15 (December 1976): 373–87.

7. Haley, *Problem-Solving Therapy,* p. 185.

8. Montalvo, "Aspects of Live Supervision," p. 344.

9. Ibid.

10. Paul Watzalwick, John H. Weakland, and Richard Fisch, *Change: Principles of Problem Formation and Problem Resolution* (New York: W. W. Norton, 1974), p. 22.

16

Social Work Supervision on Wheels

Shlomo Sharlin and Harris Chaiklin

IN SOCIAL WELFARE there is a long tradition of bringing services to people who cannot come to them. The friendly visitor, the bookmobile, or meals on wheels are all familiar. What is done much less is to bring help to service givers when they cannot get the supervision and learning experience they need. This paper reports on an attempt to do this in the north of Israel.

In the United States, as in Israel, there is an underrepresentation of rural workers, and the schools of social work have done little to prepare students for the specific problems encountered in non-urban areas.[1] Munson says:

> The only attempts schools have made to relate to rural problems have been to establish continuing education workshops. In many instances, this response is based on dwindling urban markets for continuing education rather than genuine interest in serving rural areas. Many times the continuing education programs are weak and inadequate because the urban-based faculty are unable to translate their knowledge and skills to appropriate interventive strategies needed in rural areas. Many universities have a requirement that continuing education courses, unlike campus courses, be self-supporting. This inhibits schools reaching out to rural areas, and when they do, the high registration fees necessitated by the self-sufficiency requirement compels many low-paid workers to forego the experience.[2]

Given the deficiencies in their education, it is little wonder that rural social workers often suffer from a sense of personal isolation and complain

---

An earlier version of this paper was presented at 105th Annual Forum of the National Conference on Social Welfare, Los Angeles, California, May 1978. Reprinted by permission of the authors.

about a lack of professional stimulation. Existing agencies are frequently understaffed. Opportunities for supervision and to supervise are severely restricted. If workers grew up in an urban area, they often find it difficult to make the transition to rural living. Unmarried workers often feel their chances of marriage are diminished. In a country like Israel, all these problems are compounded where so few people in rural areas have advanced education or technical training.

To counter this professional malaise, raise the level of technical skill, and give workers a sense of identity with and pride in their profession, the senior author has designed a program to bring onsite and ongoing supervision to workers in the Galilee. The demonstration is supported by the Ministry of Labor and Social Affairs under the auspices of the Richard Crossman Chair at Haifa University.

Few workers in the northern region receive any consistent supervision. The Ministry offers statewide and regional workshops which last from one to three days. When these are given in a large city, workers spend considerable time traveling. The programs are "one-shot" affairs and are not part of an integrated system of professional development. While the workshops do something to raise the level of services, they do not substitute for sustained supervision.

THE PROJECT

Given the workers' needs and the size of their job responsibilities, it was decided that the initial approach would be to focus on case management and to teach treatment techniques in relation to this goal. In selected situations, the supervisor is available for short-term or crisis intervention. For the most part the emphasis is on long-term work and prevention. This reflects the client needs in the area. Many are recent immigrants. Experience has shown that when they have difficulty integrating into the society and turn to public welfare, they tend to become long-term clients.[3] In developing a supervision-education model for community work, the same principles used in casework were followed.

Supervisory intervention with workers progresses through five levels. There is no need to follow the levels in order or to include all levels. The aim is to individualize the content so that it meets the workers' needs. The levels are:

1. Individual worker supervision with the goal of case management and teaching professional skills and knowledge.
2. Small group supervision with the same goals as in level one. Usually this is done within one agency. Where the learning issue concerns the whole group, formal teaching and sociodrama are also introduced on a selective basis.

3. Acquiring and using management and administrative perspectives. In rural areas where there are many single workers or small agencies, every service person is to some extent an administrator.
4. Learning service coordination by working with representatives of several agencies that serve an area. Even in rural areas there is the multi-agency family that gets called multi-problem because agencies are either not comprehensive or they do not hold case conferences to provide an integrated case plan for such families.
5. Working with community leaders from clusters of villages so that social workers and community leaders can share problems and move toward initiating appropriate regional service plans.

The university and its school of social work play a unique and vital role in initiating and sustaining the project. There are mutual benefits to both the school and the field. In a country short of resources and personnel, it is only the university that can effectively commit the equipment and personnel necessary for a successful project. This does not imply that the mobile lab is a "hothouse flower" that can only demonstrate its principle when conditions are ideal. The aims of the project and the equipment and personnel needed are well within the capability of any large public or private agency. The university does have some advantage due to its ability to shift personnel into a project and then back to hard money. Many a good demonstration has foundered due to the inability to hire professionals with the appropriate level of skill. In Israel there is the additional fact that laws governing employment make it difficult to hire people for time-limited periods.

Aside from the material advantage to the university base, there is an operational advantage. Usually agency supervisors must combine teaching, case management, and administrative responsibilities. The university supervisors can maximize the teaching component; what they really are offering is consultation. They do not have to make decisions as to whether a worker should get a negative evaluation, carry a bigger caseload because of demands on the agency, or even if they should get a reprimand for repeatedly being late for work.

It is probable that all supervision in social work suffers from combining too many functions. An evaluation all too often is a statement of whether or not the worker has followed the bureaucratic rules with good humor and not an estimate of professional competence. This does not say that administrative judgments should not be made; only that it is not logical to expect them to be made with other judgments in the context of the same relationship. The model of consultation-supervision developed for this project has implications which can be examined for application to the field as a whole.

Advantages accrue to the school because field instructors and faculty get more direct and current contact with practice than is the usual case with university faculty. This benefit extends to almost all the faculty with practice expertise, because if they are not working on the project, they are often called in as expert consultants. This helps the students because they are often denied the chance to get the feeling that comes from working with someone who demonstrates superior practice in action.

Another and important gain is that the school creates a pool of case materials for teaching which is directly relevant to the students' current learning and future practice. This is particularly important in a small country like Israel. It is not possible to develop a complete practice literature in Hebrew. Most of the literature comes from English and American sources. While practice theory and principles are universal, there are two problems connected with depending on printed case materials. The first is that there is often a long time span before records make their way into print. It is hard to relate to a case where the content seems unrelated to anything that anybody is currently seeing. The second is that Israel contains a surprisingly large number of racial, ethnic, and religious groups. Aside from the indigenous population, over half the nation's citizens were born somewhere else. While there may be ethnographic studies on these groups, there is no practice literature in any language. Through the use of current written and videotape materials, the faculty is able to relate practice principles to specific groups and to the general problem of acculturation and assimilation.

PROJECT OPERATIONS

Present personnel include a full-time director and five half-time supervisors. The supervisors are also faculty members. There are three service teams, two specializing in group and community work and one in casework. The staff are multi-method trained so that they switch teams when necessary. Expert consultants are available to help with specific issues. Great use is made of portable television and recording equipment. This is backed up by the school's audio-visual studio and laboratory.

Services were initially offered in towns along the Lebanese border. This is the poorest and most remote section in the developing rural north of Israel. The population in the entire North just about reaches that of Tel Aviv; yet the land area is one-third of the country. Many of the settlements have a high proportion of North African immigrants who tend to be very poor and find adjusting to the country very difficult. There is a shortage of social workers. There is also a high turnover in the work staff because workers feel isolated and under pressure from working with a demanding client population.

The project commenced operations in February, 1977. The initial task was a need survey. This concentrated on three areas. The first was to identify and plot on a map the location of all services offered in the region. This included a clear description of the service. The second area was to develop a profile of the workers. This included a job description and a report on the amount and nature of present and past supervision. Along the border all workers are employed by what in the United States is the equivalent of a State Department of Welfare. Third, all agency directors were interviewed to get their estimate of needs and priorities.

Once the information gathered was collated, a series of meetings was held with key agency people and with representatives from the Ministry of Labour and Social Affairs. These meetings became the basis for developing the first two project service contracts. These initial ventures were used to test and make changes in the project intervention model. These will be briefly described because they illustrate the way the project accomplished its goals.

HATZOR DEPARTMENT
OF SOCIAL SERVICES

The first unit worked with the local department of social services in the town of Hatzor. The workers had no professional training; they had no prior exposure to even basic casework concepts. Through consultation with management and worker representatives, a series of six training sessions was agreed on. These meetings, held about ten days apart, focused on basic interviewing techniques and elemental principles of casework service delivery.

The first meeting was a warm-up session designed to acquaint the workers with closed circuit TV procedures and other aspects of the training process. Workers were given a group process task to solve. This was filmed and replayed for analysis. A group process task was chosen because this required participation by all group members. Many role-play situations involve only an interviewer and interviewee, and other members of the group become observers. This does not maximize learning possibilities. Once a learning group has been formed, role play on this model becomes possible because workers have mastered the technique of identifying issues related to their work as they observe someone else. The group process task was to have workers share information about their job roles. It was successful in generating a training group where all members participated, and it was a measure of how isolated they were.

The second meeting was devoted to how to handle and use silence in the interview.[4] Two members of the group were videotaped as they role-played situations they had experienced in relation to silence. The simulation was then replayed and discussed. After a break, a university laboratory film on this subject was shown.[5] The two experiences were then reviewed and compared. Workers were able to see that what they had experienced with their clients was not unique, and that there was knowledge about how to deal with such situations.

The third session dealt with problem clients. Each member of the group was asked to prepare a list of "typical" problem clients. These were combined into a unified list, and then the group took turns role-playing. As in session two, this was videotaped, replayed, and then contrasted with a lab teaching film. The comparison between the workers' tape and the school film enabled the workers to see themselves more clearly as they related to their clients.

The fourth session was devoted to role-playing practice situations related to violence and confrontation between worker and client. In Israel physical violence is seldom the concern. Instead, a combination of clashing cultures, cultural groups where threat is a way of life, and poor practice involving inconsistency and broken promises, result in many stormy office encounters.[6] As the workers became aware of these patterns and their reactions to them, they could sort out cultural behavior from skill needs. They began to focus on their learning needs.

The fifth session continued themes developed in the fourth session. The specific focus was on the demanding client. There was a demonstration of how to prevent escalation and confrontation in client encounters. Various ways were considered of how to respond to the question, "When will the check come?" The workers began to see how they could develop a variety of non-provoking responses to the question.

Evaluation and Outcome

The group was enthusiastic about the experience, and they unanimously asked that the contract be extended for six months. They also asked for help in developing a professional library.

This experience reflects the workers' desire to do a good job and their willingness to use help. This is all the more striking because Israel is an educationally status-conscious country. People usually try to get university credit, or a certificate that can be used for credit, for almost any quasi-academic effort they undertake. While it is not beyond the realm of possibility that the traveling lab will offer credit in the future, it was not a part of what was offered in this experience. This suggests that the quantity and quality of professional direction is at least one element in determining whether or not workers will remain in rural areas.

MOUNT HERMON DEPARTMENT
OF SOCIAL SERVICES

The training experience conducted by the lab's second team was with the Mount Hermon Department of Social Services. Here most of the workers had the B.A. and did not have much question about their casework skills. Their concern was with the community organization and community development tasks that were a normal part of their work. Some of this difficulty comes from the structure of Israeli social work education which follows the American plan of introducing specialization early. In rural areas the basic need is for a generic worker.

The format for these meetings was the same as for the first set. The initial session was devoted to getting acquainted with the equipment and getting feedback from videotape and colleagues. The second meeting dealt with basic procedures for conducting a social survey. This is an essential and often overlooked step in any community organization activity. Somewhat to the surprise of the group, almost 200 social and other community services were identified. This underscores an important fact about services in rural areas. It is not that the services do not exist, they are often mandated; but it is lack of information, coordination, and/or competent personnel that often prevents their delivery.

The third meeting was devoted to decision making in the community organization process. This was accomplished by using a simulation game for decision making. Special attention was given to group-community processes and resolving conflicts when different community groups attempt to set common priorities for action.

The fourth meeting summed up previous material, and then theories of community organization were used to show how the experience could be integrated and generalized. These ideas and techniques were used to suggest a model for shaping projects or community services. The analytic framework was then dry run to assess a local kibbutz project.

In the fifth session a group member presented a plan for resolving a community issue. Two discussion groups then independently reviewed the plan. They then met to agree on a single plan.

The final meeting was devoted to summarizing and reviewing selected portions of tapes from previous sessions. The staff then developed a concise listing of the principles of group process and community work which they had acquired.

Evaluation and Outcome

As with the other group, the response was positive and the staff voted to extend the contract six months. Even though the workers in this office were professionally trained, they said in the last session that the focus on community work had made them more aware of the way they functioned as a professional group, and that they did not easily identify with the ministry. In Israel, as in the United States, to be associated with welfare carries a stigma for the giver as well as the receiver. In addition to the problem of early specialization, the problem of overall competence came into focus. The workers concluded they were not as skilled as they originally thought. Perhaps many workers feel bad about their job not only because of inadequate resources, but also because they do not know how to do the job.

It is a tribute to these workers that they honestly faced the problem. This demonstrates the value of the lab. In planning for future work, the workers' topics included looking at their professional cohesion in the Department of Social Services; the role of the ministry in the region and in the kibbutzim and moshavim; and the professional responsibility of qualified social workers to serve all of the population at risk.

The workers also decided that they wanted to enrich their data bank, so they made plans for a continuing social survey that would include all the locations they served. Finally, they decided to broaden their contacts and establish cooperative relationships with other workers, district supervisors, and town managers in the area. Out of this they hoped to establish an ability to confront community-level problems in the region.

COMPARISON

Other than the greater sophistication and emphasis on theory in group two, there was a close similarity in the training process and outcomes. Videotape with lecture and playback is effective for training and supervision.[7] Both groups focused on specific technical skills that they needed, and both groups identified learning and resource needs that they wanted to continue developing.

SUMMARY AND CONCLUSION

This paper has presented a way to train and supervise social workers in rural areas. Using standard principles of supervision, the project emphasized mobility of personnel and diversity in using their skills. The help which rural workers need can be brought to them. Social work supervision on wheels cannot compensate for material inadequacies in services which often make work in rural areas arduous and frustrating; but it has demonstrated that workers in these areas are responsive to efforts to help them improve their professional skills.

What this underscores is that social workers, like any other workers, want to feel competent. Bringing training and supervision to workers in remote areas does not guarantee that they will stay there; but the project has shown that it probably would be wise to include efforts to upgrade skill in any plan to try to retain workers in rural areas.

This project also highlights that supervision is one of the weakest links in the structure of the profession. In social work education and in the profession, little formal attention is given to preparation for supervision or teaching about it. The most the student can hope for is a single course. Agency workers who supervise students occasionally get some orientation from the school. Most people try to learn to supervise by practicing on students. It does not help either of them very much. Poor practices are picked up and perpetuated.

Few schools use in a systematic way the training techniques developed in this project. Clearly it is time to give more attention to the sustained use of audio-visual techniques. Training for supervision should be formalized in schools and agencies. It is possible that service throughout the whole field could be improved if supervisors were able to make their performance expectations clear and their teaching technique precise.

Beyond what the workers and the agencies gained, the school has found that the project has made important contributions and raised some questions about its program. The mobile lab is now used as a field placement. It quickly has become one of the more desired placements. The movies made for training are not only used in the classroom but are in increasing demand by other agencies. The library of films is becoming a major asset in the educational program.

Plans are under way to allow the lab to become an emergency ambulance for shock treatment and crisis intervention. While emergency mental health intervention can be used anywhere, the tension along the border areas makes this a desirable feature of the lab's activities.

An issue raised for the school, and by implication for the profession, comes from its use of expert consultants from other disiciplines. They have made important contributions to the successful accomplishment of the lab's goals. Plans are under way to develop interdisciplinary teams. The problem which is highlighted is the fact that in Israel the terminal professional degree is still the bachelor's. This will probably continue to be the case for a while. Field-work training in social work education has been an experience where students often find that they do not have clear standards, and they do not feel well prepared when they finish. Other professions seem better prepared and stronger in this respect.

By giving the students field experience that allows them to work with other disciplines, it has been possible for the school to sharpen its educational stance and to develop confidence in students.

The project has brought the school to the field. This has taken a lot of work, but it leaves the school feeling it has made its educational program move toward meeting the educational and practitioner needs of the profession and the country.

NOTES

1. Gwen K. Weber, "Preparing Social Workers for Practice in Rural Social Systems," *Journal of Education for Social Work* 12 (Fall 1975), pp. 108–109.

2. Carlton Munson, "Social Work Manpower and Social Indicators: Rural and Urban Differences," *Human Services in the Rural Environment* 3 (April 1978), pp. 35–36.

3. Don Handelman, "Bureaucratic Transactions: The Development of Official-Client Relationships in Israel," in *Transaction and Meaning*, ed. by Bruce Kapferer (Philadelphia: Institute for the Study of Human Issues, 1976), pp. 223–275.

4. This is a common social work problem. See Norman A. Polansky et al., *Roots of Futility* (San Francisco: Jossey-Bass Inc., 1972), pp. 172 ff.

5. Shlomo Sharlin and Richard Goldman, "A Laboratory for Development of Specific Skills by Social Workers," *Educational Technology* XV (January 1975), pp. 39–42.

6. Emanuel Marx, *The Social Context of Violent Behavior* (London: Routledge & Kegan Paul, 1976), pp. 32–43.

7. Bonnie C. Rhim, "The Use of Videotapes in Social Work Agencies," *Social Casework* 57 (December 1976), pp. 644–650.

PART IV

Organizational Authority and Professional Autonomy

INTRODUCTION

AUTHORITY HAS ALWAYS troubled mankind. Charles Loring Brace, writing in 1872 of his own role as a supervisor, was probably the first social worker to articulate the precarious balance that has to be maintained; he pointed out that employee selection and training involve choosing the right man for the place, making him feel that social work is a profession and life-calling, and showing him the utmost respect and confidence, while at the same time holding him to the strictest accountability.[1] This is no simple feat, and whether or not Brace achieved his goal is lost in the history of social work; however, the profession still struggles with the accountability–confidence issue daily.

There have been many changes since Brace's time, especially in the growth of organizations and the formalization of the profession. The dilemma of modern man as a creature of organizations has evolved from Durkheim's belief that division of labor would not destroy the notion that "to be a person is to be an autonomous source of action"[2]; to Weber's idea that the principles of organizational hierarchy and the concepts of superordination and subordination did not mean that higher authorities should simply take over the business of the lower group;[3] to the recent, vivid description of the "social ethic" by William Whyte, defining the struggle of the individual for autonomy in complex organizations. Whyte presents the problem of individualism within modern organizations because of the inherent challenge to authority involved. He recommends that we cooperate with organizations but also resist them; and he is optimistic about the outcome, holding that organizations have been created by humans and certainly can be changed by humans.[4]

Social work is caught up in the changes and problems of an evolving organizational society; in fact, social work has been described as a product of these changes.[5] Scott Briar has succinctly applied Whyte's concept of the issue for the profession by calling attention to the fact that 90 percent of casework is practiced in bureaucratic organizations, and that the demands of these organizations encroach upon professional autonomy. He holds that every attempt by the agency to make routine some condition or aspect of professional practice amounts to a restriction of professional discretion, and for that reason probably should be resisted by practitioners. There is a limit to the autonomy and discretion an organization can grant the practitioner, but no one knows just where that limit is, and we cannot know until we have tried to reach it.[6] The area in which much of the knowledge about the limits of practice has evolved is supervision. Hughes has epitomized the issue of professionals by asking the question: What orders does one accept from an employer, especially one whose interests may not always be those of the professional and his clients?[7]

The problem of control in modern professions and organizations leads to a number of questions especially appropriate to social work. Supervision, as we have noted, has been traditionally summarized functionally as administration, teaching, and helping.[8] If so, what are the limits of control in these functions? What are the best means of carrying out these functions structurally? If helping and teaching are major functions of supervision, what is appropriate to teach, and how is supervision to help the experienced as opposed to the inexperienced worker?

The article by Kadushin uses an interactional framework organized around game theory, as popularized by Eric Berne in *Games People Play*. Game strategies are explained through the projected outcome for the supervisee or supervisor. Game playing is viewed as a ploy, based on unrealistic expectations by both participants, and as a means of avoiding risk and loss of control. This frame of reference is used to define interactionally and explain behavior in the supervisory relationship through three categories: manipulating demand levels, redefining the relationship, and reducing power disparity.

Whereas Kadushin emphasizes the games played by supervisees, Hawthorne uses the same perspective to explore those played by supervisors, particularly in relation to the exercise of authority. Supervisors are required to exercise many forms of authority that they find unfamiliar and alien; these are defined as administrative, evaluative, educational, parental, and consultative. To deal with authority, supervisors use the defensive game-playing strategies of abdication and power. In the former, the supervisor manipulates the situation so that authority cannot be exercised; and in the latter, the supervisor takes an omnipotent position where deviation from the rules is portrayed as impossible. Both categories achieve the same goal: avoiding clarity and preventing challenges to the supervisor's authority.

Whereas Kadushin and Hawthorne explore the interactional aspects of authority in supervision, Wasserman describes the bureaucratic and organizational problems that serve as the background for both the supervisee and the supervisor in game-playing arrangements. His descriptions of workers and supervisors in public welfare are helpful in understanding how systems promote defensive game-playing rather than rational behavior. According to Wasserman, supervisees are in conflict over "serving two masters"—the autonomous professional self and the employing organization—and supervisors are viewed as insufficiently competent to be helpful. The workers perceive supervision as bureaucratic control irrelevant to implementing social work values, knowledge, and skills; and they view the administration as aloof and uncommitted, attributes that encourage the treatment of clients as objects rather than people.

The article by Levy provides an ethical framework for conducting supervision to avoid the interactional problems identified by Kadushin and Hawthorne and the organizational conflicts documented by Wasserman. Levy defines the characteristic sources of power that the supervisor has available, based on which is a set of principles that can serve as a supervisory code of ethics. The principles are behavior-oriented and include the following: (1) an ethical supervisory act is based not on the best course of action but on the right one; (2) job assignment should be consistent with the worker's capability; (3) supervisors owe workers the tools to do a good job; (4) supervisors must insure that workers' aspirations and opportunities are correlated; and (5) supervisors must make their expectations clear, and must explain how performance is to be evaluated.

The article by Munson traces the history of the literature of supervision in relation to the theory of functional control as a means of insuring the continuity and smooth functioning of the societal system through the organizational and supervisory process. Role theory is used to unite the interactional and organizational problems raised by other articles in this section and to clarify means of confronting these issues in the supervisory relationship. The notion is presented that the traditional view of controlled practice through supervision is damaging to the profession, and suggestions are made for conceptualizing supervision to promote autonomy. A role-theory perspective is applied to supervision as opposed to a psychologically oriented model, and Merton's social mechanisms are used to explore areas of consensus and conflict in practice. A broad conception of supervisory role performance is presented which can be used for the application of Levy's code of ethics. Roles in supervision are applied to Merton's social mechanisms: (1) importance of various statuses, (2) differences in power, (3) observability of activity, (4) observability of conflicting demands, (5) mutual social support, and (6) abridging the role-set.

NOTES

1. Charles Loring Brace, *The Dangerous Classes of New York and Twenty Years Work Among Them* (New York: Wynkoop and Hallenbeck, 1872; reprint ed., New York, National Association of Social Workers Classic Series, 1973), p. 443.

2. Emile Durkheim, *The Division of Labor in Society* (New York: The Free Press, 1964), p. 403.

3. Max Weber, "Bureaucracy," in Edgar A. Schuler *et al.*, eds., *Readings in Sociology* (New York: Thomas Y. Crowell Company, 1971), pp. 348–349.

4. William H. Whyte, *The Organization Man* (New York: Simon and Schuster, 1956), pp. 3–14.

5. Everett C. Hughes, "Professions," *Daedalus* (Fall 1963), p. 658.

6. Scott Briar, "The Current Crisis in Social Casework," in Robert W. Klenk and Robert M. Ryan, eds., *The Practice of Social Work* (Belmont, Cal.: Wadsworth Publishing Company, 1970), p. 96.

7. Hughes, *op. cit.*, p. 665.

8. Dorothy Pettes, *Supervision in Social Work: A Method of Student Training and Staff Development* (London: George Allen and Unwin Ltd., 1967), p. 15.

17

Games People Play in Supervision

Alfred Kadushin

GAMESMANSHIP HAS HAD a checkered career. Respectably fathered by an eminent mathematician, Von Neumann, in his book *The Theory of Games and Economic Behavior,* it became the "Art of Winning Games Without Actually Cheating" as detailed by Potter in *Theory and Practice of Gamesmanship.*[1] It was partly rescued recently for the behavioral sciences by the psychoanalyst Eric Berne in *Games People Play.*[2]

Berne defines a game as "an ongoing series of complementary ulterior transactions—superficially plausible but with a concealed motivation."[3] It is a scheme, or artfulness, utilized in the pursuit of some objective or purpose. A ploy is a segment of a game.

The purpose of engaging in the game, of using the maneuvers, snares, gimmicks, and ploys that are, in essence, the art of gamesmanship, lies in the payoff. One party to the game chooses a strategy to maximize his payoff and minimize his penalties. He wants to win rather than to lose, and he wants to win as much as he can at the lowest cost.

Games people play in supervision are concerned with the kinds of recurrent interactional incidents between supervisor and supervisee that have a payoff for one of the parties in the transaction. While both supervisor and supervisee may initiate a game, for the purposes of simplicity it may be desirable to discuss in greater detail games initiated by supervisees. This may also be the better part of valor.

WHY GAMES ARE PLAYED

To understand why the supervisee should be interested in initiating a game, it is necessary to understand the possible losses that might be anticipated by him in the supervisory relationship. One needs to know what the supervisee is defending himself against and the losses he might incur if he eschewed gamesmanship or lost the game.

The supervisory situation generates a number of different kinds of anxieties for the supervisee. It is a situation in which he is asked to undergo some sort of change. Unlike the usual educational situation that is concerned with helping the student critically examine and hence possibly change his ideas, social work supervision is often directed toward a change in behavior and, perhaps, personality. Change creates anxiety. It requires giving up the familiar for the unfamiliar; it requires a period of discomfort during which one is uneasy about continuing to use old patterns of behavior but does not, as yet, feel fully comfortable with new behaviors.

The threat of change is greater for the adult student because it requires dissolution of patterns of thinking and believing to which he has become habituated. It also requires an act of disloyalty to previous identification models. The ideas and behavior that might need changing represent, in a measure, the introjection of previously encountered significant others—parents, teachers, highly valued peers—and giving them up implies some rejection of these people in the acceptance of other models. The act of infidelity creates anxiety.

The supervisory tutorial is a threat to the student's independence and autonomy. Learning requires some frank admission of dependence on the teacher; readiness to learn involves giving up some measure of autonomy in accepting direction from others, in submitting to the authority of the supervisor-teacher.

The supervisee also faces a threat to his sense of adequacy. The situation demands an admission of ignorance, however limited, in some areas. And in sharing one's ignorance one exposes one's vulnerability. One risks the possibility of criticism, of shame, and perhaps of rejection because of one's admitted inadequacy. In addition, the supervisee faces the hazard of not being adequate to the requirements of the learning situation. His performance may fall short of the supervisor's expectations, intensifying a sense of inadequacy and incurring the possibility of supervisory disapproval.

Since the parameters of the supervisory relationship are often ambiguous, there is a threat that devolves not only from the sensed inadequacies of one's work, but also from the perceived or suspected inadequacies of self. This threat is exaggerated in the social work supervisory relationship because so much of self is invested in and reflected by one's work and because of the tendency to attribute to the supervisor a diagnostic omniscience suggesting that he perceives all and knows all.

The supervisor-supervisee relationship is evocative of the parent-child relationship and as such may tend to reactivate some anxiety associated with this earlier relationship. The supervisor is in a position of authority and the supervisee is, in some measure, dependent on him. If the supervisor is a potential parent surrogate, fellow supervisees are potential siblings competing for the affectional responses of the parent. The situation is therefore one that threatens the reactivation not only of residual difficulties in the parent-child relationship but also in the sibling-sibling relationship.

The supervisor has the responsibility of evaluating the work of the supervisee and, as such, controls access to important rewards and penalties. School grades, salary increases, and promotional possibilities are real and significant prizes dependent on a favorable evaluation. Unlike previously encountered evaluative situations, for instance working toward a grade in a course, this is a situation in which it is impossible to hide in a group. There is direct and sharply focused confrontation with the work done by the supervisee.

These threats, anxieties, and penalties are the losses that might be incurred in entering into the supervisory relationship. A desire to keep losses to a minimum and maximize the rewards that might derive from the encounter explains why the supervisee should want to play games in supervision, why he should feel a need to control the situation to his advantage.

Supervisees have over a period of time developed some well-established, identifiable games. An attempt will be made to group these games in terms of similar tactics. It might be important to note that not all supervisees play games and not all of the behavior supervisees engage in is indicative of an effort to play games. However, the best supervisee plays games some of the time; the poorest supervisee does not play games all of the time. What the author is trying to do is to identify a limited, albeit important, sector of supervisee behavior.

MANIPULATING DEMAND LEVELS

One series of games is designed to manipulate the level of demands made on the supervisee. One such game might be titled "Two Against the Agency" or "Seducing for Subversion." The game is generally played by intelligent, intuitively gifted supervisees who are impatient with routine agency procedures. Forms, reports, punctuality, and recording excite their contempt. The more sophisticated supervisee, in playing the game, introduces it by suggesting the conflict between the bureaucratic and professional orientation to the work of the agency. The bureaucratic orientation is one that is centered on what is needed to insure efficient operation of the agency; the professional orientation is focused on meeting the needs of the client. The supervisee points out that meeting client need is more important, that time spent in recording, filling out forms, and writing reports tends to rob time from direct work with the client, and further that it does not make any difference when he comes to work or goes home as long as no client suffers as a consequence. Would it not therefore be possible to permit him, a highly intuitive and gifted worker, to schedule and allocate his time to maximum client advantage and should not the supervisor, then, be less concerned about the necessity of his filling out forms, doing recording, completing reports, and so on?

For the student and recent graduate supervisee oriented toward the morality of the hippie movement (and many students, especially in social work, are responsive to hippie ideology, often without being explicitly aware of this), professional autonomy is consonant with the idea of self-expression—"doing your thing." Bureaucratic controls, demands, and expectations are regarded as violations of genuine self-expression and are resented as such.

It takes two to play games. The supervisor is induced to play (1) because he identifies with the student's concern for meeting client needs, (2) because he himself has frequently resented bureaucratic demands and so is, initially, sympathetic to the supervisee's complaints, and (3) because he is hesitant to assert his authority in demanding firmly that these requirements be met. If the supervisor elects to play the game, he has enlisted in an alliance with the supervisee to subvert agency administrative procedures.

Another game designed to control and mitigate the level of demands made on the supervisee might be called "Be Nice to Me Because I Am Nice to You." The principal ploy is seduction by flattery. The supervisee is full of praise: "You're the best supervisor I ever had," "You're so perceptive that after I've talked to you I almost know what the client will say next," "You're so consistently helpful," "I look forward in the future to being as good a social worker as you are," and so on. It is a game of emotional blackmail in which, having been paid in this kind of coin, the supervisor finds himself incapable of firmly holding the worker to legitimate demands.

The supervisor finds it difficult to resist engaging in the game because it is gratifying to be regarded as an omniscient source of wisdom; there is satisfaction in being perceived as helpful and in being selected as a pattern for identification and emulation. An invitation to play a game that tends to enhance a positive self-concept and feed one's narcissistic needs is likely to be accepted.

In general, the supervisor is vulnerable to an invitation to play this game. The supervisor needs the supervisee as much as the supervisee needs the supervisor. One of the principal sources of gratification for a worker is contact with the client. The supervisor is denied this source of gratification, at least directly. For the supervisor the principal source of gratification is helping the supervisee to grow and change. But this means that he has to look to the supervisee to validate his effectiveness. Objective criteria of such effectiveness are, at best, obscure and equivocal. However, to have the supervisee say explicitly, openly, and directly: "I have learned a lot from you," "You have been helpful," "I am a better worker because of you," is the kind of reassurance needed and often subtly solicited by the supervisor. The perceptive supervisee understands and exploits the supervisor's needs in initiating this game.

REDEFINING THE RELATIONSHIP

A second series of games is also designed to mitigate the level of demands made on the supervisee, but here the game depends on redefining the supervisory relationship. As Goffman points out, games permit one to control the conduct of others by influencing the definition of the situation.[4] These games depend on ambiguity of the definition of the supervisory relationship. It is open to a variety of interpretations and resembles, in some crucial respects, analogous relationships.

Thus, one kind of redefinition suggests a shift from the relationship of supervisor-supervisee as teacher-learner in an administrative hierarchy to supervisor-supervisee as worker-client in the context of therapy. The game might be called "Protect the Sick and the Infirm" or "Treat Me, Don't Beat Me." The supervisee would rather expose himself than his work. And so he asks the supervisor for help in solving his personal problems. The sophisticated player relates these problems to his difficulties on the job. Nevertheless, he seeks to engage the supervisor actively in a concern with his problems. If the translation to worker-client is made, the nature of demands shifts as well. The kinds of demands one can legitimately impose on a client are clearly less onerous than the level of expectations imposed on a worker. And the supervisee has achieved a payoff in a softening of demands.

The supervisor is induced to play (1) because the game appeals to the social worker in him (since he was a social worker before he became a supervisor and is still interested in helping those who have personal problems), (2) because it appeals to the voyeur in him (many supervisors are fascinated by the opportunity to share in the intimate life of others), (3) because it is flattering to be selected as a therapist, and (4) because the supervisor is not clearly certain as to whether such a redefinition of the situation is not permissible. All the discussions about the equivocal boundaries between supervision and therapy feed into this uncertainty.

Another game of redefinition might be called "Evaluation Is Not for Friends." Here the supervisory relationship is redefined as a social relationship. The supervisee makes an effort to take coffee breaks with the supervisor, invite him to lunch, walk to and from the bus or the parking lot with him, and discuss some common interests during conferences. The social component tends to vitiate the professional component in the relationship. It requires increased determination and resolution on the part of any supervisor to hold the "friend" to the required level of performance.

Another and more contemporary redefinition is less obvious than either of the two kinds just discussed, which have been standard for a long time now. This is the game of "Maximum Feasible Participation." It involves a shift in roles from supervisor-supervisee to peer-peer. The supervisee suggests that the relationship will be most effective if it is established on the basis of democratic participation. Since he knows best what he needs and wants to learn, he should be granted equal responsibility for determining the agendas of conferences. So far so good. The game is a difficult one to play because in the hands of a determined supervisee, joint control of agenda can easily become supervisee control with consequent mitigation of expectations. The supervisor finds himself in a predicament in trying to decline the game. For one, there is an element of validity in the claim that people learn best in a context that encourages democratic participation in the learning situation. Second, the current trend in working with the social agency client encourages maximum feasible participation with presently undefined limits. To decline the game is to suggest that one is old-fashioned, undemocratic, and against the rights of those on lower levels in the administrative hierarchy—not an enviable picture to project of oneself. The supervisor is forced to play but needs to be constantly alert in order to maintain some semblance of administrative authority and prevent all the shots being called by the supervisee-peer.

REDUCING POWER DISPARITY

A third series of games is designed to reduce anxiety by reducing the power disparity between supervisor and worker. One source of the supervisor's power is, of course, the consequence of his position in the administrative hierarchy vis-à-vis the supervisee. Another source of power, however, lies in his expertise, greater knowledge, and superior skill. It is the second source of power disparity that is vulnerable to this series of games. If the supervisee can establish the fact that the supervisor is not so smart after all, some of the power differential is mitigated and with it some need to feel anxious.

One such game, frequently played, might be called "If You Knew Dostoyevsky Like I Know Dostoyevsky." During the course of a conference the supervisee makes a casual allusion to the fact that the client's behavior reminds him of that of Raskolnikov in *Crime and Punishment*, which is, after all, somewhat different in etiology from the pathology that plagued Prince Myshkin in *The Idiot*. An effective ploy, used to score additional points, involves addressing the rhetorical question: "You remember, don't you?" to the supervisor. It is equally clear to both the supervisee and the supervisor that the latter does not remember—if, indeed, he ever knew what he cannot remember now. At this point the supervisee proceeds to instruct the supervisor. The roles of teacher-learner are reversed; power disparity and supervisee anxiety are simultaneously reduced.

The supervisor acquiesces to the game because refusal requires an open confession of ignorance on his part. The supervisee in playing the game well co-operates in a conspiracy with the supervisor not to expose his ignorance openly. The discussion proceeds under the protection of the mutually accepted fiction that *both* know what they are talking about.

The content for the essential gambit in this game changes with each generation of supervisees. The author's impression is that currently the allusion is likely to be to the work of the conditioning therapists—Eysenck, Wolpe, and Lazarus—rather than to literary figures. The effect on the supervisor, however, is the same: a feeling of depression and general malaise at having been found ignorant when his position requires that he know more than the supervisee. And it has the same payoff in reducing supervisee anxiety.

Another kind of game in this same genre exploits situational advantages to reduce power disparity and permit the supervisee the feeling that he, rather than the supervisor, is in control. This game is "So What Do *You* Know About It?" The supervisee with a long record of experience in public welfare makes reference to "those of us on the front lines who have struggled with the multiproblem client," exciting humility in the supervisor who has to try hard to remember when he last saw a live client. A married supervisee with children will allude to her marital experience and what it "really is like to be a mother" in discussing family therapy with an unmarried female supervisor. The older supervisee will talk about "life" from the vantage point of incipient senility to the supervisor fresh out of graduate school. The younger supervisee will hint at his greater understanding of the adolescent client since he has, after all, smoked some pot and has seriously considered LSD. The supervisor trying to tune in finds his older psyche is not with it. The supervisor younger than the older supervisee, older than the younger supervisee—never having raised a child or met a payroll—finds himself being instructed by those he is charged with instructing; roles are reversed and the payoff lies in the fact that the supervisor is a less threatening figure to the supervisee.

Another, more recently developed, procedure for "putting the supervisor down" is through the judicious use in the conference of strong four-letter words. This is "telling it like it is" and the supervisor who responds with discomfort and loss of composure has forfeited some amount of control to the supervisee who has exposed some measure of his bourgeois character and residual Puritanism.

Putting the supervisor down may revolve around a question of social work goals rather than content. The social action-oriented supervisee is concerned with fundamental changes in social relationships. He knows that obtaining a slight increase in the budget for his client, finding a job for a client, or helping a neglectful mother relate more positively to her child are not of much use since they leave the basic pathology of society undisturbed and unchanged. He is impatient with the case-oriented supervisor who is interested in helping a specific family live a little less troubled, a little less unhappily, in a fundamentally disordered society. The game is "All or Nothing at All." It is designed to make the supervisor feel he has sold out, been co-opted by the Establishment, lost or abandoned his broader vision of the "good" society, become endlessly concerned with symptoms rather than with causes. It is effective because the supervisor recognizes that there is some element of truth in the accusation, since this is true for all who occupy positions of responsibility in the Establishment.

CONTROLLING THE SITUATION

All the games mentioned have, as part of their effect, a shift of control of the situation from supervisor to supervisee. Another series of games is designed to place control of the supervisory situation more explicitly and directly in the hands of the supervisee. Control of the situation by the supervisor is potentially threatening since he can then take the initiative of introducing for discussion those weaknesses and inadequacies in the supervisee's work that need fullest review. If the supervisee can control the conference, much that is unflattering to discuss may be adroitly avoided.

One game designed to control the discussion's content is called "I Have a Little List." The supervisee comes in with a series of questions about his work that he would very much like to discuss. The better player formulates the questions so that they have relevance to those problems in which the supervisor has greatest professional interest and about which he has done considerable reading. The supervisee is under no obligation to listen to the answer to his question. Question 1 having been asked, the supervisor is off on a short lecture, during which time the supervisee is free to plan mentally the next weekend or review the last weekend, taking care merely to listen for signs that the supervisor is running down. When this happens, the supervisee introduces Question 2 with an appropriate transitional comment and the cycle is repeated. As the supervisee increases the supervisor's level of participation he is, by the same token, decreasing his own level of participation since only one person can be talking at once. Thus the supervisee controls both content and direction of conference interaction.

The supervisor is induced to play this game because there is narcissistic gratification in displaying one's knowledge and in meeting the dependency needs of those who appeal to one for answers to their questions, and because the supervisee's questions should be accepted, respected, and, if possible, answered.

Control of the initiative is also seized by the supervisee in the game of "Heading Them Off at the Pass." Here the supervisee knows that his poor work is likely to be analyzed critically. He therefore opens the conference by freely admitting his mistakes—he knows it was an inadequate interview, he knows that he should have, by now, learned to do better. There is no failing on the supervisor's agenda for discussion with him to which he does not freely confess in advance, flagellating himself to excess. The supervisor, faced with overwhelming self-derogation, has little option but to reassure the supervisee sympathetically. The tactic not only makes difficult an extended discussion of mistakes in the work at the supervisor's initiative, it elicits praise by the supervisor for whatever strengths the supervisee has manifested, however limited. The supervisor, once again, acts out of concern with the troubled, out of his predisposition to comfort the discomforted, out of pleasure in acting the good, forgiving parent.

There is also the game of control through fluttering dependency, of strength through weakness. It is the game of "Little Old Me" or "Casework à Trois." The supervisee, in his ignorance and incompetence, looks to the knowledgeable, competent supervisor for a detailed prescription of how to proceed: "What would *you* do next?" "Then what would *you* say?" The supervisee unloads responsibility for the case onto the supervisor and the supervisor shares the case load with the worker. The supervisor plays the game because, in reality, he does share responsibility for case management with the supervisee and has responsibility for seeing that the client is not harmed. Further, the supervisor often is interested in the gratification of carrying a case load, however vicariously, so that he is somewhat predisposed to take the case out of the hands of the supervisee. There are, further, the pleasures derived from acting the capable parent to the dependent child and from the domination of others.

A variant of the game in the hands of a more hostile supervisee is "I Did Like You Told Me." Here the supervisee maneuvers the supervisor into offering specific prescriptions on case management and then applies the prescriptions in spiteful obedience and undisguised mimicry.

The supervisee acts as though the supervisor were responsible for the case, he himself merely being the executor of supervisory directives. Invariably and inevitably, whatever has been suggested by the supervisor fails to accomplish what it was supposed to accomplish. "I Did Like You Told Me" is designed to make even a strong supervisor defensive.

"It's All So Confusing" attempts to reduce the authority of the supervisor by appeals to other authorities—a former supervisor, another supervisor in the same agency, or a faculty member at a local school of social work with whom the supervisee just happened to discuss the case. The supervisee casually indicates that in similar situations his former supervisor tended to take such and such an approach, one that is at variance with the approach the current supervisor regards as desirable. And "It's All So Confusing" when different "authorities" suggest such different approaches to the same situation. The supervisor is faced with "defending" his approach against some unnamed, unknown competitor. This is difficult, especially when few situations in social work permit an unequivocal answer in which the supervisor can have categorical confidence. Since the supervisor was somewhat shaky in his approach in the first place, he feels vulnerable against alternative suggestions from other "authorities" and his sense of authority vis-à-vis the supervisee is eroded.

A supervisee can control the degree of threat in the supervisory situation by distancing techniques. The game is "What You Don't Know Won't Hurt Me." The supervisor knows the work of the supervisee only indirectly, through what is shared in the recording and verbally in the conference. The supervisee can elect to share in a manner that is thin, inconsequential, without depth of affect. He can share selectively and can distort, consciously or unconsciously, in order to present a more favorable picture of his work. The supervisee can be passive and reticent or overwhelm the supervisor with endless trivia.

In whatever manner it is done, the supervisee increases distance between the work he actually does and the supervisor who is responsible for critically analyzing with him the work done. This not only reduces the threat to him of possible criticism of his work but also, as Fleming points out, prevents the supervisor from intruding into the privacy of the relationship between the worker and the client.[5]

SUPERVISORS' GAMES

It would be doing both supervisor and supervisee an injustice to omit any reference to games initiated by supervisors—unjust to the supervisees in that such omission would imply that they alone play games in supervision and unjust to the supervisors in suggesting that they lack the imagination and capacity to devise their own counter-games. Supervisors play games out of felt threats to their position in the hierarchy, uncertainty about their authority, reluctance to use their authority, a desire to be liked, a need for the supervisees' approbation—and out of some hostility to supervisees that is inevitable in such a complex, intimate relationship.

One of the classic supervisory games is called "I Wonder Why You Really Said That?" This is the game of redefining honest disagreement so that it appears to be psychological resistance. Honest disagreement requires that the supervisor defend his point of view, present the research evidence in support of his contention, be sufficiently acquainted with the literature so he can cite the knowledge that argues for the correctness of what he is saying. If honest disagreement is redefined as resistance, the burden is shifted to the supervisee. He has to examine his needs and motives that prompt him to question what the supervisor has said. The supervisor is thus relieved of the burden of validating what he has said and the onus for defense now rests with the supervisee.

Another classic supervisory game is "One Good Question Deserves Another." It was explicated some years ago by a new supervisor writing of her experience in an article called "Through Supervision With Gun and Camera":

> I learned that another part of a supervisor's skills, as far as the workers are concerned, is to know all the answers. I was able to get out of this very easily. I discovered that when a worker asks a question, the best thing to do is to immediately ask for what she thinks. While the worker is figuring out the answer to her own question (this is known as growth and development), the supervisor quickly tries to figure it out also. She may arrive at the answer the same time as the worker, but the worker somehow assumes that she knew it all along. This is very comfortable for the supervisor. In the event that neither the worker nor the supervisor succeeds in coming up with a useful thought on the question the worker has raised, the supervisor can look wise and suggest that they think about it and discuss it further next time. This gives the supervisor plenty of time to look up the subject and leaves the worker with the feeling that the supervisor is giving great weight to her question. In the event that the supervisor does not want to go to all the trouble, she can just tell the worker that she does not know the answer (this is known as helping the worker accept the limitations of the supervision) and tell her to look it up herself. . . .[6]

IN RESPONSE TO GAMES

Before going on to discuss possible constructive responses to games played in the context of supervision, the author must express some uneasiness about having raised the subject in the first place, a dissatisfaction similar to the distaste felt toward Berne's *Games People Play*.

The book communicates a sense of disrespect for the complexities of life and human behavior. The simplistic games formulas are a cheapening caricature of people's struggle for a modicum of comfort in a difficult world. A perceptive psychiatrist said in a critical and saddening review of the book:

> It makes today's bothersome "problems" easily subject to a few home-spun models—particularly the cynical and concretely aphoristic kind that reduces all human experiences to a series of "exchanges" involving gain and loss, deceit or betrayal and exposure, camouflage and discovery.[7]

There are both a great deal more sensible sincerity and a great deal more devious complexity in multidetermined human interaction than is suggested by *Games People Play*.

However, the very fact that games are a caricature of life justifies discussing them. The caricature selects some aspect of human behavior and, extracting it for explicit examination, exaggerates and distorts its contours so that it is easier to perceive. The caricature thus makes possible increased understanding of the phenomenon—in this case the supervisory interaction. The insult to the phenomenon lies in forgetting that the caricature is just that—a caricature and not a truly accurate representation. A perceptive caricature, such as good satire, falsifies by distorting only elements that are actually present in the interaction in the first place. Supervisory games mirror, then, *some* selective, essentially truthful aspects of the supervisory relationship.

The simplest and most direct way of dealing with the problem of games introduced by the supervisee is to refuse to play. Yet one of the key difficulties in this has been implied by discussion of the gain for the supervisor in going along with the game. The supervisee can only successfully enlist the supervisor in a game if the supervisor wants to play for his own reasons. Collusion is not forced but is freely granted. Refusing to play requires the supervisor to be ready and able to forfeit self-advantages. For instance, in declining to go along with the supervisee's requests that he be permitted to ignore agency administrative requirements in playing "Two Against the Agency," the supervisor has to be comfortable in exercising his administrative authority, willing to risk and deal with supervisee hostility and rejection, willing to accept and handle the accusation that he is bureaucratically, rather than professionally, oriented. In declining other games the supervisor denies himself the sweet fruits of flattery, the joys of omniscience, the pleasures of acting the therapist, the gratification of being liked. He has to incur the penalties of an open admission of ignorance and uncertainty and the loss of infallibility. Declining to play the games demands a supervisor who is aware of and comfortable in what he is doing and who is accepting of himself in all his "glorious strengths and human weaknesses." The less vulnerable the supervisor, the more impervious he is to gamesmanship—not an easy prescription to fill.

A second response lies in gradual interpretation or open confrontation. Goffman points out that in the usual social encounter each party accepts the line put out by the other party. There is a process of mutual face-saving in which what is said is accepted at its face value and "each participant is allowed to carry the role he has chosen for himself" unchallenged.[8] This is done out of self-protection since in not challenging another one is also insuring that the other will not, in turn, challenge one's own fiction. Confrontation implies a refusal to accept the game being proposed by seeking to expose and make explicit what the supervisee is doing. The supervisory situation, like the therapeutic situation, deliberately and consciously rejects the usual rules of social interaction in attempting to help the supervisee.

Confrontation is, of course, a procedure that needs to be used with some regard for the supervisee's ability to handle the embarrassment, discomfort, and self-threat it involves. It needs to be used with some understanding of the defensive significance of the game to the supervisee. It might be of importance to point out that naming the interactions that have been described as "games" does not imply that they are frivolous and without consequence. Unmasking games risks much that is of serious personal significance for the supervisee. Interpretation and confrontation here, as always, require some compassionate caution, a sense of timing, and an understanding of dosage.

Perhaps another approach is to share honestly with the supervisee one's awareness of what he is attempting to do but to focus the discussion neither on the dynamics of his behavior nor on one's reaction to it, but on the disadvantages for him in playing games. These games have decided drawbacks for the supervisee in that they deny him the possibility of effectively fulfilling one of the essential, principal purposes of supervision—helping him to grow professionally. The games frustrate the achievement of this outcome. In playing games the supervisee loses by winning.

And, if all else fails, supervisees' games may yield to supervisors' counter-games. For instance, "I Have a Little List" may be broken up by "I Wonder Why You Really Asked That?" After all, the supervisor should have more experience at gamesmanship than the supervisee.

NOTES

1. John Von Neumann, *Theory of Games and Economic Behavior* (Princeton, N.J.: Princeton University Press, 1944); Stephen Potter, *Theory and Practice of Gamesmanship* (New York: Henry Holt & Co., 1948).

2. New York: Grove Press, 1964.

3. *Ibid.*, p. 84.

4. Erving Goffman, *The Presentation of Self in Everyday Life* (Garden City, N.Y.: Anchor Books, Doubleday & Co., 1959), pp. 3–4.

5. Joan Fleming and Therese Benedek, *Psychoanalytic Supervision* (New York: Grune & Stratton, 1966), p. 101. *See* Norman Polansky, "On Duplicity in the Interview," *American Journal of Orthopsychiatry*, Vol. 37, No. 2 (April 1967), pp. 568–579, for a review of similar kinds of games played by the client.

6. H.C.D., "Through Supervision With Gun and Camera," *Social Work Journal*, Vol. 30, No. 4 (October 1949), p. 162.

7. Robert Coles, *New York Times*, Book Review Section (October 8, 1967), p. 8.

8. Erving Goffman, *Ritual Interaction* (Garden City, N.Y.: Anchor Books, Doubleday & Co., 1967), p. 11.

18

Games Supervisors Play

Lillian Hawthorne

WHAT ARE GAMES? Why do people play them? Is game-playing honest? Is it an effective strategy?

Games are defined by Berne as "an ongoing series of complementary ulterior transactions . . . often superficially plausible . . . and progressing to a well-defined, predictable outcome." [1] Four components of this basic statement warrant further definition.

First, the desired outcome of the game is to achieve a payoff for its initiator. For this reason, the essential function of all preliminary moves is to set up conditions that will insure this outcome. The purpose of the payoff is to obtain some internal or external advantage leading to a new or confirmed homeostasis.

A second factor is the ulterior quality of the transactions. This means that "by definition . . . games must have some element of exploitation in them." [2] That is, the initiator seeks to achieve maximum reward at minimum cost and directs his strategies toward this purpose regardless of the effects on his partner in the game.

A third component of the definition is complementarity. The game requires the participation of a responsive, active partner if it is to proceed toward its desired conclusion. As if in contradiction, there must also be some benefit to the partner. Despite the initiator's achievement, the partner must derive a secondary gain, or he will be unwilling to continue playing.

The fourth factor is superficial plausibility. The strategies of the game are not conjured up out of fantasy but have some connection with reality. This connection may be selective in that it can be distorted or misinterpreted to serve the purpose of the game and, at the same time, can be exploited to justify its perpetuation.

DEFENSIVE GAME-PLAYING

Kadushin relates games that are played in the supervisory situation to "the kinds of recurrent interactional incidents between supervisor and supervisee that have a payoff for one of the parties in the transaction." [3] Although his article focuses chiefly on games initiated by supervisees, he does suggest as a possible motivation for supervisors' games the need for defenses against

> . . . felt threats to their position in the hierarchy, uncertainty about their authority, reluctance to use their authority, a desire to be liked, [or] a need for the supervisee's approbation. . . .[4]

In this article, the author will focus on certain games that are played by supervisors and relate principally to problems concerning the supervisors' definition and use of authority. The material presented is based on reading, observation, and personal experience. The author has witnessed these games being played, has been induced to play them, and has even initiated them herself.

Many supervisors, especially new ones, have difficulty adjusting to their new authority. As Reynolds notes, "The balance which they have worked out for their personal lives between dominance and submission is upset by the new responsibility." [5] The supervisory relationship is complex, intense, and intimate. Within this framework, the supervisor must exercise several different kinds of authority—administrative, evaluative, educational, parental, and consultative. It requires effort and experience to integrate these into a comfortable and effective identity. Sometimes the effort is hampered by the supervisor's unfamiliarity with the requirements of his role, by difficulties stemming from personal experiences with authority, or by discomfort in the one-to-one relationship.

The games that will be described are attempts on the part of supervisors to deal with the difficulties surrounding authority. They do not, however, actually resolve the problem, but merely deal with it through different and seemingly contradictory kinds of avoidance. These games fall into two general categories that use almost opposite kinds of strategies but are motivated by the same payoff—the avoidance of a clear definition and exercise of supervisory authority. The first category is referred to as "games of abdication" and the second as "games of power."

In games of abdication, the supervisor deliberately relinquishes authority, manipulates the circumstances so that he is unable to exercise authority, projects the responsbility elsewhere, or uses inappropriate kinds of authority. Perlman describes professional authority as "carrying those rights and powers that are inherent in special knowledge and are vested in special functions." [6] Although she associates this with the case-work process, her point is equally valid in the supervisory relationship. There too, "it is the very assumption that the person carries this authority which infuses the relationship with safety and security and strengthens the response to guidance." [7]

In the second type of game, the supervisor sees his authority as omnipotent and sets up a closed system where every member participating has a fixed assignment from which deviation or negotiation is not permissible. Towle refers to this as "the cult of passivity" in which supervisors deliberately generate helplessness or submission on the part of their supervisees, "perhaps because they themselves experienced this kind of supervision or because for varied reasons they are not secure in their responsibility. . . ." [8]

Although seemingly contradictory in the techniques used, both types of game, if successful, achieve the same payoff for the supervisor. His authority is never clearly defined or validated and, at the same time, his position as supervisor is retained and reinforced.

GAMES OF ABDICATION

One of the most common games of abdication is "They Won't Let Me." Here the supervisor expresses the desire to take or permit some requested action, but does not do so and does not even attempt to explore the possibility of doing so, because his superior in the agency, the regulations, or customary practice will not allow it. "I know this family might be eligible for a special allowance but the deputy won't approve it." "I'd really like to let you make an evening home visit, but no one in the agency does that." "I know this meeting is covering material you're already familiar with, but you're required to attend anyway." The supervisor protects himself from making decisions, from taking risks, from becoming involved in change by projecting onto others the responsibility for his inaction and indecision. By doing this, he accomplishes two things at the same time. He preserves his image by expressing the desire and willingness to take some action and he avoids risking that image by surrendering his authority to anonymous, superior powers. "I'd really like to do it if I could, but they won't let me."

Another common game in this category is "Poor Me." Here the supervisor is so involved with the details of administrative requirements—statistics, reports, surveys—that he has no time for other supervisory tasks. "I wish I had time to discuss that case with you, but I have to complete this report for the deputy." "We'll have to postpone the unit meeting because I was just handed this survey that has to be done immediately." "I'm sorry about having to cancel our weekly conference, but you have no idea how busy I am with these monthly lists for the director."

This results in a reversal of roles in which the supervisor instructs the worker to sympathize with him and not to impose any additional demands. By using these techniques of role reversal and environmental manipulation, the supervisor achieves a double payoff—he retains his positive and sympathetic image and avoids his role responsibilities toward his supervisees.

A third example of a game of abdication appears in two basic variations, "I'm Really One of You" or "I'm Really a Nice Guy." In the first variation, the supervisor seeks approval by supporting his supervisees in all complaints against agency policy, requirements, or expectations. He even relates incidents from his own experience in which he successfully ignored or circumvented agency practices. However, none of his past experiences involved direct confrontation of the disputed issues, nor does his attitude imply any planned action directed at changing regulations.

In the second variation, the supervisor seeks approval and even affection on the basis of personal qualities rather than professional competence. He is an attractive and affable person who socializes freely with his supervisees, or he is a devoted husband and father who relates compassionate and endearing anecdotes about his family. Once the supervisor has been accepted as "one of the crowd" or "really a nice guy," no reasonable supervisee could be critical or demanding of him or become dependent. Whatever variation is used, a double purpose is achieved—the supervisor establishes a benevolent image and is not called on to exercise his supervisory authority.

Another classic game of abdication is referred to by Kadushin as "One Good Question Deserves Another." Here the supervisor invariably responds to questions by asking the worker what he thinks. This transfers the responsibility back to the supervisee at the same time as the supervisor retains his reputation for omniscience. Other ploys are to assign the worker to do some research on the question or to schedule it for fuller discussion at a later date. The worker is thus made to feel that he has raised a significant issue and that his independence of thought and action are being fostered. At the same time, the supervisor has avoided answering, instructing, clarifying, or deciding anything.

There is some essential validity in each of these games, which is what makes them so difficult to deal with and also makes it possible for supervisors to be unaware that they are even playing these games. There are agency policies, requirements, and limitations that restrict supervisory authority and prohibit certain pactices. There are administrative require-ments that may be demanding and time consuming. Certainly it is pleasant for a supervisor to be personable as well as proficient, to be democratic as well as authoritative. Indeed, encouraging independent solutions is a valuable teaching technique. The point is to what extent has the reality of the situation been manipulated to justify or perpetuate the game? Have other options been attempted or even considered? To what extent do the advantages of playing the game outweigh the benefits of solving the problem?

The supervisee acquiesces in these games for various reasons: he is in a vulnerable position in the relationship, he recognizes the essential reality in some of the situations, he likes the supervisor, or he senses the possible advantages that participation gives him. As Kadushin points out:

> The simplest and most direct way of dealing with the problem of games . . . is to refuse to play. The supervisee can only successfully enlist the supervisor in a game if the supervisor wants to play for his own reasons. Collusion is not forced but is freely granted. Refusing to play requires the supervisor to be ready and able to forfeit self-advan-tages.[9]

He also adds that agreeing to play the game implies a mutual face-saving agreement. By not challenging the other, the player insures that he will not be challenged in turn. For the supervisee, the payoff in games of abdication is that few demands or expectations are made of him, few controls are placed on him, few pressures disturb him. He is effectively freed—or abandoned—to do whatever he wishes.

GAMES OF POWER

Games of power can be further divided into subgroups that are distinguished by the degree of benevolence involved. The first two games in this category are less benevolent than the last two, although their strategies are similar and their motivations identical.

The first game is called "Remember Who's Boss." Here the super-visor defines his role as one of absolute power and permits no contra-dictions, disagreements, or negotiations. The supervisor is the critical parent who insists on undeviating obedience. "This is the way things are always done in my unit." "My workers always notify me before leaving for home visits and after coming back." "Everyone in my unit knows I expect them to be at their desks on time." This supervisor implements his control in two ways: (1) explicitly, by frequent reminders of his power, especially in preparing evaluations, and (2) implicitly, by establishing a possessive relationship with his supervisees that clearly delineates his positive as master ("my workers," "my unit").

The supervisor who is most successful at this game is generally one who is a veteran in the agency and who has an impeccable reputation for meeting bureaucratic requirements. The payoff is that the supervisor never has to defend or validate himself because he has placed himself beyond reach. His omnipotence is unquestioned and his closed system remains tightly locked.

"I'll Tell on You" is the name of the second game. It is similiar to the first, except that it relies on a second-hand use of power. The supervisor exercises control by repeated threats of reporting to a higher power—the deputy, director, or administrative board. The supervisor places himself in a weaker position than he held in the first game because he has delegated his power of punishment to the next highest level of authority. For this second-hand control to be effective, he must periodically carry out his threats and is therefore dependent on the hierarchy to validate his power. The payoff in this game would appear to be less effective than in "Remember Who's Boss" because of the supervisor's diminished power. However, many supervisors prefer playing this game because they achieve sufficient power to preserve their status and, at the same time, the burden of disciplinary responsibility is transferred to others. Also the supervisor enjoys the advantage of power by association, which is both flattering and safe.

The next two games are more benevolent in their techniques than the preceding ones, but are similar in that they establish an inflexible and unvalidated relationship of authority. The first is called "Father Knows Best" or "Mother Knows Best," depending on the sex of the supervisor. The supervisor cloaks his control in the garment of parental wisdom and experience. "I'm only telling you this for your own good." "I've had years of experience, so I know what I'm talking about." "This is what has always worked for me, so I know it will work for you." The supervisor is using not his professional competence or knowledge to validate his authority, but his external position—his status, seniority, and past experience.

In this game he assumes the role of wise and guiding parent, and the supervisee the role of helpless, dependent child. But beneath the benevolent role of parent, the superior-subordinate relationship is clearly structured. Any potential threat to the supervisor's power becomes translated into an implicit attack on the act of parenting. As a result, the supervisee is effectively disarmed, and the supervisor retains both his image as benign parent and his undiminished control.

The last game in this category either takes the form of "I'm Only Trying To Help You" or "I Know You Really Can't Do It Without Me." Both are variations of the pseudo-benevolent approach to power and both are based on the assumption of failure or incompetence on the part of the partner. In these variations, control is exercised in the disguise of help, but success is never actually expected or even sought. If anything goes wrong, it is the supervisee's fault because he did not use the proffered help or used it incorrectly. Success is due solely to the supervisor's intervention and not to the worker's action, because recognition of success would threaten their positions in the game. The supervisor assumes that the supervisee is helpless and inadequate and therefore expects little of him. He offers to share the work load because otherwise it would not be properly handled. All this is presented in the form of concern and help.

The message of lowered expectations is clear; the supervisee is instructed not to be competent or independent. He thereby safeguards the supervisor's own need to be effective and indispensable. The success of this game depends on the supervisee's inability to be "helped" or to conform to the supervisor's lower expectations. Towle distinguishes this supervisor from the effective one who "does not waive demands, but . . . affords a relationship oriented to current reality on the assumption that the worker can use it." [10]

The element of reality in each of these situations must be acknowledged. The supervisor does have a responsibility to serve as critic, judge, and controller of the supervisee's actions. The supervisor does have an obligation to keep the administration reliably informed about workers' performances. The supervisor generally does have more professional experience, greater familiarity with and knowledge of agency operations, and often more personal maturity than the worker. The supervisor should attempt to help workers with particular problems and, if necessary and appropriate, adjust their expectations. Again the question is to what extent these realities are exploited as part of the game instead of used as part of the process of resolving problems.

There is also the fact of the supervisee's acquiescence in the games. The supervisee may agree to play the game because he has little alternative in dealing with an authoritarian supervisor. Or he may derive a payoff himself—the benefits of the passive and dependent role. He is relieved of responsibility; he is absolved from making plans or decisions; he escapes all risks. By accepting this role of child toward the powerful parent, the worker reaps the advantages of dependence and irresponsibility. As Scherz points out:

> Dependence is not in and of itself evil, but the unwholesome childish dependence which is stimulated when job responsibilities are ill defined and ill used has created problems in both casework and supervisory practice. Mature interdependence, which results from the appropriate use of the strength of others without loss of self-identity, is actually highly desirable. . . .[11]

RESPONSES TO GAMES

Responses to games can come from the supervisee or from the supervisor himself. The superivsee is generally in too vulnerable a position to deal with games through open confrontation, which Kadushin defines as "a refusal to accept the game being proposed by seeking to expose and make explicit what is being done." [12] To this point, Austin suggests that "if supervisors are not fearful themselves, they can let workers tell them what helps them and what bothers them in their ways of working." [13] But it can be seen that the supervisor's very need to play these games implies the absence of the kind of relationship or environment that would make such an exchange possible. If the supervisee is also willing to forego his own advantages and assume some risks, there are other ways in which he can refuse to play the game.

With the abdicating supervisor, he can present his needs for professional help explicitly, persistently, and in a nonthreatening way. He can clearly and honestly share with the supervisor his professional needs and his concerns about fulfilling them effectively. He can use the countergame "I Know You Can Help Me," thus appealing to the supervisor's expertise and experience, or the one "I Know You Can Help Me Get Help," appealing to the supervisor's parental instincts to direct him to other appropriate sources of help. This last countergame must be practiced with caution for fear that it could impugn the supervisor's ability or undermine his role. Or the worker can turn to an available consultant —adviser or specialist in staff training—for intervention. In this case, the supervisee must be clearly aware of his real needs and be able to present them objectively and without recrimination.

With the authoritarian supervisor, confrontation is probably inadvisable, but a process of gradual interpretation may be possible. The supervisee can attempt to expand the constraints by testing independent ideas and by validating his right to independence through achievement. In following this course, he must be meticulously careful to operate within agency policies, and procedures.

He can counteract the threat of "I'll Tell on You" by honestly acknowledging the supervisor's responsibility to evaluate him and accepting responsibility for his own actions. Or he may play the countergame "I Learned Everything I Know from You," which will preserve the supervisor's influence at the same time as it validates his own independent performance. At all times, the supervisee must be careful to focus his attention on the professional problem and not on the dynamics of personal behavior.

For the supervisor to deal with his own games is a more complex and subtle task. He may not be consciously aware that he is playing these games, because each one is partly rooted in reality and may appear superficially reasonable and appropriate. The supervisor who plays these games consciously may be doing so to protect himself from feelings of insecurity. He will understandably be reluctant to

> . . . risk and deal with supervisee hostility and rejection. . . . In declining other games the supervisor denies himself the sweet fruits of flattery, the joys of omniscience, the pleasures of acting the therapist, the gratification of being liked. He has to incur the penalties of an open admission of ignorance and uncertainty and the loss of infallibility.[14]

The supervisor must examine his own feelings and needs concerning his professional role. He must decide what he wants to give as a supervisor and what he wants to get, and whether these are appropriate and congruent. He must be sensitive to the responses of the supervisee and the meaning his behavior communicates. Is the worker generally acquiescent or open? Is he conforming or concerned? Is he anxious or active? The supervisor must examine to what extent his own behavior has programmed these kinds of responses and what benefits he has derived from those responses. In other words, he must become aware of the payoffs from the games he plays and he must assess honestly whether these are compatible with his supervisory role. He must explore whether a professionally responsible position can be better maintained through other kinds of behavior, such as "good" games. Berne defines these as games

> . . . whose social contribution outweighs the complexity of their motivations . . . and which contribute both to the well-being of the other players and to the unfolding of the one who is "it." [15]

The supervisor who experiences discomfort in his role and dissatisfaction with his gamesmanship may also turn to a consultant for help. Unfortunately, this rarely happens unless the games are not working, at which point intervention is sought as a corrective measure by the other person in the game. The more aware of and comfortable with himself the supervisor is, the less need he will have for gamesmanship. As Reynolds wrote:

> Once a supervisor has given up trying to answer all questions, and knows that his skill consists in drawing others out, clarifying responsibilities, contributing what is known from theory and experience, his position is no longer terrifying but rather exhilarating. A leader, no less than those who are led, is sustained by the sharing of responsibility, not only with those who may be above him but just as truly with all those with whom he works.[16]

The supervisor who continues to rely on these games to defend himself actually loses by winning, for he deprives himself of both the tasks and the joys of his role.

NOTES

1. Eric Berne, *Games People Play* (New York: Grove Press, 1964), p. 48.
2. Ibid., p. 163.
3. Alfred Kadushin, "Games People Play in Supervision," *Social Work*, 13 (July 1968), p. 23 [Chapter 17 above, p. 182].
4. Ibid., p. 30.
5. Bertha Reynolds, *Learning and Teaching in the Practice of Social Work* (New York: Farrar & Rinehart, 1942), p. 305.
6. Helen Harris Perlman, *Social Casework* (Chicago: University of Chicago Press, 1957), p. 69.
7. Ibid., p. 69.
8. Charlotte Towle, "The Place of Help in Supervision," *Social Service Review*, 37 (December 1963), p. 404.
9. Kadushin, op. cit., p. 31.
10. Towle, op. cit., p. 405.
11. Frances Scherz, "A Concept of Supervision Based on Definitions of Job Responsibility," *Social Casework*, 39 (October 1958), p. 442 [Chapter 8 above, p. 81].
12. Kadushin, op. cit., p. 321.
13. Lucille Austin, "Basic Principles of Supervision," *Social Casework*, 33 (December 1952), p. 416 [Chapter 7 above, p. 64].
14. Kadushin, op cit., p. 31.
15. Berne, op. cit., p. 163.
16. Reynolds, op. cit., p. 305.

19

The Professional Social Worker in a Bureaucracy

Harry Wasserman

THE PROFESSIONAL SOCIAL WORKER in a public welfare bureaucracy serves two masters—his professional self, embodying intellectual and moral criteria, and his employing organization, with its demands and constraints. In a previous article the author discussed the general question of the comparative influence of social work education and structural constraints on social work practice.* In this article he discusses specifically the neophyte professional social worker's life in a bureaucracy. Some of the areas that will be explored are the following: How does the bureaucratic structure support or constrain the worker's professional activities? What is the nature of the transactions and interactions he makes in order to perform his role as efficiently and effectively as possible? How does he maneuver within the bureaucracy to gain what he needs for his clients? In what ways does the bureaucratic structure manipulate him?

POSITION OF RELATIVE POWERLESSNESS

The formal organization of the agency involved in this study places the professional social worker at one of the lower levels of authority

---

* The study on which this article and the author's previous article were based involved observing twelve new professional social workers over a two-year period. For an overall discussion of the study and some general theoretical considerations, *see* Harry Wasserman, "Early Careers of Professional Social Workers in a Public Child Welfare Agency," *Social Work*, Vol. 15, No. 3 (July 1970), pp. 93–101; Chapter 24 below.

and power. Administratively he is responsible to the following ascending hierarchy; a supervisor who is his immediate superior, a deputy director who fills the role of a chief of supervisors, a district director, and higher administrators who are physically and operationally removed from the worker's daily activities because they are located in the agency's central office. Operationally, however, it is the supervisor to whom the worker turns for expertise, guidance, and organizational support.

An analysis of supervisor-worker transactions reveals some aspects of the way the bureaucratic structure works. Each supervisor is administratively responsible for five workers and generally meets with each one on a regular basis (e.g., once a week or once every two weeks). The supervisor is also available as an emergency consultant at unscheduled times. During supervisory conferences, the worker explains what he has been doing, discusses problems in case management, negotiates for the fulfillment of clients' material needs, and seeks advice and guidance concerning the problems of specific clients. This practice is fairly typical of supervisor-worker transactions. It is quite striking, however, that the supervisor rarely meets with his five workers as a group except when new regulations, rules, and procedures must be explained. During the two-year span of the study there were no group meetings with a supervisor for the purpose of discussing case problems rather than administrative procedures. This fact raises the following questions: Why are so few group meetings of supervisors and workers initiated by the supervisors? Conversely, why is it that professional social workers never insist on having group meetings to discuss and grapple with the common recurrent problems and issues they face?

There are several factors that, when acting together, militate against group meetings. The administration can more effectively maintain control over the workers if workers must deal with their supervisor as individual entrepreneurs or contractors. For instance, a particularly resourceful and ingenious young worker, who is capable of providing special items for his clients, might inadvertently disclose in formal sessions the many ways to "work the system." *

By negotiating with the worker at the formal level of supervision as if he were a private entrepreneur, the administration avoids the introduction of resourcefulness and ingenuity into the formal system. On the other hand, by accomplishing things for his clients, the worker receives gratification that sustains him in his work. Paradoxically, however, it is clear that the individual worker's successes serve to gloss over or cover

---

* In "working the system," some workers develop informal alliances with supervisors, cashiers, and clerks, who then serve as expediters. If the workers are relatively moderate in their demands, they can be quite successful in obtaining material goods for their clients, as well as jobs, housing, and medical care. Evidently, these alliances are known to those who must process special requests, and the worker may discuss some of his moves with others, but the extralegal moves are kept secret.

up the harsh inadequacies of the system. In struggling for successful outcomes within his own caseload, the worker tends to forget that the penurious institutional resources are abrasive and harmful to significant numbers of families and children whose social workers are less endowed with the qualities of resourcefulness and ingenuity.

The questionable legal maneuvers to protect clients from what, in the worker's opinion, are excessively harsh rules and regulations are justified by the worker as "situation ethics." [1] For example, the worker obtains an increase in a foster family's monthly grant because the foster child has a behavior disorder (the child actually does not, but the worker feels that because the foster parents are doing a good job they deserve a few extra dollars per month); an adolescent foster child earns enough money to necessitate recomputing his grant, but the worker "forgets" about it; or an AFDC mother has a friend who contributes financially, but the worker "forgets" about it. Although the worker may try to convince himself of the validity of his position, he does not quite succeed. He feels guilty, tense, and uneasy when he has acted in a questionable, unethical manner.

WORKERS' PERCEPTION OF SUPERVISION

Most of the workers in the study had more than one line supervisor during their period of employment with the agency; only three of the twelve judged their supervisors to be competent and therefore helpful. The majority of these young workers perceived the supervisory position to be primarily a bureaucratic control device; thus the way the supervisors functioned had little or nothing to do with social work values, knowledge, and skills.

The supervisor performs the function of organizational mediator; he makes judgments and decisions about workers' claims and demands on behalf of their clients on the basis of the agency's scarce resources. In other words, he negotiates on behalf of the organization with the worker who represents the clients.

The supervisor rarely sees the worker's clients except in emergencies. His role is to talk about clients, not to them. Thus he only knows the client through the worker and must make reasoned judgments and decisions based on a complex of variables that includes the client's actual situation, the worker's perception and definition of that situation, and the agency's capacity to provide an item or series of items. If the supervisor is responsible for five workers with a total of 175–200 cases or more, one questions whether he can make reasoned and balanced judgments about any problematic human situations, particularly when he must base his judgments on what the workers say about clients.

The majority of the new workers viewed their supervisors as insecure and frightened people who were unsure of their authority and power, conforming, lacking courage, unwilling to take a stand on critical issues involving either workers or clients, and more sensitized and attuned to organizational demands and needs than to those of the clients. They also believed that the system wanted passive, uninspired people in supervisory positions, that the need for supervisors with master's degrees was just another manifestation of our "credential society"; [2] that credentials and comformity were more important for system maintenance than knowledge, competence, and skill; and that image and facade were valued more highly than reality and substance.

The agency's utilization, whenever possible, of graduate social work supervisory personnel and the lack of resistance of supervisory personnel to the impediments of the system probably accounted, in part, for the noticeable increase in cynicism among the new workers during the two-year period of study. This growing cynicism, plus the frustrations of working with difficult clients (many of whom were chronically in disastrous situations) and the cumulative reactions of physical and emotional fatigue, inevitably produced situations of great stress. The workers protected themselves in such situations, but the cost was the reinforcement of their natural defense mechanisms to the point of rigidity and brittleness.* Functionally this meant that they worked with many of their clients in a routine, uninspired way.

There are two solutions to such a dilemma. The worker can remain in the agency and eventually be promoted to a supervisory position, which will remove him from the clients, or he can leave the agency for another job (the solution chosen by six of the workers in the study.) † If he remains and becomes a supervisor, he will adapt to the system. He may rationalize that he will do things differently and try to change the system, but he realizes that because bureaucracies do not change easily, structural change is a tremendously difficult, long-term undertaking. As Dahrendorf explains:

> Bureaucratic organizations typically display continuous gradations of competence and authority and are hierarchical. Within dichotomous organizations class conflict is possible; within hierarchical organizations it is not. This difference has an important consequence for the definition of bureaucratic roles. Insofar as bureaucratic roles are defined

---

* As reported in Wasserman, op. cit., three of the twelve new professionals in the study suffered from psychiatric difficulties that they believed were triggered by their work situations.

† At the termination of the study, eight of the twelve new professionals had left the agency. Six of the resignations were voluntary and two were involuntary (one worker was drafted into the armed forces; the other moved to another city as a consequence of her husband's employment situation).

in the context of a career hierarchy, they do not generate a [class] conflict of interest with other bureaucratic roles.[3]

This means that all employees of a bureaucracy, regardless of their hierarchical status, are essentially ". . . on the same side of the fence that divides the positions of dominance from those of subjection."[4] In the long run, it is extremely difficult for a professional social worker in a bureaucracy to be an impassioned advocate for his clients, because in so doing he must come into conflict with agency administrators as well as professional colleagues. If he cannot mobilize the support of both colleagues and welfare rights or other organizations that represent clients, he will be forced to leave the agency. If the new professional remains in the agency and eventually moves to the position of supervisor, he is constrained to "play the game," which includes accepting the meager systemic inputs and the dysfunctional aspects of the bureaucratic structure.*

WORKERS' VIEW OF THE ADMINISTRATION

Almost invariably the new professionals in this study looked on the higher administrators of the agency as "them." The administrators were not quite "the enemy," but they were viewed as being unconcerned about the worker's involvements with his clients, except when financial accountability was an issue. The most important indication of the administrators' lack of concern for clients, according to the observations of the workers, was the nature of the communication system, which was generally a one-way flow from top to bottom.

One of the assumptions of the "rational" system of organization is that knowledge, competence, authority, and important decision-making are at the top of the organizational pyramid and ignorance, passivity, and capacity for routine performance are on the bottom. As Blau and Scott point out, when the need for a highly coordinated organization is imperative, communication is of low organizational value.[5] This generalization also applies to the agency in which the flow of information from top to bottom is considered the normal pathway and direction of communication. It is true that workers can write memorandums to higher administrators through their supervisor, but these are rarely acted on. Therefore, the workers virtually have no way to voice their work needs, observations, good ideas, or creative innovations.

---

* In a bureaucracy a skeleton of "permanent cadre"—supervisors and administrators, professional and nonprofessional—maintain the system. Many of them have become thoroughly acclimated to the system. Little research has been done on either the self-concepts or the sociological functions of these long-term employees.

The social work education of these neophyte professionals apparently gave them no experience in working together as members of a professional collectivity, e.g., in identifying their clients' needs or gaps in programs, social resources, and social utilities. As a professional group with a sense of collective responsibility, social workers do not pressure the system on behalf of clients—they accept the system. For example, the workers studied were prone to make such statements as the following: "You can't fight city hall," "The county supervisors [commissioners] are the real bosses," "What's the use of trying to change things when it's impossible to do so," and so forth. Such statements connote more than poor morale; they are part of a system of beliefs. Such defeatism and cynicism (as cognitive and emotional "sets") are psychological reflections of what Kenniston calls the "institutionalization of hypocrisy":

> Of course, no society ever fully lives up to its own professed ideals. In every society there is a gap between creedal values and actual practices, and in every society, the recognition of this gap constitutes a powerful motor for social change. But in most societies, especially when change is slow and institutions are powerful and unchanging, there occurs what can be termed institutionalization of hypocrisy.[6]

The social welfare bureaucracy only expresses the profound hypocrisy of a larger society. The agency is neither the conspiracy of a small group nor the perpetual fiefdom of cruel men who have deliberately decided to harm or destroy families and children. The agency's cruelty reflects society's pejorative attitudes about broken poor families who must rely on the public for special kinds of aid.

Dahrendorf explains the purposes and functions of bureaucracies and their power position in society as follows:

> . . . although . . . [bureaucracies] always belong to the ruling class, because bureaucratic roles are roles of dominance, bureaucracies as such never are the ruling class. Their latent interests aim at the maintenance of what exists; but what it is that exists is not decided by bureaucracies, but given to them. . . .[7]

Dahrendorf's conceptualization of the purposes and functions of bureaucracies is dramatically illustrated by the fact that financial accountability is the supreme value, and all other values are subordinate to it. For example, the social worker with a master's degree is not permitted to make a judgment or decision about a client's need for an extra grocery order; he must obtain authorization from two higher supervisor-administrators. If translated into whether the professional social worker is capable of making judgments and decisions about a client whose immediate future is hunger, the overriding organizational value of financial accountability means, in an objective sense, indignity and humiliation for the worker. Subjectively, some of the new workers felt this indignity and humiliation; others did not.

CLIENTS AS OBJECTS

Bureaucratic inefficiency is usually equated with an excessive amount of menial activities, e.g., red tape, paper work, and the like. The new professionals in the study complained about the amount of paper work, but, when emotionally unable to see clients, even the most committed workers found respite in paper work and other office routines. Most professional social workers protest that such routine activities as maintaining files, keeping records, and collating statistics are beneath their professional competence; yet it is such menial work that allows them to objectify their clients, i.e., to regard them as objects rather than people. To preserve his mental health, a worker must not be too sensitive about the clients' plight or become too involved with their "outcomes." Thus although bureaucratic procedures that cause dehumanization of clients are severely criticized, they are probably a psychic necessity for some workers.

What then is questionable and inevitably harmful in the process of client "objectification"? It is that the bureaucracy tends to dehumanize recipients by viewing them as cases and numbers or as objects related to financial accountability. If it is inevitable that workers will dehumanize their clients because psychologically they need to perceive them as abstractions, what does finally intervene on behalf of the client? It is simply the "sometimes" humanity of the worker. The word sometimes is critical, because it is psychologically impossible for a worker constantly to be a feeling, responsive human who is prepared at all times to cope with human disorder and disaster. However, the fact that the worker sometimes treats the client as a worthwhile human being keeps the system partially viable and, more important, the client feels that someone does care for him.

However, the cumulative effects of insufficient resources, bureaucratic structure, and personal fallibility finally can force the workers toward

> working on a different set of problems from those the . . . [organization] has set for them. . . . There is a sharp distinction that must be made between behavior that *copes* with the requirements of a problem and behavior that is designed to *defend* against entry into the problem. It is the distinction one might make between playing tennis on the one hand and fighting like fury to stay off the tennis court altogether on the other.[8]

The worker can defend himself by becoming overinvolved in paper work, a specific case, informal meetings with colleagues, aimless driving, and so on. In other words, he can spend a large amount of time avoiding meaningful encounters with clients.

The bureaucratic system stimulates and reinforces defending rather than coping behavior by keeping the worker off balance. The constant changes in caseloads, rules, regulations, and procedures imposed from above produce a state of insecurity and instability in the worker. Thus the new professional's underinvolvement in initiating or participating in the creation of policies and procedures was undoubtedly another important cause of excessive defending behavior and low morale.

INFORMAL ORGANIZATIONS

According to Gouldner, informal organizations are "spontaneously emergent and normatively sanctioned structures in the organization." [9] Although one of the latent functions of the informal organization is to permit people to act as people rather than as occupants of specific positions or as incumbents of a structured role, organizational theorists generally assume that the informal organization in a bureaucracy tends to support the goals of the formal organization.

The informal organization—which must be understood specifically in this context as small groups of two or more people who are peers—primarily serves two functions: (1) it is the focal point for expressing complaints about the agency and (2) it is the most important social system for providing emotional support for workers and a sense of mutuality among them. [10] Workers let off steam in their informal meetings with colleagues while working at their desks, when they meet other workers accidentally in the halls, and during planned and unplanned coffee breaks. Their complaints cover a wide range of difficulties involving clients, other workers, supervisors, bureaucratic obstacles, and so on.

More important than the content of the complaints, however, are the latent functions of these informal gripe sessions: They provide emotional support for the worker in the sense that he can talk to a peer who understands, and they are a mechanism for draining off and deflecting the worker's need for a more formally organized, systematic approach to his problem as a worker in a bureaucracy. Thus although some of the verbal attacks against the agency are subversive in the sense that they frequently carry a high anti-authority component, the complaining done in the informal group is essentially functional to the maintenance of the formal system's equilibrium. As Coser has shown, much social conflict can be encapsulated within a social structure; in fact social conflict often supports it. [11]

In district offices where there were other professional workers, the new professionals were members of small informal groups. In those offices in which there were few, if any, professional social workers, the new professional was almost totally isolated. The workers who gave and received emotional support from informal relationships unquestionably had higher morale than those who were deprived of this experience. When the new worker was the only professional or one of few professionals, he tended to reject the camaraderie of the nonprofessionals because he saw himself as different from them. This was probably a defensive reaction against the nonprofessionals, who saw him as a threat because he was engaged in the same work but received greater financial rewards and a higher status.

CONCLUSION

The large public welfare agency—with its bureaucratic structure—is the embodiment of a profound moral ambivalence toward the people it serves. On the one hand, its manifest purpose is to help needy persons; on the other hand, its latent function is to "punish" those who are unable to maintain independent successful lives by failing to provide conditions by which they can help themselves or be helped. Its main aim is financial accountability—not accountability to the people it serves.

The social worker in such a bureaucracy is caught up in this brutal intersection of contradictory values. If he actually tries to help his clients and "buck" the organization, he often suffers from emotional and physical fatigue and becomes cynical and defeatist about the nature of social work. If he adapts to the bureaucracy, he at best experiences massive frustration; at worst he becomes a "mindless functionary." [12]

It is time for the social work profession, bureaucrats, and schools of social work to stop hiding their knowledge of bureaucracies. What we now need are new ideas, concepts, and models—in short, a new vision to reconstruct our working lives and new ways to relate to each other and to those we serve.

NOTES

1. Joseph Fletcher, *Situation Ethics* (Philadelphia: Westminster Press, 1966).
2. *See* Edgar Z. Friedenberg, "Status and Role in Education," *Humanist,* Vol. 28, No. 5 (September–October 1968), p. 13.
3. Ralf Dahrendorf, *Class and Class Conflict in Industrial Society* (Stanford, Calif.: Stanford University Press, 1959), p. 296.
4. Ibid.
5. Peter M. Blau and W. Richard Scott, *Formal Organizations: A Comparative Approach* (San Francisco: Chandler Publishing Co., 1962), p. 242.

6. Kenneth Kenniston, "Youth, Change and Violence," *American Scholar*, Vol. 37, No. 2 (Spring 1968), p. 239.

7. Dahrendorf, op. cit., p. 300.

8. Jerome S. Bruner, *Toward a Theory of Instruction* (Cambridge, Mass.: Harvard University Press, 1966), pp. 3–4.

9. Alvin W. Gouldner, "Organizational Analysis," in Robert K. Merton et al., eds., *Sociology Today* (New York: Basic Books, 1959), p. 406.

10. *See* Earl Bogdanoff and Arnold Glass, *The Sociology of the Public Assistance Caseworker in an Urban Area.* Unpublished master's thesis, University of Chicago, 1954.

11. Lewis A. Coser, *The Functions of Social Conflict* (London: Routledge & Kegan Paul, 1956).

12. Hannah Arendt, *Eichmann in Jerusalem: A Report on the Banality of Evil* (New York: Viking Press, 1964), p. 289.

20

The Ethics of Supervision

Charles S. Levy

CONSIDERABLE ATTENTION has been paid in the social work literature to the purposes, skills, and processes of supervision. But the subject of ethics in supervision has been virtually neglected. This article discusses some of the reasons for according to ethics in supervision a high priority, particularly because of current conditions in the field.

Six conditions that presently exist in social work make the formulation and implementation of an ethic for supervision in social work more imperative than ever before: (1) resources for social work training and education have been reduced or eliminated, (2) social agencies are finding it difficult to raise funds for their programs, (3) what was formerly a tight labor market has become a tight job market, (4) social work education at the bachelor's degree and associate degree levels has increased, (5) agencies are employing greater numbers of paraprofessional personnel, and (6) professional personnel are increasingly deployed in supervisory positions.

NATURE OF SUPERVISION

Supervision has been described as an administrative process designed to improve services to clients through the "development of the worker's skill in the employment of agency-structured processes." [1] Though intended to facilitate the agency's work, supervision implies a teaching function because ideally it is aimed at the "continued development of staff competence." [2] In other words, it is not inconsistent with the supervisor's administrative accountability for him to be guided in his supervisory practice as much by his supervisees' learning needs as by agency demands and the supervisee's responsibility to clients. Williamson's early definition of supervision went so far as to recommend a concern for supervisees' satisfaction:

> [Supervision is] a process by which workers . . . who, as individuals, have a direct responsibility for carrying out some part of the agency's program plan, are helped by a designated staff member to learn according to their needs, to make the best use of their knowledge and skills, and to improve their abilities so that they do their jobs more effectively and with increasing satisfaction to themselves and to the agency.[3]

The following is perhaps a more extended conception of the supervisor's responsibility:

> . . . the social work supervisor, by virtue of the role to which he is assigned in the agency and by virtue of the relationship through which he activates that role, helps his supervisee to do a better job for the agency and to become a creative and proficient social worker in his own right. Through the supervisory process, the social work supervisor helps the supervisee become equipped to undertake greater or different responsibilities within the same agency or in another agency. Through the supervisory process, the social work supervisor encourages the supervisee to participate in research and otherwise to make his practice the medium for the conscious examination not only of his own practice but social work practice in general, and for the development of social work theory. These gains are not designed for the advancement of the agency's purposes alone, but they will accrue to the agency just as the social worker, who comes to the agency after a salutary developmental experience in another agency, will bring his gains with him to the advantage of the clientele he will be serving in the new setting.[4]

This conception of the nature of supervision in social work may seem idealistic, if not excessive, but it describes what supervision ought to and can be. Moreover, it provides the framework within which the ethics of supervision in social work may be optimally conceived.

EMPHASIS ON ETHICS

Despite the genuine need for social workers today, there are fewer jobs (or at least fewer job choices) for professionally educated social workers (those with master's degrees) than there have been for at least a generation. The jobs that are available put a greater premium on supervisory skill and responsibility than ever before, since so many positions have been opened to personnel with no or limited formal professional education.

The trend in the 1950s and early 1960s to devalue supervision as a developmental process affecting professionally educated social workers has reversed in the direction of emphasizing the supervisory role of professionally educated social workers in relation to paraprofessional personnel and graduates of bachelor's and associate degree social work programs. The mobility and opportunities of these nonprofessional personnel are limited unless they have access to additional professional credentials. But their access has been considerably circumscribed in the last year or so because resources for scholarships, traineeships, and educational leaves have diminished. When they do have such access, the tight job market for professionally educated social workers may restrict their professional aspirations. In short, social work personnel are in a bind, and their supervisors hold more power than they have for some time. Therefore, a special and perhaps enforceable set of ethics is required to guide the supervisor's conduct.

Goldhamer and Shils defined power as the extent to which a person "influences the [covert or overt] behavior of others in accordance with his own intentions," and Weber has described it as "the probability that one actor within a social relationship will be in a position to carry out his will, despite resistance." [5] Thibaut's and Kelley's conception of power as fate and behavior control is especially relevant to the supervisor-supervisee relationship in social work:

> If two persons interact, the pattern of outcomes given in their interaction matrix indicates that each person has the possibility of affecting the other's reward-cost positions and, thereby, of influencing or controlling him. . . . In other words, the matrix reveals that each person has certain possibilities for exercising power over the other. [Conversely, the effect may be dependence.] . . . If, by varying his behavior, A can affect B's outcomes *regardless of what B does*, A has *fate control* over B. . . . The larger the range of outcome values through which A can move B, the greater his fate control over B.
>
> A second kind of power is called *behavior control*. If, by varying his behavior, A can make it desirable for B to vary his behavior too, then A has behavior control over B. . . . The amount of this behavior control will depend upon the values to B of the various outcomes. . . . B's outcomes vary not as a function either of A's behavioral choices (fate control) or of his own but as a function of the interaction between them. [6]

SOURCES OF POWER

Aside from current conditions in social work that reinforce the supervisor's power over the supervisee, the following characteristics of the supervisory relationship contribute to the supervisor's control over the supervisee:

The supervisor has administratively assigned and sanctioned authority over the supervisee. The supervisory relationship is usually a condition of the supervisee's employment: i.e., a supervisor is *assigned* to the supervisee; he is not an optional figure in the supervisee's agency career. Supervisory responsibility is usually defined in terms of control over the supervisee and the supervisee's accountability to the supervisor, although a common implicit or explicit component of that responsibility is the provision of assistance and guidance.

The supervisor mediates the relationship between the supervisee and the agency. Depending on the supervisor's position in the agency hierarchy and the function he performs in it, he represents and interprets the supervisee to those in higher authority and in turn determines whether and how the agency will be represented and interpreted to the supervisee. The higher the supervisor's hierarchical position, of course, the greater his potential influence and control over the supervisee will be.

The supervisor usually has a role to play in hiring or firing the supervisee. The higher his hierarchical position in the agency, the greater his immediate jurisdiction over the supervisee's job and the greater his power over the supervisee will be. However, any supervisor has some jurisdiction over his supervisee's job, because he is in a position to judge the supervisee's job performance. The more the supervisee needs the job and the less mobile he feels because of his personal or professional limitations or limited job opportunities, the less independent he tends to feel. As Mills points out:

> In almost any job, the employee sells a degree of his independence; his working life is within the domain of others; the level of his skills that are used and the areas in which he may exercise independent decisions are subject to management by others.[7]

The supervisor is certainly one of these "others" and often a significant one in the supervisee's life.

The supervisor controls the supervisee's salary increases and promotions and determines the kind of entries that will appear in his record. Thus although the supervisee's job may not be threatened, his status and movement in it are likely to be contingent on the supervisor's appraisal of his performance—however accurate or inaccurate, relevant or irrelevant.

> The comparative intimacy of the supervisory relationship and the recognized factors of control in it tend to make it a sphere in which one can do, with comparative safety, many of the things one might like to do in other relationships, in which one is held back for one reason or another. . . . It must be recognized . . . that it is possible to misuse a situation in which there are so many factors favorable to one party in the relationship. . . . This inequality is epitomized, so to speak, in the super-

visor's power to evaluate. This is a power of which the supervisee is conscious.[8]

Implicit in the following admonitory statement regarding the supervisor's authority to grant salary increases is the nature of the power this authority implies and the possibility of abusing it:

> Authority over the granting of increases is not designed as a punitive device for irresponsible use. It is definitely *not* a license for a supervisor to penalize an employee without fully explaining the reason for the penalty or without an opportunity for the employee to present his side of the case fully to someone other than the supervisor.[9]

Although the supervisor is not inevitably more professionally competent than the supervisee, he almost invariably knows more than the supervisee about some things. To the extent that he does, he has power to wield over the supervisee. If he is also more experienced in and knowledgeable about the supervisee's job, his power is increased. Perlman has alluded to "knowledge and know-how" as a source of power that certainly affects an uneducated or inexperienced supervisee.[10] The supervisor may not possess greater professional wisdom and acumen than the supervisee, but if the supervisee *believes* he does, the supervisor has power over him. This is understandable because the supervisee reacts to the supervisor "as a symbol of a system and not just a person." [11]

Although some indigenous nonprofessional workers may be cynical about a supervisor's professional knowledge, the supervisor, as part of management, is likely to have knowledge and information to which the supervisee does not have ready access. Thus the supervisor is a channel of communication and may, if he wishes to achieve some strategic end, parcel out information or withhold it altogether. This ability to censor information is a form of managerial power that may be "converted to personal influence." [12]

The supervisor's stance of possessing superior knowledge—whether his knowledge is actual or the supervisee merely believes it is—becomes a "manipulative controlling device." Therefore, if the supervisee's judgment differs from his supervisor's, the supervisor may accuse him of being unable to accept supervision.[13] Although the supervisor may genuinely believe he is right, his position permits him the unilateral option of deciding so, and the insecure or uncertain supervisee has neither the competence nor choice to doubt him.

The supervisor expects, if not requires, the supervisee to reveal much about himself in the supervisory relationship. Thus the supervisee exposes himself to the risk of having such revelations used inappropriately or misused, at least in ways that are disadvantageous to him. Obviously, it is invalid to discuss, during supervisory conferences, information that is related more to the supervisee's private life than his job performance.

But this may happen unless both supervisee and supervisor exercise self-discipline in their relationship.

However, even if their discussions are relevant to the supervisee's job and to the agency, the supervisor is in a position to use or misuse whatever the supervisee reveals. In fact, if the supervisee fails to identify weaknesses and impediments he is aware of in his own performance and development as a practitioner, he may be viewed as aborting or hindering his opportunities to receive the supervisor's professional help and guidance, which are considered legitimate supervisory functions. The supervisor, on the other hand, is not expected to reciprocate. He is expected to exercise sufficient control over his conversations with the supervisee to keep the focus of attention on the supervisee and his job, unless discussing his own role will implement his supervisory function in relation to the supervisee. The important implication is not that the supervisor will misuse information the supervisee reveals, but that such abuse is possible and the supervisee feels vulnerable as a result.

The supervisor's influence extends beyond the supervisee's tenure on the job. Judgments about the supervisee's performance in the agency, as well as the way in which these judgments are phrased, affect the supervisee long afterward. For example, the less accurate or fair the supervisor's reference letter is, the more it can skew the supervisee's future job opportunities.

Reynolds long ago assembled a set of principles governing the supervisor's responsibility to write reference letters that are timely, current, job related, and so on.[14] These principles attest to the enduring nature of the supervisor's fate and behavior control over the supervisee and suggest the relative powerlessness of supervisees who find themselves haunted and victimized by written judgments that may not have been or no longer are fair estimates of their performance (or perhaps are not germane in substance or interpretation to the purposes for which they are used).

ETHICAL IMPLICATIONS

No doubt there are many other sources of supervisory power, but those just mentioned demonstrate the importance of a code of ethics for supervisors. The fate and behavior control that supervisors can wield over supervisees dictates at least restraint and at best creativity in performing their supervisory function. Guides are essential not only with respect to the skills a supervisor must have, but with respect to the ethics required. London's comment about power in the behavioral sciences in general applies as well to supervision:

> Control means power. Behavior control means power over people. . . .
> The moral problem of behavor control is the problem of how to use
> power justly. . . . All good people who have power over others, even just
> a little power for just a little while, need access to an ethic that can
> guide their use of it.[15]

This view of the supervisor's power does not assume that the power
is unilateral in nature or that the supervisee is completely powerless.
Nor does it assume that formal or informal regulatory media to contain
the supervisor's relative power or protect the supervisee are absent. Such
media indeed exist, and supervisees are hardly bereft of power. Some
supervisees—especially, perhaps, untrained personnel—are masters at the
"negotiation of systems": i.e., the use of organized pressure and even
intimidation to effectively restrain wayward or cowed supervisors. Nevertheless, the nature and sources of supervisory authority and the characteristics of the supervisory function and relationship compel the conclusion that the supervisor is in an advantageous position, although the
degree of his advantage varies. Therefore, a code of ethics for supervision inheres in the nature of the supervisory situation. An understanding of that situation as it affects the supervisee suggests the following
principles that might serve as a guide for ethical use of the supervisor's
power.

1. The supervisor must regard an ethical act not as the *best* or most
practical course in a given circumstance, but as the *right* thing to do
because of the supervisee's relatively disadvantageous position. An ethical act is not measured by its consequences but by its intentions and
whether it is consonant with specific values. As Edel points out, "Ethical
principles are themselves values." [16]

Kant regarded ethics as "a doctrine of ends" and as supplying laws
for the maxims of action rather than for the actions themselves.[17] Supervisory practice in an agency can hardly be guided less by agency values
than the agency's service to clients. In fact, supervisory practice may
serve as a model for helping relationships with others and thus inspire
ethical practice and the application of those values that the agency and
the social work profession assert they believe in. The supervisor's scrupu-
lous regard for the supervisee's welfare and development therefore stems
not only from the definition of the supervisor's function in the agency but
from his concern for the supervisee as a human being—a concern to
which the supervisor is committed as a professional social worker.

2. When the supervisor participates in the process of employing the
supervisee and fashioning his job assignment, he is subject to ethical
constraints that transcend his professional responsibility. Ethics demand
his unbiased consideration and a considerate approach in evaluating the

supervisee for the job. The supervisee should be assigned to a job in which he can succeed and one that is worthy of him—whether or not it proves to be practical for the agency.

3. The supervisor *owes* the supervisee a good start, and it is his ethical obligation to provide whatever the supervisee needs to do his job. Even if the supervisor is never held accountable for the supervisee's ultimate failure in the job, he should feel the personal accountability that results from ethical responsibility if the supervisee's failure may be attributed in any way to his negligence in providing assistance or opportunities that might have led to the supervisee's success.

True, social work supervision is by definition a helping process concerned with

> teaching certain contents of knowledge and skill and helping workers to learn. [But] this helping relationship may facilitate or obstruct the learning process, depending on its nature. . . .
>
> The supervisor's gratification in a worker's dependence is sometimes a factor operating against the worker's development. This gratification may have led the supervisor to impose help, to be authoritative, and to show approval of a worker's submissive response.[18]

If the supervisor emphasizes getting the job done (both his own and the supervisee's) then these incidental consequences are rarely cause for concern. Indeed, the supervisee may perform his assigned agency task better if his supervisor gives him explicit instructions and handles him authoritatively. It is more a matter of ethics than skillful supervisory practice for the supervisor to be concerned about what happens to the supervisee in the process, although better performance and service may well result from ethical as well as competent supervisory practice.

> There are sometimes indications that staff members incorporate in their performance, and in reports of their performance, elements which have either met the test of previous . . . approval, or are sure to be received with such approval. . . . It is not uncommon for professional workers in an agency to engage in a process of "second-guessing" which causes them to be more concerned about what is likely to meet with [supervisory] approval than with what will produce better services.[19]

But the ethical issue is not better service (although that is certainly an important administrative issue), but the supervisor's obligations to the supervisee. The supervisee's growth on the job, whether or not it benefits the agency and its clientele, is the supervisor's legitimate ethical concern since the supervisory relationship places the supervisor between the supervisee and his potential for professional growth, no matter who may ultimately benefit from it: the present agency and its clientele or another agency and its clientele. In other words, the supervisee's creative development is the supervisor's responsibility, even if such development constitutes growth beyond the boundaries of agency utility. The dead-end job, which paraprofessionals are often concerned about, need not be a dead end in the long run if it paves the way for professional movement elsewhere.

4. The supervisor owes it to the supervisee to determine whether there is a correlation between the supervisee's aspirations and opportunities. The paraprofessional or indigenous nonprofessional staff member may, like Alfred Doolittle, have aspirations unsuited to his capacities, opportunities, or preferences. In addition, the supervisor owes it to the supervisee to look ahead to what the supervisee will face when he leaves the agency, including the resumption of normal ties to persons with whom he may have had a different kind of relationship temporarily. Although these concerns go beyond the supervisor's job description, they are his ethical responsibility. The supervisor therefore addresses himself not only to the immediate situation, but to its future consequences for the supervisee.

5. Ethics as well as practicality demand that the supervisee understand what he is expected to do in his job and the basis on which his performance will be appraised. Ethics are the enemy of "catch-22s" and "mickey-mousing." Few laws or administrative regulations exist to restrain a supervisor from committing such offenses, and therefore he must rely on his own conscience and awareness, which are the instruments of ethics. Whatever the administrative procedures and however simply they may be satisfied, the supervisor has the ethical responsibility to let the supervisee know where he stands on his job and why. He also shares responsibility for the supervisee's standing to the extent that his failure to provide effective help has affected that standing.

Because the supervisor has power over the supervisee, it is his ethical responsibility to make sure that written evaluations and references based on them are accurate, relevant to the supervisee's job and expectations of him in it, considerate of the circumstances under which the job was done, and sensitive to the possibility that such information may be misused, misinterpreted, or outdated.

Thus ethics are important in all phases of the supervisory relationship, including before it is formally initiated and after it has ended, insofar as its consequences follow the supervisee. Ethics in supervision need not imply a favorable result for the supervisee, only a just consequence for him. The outcome need not be beneficial to the supervisee, only appropriate. Ethics need not result in special advantage for the supervisee, only equity for him. They need not provide the supervisee with preferential opportunities, only safeguards against the genuine hazards he faces because in so many respects he and the supervisor are not equals.

NOTES

1. Sidney S. Eisenberg, *Supervision in the Changing Field of Social Work* (Philadelphia: Jewish Family Service of Philadelphia and the University of Pennsylvania School of Social Work, 1956), p. 51.

2. Frances H. Scherz, "A Concept of Supervision Based on Definitions of Job Responsibility," *Social Casework* 34 (October 1958) pp. 435–443 [Chapter 8 above]; and *Social Agency Responsibility in Extending Professional Education* (New York: Council on Social Work Education, 1956), p. 3.

3. Margaret Williamson, *Supervision: Principles and Methods* (New York: Woman's Press, 1950), pp. 6–7.

4. Charles S. Levy, "In Defense of Supervision," *Journal of Jewish Communal Service*, 37 (Winter 1960), p. 201.

5. Herbert Goldhamer and Edward A. Shils, "Types of Power and Status," *American Journal of Sociology*, 45 (September 1939), p. 171; and Max Weber, *The Theory of Social and Economic Organization*, Talcott Parsons and A. M. Henderson, trans. (Glencoe, Ill.: Free Press, 1964).

6. John W. Thibaut and Harold H. Kelley, *Social Psychology of Groups* (New York: John Wiley & Sons, 1959), pp. 100–104.

7. C. Wright Mills, *White Collar* (New York: Oxford University Press, 1956), p. 224.

8. Herbert H. Aptekar, "The Significance of Dependence and Independence in Supervision," *Social Casework*, 35 (June 1954), p. 239.

9. *Motivating Employees Through Within-Grade Pay Increases*, Personnel Management Series No. 17 (Washington, D.C.: U.S. Government Printing Office, November 1965).

10. Helen Harris Perlman, "And Gladly Teach," *Journal of Education for Social Work*, 3 (Spring 1967), pp. 43–44.

11. Herbert H. Aptekar, "Supervision and the Development of Professional Responsibility: An Application of Systems Thought," *Jewish Social Work Forum*, 3 (Fall 1965), p. 11.

12. Peter M. Blau, *Exchange and Power in Social Life* (New York: John Wiley & Sons, 1964), pp. 206–207.

13. Peter M. Blau and W. Richard Scott, *Formal Organizations: A Comparative Approach* (San Francisco, Calif.: Chandler Publishing Co., 1962).

14. Bertha Reynolds, *Learning and Teaching in the Practice of Social Work* (New York: Rinehart & Co., 1942), pp. 267–271.

15. Perry London, *Behavior Control* (New York: Harper & Row, 1971), pp. 250–252.

16. Abraham Edel, *Method in Ethical Theory* (Indianapolis, Ind.: Bobbs-Merrill Co., 1963).

17. Immanuel Kant, *Kant's Critique of Practical Reason and Other Works on the Theory of Ethics*, Thomas Kingsmill Abbott, trans. (4th ed., London, England: Longmans, Green & Co., 1889), pp. 291 ff.

18. Charlotte Towle, *Common Human Needs* (rev. ed.; New York: National Association of Social Workers, 1965), pp. 147 and 149.

19. Charles S. Levy, "The Staff Member: Leader or Liaison," paper presented at the Annual Staff Conference, National Jewish Welfare Board, Lakewood, N.J., February 13, 1957.

21

Professional Autonomy and Social Work Supervision

Carlton E. Munson

THE ISSUE

> In France there is a man in the Ministry of Agriculture who has worked out what the profit margin should be for pluckers of Angora rabbits.[1]

IT WOULD SEEM that the fellow in the French Ministry of Agriculture has achieved with Angora rabbits what social work has accomplished with supervision. In spite of intensive theoretical study, social work is still faced with the dilemma of precisely what the role of supervision is in social work practice. The dilemma over autonomous practice versus controlled practice is the issue addressed in this paper.

Supervision has been around as long as social work. Even "during the years of 'friendly visiting' . . . caseworkers were *told* the rules and shown how to do the job." [2] As social workers engaged in the struggle to achieve professional status and separate casework from the role of the friendly visitor,[3] supervision continued to play an important part. While historically supervision has been basic to social work, it also has been essential to the role of social work in relation to society. In fact, it has been the cement of the relationship between social work and society. This theme runs throughout the literature. In an early article we are told:

> Our focus on the family grows out of conviction that it is the key unit of society and that a healthy family is the best milieu for the development of mature, happy, productive human beings, ready to live fully and constructively. This knowledge is basic to all social work, but family

Reprinted with permission of the Council on Social Work Education. From *Journal of Education for Social Work*, Vol. 12 (Fall 1976), pp. 95–102.

agencies have the special task of preserving, building, nurturing, and preventing breakdown of what is healthy in the family.[4]

That this view is still predominant is stated succinctly in a recent article: "The organizational structures of social work agencies reflect the dominant ideologies and structures of the larger society." [5] These citations demonstrate the long-standing "functional" nature of social work.

If supervision is the link that connects social work to the social welfare desires of society, then it can be said that the administrative component of supervision is the tool used to ensure that the tie remains strong. Throughout the literature, the administrative character appears over and over and is epitomized by the comment that "the purpose of the supervisory relation is . . . that of getting the job done." [6] There has been little change in the basis for supervision. As Mandell pointed out, "there is little documented evidence of a large-scale thrust toward changing the structure of supervision." [7]

Historically the situation became more confused when the teaching function was added to that of administration. Teaching has usually been viewed as directly related to, and often an extension of the administrative role: "the supervisor has nothing better at his disposal to ensure better service to the client and the community than good methods of teaching." [8] The teaching function has to a certain extent become intertwined with administration to lead to more control of workers. This becomes apparent when casework techniques are applied in supervision. Austin stated that "supervision is to be distinguished from consultation, which is based on voluntary interrelations and does not carry the same evaluation responsibility." She went on to give an account of the therapeutic role of supervision: "Learning is made usable, largely, through the support of a positive supervisory relationship which leads the worker to new insights about people, including himself." [9]

The literature is full of material on the control through casework teaching aspect of supervision. However, almost ten years later Austin changed her views somewhat about the role of supervision and was one of the first commentators to crystalize the emerging issue of control versus autonomy:

> For many years the idea of "close" supervision . . . was an ideal goal for agencies and workers alike. . . . Since 1953 however, dissatisfaction has been expressed with the system, particularly by the practitioners. . . . They want the rights and reponsibilities for decision making and self-direction.[10]

This is a precise statement of the issue, and it is understandable that this question should emerge alongside the formalization of professionalization in social work. As long as supervision served "as a way of training staff, paid or volunteer, to do the job at hand—to help people according to the function and policies of the early social agencies," [11] then control was accepted. But as social work training moved into the university, became quite lengthy, and fostered and taught professionalism, the question of autonomy started to rear its ugly head in the literature and in agencies.

In many instances the quest for independence among workers has been handled by supervisors falling back on their old reliable casework knowledge. When workers offer disagreement or make efforts at self-direction, this is judged as resistance, hostility, a problem with authority, lack of maturity, overly aggressive behavior, or whatever fits the supervisor's style. Kadushin probed the supervisor's motivations in this circumstance:

> This is the game of redefining honest disagreement so that it appears to be psychological resistance. Honest disagreement requires that the supervisor defend his point of view, present the research evidence in support of his contention, be sufficiently acquainted with the literature so he can cite the knowledge that argues for the correctness of what he is saying. If honest disagreement is redefined as resistance, the burden is shifted to the supervisee. [12]

Increasingly during the 1960s questions were raised about the problems between fostering professional behavior and exercising regulation of workers through supervision. Scherz questioned the concept that caseworker development depends on the kind and extent of supervision, and said "we know that the most effective learning is learning that is self-motivated." She went on to raise serious questions about supervisors functioning administratively to ensure the competency of services delivered by others: "The supervisor is not responsible for, and cannot share responsibility with, the caseworker for either the kind or quality of service given in a case," and as far as professional growth is concerned, "the supervisor cannot make caseworkers competent by injecting knowledge into them." [13]

Debate continues to appear on both sides of this issue today. The traditional view that "the goal of effective supervision should be improved functioning of the professional staff" [14] is widely accepted, and Epstein perpetuated this when she asked: "Is autonomous practice possible in social work?" indicating that "the answer is a qualified yes." [15] Mandell and others pointed to the strong leanings toward autonomy and the resulting problems and conflicts. [16] Some observers have tried to reconcile the problems of individualism and accountability. Leader, in a relatively old and largely unheeded article, recognized that the value of supervision is accepted, but at the same time there is much dissatisfaction with and questioning of some practices. He called for clear standards for supervising various levels of practice, time limits to be placed on duration of supervision, and evaluations to be used for practice growth, not salary increases.[17]

Much has been written about the contribution of supervision to professionalism, but little has been said about the contributions of professionalism to supervision. Berl took a slightly different approach by holding that "social workers have a tendency to define supervision as a professional, rather than an institutional operation," but went on to unite the relationship between institutional and professional aspects of supervision:

> As a professional operation, supervision has certain defined norms and values, but these do not exist in vacuum; they are an intrinsic part of the norms and values of our society. It is true that a profession has an identity of its own, within the larger entity. Supervision, therefore, should be viewed as an institutional as well as a professional operation.[18]

The relationship between the norms and values of society and social work mentioned by Berl are seen as problematic and related to supervision by Wasserman.[19] Although there has been much theoretical discussion of supervision, there has been little scientific study, and this is where Wasserman provided some keen insights on the intensity of the problem. He studied 12 newly graduated social workers who were employed in the foster care division of a welfare department: "at least one-half of the new professional social workers suffered varying degrees of physical fatigue and emotional upset." The problems of the workers were related to an array of working conditions, but the predominant source of difficulty was supervision. In spite of having to rely on supervisors for decisions, they did not consider most of the supervisors knowledgeable enough to make decisions, and they "had little sense of being members of a professional collectivity with whom they could consult on the basis of common experiences, concerns and needs." Wasserman arrived at the estimation that:

> The major conclusions to be drawn from these observations of new professionals in a public child welfare agency is that the knowledge, skills and values (the social work perspective) that graduate students presumably acquire . . . are essentially of little use in a work situation in which structural constraints dictate the decision-making process. . . . The principal question that emerges from this report can be stated as follows: What are the facilitating conditions under which professional social work can be practiced? . . . Although this hypothesis may fall under the rubric of an "unthinkable thought," failure to ponder its possible validity jeopardizes the future of the profession and its purposes and functions in society.[20]

If we take Wasserman with his conclusions and views seriously, then the crucial element in the deprofessionalization of social work might be the failure to resolve the conflicts around supervision rather than the shift in values in society as argued by Specht.[21]

We will now turn our attention to a conceptual framework for dealing with this conflict through use of role theory. Wasserman identified the task that remains for the profession:

> It is time for the social work profession, bureaucrats, and schools of social work to stop hiding their knowledge of bureaucracies. What we now need is new ideas, concepts and models—in short a new vision to reconstruct our working lives and new ways to relate to each other and to those we serve.[22]

ROLES IN SOCIAL WORK SUPERVISION

From a sociological perspective, all the literature previously cited establishes supervision as an element in the functional nature of social work. Martindale tells us that in sociological theory "functionalism reaches its distinctive subject matter when it takes the organism-like system . . . as the primary subject matter of sociological analysis, studying all other items as system-determined and system-maintaining." [23] Since this has been, and remains the unit of analysis of supervision, the individual worker necessarily must be viewed in relation to the social system.

Merton identifies the uses of the functional approach on three levels:

> Substantially, these postulates hold first, that standardized social activities or cultural items are functional for the *entire* social or cultural system; second, that *all* social and cultural items fulfill sociological functions; and third, that these items are consequently indispensable.[24]

This is associated directly with the issue presented in the first part of this paper of control (organic view) versus autonomy (individualistic view) in supervision. This leads into Merton's questioning of the third functional postulate of how indispensable an item is. In these days of questioning the function of the profession, the issue of how indispensable to the system both supervision and social work itself are becomes crucial when viewed from a functionalist perspective. It is possible to argue that supervision has become dysfunctional for social work, but we would rather sacrifice our professionalism than give up our outdated and tradition-bound view of supervision.

This fits perfectly Merton's "modes of adjustment" in the category of "ritualism," which is not compatible with "cultural goals" but fits "institutionalized means." [25] Merton sheds further light on this problem in recognizing that "just as rigidities in social organization often balk and block the satisfaction of new wants, so rigidities in individual behavior may block the satisfaction of old wants in a changing social environment." [26] This succinctly touches the issue of supervision as described by Mandell.

The notion has been put forth that the failure of supervision to keep pace with social change has contributed heavily to social work deprofessionalization. Attention is now turned to how supervision processes could be altered to enhance rather than detract from professionalism. Merton's idea of role-set will be used in this analysis. It seems that Merton's frame of reference lends itself to this type of analysis since his early theoretical work was in the social action school of thought. Only later did he move to a functionalist approach.[27] Merton's work in both these perspectives seems to give him a unique awareness of the individual in the system, which is especially relevant to the problems of supervision.

Sociologists have for a long time recognized the importance of role theory in analyzing behavior.[28] Merton went back to Linton's theories on role and status. Linton defined status as "a position in a particular pattern" representing the individual's "position with relation to the total society," which "is simply a collection of rights and duties," while "role represents the dynamic aspect of status." Linton further stated that "the more perfectly the members of any society are adjusted to their statuses and roles the more smoothly the society will function." [29] This is critical for social work and supervision.

Social work education devotes a great deal of time to the generic aspects of the profession at the most general level, but little discussion has been geared to the generic rules and obligations regulating social work. The Code of Ethics established by the National Association of Social Workers seems to have been of little help because of its vagueness and inconsistency. While social workers continue to function in a variety of agencies, there still seems to be a need for generic guidelines for performance that would aid workers and supervisors alike. Such an outline of expectation would help at the macro level, but more specific rules are needed at the micro level, and this is where Merton's role-set is of value.

The middle-range theory of role-set holds that each status a person occupies in a society does not involve one role, but an array of associated roles, and the various statuses held by the person constitutes a status-set.[30] A social worker takes many roles in delivering service—that of helper, teacher, leader, rule giver, authority figure, evaluator, consultant, interpreter, among others. At the same time when it comes to supervision, several new and reversed roles are required of the worker in the form of the helped, learner, follower, rule recipient, subordinate figure, the evaluated, and so on.

The status-position social worker in most cases includes roles that are reciprocal to a specific alter position.[31] In the first instance, it is the reciprocal position of client and in the latter, the position of supervisor. Through the sociological definition of the situation, the personality of the individual actors in these roles takes on less significance and the important question becomes: How can the role conflicts be kept to a minimum? Rather than viewing the strain as arising from the situation, social work supervisors, for reasons explained earlier, have located the stress in the personality of the individual. Since individuals vary so much, this perspective does not lend itself to establishment of consistent standards. Situational analysis however, remains more constant. Linton explained the clarity of this view by stating: "A status, as distinct from the individual who may occupy it, is simply a collection of rights and duties."[32]

Not only does the role-set frame of reference offer more clarity than the personality system analysis, but it also offers a base for testing a number of practices and making connections among a number of practices. If social work theoreticians would launch such an analysis there would be no room for the hazy, personality-oriented ideas of writers like Levinson, Levine, Chichester, and Austin. More emphasis needs to be placed on the specific, task-related concepts of Mandell, Epstein, Wasserman, Leader, Widem, Fizdale, Scherz, and Feldman.

Merton, in an article on role-sets, identified six "social mechanisms" that are basic to consensus and conflict.[33] These six mechanisms will be discussed as a model for analyzing the problems of supervision. The first is *relative importance of various statuses*. Merton tells us that differing statuses in a given role social structure have different levels of importance and that status-occupants at different levels view differently certain role relationships.[34] This is to be expected, but what seems to be critical is that in the status relationship of supervisor-worker-client, the value assigned by each actor to given factors must be identified and mediated. What a worker sees as important in his relationship with the client, the supervisor might view as of marginal importance and place emphasis on other elements. This needs to be defined in the supervisory relationship and agreement reached on who has the responsibility for decision making and what gets implemented in service.

The second social mechanism is *differences of power of those in the role-set*. This picks up where the first mechanism left off because the assignment of value to varying behaviors in relationships leads to dealing with who has the responsibility for decision making and what gets implemented in service. Merton says that power means "the observed and predictable capacity to impose one's will in a social action, even against the opposition of others taking part in that action."[35] If supervisors and workers cannot agree on what action to take in a given situation, then the issue becomes who has the power to do what and who must accept responsibility for the consequences of a disputed action. Scherz is quite emphatic that only the professional worker can be responsible for his practice,[36] but little attention has been devoted to the resulting tension and conflict this produces in the supervisory relationship. Because of the power involved, it has been expected that in disagreements the worker must yield. But under what conditions should the supervisor yield?

The third mechanism is *insulation of role-set activities from observability by members of the role-set*. This raises many points of contention for supervision. If the teacher-learner roles are considered legitimate functions in supervision, then ground rules must be established for what worker activities are to be observed by the supervisor and what supervisor performance is to be observed by the worker. A key question is: What are to be the conditions of this observation on both sides? It appears that currently observability in these relationships is nil and all supervisory activity takes place in the context of "the unseen client." [37]

The fourth social mechanism is *observability of conflicting demands by members of a role-set*. As long as actors remain ignorant of conflicting demands, there is little problem, but with the rise of professionalism in social work, conflicting demands and the resulting problems have become acute in supervision. The sooner we come to view conflict as healthy, and in some cases ultimately beneficial to the client, the better. Merton has defused this proposition this way: "when it becomes plain that the demands of some are in full contradiction with the demands of others, it becomes, in part, the task of members of the role-set . . . to resolve these contradictions, either by a struggle for over-riding power or by some degree of compromise." [38]

The fifth mechanism is *mutual social support among status-occupants*. This is an important functional mechanism that social work has not utilized to any great extent in dealing with supervision strains. Merton points out that contrary to what the status-occupant may believe, he is not alone in his role-set.[39] Social work has not used to any large extent peer support to deal with the demands of supervision or peer evaluation, to establish norms and values of supervision. A brief review of the literature seems to reveal utilization of group supervision as a way to dilute and redirect through peer group pressure authority in supervision rather than fostering mutual support. Utilizing group supervision as a response to supervisor strain can be more devastating to the worker than the one-to-one relationship.

The sixth social mechanism is *abridging the role-set*. Merton is not completely clear about this. He talks of role relationships being broken off when incompatible demands become too great, leading to greater role consensus among those who remain.[40] This is descriptive of Mandell's comment that many social workers are dealing with the role strain of supervision by leaving agencies and entering private practice.[41] If this is taking place, then the profession needs to assess whether this has positive or negative implications over the long view. If it is found desirable to have workers remain in agencies, then this mechanism could be modified and used to analyze what conflicting demands could be eliminated from the supervisory relationship. Also, under this social mechanism the values instilled in workers by the schools and the values demanded by agencies of workers could be compared, studied, and integrated.

CONCLUSION

This then is a proposal to use the role-set as defined by Merton to build a model for confronting the issue of autonomy versus control in supervision. It can be recognized from the social mechanisms applied by the writer to supervision that social work practice at this stage is not completely autonomous, and the profession by and large functions within the confines of "organizational necessities." [42] No grand schemes for final resolution of the problems of supervision have been attempted, but a model has been advocated for making the best of a difficult situation.

NOTES

1. Sanche de Gramont, *The French: Portrait of a People* (New York: G. P. Putnam's Sons, 1969), p. 211.

2. Norma D. Levine, "Educational Components of Supervision in a Family Agency," *Social Casework*, Vol. 31 (June 1950), p. 245.

3. See Everett C. Hughes, "Professions," *Daedalus*, Vol. 92 (Fall 1963), p. 659; and Mary Burns, "Supervision in Social Work," in *Encyclopedia of Social Work*, ed. Harry L. Lurie (New York: National Association of Social Workers, 1965), p. 785.

4. Levine, *op. cit.*, p. 246.

5. Betty Mandell, "The 'Equality' Revolution and Supervision," *Journal of Education for Social Work*, Vol. 9 (Winter 1973), p. 43 [Chapter 27 below, p. 311].

6. Sidney Berkowitz, "The Administrative Process in Casework Supervision," *Social Casework*, Vol. 33 (December 1952), p. 421.

7. Mandell, *op. cit.*, p. 51.

8. Yonata Feldman, "The Teaching Aspect of Casework Supervision," *Social Casework*, Vol. 31 (April 1950), p. 156.

9. Lucille Austin, "Basic Principles of Supervision," *Social Casework*, Vol. 33 (December 1952), pp. 415 & 416 [Chapter 7 above, pp. 56–57].

10. Lucille Austin, "The Changing Role of the Supervisor," *Smith College Studies in Social Work,* Vol. 31 (June 1961), pp. 179–180.

11. Burns, *op. cit.,* p. 785.

12. Alfred Kadushin, "Games People Play in Supervision," *Social Work,* Vol. 13 (July 1968), p. 30 [Chapter 17 above, p. 192].

13. Frances H. Scherz, "A Concept of Supervision Based on Definitions of Job Responsibility," *Social Casework,* Vol. 39 (October 1958), pp. 436 & 437 [Chapter 8 above, p. 73].

14. G. S. Getzel et al., "Supervising in Groups As a Model for Today," *Social Casework,* Vol. 52 (March 1971), p. 154.

15. Laura Epstein, "Is Autonomous Practice Possible?" *Social Work,* Vol. 18 (March 1973), p. 11 [Chapter 14 above, p. 152].

16. Mandell, *op. cit.,* pp. 43–54.

17. Arthur Leader, "New Directions in Supervision," *Social Casework,* Vol. 38 (November 1957), pp. 462–68.

18. Fred Berl, "An Attempt to Construct a Conceptual Framework for Supervision," *Social Casework,* Vol. 41 (July 1960), p. 228 [Chapter 10 above, p. 95].

19. Harry Wasserman, "The Professional Social Worker in a Bureaucracy," *Social Work,* Vol. 16 (January 1971), p. 93 [Chapter 19 above, p. 206].

20. Harry Wasserman, "Early Careers of Professional Social Workers in a Public Child Welfare Agency," *Social Work,* Vol. 15 (July 1970), pp. 94–96, 97, & 100–101 [Chapter 24 below, p. 283].

21. Harry Specht, "The Deprofessionalization of Social Work," *Social Work,* Vol. 17 (March 1972), p. 31.

22. Wasserman, "The Professional Social Worker," p. 95.

23. Don Martindale, *The Nature and Types of Sociological Theory* (Boston: Houghton Mifflin, 1960), p. 465.

24. Robert K. Merton, *On Theoretical Sociology: Five Essays, Old and New* (New York: The Free Press, 1967), p. 79.

25. Robert K. Merton, "Social Structure and Anomie," in *Contemporary Society,* ed. John A. Perry and Murray S. Seidler (New York: Canfield Press, 1972), p. 109.

26. Robert K. Merton, "The Unanticipated Consequences of Purposive Social Action," *American Sociological Review,* Vol. 1 (December 1936), p. 901.

27. Martindale, *op. cit.,* p. 427.

28. Merton, *On Theoretical Sociology,* p. 41.

29. Ralph Linton, "Status and Role," in *Readings in Sociology,* ed. Edgar A. Schuler et al. (New York: Thomas Y. Crowell, 1971), pp. 157–58.

30. Merton, *On Theoretical Sociology,* pp. 42–43.

31. Alvin L. Bertrand, *Social Organization: A General Systems and Role Theory Perspective* (Philadelphia: F. A. Davis, 1972), pp. 72–73.

32. Linton, *op. cit.,* p. 157.

33. Robert K. Merton, "The Role-Set: Problems in Sociological Theory," in

Sociological Theory: A Book of Readings, ed. Lewis A. Coser and Bernard Rosenberg (New York: Macmillan, 1964), pp. 379–84.

34. *Ibid.,* p. 380.
35. *Ibid.*
36. Scherz, *op. cit.,* p. 445.
37. Frances T. Levinson, "Psychological Components of Supervision in a Family Agency," *Social Casework,* Vol. 31 (June 1950), p. 238.
38. Merton, "The Role-Set," p. 383.
39. *Ibid.*
40. *Ibid.,* p. 384.
41. Mandell, *op. cit.,* p. 47.
42. See Bernard Barber, "Some Problems in the Sociology of Professions," *Daedalus,* Vol. 92 (Fall 1963), pp. 678–82.

PART V

Research

INTRODUCTION

A GREAT DEAL OF THE LITERATURE analyzing social work supervision has taken the form of self-reports and theoretical formulations by senior-level practitioners and educators. The unit of analysis in these studies has been generally the individual within the organization as perceived by the supervisor, who would have to be considered as an investigator functioning as a participant-observer. These writers would be hard pressed to meet the scientific demands of modern empirical research because of their own involvement in the outcome of the study.

The few scientifically based studies of supervision have taken place in graduate schools, where types and extent of field instruction can be easily varied for experimental manipulation. However, little experimental research on field instruction has been attempted; what research has been carried out is generally of the participant–observer variety and has been generalized to agency supervision, even though the demands and goals of field instruction and professional supervision are separate and distinct. Their mixing is an outcome of the earlier conceptions of supervision as primarily a growth-oriented and educative endeavor, as discussed in Parts 1 and 2.

The paucity of empirical research is not understandable in light of the importance attached to supervision by the social work profession and most individual social workers. Supervision is viewed by most workers as the main channel of accountability, a means of protecting clients, and the chief source of professional development and support for the worker. These are important aspects, but there are few empirical referents as to how the profession is faring in these areas. Many social workers regard receiving "good" or satisfying supervision as a matter of luck. This belief makes supervision problematic, since it is considered so essential but at the same time so difficult to obtain at an effective level.

Recently there has been more empirical research as the profession and educational programs increasingly emphasize scientific methods. Much of the research is confirming the propositions of earlier armchair theorists and small-scale participant–observers, and it is documenting the negative results when weak and inadequate supervisory practices are employed.

The research reported by Kadushin is probably the largest survey of workers and supervisors ever made. The study consists of a mailed questionnaire involving 750 supervisors and 750 supervisees. A number of demographic variables are reported, but the emphasis is on perceptions of roles. For example, the perception of supervisors' power based on their expert knowledge was found to be granted more readily by the supervisees than supervisors were willing to accept. This finding is significant for supervisees' professional development and is related to the findings of Scott, Wasserman, and Munson, which found competence in supervisors to be a crucial variable in successful supervision. The majority of respondents were satisfied with their supervisory arrangements; when dissatisfaction did occur, it was mainly over the issue of autonomy. Kadushin found that there are differences between supervisor and supervisee in perceptions of the nature and amount of evaluation of performance, and this finding correlates with earlier writings about the role of evaluation, especially in relation to Levy's material on ethical principles (chapter 20 above). Kadushin's findings in several areas confirm the belief that the traditional therapeutic approach to supervision has given way primarily to a role-performance model.

Scott's study of supervision in a public welfare agency confronts the question of autonomy within an organizational framework. Two types of professional functioning within organizations are identified: autonomous, where there is a great deal of individual professional freedom and the organization functions merely as a base of operation; and heteronomous, where the professional is subordinate to the organizational administrative framework, and autonomy is not delineated clearly. Scott sees social workers as functioning in the heteronomous model. Within this context, he discusses his findings in the areas of workers' preferences in supervision and structure, differences between supervisors with high and low professional orientations, and differences in responses to supervision between workers with high and low levels of professional training.

The research by Wasserman illustrates the devastating results that can occur when sound supervisory practices are not employed. Wasserman used participant–observer research to study twelve newly graduated social workers who were employed over a two-year period in the foster-care division of a welfare department. He found that 50 percent suffered varying degrees of physical fatigue and emotional upset. The problems were related to a variety of working conditions, but supervision was viewed as the major source of difficulty. In spite of having to rely on supervisors, most of the workers did not consider them knowledgeable enough to make decisions, and the workers had little sense of belonging to a professional group. Although Wasserman's sample was small, the longitudinal nature of his study demonstrates the negative outcomes that do occur and the fact that such outcomes might not be detected in surveys. The results reveal empirically the need to develop ethical principles (such as those identified by Levy) and professional protections to insure implementation of the positive supervisory practices presented in many of the articles in this book.

Munson's research deals with the importance of structure and authority in supervision as perceived by the worker and the impact on outcomes such as supervision and job satisfaction. An in-depth interview was given to sixty-five workers in nineteen agencies in three states. The findings indicate, contrary to arguments in the theoretical literature, that the structure of supervision has little impact on perceived satisfactions; but the perception of the supervisor's authority orientation produces significant differences. Supervisors who were perceived as functioning from a competence model, as opposed to the positional-sanction one, had significantly higher levels of clinical exposure in supervision and interaction with supervisees, and their supervisees had significantly higher levels of satisfaction with supervision and job. The author discusses the relationship between authority and structure in promoting satisfaction and positive practices in supervision.

Cherniss and Egnatios studied 164 workers in mental health regarding perceived supervisory styles, satisfaction with supervision, and clinical self-confidence. They identified five styles of supervision: didactic-consultative, laissez-faire, authoritative, insight-oriented, and feeling-oriented. The findings reveal that the styles used differed from the styles the workers preferred, indicating a desire in agencies of this type for change in how supervision is practiced. The authors also found that satisfaction with supervision and clinical self-confidence of the workers varied with the style of supervision used. Laissez-faire and authoritative styles were viewed as the least productive; the workers preferred the didactic–consultative, feeling-oriented, and insight-oriented forms. The results of this study are consistent with those of previous research, and the discussion of the findings offers insights regarding the perceived supervisory needs of workers in mental health.

The articles in this section are representative of and summarize empirical attempts to test some of the earlier theoretical formulations about supervision. Some of the previous assumptions and propositions have been confirmed and others have been called into question. Scientifically based research in supervision is in its infancy, and much more research is needed. Additional studies can contribute a great deal to clarifying broad issues that face the profession and specific problems encountered by supervisors and supervisees in their daily activities. There is a need for experimental research that explores different models of supervision and their outcomes. Most of the studies reported here used role and interactional frameworks, but research based on psychological perspectives, or combining psychological and role or interactional orientations, could provide further insight. Such research is needed because workers frequently mention personality variables involving both workers and supervisors as having an effect on their attitudes toward supervision. Workers also mention that their attitudes toward supervisors vary over time, and longitudinal research could provide a more comprehensive view of the supervisory process. Considering the trends in supervision discussed in Part 6, research will probably move into a new era to deal with the complexity of variables involved.

22

Supervisor–Supervisee: A Survey

Alfred Kadushin

CURRENTLY, there has been a widespread reassessment of the different responsibilities assumed by professionals holding a master's degree in social work (MSW) and those with a bachelor's degree. Both the National Association of Social Workers (NASW) and the Council on Social Work Education (CSWE) have given explicit recognition to the Bachelor of Social Work degree (BSW) as a professional degree for entry-level positions. As a result, greater emphasis is being placed on master's degree training as preparation for supervisory, consultative, administrative, and planning tasks.

Reviewing the current manpower situation in social work and prognosticating future trends, Briggs suggests that during the 1970s

> . . . the graduate trained social worker [MSW and DSW] will become a middle manager, team leader, supervisor or staff developer, or a high level specialist-consultant-planner in social problem areas. Education for practice will reflect the shift in roles.[1]

In 1969 the board of directors of CSWE appointed a special committee to study the length of graduate school education. The committee held a series of open meetings throughout the country, which over two hundred practitioners and educators attended. The report notes that "with the bachelor's degree rapidly becoming the first degree in social work, thought needs to be given to the future development of the MSW program." [2] In many schools this process of redefinition has resulted in an "emphasis on training master's degree students for middle level management and supervisory and administrative positions." [3]

Such modification in the educational focus of the master's degree program is supported by the research on recent developments in practice. A summary of studies examining the distinct activities of BSW and MSW social workers in the same agencies notes that those with a master's degree were more involved in directing than in providing service.[4] Social workers with a bachelor's degree were likely to be providing direct service, whereas the major professional responsibility of those with a master's degree had become supervision of or consultation with the BSW worker.

This trend in the changing functions of MSW-trained workers is further confirmed by a follow-up study of recent graduates that indicates that many professionally trained workers assumed positions as administrators, supervisors, or consultants within two years of graduation.[5] A recent survey of Canadian social workers with master's degrees showed that over half "were employed in administrative, supervisory, consultative and other non-direct service positions."[6]

Despite the increasing importance of supervision as a unique responsibility of the graduate-trained professional social worker, relatively little research is available on social work supervision. A comprehensive review of research covering the period between 1965 and 1970 noted that "no significant studies of [social work] supervision have appeared" since 1965.[7]

PROJECT OVERVIEW

This article is a report of a study of supervision in social work that was conducted in 1973 through the use of a questionnaire addressed to a nationwide sample of 750 supervisors and 750 supervisees. Respondents were randomly selected from a listing of 2,600 casework supervisors and 5,300 casework supervisees in the 1972 NASW Directory.[8] Of the 1,500 social workers approached in the original and the follow-up mailing, there were 853 usable returns—469 from supervisors and 384 from supervisees. An additional 75 nonusable returns were received from respondents who were retired, in private practice, or who thought the questionnaire "too damned long." The usable responses amounted to 61 percent— a rate considered high for studies of this kind, particularly one with a long questionnaire.

Two different forms of the same basic questionnaire were used, each running about twenty pages. One was directed to supervisors and one to supervisees. The questionnaire was pretested in interviews with field instructors at the University of Wisconsin School of Social Work, Madison, Wisconsin. The returns were anonymous, and answers were keypunched and computer-analyzed.

On the whole, characteristics of the respondents mirrored NASW membership. Two-thirds of each group were female and about 90 percent of both groups had an MSW degree. Supervisors tended to be somewhat older (41–45 years of age) than supervisees (36–40 years of age). Supervisors had an average of twelve to thirteen years' paid experience in social work and supervisees, nine to eleven years. Both groups had worked in their current agency for an average of six years. Supervisors were more likely to be working in a public assistance or child welfare agency than were the supervisees, more of whom worked in a psychiatric–mental health agency, a family service agency, or in school social work. Supervisors worked in larger agencies (employing thirty to forty social workers) than did supervisees, who worked in agencies that employed eleven to twenty social workers. Therefore, the promotion of the MSW social worker from practitioner to supervisor often involves a move from a private to a public agency; from a smaller to a larger agency; and from a psychiatric–mental health, medical, or school social work setting to a public assistance or child welfare setting.

SUPERVISORY POWER

Supervisors are responsible for an average of four to five workers each. Only about 30 percent of their supervisees have an MSW degree. The largest percentage in the supervisee group are college graduates with a degree other than social work (33 percent), an additional 10 percent have an undergraduate degree with a social work major, and about 11 percent have no college degree. Thus the group of supervisees used for this study (all MSW graduates) represents only a small segment of the general group of supervisees. About half the supervisors carried a caseload in addition to their supervisory responsibilities.

The individual conference is the principal context for supervision. Supervisors meet with their supervisees in regularly scheduled conferences on the average of three to four times a month, for a period of an hour to an hour and a half each time. Although group supervisory meetings frequently supplement individual conferences, only 14 percent of the supervisors indicated that such meetings were the principal context for supervision.

The great majority of supervisees (72 percent) indicated that total supervisory time was "just about right." If there was any complaint, it was that the supervisees felt that they did not get enough time.

The majority of supervisors and supervisees noted that as the supervisee gains experience the relationship can become one of consultant-consultee, to be used when and as the participants decide. Although both groups felt strongly that this was a desirable direction in which to move, a somewhat higher percentage of supervisees (75.2 percent) felt this than did supervisors (69.5 percent).

Whereas 60 percent of the supervisees saw the relationship with their supervisors as "colleague-collaborator" and only 3 percent saw themselves as "students," 30 percent of the supervisors regarded themselves as "colleague-collaborator" and 26 percent as "teacher." Supervisees apparently have a more egalitarian perception of the relationship than supervisors are willing to concede.

To view the desirable relationship between supervisor and supervisee as that of consultant-consultee is not to press for peer supervision. Both groups interviewed showed that they were, in fact, hierarchically oriented. When asked to whom they would be most likely to turn for help in their work, 56 percent of the supervisees and 72 percent of the supervisors indicated that they would turn to the person responsible for their own supervision. Only 8 percent of the supervisees and 6 percent of the supervisors indicated that they would turn to a peer.

French and Raven identified five different bases of social power that might permit the supervisor to proscribe the behavior of his supervisee: reward power; coercive (punishment) power; positional power based on the title or office that the supervisor holds in the organization; referent (relationship) power based on the supervisee's identification with, and liking for, the supervisor; and expert power based on the supervisor's special knowledge and skill.[9]

These five bases of power were made explicit in five different statements, and both supervisors and supervisees were asked to indicate which they thought most salient to the supervisee. The intent of the question was to identify the particular source of power that supervisees accept as the basis for the supervisor's authority. Table 22–1 recapitulates these results:

T A B L E 22–1. Sources of Supervisory Power as Perceived by Supervisors and Supervisees

SUPERVISOR'S SOURCE OF INFLUENCE WITH RESPECT TO SUPERVISEE	AS PERCEIVED BY SUPERVISORS (PERCENTAGE)	AS PERCEIVED BY SUPERVISEES (PERCENTAGE)
Expert power	95.3	65.5
Positional power	2.6	21.1
Coercive power	.6	5.5
Reward power	.2	3.1
Referent (relationship) power	.6	2.1

Supervisees grant the supervisors the power of their position more readily than supervisors are prepared to accept it. In fact, the supervisors by and large reject this power and see it as resting almost exclusively in their greater expertise. For social workers, it is surprising that both groups reject the power of the relationship as being a significant factor in motivating supervisee behavior. Identification and emulation are based on what the supervisor knows ("his knowledge and good judgment because of greater training and experience") rather than on the meaning he has as a person ("because I like the supervisor and want to do things he thinks should be done"). It may be that both groups regard referent power as appropriate for behavioral change in the worker-client relationship but not as a basis for influencing behavior between autonomous professionals.

SATISFACTIONS IN SUPERVISION

Supervisors and supervisees were given different lists of satisfactions and dissatisfactions in supervision and asked to select those about which they felt most strongly. To supervisors, the three strongest sources of satisfaction were "satisfaction in helping the supervisee grow and develop in professional competence" (88 percent), "satisfaction in insuring more efficient and effective service to my clients through my supervisory activities" (75 percent), and "satisfaction in sharing my knowledge of social work and my skills with supervisees" (63 percent).

For supervisees, the principal sources of satisfaction were indicated by such statements as "Through supervision I share the responsibility and obtain support for difficult case decisions from somebody with administrative authority" (44 percent), "My supervisor helps me to deal with problems in my work with clients" (40 percent), and "My supervisor helps me in my development as a professional social worker" (34 percent).

The principal sources of dissatisfaction for supervisors were "dissatisfaction with the administration and with administrative 'housekeeping–red tape' details" (71 percent), "the loss of the direct worker-client contact and relationship" (46 percent), and "dissatisfaction from the need to get the worker to follow agency policy and procedure with which I strongly disagree" (41 percent).

Statements indicating principal sources of dissatisfaction for the supervisee were "My supervisor is hesitant about confronting agency administration with the needs of his supervisees" (35 percent), "My supervisor is not sufficiently critical of my work so that I don't know what I am doing wrong or what needs changing" (26 percent), and "My supervisor does not provide much real help in dealing with problems I face with my clients (26 percent).

By far the largest percentage of both groups seem satisfied with their current supervisory situation. About 60 percent of the supervisees reported being "extremely satisfied" or "fairly satisfied" with their supervisor; 73 percent of the supervisors were "extremely" or "fairly" satisfied with "their current assignment as supervisor." Conversely, only 6 percent of the supervisors checked "fairly" or "extremely" dissatisfied with their current assignment, whereas 15.4 percent of the supervisees were "fairly" or "extremely" dissatisfied with their current supervisor.

To determine what factors are associated with dissatisfaction, a comparison was made between supervisees who indicated the greatest satisfaction in their current supervisory experience and those who indicated the greatest dissatisfaction. Strong overall dissatisfaction with the supervisory experience is associated with certain factors at a statistically significant level ($p < .001$). These are shown by the following statements: "The supervisor shows little real appreciation of the work the supervisee does," "He is capricious and arbitrary in the use of authority," "He does not provide much real help to supervisees in dealing with client problems," "He is controlling and dominating, restricting the autonomy and initiative of supervisees," and "He is not sufficiently critical of the work of the supervisee to show him what he is doing wrong and what needs changing."

The factors associated with dissatisfaction tend to confirm the ambivalence generated by the supervisory situation. This is particularly evident in the desire for professional autonomy, because this conflicts with the supervisee's need for dependence in learning. Restrictions on autonomy and initiative are resented, but so is the fact that the supervisor does not provide much help in dealing with clients' problems. In view of the supervisors' hesitancy in being critical, it is interesting that supervisees generally, and the most dissatisfied group in particular, indicate strong resentment of the fact that supervisors are not sufficiently or specifically critical of their work. The supervisees are anxious to do a better job and look to the supervisors for help in identifying the deficiencies in their work.

Pronounced dissatisfaction with supervision is not related to such factors as sex, age, or years of experience in the profession or the agency. Nor is it associated with the size of the agency. It is, however, related to the type of agency at a statistically significant level. Supervisees who are clearly dissatisfied with the supervision are more likely to be located in public than in private agencies ($p < .05$). These respondents were found to be clustered in public assistance and medical social work agencies.

FUNCTIONS AND OBJECTIVES

The survey included a list of possible functions, and supervisors were asked to check those that currently occupied the most time and those for which they had the greatest preference. The supervisees were given the same list of functions and were asked to check those they thought were most important and those least important. Supervisees regarded "teaching the casework aspects of the job—the knowledge, skills, and attitudes that the supervisee needs for effective job performance" as the most important function of supervision. Supervisors indicated that this was their preferred function and the one that occupied most of their time. A closely related function—"case consultation, the analysis and planning of client contacts with supervisees"—was regarded by supervisees as the supervisor's second most important function. The supervisors themselves gave this function second highest preference and one that occupied a major proportion of supervisory time. Both functions are directly related to the learning activities of the supervisee and the response of both groups showed clear congruence.

On the other hand, supervisees gave high priority to the function of supervision concerned with teaching the "administrative aspects of the job—agency policy, procedures, regulations, forms, and caseload management." This was given low preference by supervisors, although it was a function that occupied a high percentage of their time. The supervisor's responsibility to serve as a channel of communication linking the administration with the workers was also seen as an important function by the supervisees, but was one of the functions for which supervisors had little preference. Some of the findings are recapitulated in Table 22–2.

Both supervisors and supervisees agreed that the most important objectives of supervision were "to insure that the client gets full entitlement to service" and "to insure the professional development of the supervisee." They also agreed that the least important objectives were "to insure that the community image of the agency is not damaged" and "to insure accountability for the use of public funds." Only 5.3 percent of the supervisors listed the latter objective as one of the two most important. Such a response might be given serious consideration at a time when the profession is being pressed to be accountable, and when accountability tends to be defined in terms of responsible concern for the use of public funds.

THE IDEAL AND THE ACTUAL

Supervisors were asked to describe their picture of an ideal supervisor by reacting to a series of statements about supervisory behavior.

TABLE 22–2. Supervisors' and Supervisees' Reactions to Supervisory Functions

Functions	Regarded as Most Preferred by Supervisors (Percentage) $n = 469$	Regarded as Most Important by Supervisees (Percentage) $n = 384$	Occupied Most of Supervisors' Time (Percentage) $n = 469$
Teaching the supervisee the casework aspects of the job—the knowledge, skills, and attitudes he needs for effective job performance	26.8	18	18.2
Case consultation—analysis and planning of client contact with supervisees	21.7	14.8	15.4
Preparing for and conducting staff meetings and training sessions with supervisees	15.5	5.4	3.4
Reading and reviewing case records in preparation for individual conferences	6.5	3.4	5.4
Facilitating the work of supervisees by coordinating their work with others in the agency and arranging for the availability of clerical help, case aides, consultation, etc.	5.8	9.8	7.5
Teaching the supervisee the administrative aspects of the job—agency policy, procedures, regulations, forms, caseload management	5.5	11.0	13.4
Acting as a channel of communication from administration to supervisees and from supervisees to administration	5.1	11.8	10.7
Helping the supervisees with morale problems related to the job	3.3	5.4	5.7
Holding evaluation conferences with supervisees	3.1	5.4	1.8
Reading and reviewing case records for assignment to supervisees	2.1	3.4	5.9
Checking and sanctioning supervisees' decisions regarding clients, procedures, budgets, reports	1.5	4.6	7.6
Other (specified)	3.1	7.0	5.0
Totals	100	100	100

Supervisees were given the same statements and asked to describe their current supervisor. The thirty-nine statements offered were designed to cluster into six different dimensions, as follows: (1) supervisor interest in supervisee ("ready and willing to meet with the supervisee and show real interest in discussing his work"), (2) empathic understanding of the supervisee ("when the supervisee is discouraged or anxious, the supervisor seems to recognize this"), (3) acceptance of the supervisee ("creates the kind of emotional atmosphere in which supervisees feel free to discuss their mistakes and failures as well as their successes"), (4) willingness to grant autonomy ("can permit the supervisee to make his own mistakes"), (5) openness ("is ready to acknowledge occasional inability to help supervisee"), and (6) competence ("has a detailed and accurate grasp of agency policies and procedures").

The ideal supervisor was seen as both a competent practitioner and a competent supervisor; one who is educationally and administratively interested in, understanding and accepting of the supervisee, open to criticism, free to acknowledge shortcomings, and ready to grant the supervisee autonomy and encourage him to be independent.

The supervisees' characterization of their actual supervisor was, as might be expected, at variance with the supervisors' picture of the ideal supervisor. Given the fact that supervisors are fallible, one might anticipate that they would be somewhat less than ideal. Although the description of the actual supervisor was, in general, a highly positive one (and this should be emphasized), the difference between the mean for the ideal characterization and the actual characterization reached statistical significance ($p < .001$) for each of the dimensions. The greatest discrepancy was in reference to the following statements: "He goes to bat for his supervisees with the administration even if this means trouble for him," "He knows how to structure conferences in order to maximize learning," and "If challenged and uncertain the supervisor does not become defensive." The least discrepancy was found in the following statements: "He is ready to share some of his own doubts about the agency and the profession with supervisees," and "He makes himself available to the supervisee outside regular conference time."

It is interesting that the greatest discrepancy between ideal and actual supervisory behavior reflects a problem that supervisees themselves listed as the principal source of dissatisfaction. This was their dissatisfaction with the supervisor's hesitancy to confront the agency administration with the needs of his supervisees.

These results call attention to a supervisory responsibility that apparently should be given greater emphasis. Whereas the supervisor represents agency administration to the supervisee, the supervisee expects the supervisor to represent his needs to the agency administration. Whatever responsibility supervisees might have to organize collectively in order to take action in their own behalf, they still feel they can legitimately ask that the supervisor use his positional authority, his prerogatives, and his direct contacts with agency administration to help supervisees meet their demands on the agency. If supervisees are to feel secure in the agency, they need the assurance that they have the support of the supervisor and are adequately represented by him in any conflict with agency administration and agency policy.

Two distinct orientations to supervision were offered for respondent reaction. One, an existential supervisee-centered orientation, views supervision as concerned with the development of the supervisee's self-understanding, self-awareness, and emotional growth. The supervisee has the principal responsibility for what he wants to learn, and the focus of supervision is on the *way* the worker does his work and the nature of his relationship to the client. The other, oriented toward the supervisee's thinking, is didactic and task-centered and sees supervision as primarily concerned with the development of the supervisee's professional skills. The supervisor has the primary responsibility for what is taught and the focus of discussion is on *what* the worker is doing and his activities in behalf of his clients.

In scaling their reactions to the different viewpoints on an eleven-point scale, both the supervisors and the supervisees tended to check the midpoint—an indication that the most desirable orientation was an even admixture of both approaches. Despite overall agreement, supervisors leaned in the direction of the didactic, task-oriented approach to professional growth somewhat more decidedly than supervisees.

One supervisory function that emerged persistently as having great importance is the educational-consultative function. Both supervisor and supervisee see the responsibility for the supervisee's professional growth and development as one of the principal objectives of supervision. Helping the professional development of the supervisee was listed by the supervisor as the strongest satisfaction in supervision. Being helped to develop as a more effective professional was listed as one of the three strongest satisfactions of the supervisee. Both saw the source of supervisory power in the supervisor's expertise—an expertise that, hopefully, can be shared and communicated. Both would like to see the supervisory relationship defined as one of consultant-consultee, the principal difference between the participants lying in the greater knowledge and skill of the consultant. All this puts great emphasis on the functional competence of the supervisor—competence as a knowledgeable and skilled practitioner and as an educator. Despite the expressive (attitudinal) components in the relationship, supervision is seen as oriented primarily toward helping the supervisee learn to do the job more effectively. Accomplishment of this task requires knowledge and competence on the part of the supervisor. Although relationship skills have been emphasized as a key factor in supervision, technical competence is a consideration of equal, if not greater, importance. Significantly, the discrepancy between the ideal and the actual is often greater with respect to technical competence than to relationship skills.

CLASSICAL DILEMMAS

There is a difference in the way in which supervisors and supervisees regard evaluation procedures. Although 75 percent of the supervisors indicated that they hold regularly scheduled evaluation conferences, only 48 percent of the supervisees indicated that such conferences are, in fact, held. There are similar differences as to whether or not a formal outline of evaluation is available to the supervisee and shared with him in advance. About 40 percent of the supervisees indicated that this is not done. If workers need a clear statement of standards and expectations in order to function productively, current evaluation procedures may present difficulties.

Both supervisors and supervisees agree that the supervisee is rarely asked to prepare his own evaluation and that the most frequent procedure for sharing the evaluation is the presentation of a written report supplemented by oral discussion. Both agree that the principal use made of the evaluation is as a "basis for retention or separation" and "as a basis for salary increases."

In addition, supervisors and supervisees agree that no use is made of modern technology to obtain data of on-the-job performance. Audio tapes, video tapes, and one-way mirrors are rarely used to observe the worker's competence; the principal basis for such assessment is the "supervisee's written case records," "the supervisee's verbal reports of case activity," and "the supervisee's correspondence and reports." The client's assessment of the worker was rarely solicited as a source of information.

However contradictory it might seem, neither supervisors nor supervisees see a conflict between the administrative-evaluatory responsibilities and the educational-consultative responsibilities of supervision. About 74 percent of the supervisors and 57 percent of the supervisees rejected the idea of such a conflict. In this respect respondents echoed the clear message telegraphed by respondents in an earlier study on supervision.[10] In that study, 73 percent of both supervisors and supervisees responded to a similar question by indicating that they saw no real conflict between the different responsibilities. All this contributed to the annoyance of the researchers who, in reporting the earlier results, wrote that respondents "refused to recognize the absurdity [of lack of conflict] and with glorious illogic insisted that the two [responsibilities] could be combined." [11]

Another classic controversy in supervision seems to have been resolved in the minds of the respondents to the recent study. This is the question of the legitimacy of the supervisors' concern with, and responsibility for, the personal problems of their supervisees. The respondents apparently make a clear distinction between professional and personal development. Supervision is seen as being primarily responsible for helping the supervisee become a better worker, rather than a better person. Both groups selected the professional development of the supervisee as one of the two principal objectives of supervision. Conversely, both groups selected "insuring the more complete development of the supervisee as a mature person" as among the three least important objectives of supervision.

Although the satisfaction "in helping the supervisee grow and develop in professional competence" was the principal satisfaction in supervision for 88 percent of the supervisors, less than 1 percent of the supervisors checked "helping supervisees with their personal problems" as a source of satisfaction. The statement of dissatisfaction least often chosen by supervisees was "My supervisor tends to become too involved in my personal problems," indicating that for most respondents this was not a problem.

Responding to admonitions that they have no right to "casework the caseworker," supervisors adhere more religiously than supervisees to the dichotomy of professional versus personal development. If anything, supervisees indicate they are more willing to accept the therapeutic intrusions of the supervisor than supervisors are to offer such help.

In response to the incomplete sentence "If personal problems came up in my work with clients I would prefer that my supervisor . . ." 48 percent of the supervisees said that they wanted the supervisor to "identify the problems and help me resolve them," while only 30 percent of the supervisors chose this response. Conversely, although 44 percent of the supervisors indicated that they would "identify the problem and help supervisees get outside help," only 11 percent of the supervisees preferred this response. Supervisors more often than supervisees saw the legitimate source of help with job-related personal problems as lying outside the supervisory relationship.

It might be noted that just as the nonconflicting combination of consultative-teaching and evaluatory-administrative responsibilities of supervision contain a seeming contradiction, there is a like contradiction in the separation of professional self and personal self. Since the worker as a person is the principal instrumentality in the social worker's job, it might be argued that in helping the supervisee develop greater personal maturity the supervisor is at the same time helping him to develop greater professional competence.

RESPONDENTS' COMMENTS

The questionnaire ended with a blank page and an invitation to respondents to share any further comments on social work supervision. Over 150 respondents (18 percent) accepted this invitation. In most instances their comments were descriptive—explanatory statements about the respondent's supervisory experience that might clarify the context of his responses. However, some substantive responses of general interest were received as well. Thirty respondents commented on the inappropriateness of traditional supervision, the need to encourage greater professional independence and autonomy, and the desirability of peer supervision or consultation. One respondent commented that, as a mature woman with considerable experience in social work, she was embarrassed to "refer to somebody as her supervisor." Other comments were concerned with the current negative attitude toward supervision (sometimes related to a general attitude toward social work). Remarks were made to the effect that supervision is "outmoded," "downgraded," "phased out," and "a bad word."

As opposed to this, other comments indicated that graduate schools of social work were not doing enough to prepare people for supervisory responsibilities. It was suggested that schools should routinely offer a course in social work supervision as part of the master's degree curriculum. Responses to the questionnaire indicated that only 47 percent of the supervisors had completed a formal course in supervision. Some respondents expressed concern about the fact that professional advancement almost always required one to accept a supervisory position, even though the person concerned might prefer to remain a direct service practitioner.

Despite the growing importance of supervision as a special responsibility of the MSW worker, relatively little research has been done on the process. The survey reported in this article was made in an effort to obtain current data on supervisory practices, procedures, and problems that would begin to fill this gap. The survey presents a descriptive overview of significant aspects of current supervisory practice in social casework.

NOTES

1. Thomas L. Briggs, "Social Work Manpower: Developments and Dilemmas of the 1970's," in Margaret Purvine, ed., *Educating MSW Students to*

Work with Other Social Welfare Personnel (New York: Council on Social Work Education, 1973), p. 28.

2. Frank M. Lowenberg, *Time and Quality in Graduate Social Work Education—Report of the Special Committee to Study the Length of Graduate Social Work Education* (New York: Council on Social Work Education, 1972), p. 31.

3. Ibid.

4. Robert L. Barker, "Conclusion: Research Findings Related to the Education of Baccalaureate Social Workers," in Robert L. Barker and Thomas L. Briggs, eds., *Manpower Research on the Utilization of Baccalaureate Social Workers: Implications for Education* (Washington, D.C.: U.S. Government Printing Office, 1972), p. 92.

5. Virginia M. Schultz, "Employment Trends of Recent Graduates," *Personnel Information,* 16 (November 1970), p. 15.

6. John Melichercik, "Social Work Education and Social Work Practice," *The Social Worker,* 41 (Spring 1973).

7. Scott Briar, "Family Services and Casework," in Henry Maas, ed., *Research in the Social Services: A Five-Year Review* (New York: National Association of Social Workers, 1971), p. 111.

8. *NASW Directory of Professional Social Workers* (Washington, D.C.: National Association of Social Workers, 1972).

9. John R. P. French, Jr., and Bertram Raven, "The Bases of Social Power," in Dorwin Cartwright, ed., *Studies in Social Power* (Ann Arbor, Mich.: Institute for Social Research, 1959).

10. Western New York Chapter, NASW, Committee on Social Work Practice, "Opinions on Supervision: A Chapter Study," *Social Work,* 3 (January 1958), pp. 18–25.

11. Ibid., p. 22.

23

Reactions to Supervision in a Heteronomous Professional Organization

W. Richard Scott

PROFESSIONAL ORGANIZATIONS ARE organizations in which members of one or more professional groups play the central role in the achievement of the primary organizational objectives.[1] Professionals are employed by many types of organizations in varying capacities but only in a relatively few of these are they expected to perform the primary operations. Thus, engineers serve as inspectors and quality control officers in many industrial firms; scientists are often employed by research and development departments of industrial concerns, but they generally are viewed as serving goals which are secondary or auxiliary to the major objectives of the enterprise. However, clinics employing physicians, law firms hiring lawyers, schools and colleges staffed by teachers and professors, and welfare agencies employing social workers—these and similar organizations depend on professional employees to carry on their central activities and achieve their primary purposes and hence may be included in the category of professional organizations.

AUTONOMOUS OR HETERONOMOUS

Two types of professional organizations may be distinguished. The first, following Weber, may be called "autonomous" in that organizational officials delegate to the group of professional employees considerable responsibility for defining and implementing the goals, for setting per-

Reprinted from "Reactions to Supervision in a Heteronomous Professional Organization," by W. Richard Scott, published in *Administrative Science Quarterly* volume 10, no. 1 (June 1965), pp. 65–81, by permission of *The Administrative Science Quarterly*, © copyright 1965 *The Administrative Science Quarterly*.

formance standards, and for seeing to it that standards are maintained.[2] The professional employees often organize themselves—as a "staff" in hospitals, as an "academic council" or "senate" in universities—to assume these responsibilities. Individual professionals are expected to be highly skilled and motivated and to have internalized professional norms so that little external surveillance is required. If necessary, however, formal or informal sanctions may be applied by the colleague group.[3]

In an autonomous professional organization, a more or less well-demarcated boundary is set up between those tasks over which the professional group assumes responsibility and those over which the administrative officials have jurisdiction. Even when a professionally trained person occupies an administrative position, the boundaries tend to remain intact so that the professional official exercises authority over subordinates on administrative procedure but is permitted only to proffer advice to them on professional tasks.[4] Specific kinds of professional organizations which are likely to conform to the autonomous pattern include general hospitals, therapeutic psychiatric hospitals, medical clinics, the better colleges and universities, and scientific institutes and research organizations devoted to basic research.[5]

In the second type of professional organization, called "heteronomous"[6] professional employees are clearly subordinated to an administrative framework, and the amount of autonomy granted professional employees is relatively small. An elaborate set of rules and a system of routine supervision controls many if not most aspects of the tasks performed by professional employees, so that it is often difficult if not impossible to locate or define an arena of activity for which the professional group is responsible individually or collectively.[7] Examples of professional organizations often corresponding to this type include many public agencies—libraries, secondary schools, social welfare agencies—as well as some private organizations such as small religious colleges and firms engaged in applied research.[8]

The basis of the proposed typology is the amount of autonomy granted to professionals by the administrative control structure. Previous research on professionals suggests that they place a high value on their autonomy. A number of studies have been conducted within autonomous structures on the reactions of professional workers to the administrative hierarchy and on the manner in which professional and administrative problems are reconciled and accommodated. However, with one notable exception,[9] there have been relatively few attempts to examine in detail the reactions of professional workers to the more severe control structures encountered in heteronomous organizations.

This article will examine some data on professionals in a heteronomous organization obtained from a case study of a public welfare agency. The focus here will be on the reactions of workers to the agency's system of routine supervision, since this is one of the critical points at which the administrative structure of the agency impinges on the individual professional worker. Since all data were obtained from a single agency, one cannot generalize to other welfare organizations, and certainly not to other kinds of heteronomous organizations.

REACTIONS TO SUPERVISION

Characteristics of Agency

All data were collected in a public social work agency located in a city of approximately 100,000. The agency served the city and its surrounding county and will be referred to as "County Agency." The two largest agency divisions were responsible for administering the Federal categorical assistance program and such child welfare functions as foster home placement and adoptions. The study focused on the professional staff of the agency. Ninety-two case workers were organized into 12 work groups, each under a supervisor. The average work group consisted of one supervisor and seven case workers. Lengthy questionnaires were returned by 90 of the 92 case workers, and interviews were conducted with 11 of the 12 first-line supervisors.

A good case can be made for regarding County Agency as an example of a heteronomous organization. Many of the restrictions on the agency program originated outside of the agency itself, as explained in this excerpt from a booklet distributed by County Agency describing its operations to the public:

> Unlike the private agency, the policies and procedures of the public welfare department as well as the amount and the kind of assistance that the department may grant, are legally prescribed. The County Council, County Commissioners, General Assembly (State Legislature) and the Congress of the United States, all have a voice in what the department may do and how it shall do it.

When asked to react to some of the specific Federal and State provisions importantly affecting agency programs,[10] case workers were found to be overwhelmingly opposed to them. For example, 84 percent of the workers felt that residence requirements governing client eligibility for assistance should be removed or reduced, and 99 percent of the workers felt that budgetary ceilings set by the State to govern the amount of assistance should be either removed entirely or raised. More generally, 88 percent of the workers expressed agreement with the statement that "the professional progress of this agency and others like it in this State is held back by the conservatism of the [State's] public and legislature."

Workers were likewise upset by certain requirements imposed by the local agency administration. In particular, 72 percent of the workers believed that their case loads were too large to allow them to perform adequate case work with their clients, and 85 percent felt that they were required to spend too much time filling out the various forms required by agency procedures. In short, workers in County Agency believed that the kind of services they could perform for clients—their professional function—was rather severely constrained by the administrative and legal framework within which they were required to operate.

County Agency did not differ greatly from other public welfare agencies in the extent to which worker autonomy in dealing with clients was limited by administrative considerations. It did appear to differ from them, however, in the extent to which its staff was professionalized. The director held graduate degrees in both social work and social work administration, and all division heads held graduate degrees in social work. All of the first-line supervisors and 42 percent of the case workers had taken at least some courses in graduate schools of social work. These figures compare favorably with those for a national sample of social workers employed in public agencies.[11]

Supervision in Social Work

Social workers, unlike many professionals, do not view supervision as superfluous if not insufferable, but as a professional necessity. The following quotation illustrates their view:

> In the eyes of the social work profession, supervision by personnel skilled in imparting knowledge and techniques and in helping workers to recognize and profit by their errors without ego destructiveness is mandatory for client welfare and professional growth.[12]

It is apparent, however, that the term "supervision" is used in a special sense by the profession; the role is defined as being that of an educator rather than an administrative superior.[13] This definition may be partly the result of the relatively short formal training period—a two-year graduate program is the basic educational requirement—and partly the result of the lack of any formal professional preparation for the majority of social workers.[14] Here then, we have a profession which regards tutorial supervision as a necessity for both trained and untrained workers and to this extent helps to legitimate the agency's control structure by providing a professional rationale for it.[15]

Type of Supervision Preferred

When workers in County Agency were asked the following question:

> Social work is one of the few professions that provides for the persistent routine supervision of both the new and the experienced worker. Do you think, all things considered, that this is a good arrangement?

exactly half (44) stated that it was "a good arrangement," the other half admitted that it had both "advantages and disadvantages," but none felt that it was "not a good arrangement." In order to determine what *kind* of supervision workers preferred, they were asked to choose between the following pairs of qualities in a supervisor:

a) A supervisor well-versed in social and psychological theory.

b) A supervisor with several years of on-the-job experience.

a) A supervisor who will require the worker to make most of the decisions.

b) A supervisor who will make most of the decisions himself.

a) A supervisor who will stick very closely to procedure.

b) A supervisor who is quite flexible with regard to procedure.

a) A supervisor who checks quite closely on your work.

b) A supervisor who lets you work pretty much on your own.

a) A supervisor who is skilled in teaching casework techniques.

b) A supervisor who is skilled in agency policy and is a good administrator.

It was recognized that a worker might have difficulty choosing between some of these pairs of qualities, but the intent was to force workers to choose between characteristics associated with a professional (*a, a, b, b, a*) as opposed to a bureaucratic approach to supervision. As might be expected, agency workers in large measure preferred professional qualities in a supervisor with the exception that as many wished their supervisor to have had on-the-job experience as desired him to be well-versed in theory. Thus of about 85 workers responding, 49 percent preferred a supervisor well-versed in theory; 95 percent, a supervisor who would let workers make their own decisions; 78 percent, a supervisor who was flexible with regard to procedure; 69 percent, a supervisor who would let them work on their own; and 70 percent, a supervisor who was skilled in teaching case-work techniques.

Worker Orientations

It is particularly important when dealing with "weaker" professions like social work to differentiate between types of workers because of the wide variations in worker training and degree of contact with the profession. Advanced training in a school of social work was selected as the basis for distinguishing between types of workers, and while this may appear to be a rather weak index of professional orientation, it may be argued that in a profession where only the minority of workers have had any exposure to professional training centers, it is not without significance. [16]

One-third (10 of 30) of the workers with some graduate training in social work stated a preference for all five of the professional characteristics as compared to one-sixth (8 of 47) of the workers lacking graduate training. This finding holds for each of the five paired choices considered separately, although in some cases the differences between the two groups of workers is small. Also, to the question,

> In general, do you feel that supervisory positions in this agency should be filled only by workers with a master's degree in social work, or by any good worker with sufficient experience?

sixty-one percent of the (33) workers with some graduate work preferred supervisory positions to be held by a person with an advanced degree as compared to 40 percent of the (53) workers lacking graduate training.

Supervisor Orientations

Supervisors, like workers, differ in the degree to which they are professionally oriented, and the same dimension—exposure to professional training centers—was employed to differentiate between types of supervisors. Since all supervisors had some graduate training in social work, however, it was decided to utilize number of hours of graduate training as the criterion measure, with the median taken as the point of division. Supervisors having 18 hours of graduate work or less were assigned to the "low-exposure" group ($n = 7$); those having more than 18 hours were assigned to the "high exposure" category ($n = 4$). All supervisors assigned by this procedure to the high-exposure group had taken at least a full year of graduate work (30 hours or more), whereas those assigned to the low-exposure group had taken only a half year's work (18 hours) or less, there being a broad gap in the distribution at the point of division.*

In order to describe the supervisors' behavior as viewed by his subordinates, workers were asked to check a series of statements if they felt that they were applicable to their present supervisor. These data, differentiated by supervisor's exposure to professional training centers, are presented in Table 23–1. It is clear that on the three descriptions of professional qualities, workers under supervisors having high exposure to training centers were more likely to see their supervisor as exhibiting

---

* As was the case with workers, there again appeared to be a positive correlation between amount of graduate work and orientation to outside reference groups. All four supervisors in the high-exposure category reported their main source of professional stimulation to come from some person or group external to the agency, whereas only two of the seven supervisors in the low-exposure category located their main source of professional stimulation outside the agency.

TABLE 23–1. Professional Training of Supervisors as Related to Descriptions by Their Workers

PROFESSIONAL AND BUREAUCRATIC QUALITIES OF SUPERVISOR	EXPOSURE OF SUPERVISORS TO GRADUATE STUDY	
	HIGH ($n = 28$)	LOW ($n = 49$)
*Professional statements**	%	%
Tries to teach and help me when I make a mistake	82	63
Has a good background in social work theory	89	45
Is a good teacher of case-work methods and techniques	64	45
*Bureaucratic statements**		
Sticks very closely to rules and procedure	43	63
Is pretty strict with workers	14	31
Checks my work very closely	36	53
Is quite expert on the laws and policies pertaining to the agency	64	69
Sometimes forces his decisions on me	14	27

* All statements preceded by "My supervisor."

these qualities than workers under supervisors with low exposure to training centers. As to bureaucratic orientation of supervisors, the data indicate that the low-exposure supervisors were more likely to be viewed as exhibiting bureaucratic qualities than the high-exposure supervisors.

These data suggest that supervisors vary in their approach to subordinates, as perceived by the suborinates themselves, and that an important determinant of their approach is their degree of exposure to professional training centers. The data also may be viewed as providing some validation for the use of degree of exposure to training centers as an indicator of professional orientation among supervisors.

There is also evidence that professionally oriented supervisors were evaluated more highly than those less professionally oriented. It was noted earlier that exactly half of the workers in the agency regarded routine supervision as "a good arrangement." However, when workers were differentiated by type of supervisor, 77 percent of the (22) workers under professionally oriented supervisors in contrast to 45 percent of the (42) workers under less professional supervisors felt that the arrangement was a good one. Also, workers were asked:

> Would you favor the agency's hiring more specialists (for example, medical social workers, psychiatric social workers) with whom you could consult with regard to some of your case problems?

TABLE 23–2. Professional Training of Supervisor as Related to Worker's Evaluation of Effectiveness

EFFECTIVENESS OF SUPERVISOR	EXPOSURE OF SUPERVISORS TO GRADUATE STUDY	
	HIGH ($n = 28$)	LOW ($n = 49$)
*Effective statements**	%	%
Is quite sure of himself and self-confident	68	45
Backs me up in conflicts with clients	68	43
*Ineffective statements**		
Has very little control over his workers	0	8
Sometimes is impatient and loses his temper	7	20
Sometimes is reluctant to make decisions that he should make	7	25

* All statements preceded by "My supervisor."

Thirty-six percent of the (25) workers under professional supervisors strongly favored the hiring of more specialists, while 60 percent of the (45) workers under less professional supervisors strongly favored such a policy, indicating that workers under professional supervisors were more likely than those under less professional supervisors to feel that they were obtaining the technical assistance needed to deal with the problems of their clients.* When asked,

> Would you prefer to be given a freer hand in working with your case load than you are given by your supervisor?

89 percent of the (28) workers under professionally oriented supervisors felt that they were given the right amount of freedom rather than stating that they preferred more freedom or that they had too much freedom, as compared to 72 percent of the (46) workers under less professional supervisors.

Finally, workers were asked to check a series of statements relating in general to the perceived effectiveness of their supervisor. These statements together with worker responses to them appear in Table 23–2. Professionally oriented supervisors were viewed as more effective in being more self-confident and more likely to come to the aid of workers in

* Since the number of professionally oriented workers under professionally oriented supervisors was slightly higher than that under less professional supervisors, these result might be due to worker rather than supervisor orientation. This, however, is not the case. Thirty-six percent of both the (11) professionally oriented workers and the (14) nonprofessionally oriented workers under professional supervisors strongly favored hiring more specialists.

their conflicts with clients. By contrast, the less professional supervisors were seen as less effective in being somewhat more likely to lack control over workers, to lose their tempers, and to resist making dcisions within their jurisdiction.

While no one of these findings taken separately is particularly convincing, the over-all pattern exhibited by the several findings supports the view that a majority of workers tended to evaluate more highly the performances of professionally oriented as compared to less professionally oriented supervisors.

LOCATION OF REFERENCE GROUPS

Worker's First Reference

To determine the type and location of professional reference groups for workers, they were asked:

> From which of the following sources do you obtain the greater part of your intellectual and professional stimulation in connection with your work?

Workers were asked to select and order three sources from the following list: (1) my colleagues here in the agency; (2) my immediate supervisor; (3) my division head; (4) the director of the agency; (5) professional people outside the agency (teachers, conference speakers, etc.); (6) professional books or journals; and (7) others (to be specified). If attention is limited to the first choice, it was found that 77 percent of the (22) workers under professionally oriented supervisors selected their own supervisor as their primary source of professional stimulation as compared to 45 percent of the (42) workers serving under nonprofessionally oriented supervisors. Professionally oriented supervisors appear to serve at least in some measure as the voice of the profession for their subordinates and are in the happy position of helping to determine the criteria by which they are evaluated by workers. This may help to account for their being more highly evaluated by their subordinates.

Supervisors, however, are not the only source of professional stimulation within the agency. It appears to be the case in this agency that workers are not only subject to a legitimate order fashioned by Federal and State law-making agencies as interpreted and implemented by the administration, but much of whatever professional influence exists is filtered through the administrative apparatus. If those workers who selected either their division head or the director of the agency as their primary source of professional stimulation are added to those selecting their immediate supervisor, nearly three-fourths (72 percent) of the workers in this agency reported their main source of professional stimulation to be a member of the administrative hierarchy of the organization.

Professional Standards

Whether the professional standards set by administrative superiors are as high and as "pure" as those set by the profession itself can be explored to some extent by comparing the evaluations of the supervisors made by professionally oriented workers and by nonprofessionally oriented workers, holding orientation of supervisor constant. It will be recalled that the indicator of professional orientation for workers is whether they have had some exposure to professional training centers *outside the agency*. If the standards obtained from the worker's exposure to professional sources external to the agency are in fact higher than those obtained by workers from their experiences within the agency, then the trained workers should be more critical of their supervisors than the untrained workers. Since workers generally tended to be more critical of the less professional than of the professional supervisor, one would expect trained workers to be highly critical of the less professional supervisor and only moderately critical of the professional supervisor, whereas the untrained worker would be only moderately critical of the less professional supervisor and only slightly critical of the professional supervisor. And indeed, 54 percent of the (13) trained workers as compared to 66 percent of the (15) untrained workers under professional supervisors felt that routine supervision was a good thing; and 25 percent of the (16) trained workers as compared to 53 percent of the (30) untrained workers under less professional supervisors upheld the value of routine supervision. And although there were no differences between groups of workers under professionally oriented supervisors concerning the desirability of hiring specialists, 36 percent of each group strongly favoring such a policy, workers under less professional supervisors conformed to the predicted pattern: 73 percent of the (15) trained workers but only 53 percent of the (30) untrained workers favored hiring specialists. This suggested that exposure to professional training centers made the trained group more critical of the professional advice received from their own supervisor.

Most of the relevant data, however, again come from the statements to which workers were asked to respond in describing their present supervisor. These data appear in Table 23–3. Since the present focus is on evaluations based on professional criteria, the proportion of workers who fail to ascribe professional characteristics, or who ascribe bureaucratic characteristics to their supervisor, or who consider their supervisor

T A B L E 23–3. Professional Training of Supervisors and Social Workers as Related to Critical Attitudes of Workers

CRITICAL ATTITUDES OF WORKERS	EXPOSURE OF SUPERVISORS TO GRADUATE STUDY			
	High Exposure		Low Exposure	
	WORKER EXPOSED ($n=13$)	WORKER NOT EXPOSED ($n=15$)	WORKER EXPOSED ($n=17$)	WORKER NOT EXPOSED ($n=32$)
	%	%	%	%
*Professional statements**				
Does *not* try to teach and help me when I make a mistake	23	13	53	28
Does *not* have a good background in social work theory	8	13	71	47
Is *not* a good teacher of casework methods and techniques	46	27	59	53
*Bureaucratic statements**				
Sticks very closely to rules and procedures	54	33	59	62
Is pretty strict with workers	23	7	23	34
Checks my work very closely	38	33	47	57
Is quite expert on the laws and policies pertaining to the agency	62	67	53	78
Sometimes forces his decisions on me	23	7	23	28
*Ineffective statements**				
Is *not* sure of himself or self-confident	38	27	59	53
Does *not* back me up in conflicts with clients	38	27	59	56
Has very little control over his workers	0	0	12	6
Sometimes is impatient and loses his temper	15	0	29	16
Sometimes is reluctant to make decisions that he should make	8	7	35	19

* All statements preceded by "My supervisor."

ineffective will be taken as an indicator of the level of criticism directed toward the supervisor.†

† Note that although these are the same questions utilized in Tables 23–1 and 23–2, wording of some of the entries has been changed for this presentation so that all percentages within the table represent negative evaluations in terms of professional criteria—that is, larger percentages indicate that a higher proportion of the workers involved were critical of their supervisor. The changes were made only to facilitate comparisons among the percentages.

The over-all pattern of the worker responses appears to be consistent with the predicted reactions, suggesting that professionally trained workers tend to be more critical of the professionalism of their supervisors. As can be seen from the professional statements, on five of the six comparisons trained workers were more critical of their supervisors than untrained workers, holding constant supervisor's exposure to professional training centers. For the bureaucratic statements, the predicted reactions held for workers under high-exposure supervisors for four of the five comparisons, but were reversed on all comparisons involving workers under low-exposure supervisors. A possible explanation for this discrepancy is that the less professionally oriented supervisors may have been less strict, less apt to check closely, and less likely to attempt to force their decisions on their better trained workers because many of these workers had at least as much training as they. There is some evidence to support the hypothesis that the less well-trained supervisors gave differential treatment to their trained and untrained workers. When workers were asked if they would prefer to have a freer hand in working with their case load than they were given by their supervisor, responses permitted were: (a) yes, would prefer more freedom; (b) have about the right amount of freedom; and (c) have too much freedom; would prefer more guidance and control from supervisor. As indicated by Table 23–4, none of the workers under professionally trained supervisors stated that they had "too much freedom," but 19 percent of the (16) trained workers as compared to 7 percent of the (30) untrained workers stated that they would prefer more supervision than they were getting at present. Obviously, the differences are so small that these findings are merely suggestive, but it appears that there is some tendency for the less professional supervisors to undersupervise their trained workers so that they desire

T A B L E 23–4. Professional Training of Social Workers and Supervisors as Related to Degree of Freedom Permitted by Supervisor

DEGREE OF FREEDOM PREFERRED	EXPOSURE OF SUPERVISORS TO GRADUATE STUDY			
	High Exposure		Low Exposure	
	WORKER EXPOSED ($n = 13$)	WORKER NOT EXPOSED ($n = 15$)	WORKER EXPOSED ($n = 16$)	WORKER NOT EXPOSED ($n = 30$)
	%	%	%	%
Have right amount of freedom	92	87	69	73
Would prefer more freedom	8	13	12	20
Have too much freedom	0	0	19	7

more control. And such a tendency would account for the unexpected reversal.

The pattern of responses for the effectiveness statements (Table 23–3) appears to be generally consistent with the original predictions. On five of the ten comparisons, trained workers were more critical of their present supervisor than the untrained workers, holding supevisory orientation constant, and did not differ from the untrained workers in their responses to the remaining statements.

SUMMARY

Data obtained from a case study of a public welfare agency have been utilized to illuminate further the attitudes toward supervision where professional workers operate within a heteronomous structure, allowing them relatively little autonomy in the conduct of their work. In this study on the reactions of workers to the agency's routine system of supervision, workers in general were found to accept the system, although the degree of acceptance was found to vary with the professional orientation of both workers and supervisors. Professionally oriented workers were more critical of the system than nonprofessionally oriented workers and workers supervised by professionally oriented supervisors were less critical of the system than workers serving under less professionally oriented supervisors. Nearly three-quarters of the workers reported some member of the agency hierarchy to be the major source of professional stimulation, indicating that most workers looked chiefly to the agency officials for their professional norms and standards rather than to a source external to the agency. That standards transmitted through the agency hierarchy were not as high as those transmitted through external sources was indicated by the finding that workers exposed to professional training centers tended to hold higher standards for supervisors—hence were more critical of their supervisor—than workers who had not had such exposure.

NOTES

1. For another definition of the professional organization, see Amitai Etzioni, *A Comparative Analysis of Complex Organizations* (New York: Free Press, 1961), p. 51.

2. In his discussion of the corporate group (an organization is a specific type of corporate group), Weber defines as "autonomous" the group whose legitimate order "has been established by its own members on their own authority. . . ." See Max Weber, *The Theory of Social and Economic Or-*

ganization, trans. by A. M. Henderson and T. Parsons (Glencoe, Ill.: Free Press, 1947), p. 148.

3. This description should not be interpreted as implying that professionals are in fact able to exercise effective control over one another or that their members are equal in ability to control. On the ability of professionals to exercise effective control, see Eliot Freidson and Buford Rhea, "Processes of Control in a Company of Equals," *Social Problems*, 11 (1963), 119–131; and on differential control among professionals, see Etzioni, *op. cit.*, p. 256.

4. See Mary E. W. Goss, "Influence and Authority among Physicians in an Outpatient Clinic," *American Sociological Review*, 26 (1961), 39–50. Goss reports that the physician-in-charge exercised authority over other physicians with respect to the scheduling of student assistants, rooms, and patients, but, although he routinely reviewed patients' charts, he was expected to offer only suggestions on patient care to his fellow physicians.

5. The following studies provide some documentation for a relatively autonomous legitimate order established and operated by professionals in each of the settings: Harvey I. Smith, "Two Lines of Authority: The Hospital's Dilemma," in E. G. Jaco, ed., *Patients, Physicians, and Illness* (Glencoe, Ill.: Free Press, 1958), pp. 468–477; Alfred H. Stanton and Morris S. Schwartz, *The Mental Hospital* (New York: Basic Books, 1954), pp. 69–80; Talcott Parsons. "The Mental Hospital as a Type of Organization," in M. Greenblatt, D. J. Levinson, and R. H. Williams, eds., *The Patient and the Mental Hospital* (Glencoe, Ill.: Free Press, 1957), pp. 118, 125–128; Goss, *op. cit.*; Burton R. Clark, "Faculty Authority," *Bulletin of the American Association of University Professors*, 47 (1961), 293–302; and Barney G. Glaser, "Attraction, Autonomy, and Reciprocity in the Scientist-Supervisor Relationship," *Administrative Science Quarterly*, 8 (1963), 379–398.

6. In the heteronomous corporate group, the legitimate order "has been imposed by an outside agency." Weber, *op. cit.*, p. 148.

7. While it is not the purpose of this paper to account for the emergence of these two types of professional organizations, it may be noted that the stronger professions do appear to enjoy a mandate which allows them "to define what is proper conduct of others toward the matters concerned with their work," which is largely denied to the weaker professions. See Everett C. Hughes, *Men and Their Work* (Glencoe, Ill.: Free Press, 1958), p. 78. Etzioni also points out that a majority of the professions found in the heteronomous type of structure are composed of women, which undoubtedly has considerable bearing on their inability to acquire a fully legitimate professional status. See Amitai Etzioni, *Modern Organizations* (Englewood Cliffs, N.J.: Prentice-Hall, 1964), p. 89.

8. For representative studies of such structures, see Robert D. Leigh, *The Public Library in the United States* (New York: Columbia University, 1950); Howard S. Becker, "The Teacher in the Authority System of the Public School," *Journal of Educational Sociology*, 27 (1953), 128–141; Harold L. Wilensky and Charles N. Lebeaux, *Industrial Society and Social Welfare* (New York: Russell Sage Foundation, 1958); and William Korn-

hauser, *Scientists in Industry: Conflict and Accommodation* (Berkeley: University of California, 1962).

9. Kornhauser, *op. cit.*

10. For a summary of these provisions, see Helen I. Clarke, *Social Legislation* (2nd ed. rev.; New York: Appleton-Century-Crofts, 1957), pp. 562–563; and *Characteristics of State Public Assistance Plans under the Social Security Act* (U.S. Department of Health, Education and Welfare, Social Security Administration, Washington, D.C.: U.S. Government Printing Office, 1956).

11. For additional information on the characteristics of the agency and the composition of its staff, see Peter M. Blau and W. Richard Scott, *Formal Organizations* (San Francisco: Chandler, 1962), pp. 254–257.

12. Lloyd F. Ohlin, Herman Pivan, and Donnell M. Pappenfort, "Major Dilemmas of the Social Worker in Probation and Parole," *National Probation and Parole Association Journal*, 2 (1956), 219.

13. See Wilensky and Lebeaux, *op. cit.*, p. 237, where they point out that "in courses in supervision in schools of social work, leadership is more often conceived in terms of education than of command. . . ."

14. According to the national survey conducted in 1950 by the Department of Labor, although two-thirds of the social workers in this country were college graduates, only two in every five had any graduate study in a school of social work and only one in five had earned a graduate degree in social work (U.S. Department of Labor, Bureau of Labor Statistics), *Social Workers in 1950* (New York: American Association of Social Workers, 1952), p. 8.

15. This view has recently begun to come under attack within the profession. Another source of stress is the often discussed problem of the social worker's independent and responsible functioning, held as a value but often impeded by agency hierarchical structure and tradition. The most prominent feature of this area of stress is the system of prolonged supervision." See Lydia Rapaport, "In Defense of Social Work," *Social Service Review*, 34 (1960), 71.

16. Exposure to professional training centers was found to be positively correlated, although not strongly, with orientation to professional reference groups external to the agency (e.g., teachers, professional books and journals, etc.). See Blau and Scott, *op. cit.*, pp. 66–67.

24

Early Careers of Professional Social Workers in a Public Child Welfare Agency

Harry Wasserman

IN THIS ARTICLE, which describes and analyzes the early career experiences of neophyte professional social workers, a fundamental issue is explored: To what extent is professional social work practice in a large public child welfare agency determined by professional education—knowledge, values, and skills—and to what extent by structural constraints that reduce professionals to the level of case aide technicians? Related to this issue is an even more serious one: Can professionally educated social workers use knowledge and skills to effect the maximum well-being of clients involved in public child welfare services? The very lives of children and their families, separated through foster placement, are determined by the quantity and quality of the resources and services they receive. Social work intervention in this precarious human situation is, like some types of medical intervention, a matter of life or death.*

The professional social worker in a public child welfare agency assumes an awesome responsibility. The intellectual, emotional, and moral development of the child who is separated from his biological parents is at stake. The satisfaction of the child's most basic needs and the formation of his character depend on the professional social worker's capacity to (1) offer the child a relationship that carries an implicit contract of concern, care, and continuity, (2) advise and guide the foster parents in their roles as temporary (sometimes permanent) substitute parents, and (3) help the child's biological parents either to resume the normal parental role or maintain a proper physical and psychological distance from

---

* Erik Erikson speaks of the "mutilation of the spirit" in young children who have been grossly deprived of the gratification of basic needs.

Copyright 1970, National Association of Social Workers, Inc. Reprinted with permission from *Social Work*, Vol. 15 (July 1970), pp. 93–101.

the child when, in the worker's judgment, they are temporarily or permanently harmful to his well-being.

In attempting to satisfy and mediate the often conflicting claims and demands of the three parties, the professional social worker must be able to fulfill the roles of wise judge, loving parent, firm advocate, and patient friend. His intellectual and emotional resources are constantly being tested; he must be able to respond in a humane manner to a diversity of troubled, often difficult, people. The fate of children and families often hangs on the correctness of the professional social worker's judgments and decisions and on the agency's capacity to offer the needed social resources.

EARLY RESPONSES TO
THE WORK SITUATION

In June 1966 twelve newly graduated social workers were employed as child welfare workers by a large public welfare agency. Eleven were assigned to work duties in the agency's foster care program and one joined a newly formed proctective services unit that offered assistance to nonaided clients, i.e., individuals and families who were not financially dependent on public funds. These new professionals were observed and interviewed intermittently for two years as they went through the experience of becoming professional social workers.[1] Although there were minor differences in the operations of their respective district offices, they carried out their functions under the same major facilitating and constraining structural arrangements, i.e., policies, programs, regulations, and procedures.

The new professionals came from five schools of social work, four of which are located in California. The seven men and five women in the group ranged in age from 27 to 46.* Seven were in their 30s, three in their 20s, and two in their 40s. Nine had had prior experience in public welfare as nonprofessionals working in one of the assistance categories. Three workers had had no prior public welfare experience. Nine had been committed by stipends to work in the agency after graduation.

Within a month it was clear that the three professional social workers without public welfare experience were disappointed in their work situations. They had expected to have relatively small caseloads and definite interview times (e.g., on a weekly basis) and had expected, through intensive casework, to work toward bringing about changes in the feelings of clients. Since the workers were responsible for from fifty to seventy children, their expectations were rendered impossible. They felt

---

* These twelve new graduate workers represented the total number who came into service in this public agency in June 1966.

disheartened and overburdened by the large numbers of biological parents, foster parents, and children with whom they had to work, and overwhelmed by the large number of emergencies they had to face on an almost daily basis.

Four of the nine workers who had had previous public welfare experience had expected that once they were in a public agency child welfare program, they could "do casework." They believed there was a special aura, a special condition pertaining to child welfare within the public welfare structure that might permit a quality of social work whereby knowledge and principles of the profession would outweigh the exigencies of caseload and bureaucratic impediments. They too were disappointed but did not suffer at the outset from massive feelings of being overwhelmed and overburdened. They were able to adapt, even though their expectations were not initially realistic. However, their capacity to cope in the past was useful in their first experience as professional social workers. Only five workers were utterly realistic about the conditions and circumstances of work. As new professionals, they expected to be confronted with all the obstacles and difficulties of a large public agency serving disorganized families and their children. It has been observed that, while they were the most realistic of those interviewed, they were in a sense the most cynical. They tended to perceive the difference between their new and old work situations as the difference between having or not having an MSW degree.

WORKING CONDITIONS

The new professional social worker's home base is usually a district office. His desk is one of many on an open floor. There is little or no privacy. He is surrounded by other workers, welfare assistants, clerks, and supervisors, all crowded together with one desk adjoining another. Telephones are constantly ringing, and there is a steady hum of conversation, typewriting, and people moving from place to place. The office is not an environment in which a worker can think clearly and calmly about the complex and painful situations he faces and the fateful decisions he must sometimes make. There is no quiet place where one can go to think for a few moments or consult with colleagues. Interviewing clients, which occasionally takes place at the agency, is carried out in a small, open cubicle. There is no privacy. In sum, the setting is not one usually conceived of as "professional"; in fact, the environmental image is more industrial than professional.

The agency, whose offices are located in a large urban area, also provides service to a large county hinterland. This necessitates a great deal of car travel by workers. The distances covered add up to a few or several hundred miles per month. Foster children from one district of the county are not necessarily placed with foster parents from that district because there is a severe shortage of foster homes in certain districts.* Some workers spend as much as 20–25 percent of their time in travel. The extensive traveling is a mixed blessing: Although it consumes much time, it represents to some workers a haven from the noise and tension of the office. Unbelievable as it may seem, some workers report that a busy freeway is more conducive to reflection on cases than the office. Some workers, however, are fearful of the heavy traffic and high speeds, and their engrossment in case analysis raises anxieties about driving.

NATURE OF THE WORK

The following are some of the reasons why children are placed in foster homes: (1) the mental illness of one of the parents, usually the mother, (2) child neglect or abuse, (3) poor physical health of one of the parents, usually the mother, (4) the inability or unwillingness of the parent(s) to continue care for reasons other than mental illness, such as the mother's employment, (5) abandonment of the family, (6) a severe mental problem affecting the well-being of the children, and (7) the deviant and unmanageable behavior of a child.

The child welfare worker is almost constantly confronted with bewildering and painful human situations in which he must make serious decisions that will affect the fate of the children who are his primary clients and, through the impact of interpersonal relationships, the fate of the parents and siblings.

The possibilities for emergency situations in public child welfare work appear to be infinite. In much of the worker's daily experience he is in contact with his clients, and a significant amount of this contact is directed toward handling emergencies: e.g., a biological parent is intruding in the foster home situation, a foster child has been expelled from school, a foster parent has fallen ill and a new foster home is needed for the child. Thus the handling of emergencies carries with it not only a major investment of work time, but demands a type of worker who either has a preemployment capacity to work on this level or is one who can learn to do so.

The majority of the workers attempted to manage their caseloads by dividing foster home situations into three types: stable, potentially unstable, and emergency. In practice the first type meant that no news is good news. Although this was often true, many times silence covered smoldering problems. Workers saw these children, their biological par-

---

* There is a chronic shortage of foster homes throughout the county, but in some districts the shortages are more severe than in others.

ents, and foster parents only when necessary—during "reaffirmation" time, which occurred once every three months. Workers knew that problems were brewing in the potentially unstable situations, but had little time to invest in assessing the difficulties; treatment was thus out of the question. The workers secretly hoped that "everything would hold." Often enough these situations deteriorated into the third type, emergency, which demanded an immediate response from the worker. Frequently the child had to be removed from one foster home and placed in another. Simultaneously placing the child in a suitable new foster home, while salvaging the old one for other children, proved to be a complicated operation.

CUMULATIVE EMOTIONAL EFFECTS

The public agency child welfare worker works extremely hard. He is constantly "running to catch up," as one worker described his pace. In responding to the many crises and emergencies, he tries to save foster homes that are "blowing up," including some foster homes that are not the most desirable. He has to move children from one home to another and attend to the well-being of biological parents who may have some children in their own homes as well as some in foster homes. In other words, he has to confront a host of multifaceted human crises in order to maintain an orderly rather than chaotic life experience for his clients.

It was the observation of this writer that at least one-half of the new professional social workers suffered from varying degrees of physical fatigue and emotional upset.* Littner suggests that child welfare work is stressful because it reactivates unconscious conflicts, i.e., the worker's childhood conflicts.[2] Although this is undoubtedly true, there is perhaps a less recondite reason for a worker's emotional ill-health: He is often overwhelmed by the cumulative impact, perhaps the cumulative terror, of a large number of cases—by the human suffering, deprivation, disorder, ignorance, hostility, and cruelty he must face as part of his everyday work situation.

The worker's own psychic health is at stake if he attempts to establish what the existentialists call a "genuine human encounter" with all the persons to whom he is supposed to render service. In order to keep reasonably calm and sane, he must withdraw emotionally from significant engagement in many interactions and transactions with parents and

---

* By order of her physician one worker had to take a month off to recuperate from the stress of work. Another worker developed a phobia of freeway driving and underwent psychiatric treatment. A third worker suffered from sleeplessness and moderate depression. All three workers believed that their somatic and psychological upsets were due to work stress.

children. In effect he chooses a few human situations in which he can insert himself as a sentient human being.

The worker's caseloads are unsolicited. Cases are assigned to him much in the same way a ticket is pulled out of a raffle box. Case assignment, which could be designed to utilize a specific worker's knowledge and skills for a particular client's benefit, is nonselective. Workers and clients are brought together for the restructuring of family life with little evident concern for the balance of strengths, weaknesses, skills, and needs that must be weighed as carefully as possible in the precarious quest for human welfare and development.

CONSTRAINTS ON THE DECISION-MAKING PROCESS

One of the paradoxes of the bureaucratic structure is that, although it has the capacity to coordinate highly paid administrative staff to make relatively easy decisions, it seems barren of expertise and moral sensitivity when difficult, fateful decisions must be made. If a worker wants to obtain an emergency grocery order for a client, for example, he cannot be the sole decision-maker. The order must be approved first by the supervisor and then by the deputy district director. If the worker needs expert guidance and advice regarding case decisions, however, he has no one to turn to unless his supervisor or an agency consultant can contribute some insights and a plan of action. Following are three examples of the problems the new workers faced:

1. Mrs. B, a 37-year-old woman with a history of alcoholism, requested the return of her children from the foster home. After a period of exploration with the client and others, the worker felt unsure about the course to take.

2. About a month after Mrs. Y returned home from a state mental hospital, she expressed the desire to have her children back. Hospital prognosis was ambiguous. A telephone call to the attending psychiatrist was not helpful. Mrs. Y refused to see a psychiatrist in an outpatient clinic. She clamored for her children. She seemed to be in fairly good shape as far as the worker could tell.

3. The worker was not sure, after working with a couple for several months, whether they should be turned over to the court as neglectful parents. The worker was not sure of his diagnosis and therefore was unclear as to how to proceed.

Only three workers felt that their supervisors or consultants had sufficient knowledge and experience to help them make proper decisions about the living arrangements and, to some degree, the future well-being of the children and families they saw. For the majority of the workers in the type of situations cited, it seemed that expertise had been banished from the system. Other workers—professional and nonprofessional—often provided consultation and emotional support when the new workers were faced with important decisions or generally frustrating work situations.

All of the workers' decisions about clients are affected by the conditions (financial and social) under which the agency operates. Some of these conditions are legally determined. Others are imposed by the bureaucratic structure that is in part a reflection of the pervasive stigmatization of families and children in need of public aid. Seven such conditions can be described here.

1. The monthly grants under Aid to Families with Dependent Children (AFDC) represent an income approximately 25 percent below the poverty level set by the federal government. The AFDC grant as a sole source of income often reinforces malnutrition in children. Some of the twelve new workers had caseloads in which half of the foster children came from AFDC families.

2. For children of all ages, but especially for older children and adolescents, there are at present few alternatives to foster home care. Some children and adolescents could benefit from placements other than traditional foster homes; for some, foster home care is destined to be an experience of failure; and for still others institutional care is not even indicated. The new forms of foster care, such as family group homes and group homes either owned or operated by the agency, are extremely scarce.[3] Foster home placement is relied on almost exclusively as a one-way, fixed strategy of aiding children who cannot live with their own parents.[4]

3. Children are not assigned to foster homes on the basis of prior study and diagnosis. Assessments of the child, his biological family, potential foster parents, and the anticipated interactions of the three parties are not made. Ideally, it is the professional social worker's task to match a child with foster parents—to aim for a fit between the two. In reality a request is made to the licensing section within the district for a foster home for the child in question. The child's sex and age are the major determinants in the choice. The subtleties of the child's personality and individual needs are rarely the considerations upon which foster home assignment is made. In any case the severe chronic shortage of foster homes does not often permit selection or choice—personal or impersonal—among alternatives.

4. Children are usually removed from their own homes and placed in foster homes in emergency situations. There are no facilities for psychiatric and psychological examinations. There is no mechanism through which a serious study of the child can be made before placing him in a new situation. Consequently when the child is assigned to the social worker, he is an unknown to the worker except for those facts that accrue

in a case record or those that surround the immediate event of placement. The task of the social worker in helping the unknown child is analogous to that of the surgeon who performs surgery without prior study of an extensive medical work-up.

5. The large urban area where the agency described here is located suffers from a critical lack of social utilities—homemaker services, day care centers, and nurseries for children, vacations for poor families, one-stop neighborhood service centers, recreational facilities for adolescents, and so on.[5] Kahn conceptualizes these social utilities as normal institutional arrangements, operating singly and as a network to meet normal human needs in contemporary urban civilization.[6]

6. The constraints limiting the worker's knowledge, imagination, and ingenuity as they affect the decision-making process are further magnified by the rigidity of the institutions connected with the welfare enterprise. The cooperation of schools, hospitals, and courts—in sum, the institutional network in which the agency's families and children are involved—is undoubtedly one of the necessary conditions for rendering effective help.

Following are three examples taken from workers' cases. They demonstrate an institutional rigidity that is linked to the prejudices against "those who have failed."

> *Case 1.* Mrs. Smith and her two children remaining at home, ages 8 and 5, lived in a small house that deserved to be called a shack. After working with Mrs. Smith for about five months, the worker succeeded in persuading her to go into public housing. Plans fell through at the last minute because the housing authority learned that Mrs. Smith had once been arrested for prostitution. The worker's intervention (the worker's agency decided not to intervene for "strategic" reasons) on behalf of her client and the two children was unsuccessful. The family remained in the bad housing for five more months until new arrangements were made.
>
> *Case 2.* The worker persuaded Mrs. Jones to allow her 4-year-old daughter to be taken three times a week to a day care center located about five miles from home. An agency volunteer would provide transportation. After the child had attended the day care center for two days, the director informed the worker that the child could not return because she was not "dressed properly" and was "not clean." The worker promised to correct this, but to no avail. The day care director made pejorative allusions to "people on welfare."
>
> *Case 3.* John Wilson was placed in a foster home for the first time in his life at the age of 10. After about ten days, he was suspended from school for fighting. Whether he was the aggressor was not clearly established. John denied that he was. He was not a boy who normally attacked others. The worker explained to the principal and the assistant principal that many children became disturbed on being removed from

their own homes and placed in a foster home. The worker could not persuade the two school officials to readmit John. Apparently he had fought with a boy from an important family. John was placed in another foster home in another school district.

A process that stigmatizes client, worker, and agency as the institutionalized symbols of "damaged goods," combined with the genuine and projected problems of client behavior, severely impedes the rehabilitative efforts of the worker. Decision-making in respect to clients' living arrangements and well-being is directly affected.

7. Although all workers had foster homes that they evaluated as inadequate, if not harmful, they were reluctant to advise the agency to drop them. The chronic shortage of foster homes, a daily frustration for all workers, does not permit the agency to divest itself of any of them unless the child is grossly neglected or abused by the foster parents. The subtly harmful psychological attitudes and behavior of foster parents have to be overlooked.

To summarize: in the agency under discussion, professional workers' decision-making was sharply constrained by an interacting set of "impersonal" factors—insufficient financial payments to AFDC families and to foster families; an overconcentration on one strategy of foster placement (the family foster home) and, hence, a lack of diverse living arrangements for children of varying ages with a wide range of personality and character structures: a severe lack of social utilities; and a process of social definition that attributes little value either to the children and families needing agency services or to the agency itself.[7]

EXPECTATIONS AND OUTCOMES

Based on his observations, the author concludes that the two principal feelings expressed by the twelve new professional social workers during the two-year period were frustration and fatigue. They felt frustrated by natural constraints that did not permit them to employ the values, knowledge, and skills that their training had prepared them to use. They were exhausted by having day after day to face critical human situations with insufficient material, intellectual and emotional resources, and support.

After two years, eight of the new professionals left the agency for other employment. Six of the eight left voluntarily and two left involuntarily.* Among the voluntary terminations were the three who had felt overwhelmed and overburdened from the beginning of their professional work experience.

* One worker was drafted into the armed forces; the second worker moved to another city as a consequence of her spouse's employment situation.

The most important point to be made about those who terminated their employment is that, with the exception of one person who was essentially negative from the beginning, they were highly ambivalent about their departure. Although these new professional caseworkers had no choice of placements, most of them accepted the assignment in the child welfare division as potentially the most fruitful within the agency. In their involvement with the children and their biological and foster parents, commitments had been made and strengthened. To undo these commitments because of cumulative frustrations and physical and emotional fatigue did not provide a satisfactory rationalization for terminating their services. Commitments are infused with values, and to restructure interests and attitudes almost always is a major crisis. These new professionals terminated their positions only after much internal struggling, reflection, and discussion with trusted others. Ambivalent feelings had not been worked out at the point of departure; the needs of the inner self had neither been appeased nor mollified.

The new professionals had a profound sense of commitment to and had established bonds of mutual affection with some of the children. They were acutely aware of the experiences of abandonment and loss many of the children had suffered and how the departure of another important person signified one more such devastating experience. Some of the workers left the agency with the sense that they were betraying the children and, in some cases, the biological and foster parents. To sever ties with a child when his future appears to be as disordered and disruptive as his past is to leave with great sadness and the feeling of having run out. But the frustrations of work were overwhelming, and the physical and emotional fatigue too debilitating. Powerful negative forces dictated the necessity to leave the public welfare field. The departure of eight out of twelve professional workers at the end of a two-year period is a high attrition rate, especially for an agency that had made great efforts to recruit new professionals.[8]

Only one worker felt his work experience to be highly satisfactory in the sense that it was both a stimulating and useful intellectual and emotional experience. For the major part of the two years this worker has been in a small experimental unit of the one-stop neighborhood services type. This decentralized unit deserves a great deal of study. It was a healthful and supportive work environment in respect to the worker's mental health and general well-being and as an organizational arrangement designed to respond to children's and families' concerns and needs.

Some of the structural features of this small unit were a collegial (nonhierarchical) relationship among professional workers and between them and the supervisor; a supervisor who fulfilled the roles of teacher and charismatic leader; professional and nonprofessional personnel (welfare assistants and aides) who were assigned progressively more difficult duties and complex responsibilities designed to stretch the perimeters of competence; and reliance on a small group of people who were naturally willing to help each other in work situations of stress, strain, and crisis. The work group was formally designed as a primary social institution in which people could interact with each other as persons rather than as occupants of bureaucratic status and role.

CONCLUSIONS

The major conclusions to be drawn from these observations of new professionals in a public child welfare agency is that the knowledge, skills, and values (the social work perspective) that graduate students presumably acquire during a two-year period of professional social work education are essentially of little use in a work situation in which structural constraints dictate the decision-making process. While it is true that some social workers are able to respond naturally to troubled human beings above and beyond the constraints of social system and structure, it is also true that professionally trained social workers have little to offer those children and families who need special attention, care, guidance, and massive social resources over a long period of time. Workers estimated that 35–60 percent of their caseloads were made up of multi-problem, hard-core families. As Glover and Reid have said, "It is folly—if not hypocrisy—to plan for and talk about providing casework services and educational resources for people who are miserably housed and hungry. . . ." [9]

Frustration as a reaction to insufficient resources and utilities and physical and emotional fatigue as a response to daily emergencies and crises were the cumulative effects during the two-year period. The workers suffered individually, except for the important support some of them received in informal work groups. They had little sense of being members of a professional collectivity with whom they could consult on the basis of common experiences, concerns, and needs.

No group meetings—initiated either by the workers or by the administrative-supervisory staff—for the purpose of discussing common diagnostic and treatment problems took place in the agency's offices during the two-year observation period. Each worker conceived of himself as a private entrepreneur except that he had to follow agency-imposed rules, regulations, and procedures. The administrative staff did not encourage formal group consultation, case analysis (except for monthly psychiatric consultation), or the collection and analysis of data, and the new professional workers did not perceive these activities to be an integral part of professional life.

The principal question that emerges from this report can be stated as follows: What are the facilitating conditions under which professional social work can be practiced? It is a question that is not dissimilar to that facing the teaching profession. There is considerable evidence today that professional teachers cannot execute their functions effectively in the urban ghetto schools.[10] Similarly the effective practice of professional social work in a public agency chronically plagued by insufficient social resources, social utilities, and expertise is dubious. Although this hypothesis may fall under the rubric of an "unthinkable thought," failure to ponder its possible validity jeopardizes the future of the profession and its purposes and functions in society.

NOTES

1. For a more complete discussion of the participant-observer role, *see* Severyn T. Bruyn, *The Human Perspective in Sociology: The Methodology of Participant Observation* (Englewood Cliffs, N.J.: Prentice-Hall, 1966).

2. Ner Littner, *The Strains and Stresses on the Child Welfare Worker* (New York: Child Welfare League of America, 1957).

3. For a discussion of new forms of foster care, *see* Donald D. Dowling, "New Methods of Care," *Annals of the American Academy of Political and Social Science,* Vol. 355 (September 1964), pp. 49–55.

4. Leon Eisenberg writes: "Is it not time that we re-examine the very nature of foster care itself? The instability of foster homes, the shortage of adequate homes, the inability to provide continuity of worker, supervision, and foster parent—all these factors combine to suggest that group homes deserve to be given more weight in planning." "The Sins of the Fathers: Urban Decay and Social Pathology," *American Journal of Orthopsychiatry,* Vol. 32, No. 1 (January 1962), pp. 5–17.

5. For a detailed analysis of the lack of day care workers, homemaker services, and other social utilities in Los Angeles, *see Planning for the Protection and Care of Neglected Children in California* (Los Angeles: National Study Service, 1965).

6. Alfred J. Kahn, "New Policies and Service Models: The Next Phase," *American Journal of Orthopsychiatry,* Vol. 35, No. 3 (July 1965), pp. 652–662.

7. Elizabeth Wickenden's comments are pertinent. She writes: "There must be enough of the service—whatever the service may be—to make it available to all those whom it has been decided are entitled to it. There is no use in saying, for instance, that every child is entitled to day care if you haven't got enough day care. This is the problem with public assistance. The problem is that people have entitlements to something of which there is not enough to go around. . . . But if a person is entitled to something that isn't as divisible as money, such as day care, or foster care, or certain

kinds of service for the aged—there must be enough. . . ." "Services—What Are the Issues," in Malvin Morton, ed., *Round Table Reader, 1967* (Chicago, Ill.: American Public Welfare Association, 1968), p. 44.

8. Alfred Kadushin writes: "Child welfare agencies, both public and private, have relatively high turnover rates. A detailed, nationwide study of full-time caseworkers in such agencies indicated that about 27 percent of the workers who are with the agency at the beginning of the year will no longer be with it by the end of the year." *Child Welfare Services* (New York: Macmillan Co., 1967), p. 593.

9. Elizabeth Glover and Joseph H. Reid, "Unmet and Future Needs," *Annals of the American Academy of Political and Social Science*, Vol. 355 (September 1964), p. 12.

10. For a commentary on the difficulties facing professional teachers in ghetto schools, *see* Jason Epstein, "New York School Revolt," *New York Review of Books* (October 10, 1968), pp. 37–40.

25

An Empirical Study
of Structure and Authority
in Social Work Supervision

Carlton E. Munson

INTRODUCTION

SUPERVISION HAS BEEN AROUND as long as social work. Even "During the years of 'friendly visiting' . . . caseworkers were *told* the rules and shown how to do the job." [1] As social workers struggled to achieve professional status and to separate casework from the role of the friendly visitor, [2] supervision continued to play an important part. Pettes observed, "The history of supervision goes back to the very beginnings of social work as a profession; indeed it is inextricably bound up with the development of the profession." [3]

The evolution of the literature on social work supervision has been characterized by concern with control. [4] As long as supervision served "as a way of training staff, paid or volunteer, to do the job at hand—to help people according to the function and policies of the early social agencies," [5] control was accepted; but as training moved into the university, became quite lengthy, and fostered and taught professionalism, the question of autonomy became crucial. Questions were raised during the 1960s about the conflicts associated with fostering professional behavior and exercising regulation of workers.

The case for control has been getting more difficult to make as emphasis on autonomy has increased in education and practice. The focus has shifted to exploration of alternative means of structuring supervision. Much of the literature on group supervision seems to reveal an attempt to utilize group methods to dilute and redirect authority. [6] Abrahamson, [7] Judd, [8] Kaslow, [9] and Epstein [10] have argued that group supervision is more effective than individual supervision in most respects, including use of authority.

Debate continues at the theoretical level of how best to exercise authority and structure supervision, partly because little is known about the attitudes of workers. The research reported here is intended to provide information about the following: How is authority perceived? Are there differential methods of exercising authority? Is group supervision more effective than individual supervision? What is the relationship between structure of supervision and exercise of authority?

METHODOLOGY OF RESEARCH

A survey was used to gather data from sixty-five workers in nineteen agencies in three states. A cluster sampling technique was employed to obtain a cross-section of social workers at various levels of education, in various settings, and in public as well as private agencies. Agencies and workers were selected at random based on agency size. Nineteen (76 percent) of the twenty-five agencies selected were used in the study, and sixty-five (93 percent) of the seventy workers originally selected were interviewed. In the majority of the descriptive variables (sex, age, and experience) the findings were similar to Kadushin's,[11] adding support for the representativeness of the sample.

An eighteen-page questionnaire containing structured and open-ended questions was administered in face-to-face interviews that lasted approximately one hour. Descriptive and attitudinal data were gathered, as each interviewee was asked to identify from a list of measures his or her perception of the structural model and the model of authority used in supervision. The structural models of traditional (individual supervision), group, and independent were based on typologies identified by Epstein.[12] The authority models of sanctioned, evaluative, mediator, and competence were based on the "source of power" in supervision identified by Levy.[13] Because of the small frequencies in the categories of evaluative ($n = 1$) and mediator ($n = 2$), these categories were combined with the sanctioned and competence models respectively for statistical analysis.

The responses to the open ended questions were categorically computerized and analyzed according to the structural and authority models to find out if differences in attitudes existed toward them.

The following variables were analyzed in relation to the perceived structural and authority models in use: (1) worker age, (2) worker years of experience, (3) degree of sharing of clinical practice between worker and supervisor, (4) interaction between worker and supervisor, (5) worker job satisfaction, and (6) worker general satisfaction with supervision. All these variables were measured at the interval level and were statistically analyzed by point biserial correlation, which provides a comparison of means and allows application of the t-tests of significance. This statistical procedure was selected because it provides for comparison of paired groups; in some agencies, combinations of supervision structures are used, and this type of analysis can explore what combinations are most productive.

FINDINGS

Major Variables

Table 25–1 presents the findings on the major variables. The average age of the workers was 34.3 years, and they had an average of 5.8 years of experience in social work. Clinical exposure was measured through a series of questions about the amount of joint interviewing, audio and video tape usage, and process recording used in supervision. It was found that virtually none of these learning techniques was being used. The possible range on this variable was 5 to 20, and the average score was 6.4. The only device reportedly used with any consistency was process recording, and even that was used infrequently. There was a fairly high level of interaction reported between supervisees and supervisors, the mean score being 30.1. Both job satisfaction (20.4) and general satisfaction with supervision (36.9) were held to be high by the workers. In summary, the workers were in their mid-thirties, with a little under six years of experience, and had high levels of interaction in and satisfaction with supervision as well as a high degree of job satisfaction, but there was almost no clinical exposure taking place in their supervision.

Structural Models of Supervision

Table 25–2 shows the distribution of the major variables, and Table 25–3 contains the correlation of the variables for the three structural

T A B L E 25–1. Mean and Standard Deviation for Major Descriptive Variables

Variable	Possible Range of Scores	Mean	Standard Deviation
1. Worker age	—	34.3	11.4
2. Worker years of experience	—	5.8	4.9
3. Clinical exposure	(5–20)	6.4	1.6
4. Interaction level	(7–42)	30.1	6.7
5. Job satisfaction	(5–30)	20.4	4.6
6. General supervision satisfaction	(8–48)	36.9	8.4

TABLE 25-2. Difference Among Means of Worker-Perceived Models of Supervision on Supervision Variables

Variable	SUPERVISION MODEL		
	Traditional ($n = 35$)	Group ($n = 11$)	Independent ($n = 19$)
1. Worker age	31.61	40.36	36.00
2. Worker experience	4.52	7.09	7.72
3. Clinical exposure	6.41	7.27	5.77
4. Interaction level	31.86	29.45	26.94
5. Job satisfaction	21.27	20.18	18.88
6. General supervision satisfaction	37.86	37.45	34.88

models. From Table 25-2 it can be determined that older workers tended to be supervised more in the group model and younger workers in the traditional model of individual supervision. Table 25-3 shows that age of the worker was significantly ($\rho = < .01$) correlated with the traditional and group model. There was a tendency to use the group model more than the independent model with older workers. Also, there was a natural progression, as experience increased, from traditional to group to independent model. The only significant ($\rho = < .05$) difference occurred between the traditional and independent models, indicating that there is some differentiation of the model used based on experience.

Clinical exposure and level of interaction did show some difference in the structural model. For the former, the group model showed the highest level, and the independent model the lowest. This outcome was expected because of the nature of the structural models, but it suggests that a lack of provision for clinical exposure is an inherent weakness of the independent model. The lowest level of interaction also occurred in the independent model, and the highest in the traditional. Although there was more clinical exposure in the group model than in the traditional one, for interaction the situation was reversed. In both clinical exposure and interaction, the independent model produced significantly lower levels of activity.

Job satisfaction and general satisfaction with supervision showed no significant difference in any of the three models—which raises a question about the theoretical argument that group supervision is the preferred model. In these two areas structure alone has little impact on outcome.

Authority Model of Supervision

Table 25-4 reflects the differences in mean scores on each variable according to the authority perceived by the worker. Originally four types of authority were identified: sanctioned, evaluative, mediator, and

TABLE 25–3. Difference Among Variables of Worker-Perceived Models of Supervision (by Point Biserial Correlation Coefficients)

Variable	SUPERVISION MODEL								
	Traditional with Group			Traditional with Independent			Group with Independent		
	r_{pbi}*	tf	p	r_{pbi}	t	p	r_{pbi}	t	p
1. Worker age	-.41	-3.02	<.01	-.19	-1.39	N.S.	.17	.89	N.S.
2. Worker experience	-.25	-1.73	N.S.	-.31	-2.36	<.05	-.06	-.31	N.S.
3. Clinical exposure	-.22	-1.51	N.S.	.44	3.53	<.001	.45	2.61	<.02
4. Interaction level	.17	1.16	N.S.	.35	2.69	<.01	.16	.84	N.S.
5. Job satisfaction	.11	.74	N.S.	.23	1.70	N.S.	.14	.74	N.S.
6. General satisfaction	.02	.13	N.S.	.17	1.24	N.S.	.14	.73	N.S.

*r_{pbi}—Point biserial correlation coefficient. Positive and negative signs only indicate the direction of the difference in means.

†t—Two-tailed test.

T A B L E 25–4. Difference Among Variables of Worker-Perceived Sanctioned and Competence Models of Authority (by Point Biserial Correlation Coefficients)

Variable	Sanctioned ($n = 24$) MEAN	Competence ($n = 41$) MEAN	r_{pbi}*	t†	p
1. Worker age	36.65	32.43	.085	.67	N.S.
2. Worker experience	7.08	4.74	.23	1.87	$<.05$
3. Clinical exposure	5.82	6.66	−.25	−2.04	$<.05$
4. Interaction level	26.69	32.76	−.43	−3.77	$<.001$
5. Job satisfaction	18.86	21.46	−.27	−2.22	$<.05$
6. General supervisor satisfaction	31.56	40.61	−.52	−4.83	$<.001$

Column group header over the first two data columns: PERCEIVED SUPERVISORY AUTHORITY MODEL

*r_{pbi}—Point biserial correlation coefficient. Positive and negative signs only indicate the direction of the difference in means.
†t—Two-tailed test.

competence. Because of the small frequencies in the evaluative ($n = 1$) and mediator (2) categories, the former was combined with sanctioned and the latter with competence. The failure of the workers to perceive authority in the role of the supervisor as mediator of the worker–agency relationship raises questions about this perception of authority in practical use even though it has been cited in the literature as an important aspect of supervision.[14] The majority of workers (63 percent) saw their supervisors as deriving authority from their competence, and 24 workers (37 percent) from the sanctioned model. This finding is consistent with Kadushin's survey, where he found that 65 percent of workers viewed supervisory authority as originating from "expert power" (competence) and 21 percent from "positional power" (sanctioned).

The means were significantly different for the sanctioned and competence models, in contrast to the structural models, on five of the six variables. Worker age had little bearing, but more experienced workers tend to view supervisors in the sanctioned model. Logically this finding is to be expected since as workers gain experience their own competence increases and the supervisor is seen more as a peer professionally and as an agency representative in the supervisory role, whereas for the inexperienced worker the supervisor is a source of professional growth and knowledge.

Clinical exposure and level of interaction were significantly different for the two models. The supervisor who is seen as exercising authority from competence engages in more sharing of clinical practice through use of joint interviewing, electronic recording devices, and written case materials. The competent supervisor interacts more frequently with the worker, is more pleasant, is more open and honest, is approachable, expresses appreciation for good work, is clear and concise in communication, and socializes with the worker. The supervisor who is perceived as using the sanctioned model is more likely to use the position as the basis of interaction, which becomes limited to a formal relationship.

Job satisfaction and supervision satisfaction were found to be significantly higher for the competency model. As regards job satisfaction, the competent supervisor showed concern for staff welfare as well as output, was stable and consistent in expectations, and was able to solve problems and effectively deal with staff conflicts. However, attitude toward the agency and adequacy of salary were also higher for the competency model. The competent supervisor did show high levels of respect for the worker as a professional, was fair in evaluating the worker's performance, and made supervisory sessions a worthwhile, productive experience.

DISCUSSION, INTERPRETATIONS, AND CONCLUSIONS

It is difficult to discuss the use of structure and of authority in supervision separately; historically the literature has made few if any distinctions between the two. There is a certain degree of authority inherent in the supervisory relationship. Pruger has pointed out that the worker must be attentive to and understand legitimate authority, but "there still exists significant autonomy for the individual, if he consciously recognizes and uses it." [15] For social workers to expand and at the same time recognize the limits of autonomy, a distinction must be made between structure and authority. Pruger unites the two concepts: " . . . if . . . autonomy is lost, it must be because it was . . . given up, rather than because it was structurally precluded." [16] The idea that authority and structure in supervision are two different but related concepts is supported by the findings of this study since the structural models did not produce significantly different outcomes; however, the perceptions of authority models did show major significant differences.

Although there have been increasing demands for worker autonomy, the findings of this study indicate that this struggle has had little impact on the structure of supervision. Group supervision has been viewed as an alternative structure to promote autonomy, but the findings of this research and reports of others [17] show that it has not been implemented on a broad basis. Kaslow attributes this dearth to the fact that supervisors lack the skills or confidence to use group methods.[18] If this is the case then the issue becomes whether or not the supervisor is seen by the worker as being competent in the position. The failure to use group methods widely could also be related to the supervisor's fear of loss of control and feeling of threatened authority. The findings of this study would indicate that there are specific behaviors supervisors can manifest to promote worker regard for their competence and decrease the resistance to group supervision, thereby increasing the degree of autonomy.

Widen has defined supervision as a creature of agencies rather than as a professional enterprise. It is his view that the literature has explored the supervisory process but not the structure which " . . . is particularly sensitive to the life style of the agency as a social institution," [19] and the result is that " . . . each agency that has a formal supervisory structure has a philosophy of supervision." [20] Often the problem of autonomy and supervision is expressed as a struggle between the individual professional worker and the agency, and the supervisor, who is usually a member of the same professional group, is put in conflict when expected to mediate this relationship. As long as the issue is viewed in this way, little substantial change will occur, especially considering that virtually no workers view the supervisor role as one of mediation. Supervisors' failure to use the mediator model could be the result of a conscious attempt to avoid role conflict and strain—most supervisors know the consequences of such role performance—but at the same time the supervisee is left with the problem of how to confront the organization. Only when the profession as a group addresses this issue through its organizations will systematic, standardized principles be established to guide agencies in their practices. Organizational issues can only be resolved at the organizational level.

In addressing the issue of supervision at the professional level, the findings of this research would indicate that the unit of analysis should not necessarily be the structure of supervision itself but the content and means of implementation. Autonomy will be best achieved when the worker is free to select the model to be used rather than having one imposed by theoreticians, agencies, and supervisors. Given the diversity in the resources and size of the agency and the education, experience, personalities, and supervisory preferences of the worker, it seems unrealistic to seek one best model of supervision; and it is my belief, based on the findings of this study, that a flexible system is attainable.

There is a certain degree of authority in the supervisory relationship, based on the notion that "in pre–World War II organization theory, efficiency was assumed to result from specialization of task and strict adherence to a hierarchic chain of command." [21] Based on the findings of this study that clinical exposure, interaction, job satisfaction, and supervisory satisfaction were significantly higher in the competence than the sanctioned model, the latter is the more productive model in all respects. Our findings are quite similar to those of a sociological study in which an association was found among authority styles, verbal aggression toward the supervisor, productivity, and job satisfaction.[22] If this distinction is valid, then agencies, the profession, and supervisors must strive to attain a perception of competence to achieve the most effective functioning of the organization and at the same time provide high levels of satisfaction among workers.

The most difficult task remains for the profession and agency managers: If the competence model produces better outcomes, then what makes workers see their supervisors as competent? Responses from workers indicate that such perceptions involve personal characteristics, genuine interest and support of the supervisor in what the worker is doing, organizationally manipulable behaviors such as availability and appropriate levels and timing of control, and superior skill and knowledge of the supervisor concerning the task and position to be supervised.

Agencies must make hard decisions about who becomes and remains a supervisor, and supervisors must make firm choices about what to control and when to control it. Authority involves the ability to influence, but the subjective responses of workers in this study would indicate that they should also be able to influence their supervisors. If they actually were doing so, then supervisors would be truly viewed as having the role of mediators.

> A greater amount of total control, whereby subordinates can actually influence their supervisors, will heighten, not lower, the organization's performance. However, when subordinates obtain a measure of expertise but are given no control, morale and willingness to contribute to the organization decreases.[23]

Workers, as they indicated in this study, will continue to look for supervisors "who are smarter than we are" and will want to feel that "I work for my supervisor, not the agency"; but at the same time they will contend that supervision is no good if you have to tell a client "I will have to talk this over with my supervisor and let you know" and that good supervision only exists "when you know you are supervised, but are not aware of it every moment." The workers' words speak for themselves.

NOTES

1. Norma D. Levine, "Educational Components of Supervision in a Family Agency," *Social Casework* 31 (June 1950), p. 245.
2. See Everett C. Hughes, "Professions," *Daedalus* 92 (Fall 1963), p. 659;

Mary Burns, "Supervision in Social Work," *Encyclopedia of Social Work,* Harry L. Lurie, ed. (New York: National Association of Social Workers, 1965), p. 785.

3. Dorothy Pettes, *Supervision in Social Work: A Method of Student Training and Staff Development* (London: George Allen and Unwin, Ltd., 1967), p. 15.

4. For examples see Frances T. Levinson, "Psychological Components of Supervision in a Family Agency," *Social Casework* 31 (June 1950), pp. 237–245; Elizabeth Chichester *et al.,* "Field Work Criteria for Second-Year Casework Students," *Social Casework* 31 (June 1950), pp. 229–237; Alfred Kadushin, "Games People Play in Supervision," *Social Work* 13 (July 1968), pp. 23–32 [Chapter 17 above]; Pettes, *op. cit.,* pp. 15–25.

5. Burns, *op. cit.,* p. 785.

6. See Arthur C. Abrahamson, "Group Methods in Field Work Teaching," *Social Casework* 35 (February 1954), pp. 68–71; Elizabeth E. Chichester, "Group Meetings as an Aid to Student Supervision," *Social Casework* 36 (June 1955), pp. 264–269; Ruth Fizdale, "Peer-Group Supervision," *Social Casework* 39 (October 1958), pp. 443–450 [Chapter 12 above]; Jadwiga Judd *et al.,* "Group Supervision: A Vehicle for Professional Development," *Social Work* 7 (January 1962), pp. 96–102; Tsuneko Apaka *et al.,* "Establishing Group Supervision in a Hospital Social Work Department," *Social Work* 12 (October 1967), pp. 54–60; G. S. Getzel *et al.,* "Supervising in Groups as a Model for Today," *Social Casework* 31 (March 1971), pp. 154–163.

7. Abrahamson, *op. cit.,* p. 71.

8. Judd, *op. cit.,* p. 96.

9. Florence W. Kaslow, "Group Supervision," in Florence W. Kaslow, ed., *Issues in Human Services* (San Francisco: Jossey-Bass, 1972), p. 118.

10. Laura Epstein, "Is Autonomous Practice Possible?" *Social Work* 18 (March 1973), p. 6 [Chapter 14 above, p. 144].

11. Alfred Kadushin, "Supervisor-Supervisee: A Survey," *Social Work* 19 (May 1974), pp. 288–297 [Chapter 22 above].

12. Epstein, *op. cit.,* pp. 5–12.

13. Charles S. Levy, "The Ethics of Supervision," *Social Work* 18 (March 1973), pp. 14–21 [Chapter 20 above].

14. See Epstein, *op. cit.,* p. 6; and Levy, *op. cit.,* p. 16.

15. Robert Pruger, "The Good Bureaucrat," *Social Work* 18 (July 1973), p. 28.

16. *Ibid.,* p. 28.

17. Betty Mandell, "The 'Equality' Revolution and Supervision," *Journal of Education for Social Work* 9 (Winter 1973), p. 51 [Chapter 27 below, p. 321]; and Kaslow, *op. cit.,* p. 117.

18. Kaslow, *op. cit.,* p. 117.

19. Paul Widen, "Organizational Structure for Casework Supervision," *Social Work* 7 (October 1962), p. 79.

20. *Ibid.,* p. 84.

21. Philip M. Marcus and Dora Marcus, "Control in Modern Organizations," in Merlin B. Brinkerhoff and Phillip R. Kung, eds., *Complex Organizations and Their Environments* (Dubuque, Iowa: W. C. Brown, 1972), p. 234.

22. Robert C. Day and Robert L. Hamblin, "Some Effects of Close and Punitive Styles of Supervision," in Gerald D. Bell, ed., *Organizations and Human Behavior: A Book of Readings* (Englewood Cliffs, N.J.: Prentice Hall, Inc., 1967), pp. 172–181.

23. Marcus and Marcus, *op. cit.*, p. 243.

26

Clinical Supervision
in Community Mental Health

Cary Cherniss and Edward Egnatios

PERHAPS MORE THAN ANY other occupational group, mental health clinicians use supervision and consultation to further their own professional development. The quality of their supervision often seems to be the most important single factor affecting their job satisfaction, especially in the case of newer, less experienced clinicians. When asked, clinicians report that supervision is of prime importance in their training and early career. For instance, in a study of practicing psychotherapists, conducted by Henry, Sims, and Spray, the respondents cited supervision as their single most important socialization experience; 90 percent of the respondents considered additional supervision received after their formal training had ended to be valuable.[1] In another study, Cherniss and Egnatios found a significant correlation between frequency of supervision and the reported job satisfaction of community mental health clinicians.[2] Those who received supervision regularly and frequently were more satisfied with their jobs.

Much of the literature on supervision in clinical agencies has defined three basic types: "laissez-faire" supervision, "close" supervision, "professionally oriented" supervision. In laissez-faire supervision, the supervisor leaves the supervisee alone most of the time and is rarely available for consultation on work problems. Standards of performance and expectations often are unclear. Close supervision represents the opposite extreme in which the supervisor allows the supervisee little autonomy and closely observes and evaluates the supervisee's performance. In professionally oriented supervision, the supervisor, who is skilled in practice and teaching, allows considerable autonomy but remains easily accessible to provide help when it is needed and is flexible in enforcing the agency's policies. Scott, Kadushin, and Hall and Schneider all found that workers in various mental health, religious, or social welfare occupations preferred the active, supportive approach of the professionally oriented supervisor.[3]

Clinical supervision serves the dual functions of professional development and organizational control. The critical function of professional development distinguishes clinical supervision from the supervision characteristics of other work. Organizational psychologists have found that most workers value supervisors who are considerate, friendly, and worker oriented.[4] However, mental health professionals find interpersonal sensitivity in a supervisor to be less important than technical skills and competence.[5] Of course, the typical staff member of a mental health agency probably would like a supervisor who is both nice and knowledgeable, but the skilled clinician who can teach others seems to be more valued as a supervisor than is the individual who is friendly but not helpful. In fact, one group of social workers wanted their supervisors to be more critical of their performance as a way of improving the workers' skill.[6]

PROFESSIONAL DEVELOPMENT

Given the importance of the function of professional development in clinical supervision, surprisingly little research has focused on this particular aspect. Most studies on the clinical process have focused on the client or on the techniques and personalities of the clinicians. It is hard to find an empirical study of the therapist's supervisor or of the supervisory process itself, and therefore several areas are open to investigation. Some questions that could be answered include the following: What are the ways in which supervisors actually try to enhance professional development? What are the different behavioral styles or approaches that are used? Are certain supervisory approaches preferred over others?

Professionally oriented supervision seems to be preferred to laissez-faire or close supervision. However, the professionally oriented supervisor, meeting one to two hours weekly with a supervisee, can use a variety of behavioral styles to enhance the supervisee's professional development. In one of the few studies to distinguish among the different styles of "professional development" in clinical supervision, Kadushin identified two approaches: the "supervisee-centered" approach—emphasizing self-awareness, emotional growth, and relationships with clients; and the "task-centered" approach—emphasizing the development of specific technical skills and behaviors.[7] The sample of social workers in his study indicated a preference for a mixture of the two approaches. However, the supervisors surveyed in the same study seemed to emphasize the task-centered approach to a degree that the supervisees considered less than optimal.

In an attempt to replicate and extend Kadushin's work on different styles of clinical supervision the present authors, under the auspices of the University of Michigan, undertook a study in 1975, the purposes of which were to delineate the different approaches to clinical supervision, to assess staff preferences for different approaches, and to determine the extent to which the different approaches actually are emphasized in supervision. The present study was based on previous informal interviews conducted with social workers and clinical psychologists employed in mental health agencies. It addressed several specific questions concerning supervisory styles. First, do mental health professionals prefer certain supervisory styles over others? Second, which styles actually are emphasized in the clinical supervision currently received? Third, to what extent is a supervisor's emphasis of a particular style correlated with the supervisee's general satisfaction with his or her supervision? Fourth, to what extent is a supervisor's style associated with the supervisee's self-confidence as a clinician? (Clinical self-confidence was chosen as a variable for study because there is some evidence to suggest that a mental health professional's confidence in his or her own methods and abilities is a powerful ingredient in the psychotherapeutic process.[8] Novice staff were examined separately on this point, since the authors assumed that the supervisor's style would influence more strongly the self-confidence of less experienced clinicians.)

METHODOLOGY

The participants in the study were 164 line staff and their immediate supervisors working in 22 community mental health programs in three counties in Michigan. Six programs were located in predominantly urban areas, three were located in rural areas, and the rest were in predominantly suburban areas. There were ten counseling agencies that could also provide consultation and education services, five day treatment programs serving adults or children, two drug abuse or alcoholism programs, two emergency services programs, one mental retardation program, one inpatient program, and one program connected with a probate court. The sample for this part of the research included social workers, psychiatrists, nurses, psychologists, and nonprofessionals, the educational levels of whom ranged from high school graduates to doctorates in medicine and psychology. There were 75 men and 89 women.

All line staff employed at least half time in the programs were asked to participate. Of the 174 staff members eligible to participate, 164 agreed to do so, providing a response rate of 94 percent. The staff in only one program refused to take part. In return for participating, the staff members were promised quick feedback of data so their program could be compared to others. Written data were provided to all program heads within 90 days of collection. Oral feedback was also given at staff meetings for all members of programs wishing it. The research design identified five types of supervision to be investigated: laissez-faire, authoritative, didactic consultative, insight oriented, and feelings oriented. *Laissez-faire* and *authoritative* supervisory styles correspond to the laissez-faire and close supervision studied previously. In these styles, the function of professional development is minimal. The other three styles represented different ways in which a professionally oriented supervisor might attempt to foster learning and professional development in supervisory sessions.

In the *didactic-consultative* approach, the supervisor offers advice, suggestions, and interpretations concerning the dynamics of clients and clinical technique. The supervisee is not given orders and expected to carry them out, as in the authoritative approach. Rather, the supervisor functions like a consultant who offers comments and formulations intended to help the supervisee deal with uncertainties and problems.

The second style of supervision fostering professional development is called *insight oriented*. In this approach, the supervisor asks questions designed to stimulate the supervisee to think through and solve problems on his or her own. Typical questions would be these: "Why do you think the client said that?" "Do you think his current conflicts with his wife are related to some earlier event in his life?" "What do you think would be the best way to desensitize this particular phobia?"

The third supervisory style dealing with professional development— *feelings oriented*—encourages the supervisee to question and reflect about his or her own emotional response to clinical work and the way in which it might be affecting the process. It is similar to the approach Kadushin called "supervisee centered." [9] The supervisor encourages the supervisee to discuss his or her own conflicts, asking questions and making interpretations as the supervisee discusses a case.

QUESTIONNAIRES

Participating staff completed questionnaires that requested background information and sought answers to measures dealing with supervisory styles, satisfaction with supervision, and clinical self-confidence. These measures will be discussed at length. Staff filled out the questionnaires during regular staff meetings, after having been briefed by one of the authors on the nature of the study. The average time for completion of the questionnaire was 40 minutes.

Supervisory Styles

Respondents were given a one-paragraph description similar to the descriptions above of each of the five supervisory styles. Following each description, they were asked first to rate the extent to which their current primary supervisor resembled the description, using a 7-point Likert-type scale, $1 =$ "disagree" and $7 =$ "agree." Then they were asked to rate the extent to which they would like their supervisor to resemble the description, using the same Likert-type format. In this way, an "actual" and a "preferred" score for each style was obtained from each staff member.

Satisfaction with Supervision

The "supervision" scale from the Job Descriptive Index (JDI) was used to measure the general level of staff satisfaction with supervision. JDI is a standardized job-satisfaction questionnaire consisting of several scales measuring different facets of the job.[10] The supervision scale contains 18 adjectives describing supervisors (for example, "asks my advice," "hard to please," "knows job well," "lazy"). For each adjective, the respondent marks yes if the adjective roughly describes his or her supervisor, no if the adjective does not accurately describe the supervisor, and "?" if the respondent is not sure or cannot decide. Responses are tallied in a simple scoring system to obtain a single numerical score representing satisfaction with supervision.

Clinical Self-Confidence

Respondents were asked to indicate how confident they feel when engaged in psychotherapy or counseling with individuals. Staff used a 4-point Likert-type scale with $1 =$ "very effective and competent" and $4 =$ "poor and ineffective" to rate their self-confidence. They also could indicate "cannot judge." There was a moderately strong, positive correlation between the clinical self-confidence measure and the number of years of experience in the mental health field ($r = .38, p < .0001$).

RESULTS

The participating staff members indicated a strong preference for the three styles of supervision that are associated with professional development. The mean ratings presented in Table 26–1 suggest that didactic-consultative, insight-oriented, and feelings-oriented supervision

TABLE 26–1. Mean Ratings of Actual and Preferred Supervisory Behavior

Behavior	Actual Level	Preferred Level	Difference
Didactic consultative	4.97	5.40	−.43
	(150)	(148)	
Laissez-faire	2.46	1.95	.51
	(151)	(147)	
Authoritative	2.46	2.37	.11
	(150)	(147)	
Insight-oriented	4.54	5.63	−1.09
	(151)	(147)	
Feelings-oriented	4.48	5.37	−.89
	(149)	(147)	

Note: Numbers in parentheses refer to the number of respondents on the basis of which the mean score was computed. Numbers differ because of missing data.

are preferred to authoritative and laissez-faire approaches. Paired t tests were performed to test for statistical significance of the differences between the preference ratings, using the procedure described by Dixon and Massey.[11] The results indicated that preferences for didactic-consultative, insight-oriented, and feelings-oriented supervision were significantly greater than preferences for authoritative and laissez-faire styles ($p < .0001$). The preferences for didactic-consultative, insight-oriented, and feelings-oriented styles were not significantly different from one another, however, which suggests that staff probably prefer these three approaches about equally.

Staff members' ratings of their actual supervision suggested that the dominant style emphasized by supervisors is didactic-consultative. (See Table 26–1.) Using the same type of paired t test used for the analysis of preference ratings, the mean rating for didactic-consultative supervision was significantly higher than the ratings for laissez-faire and authoritative supervision ($p < .0001$), feelings-oriented supervision ($p < .009$), and insight-oriented supervision ($p < .02$).

The greatest discrepancy between the actual and preferred levels occurred for insight-oriented supervision; however, the discrepancy for feelings-oriented supervision also was large. (See Table 26–1.) Paired t tests indicated that the discrepancy scores for these two styles were significantly higher than any of the other discrepancy scores ($p < .008$), thus suggesting that staff would like more emphasis on insight-oriented and feelings-oriented styles and less emphasis on the laissez-faire style. The staff seem to feel that the extent to which supervisors are authoritative is just about right, based on the minimal discrepancy between actual and preferred ratings for this dimension. Although staff seem to want their supervisors to be more active and available, they do not want them to be more directive.

Ratings for 4 of the 5 supervisory styles were significantly correlated with satisfaction with supervision. As the data in Table 26–2 suggest, the correlations between the levels of insight-oriented, feelings-oriented, and didactic-consultative supervision were positively correlated with the score obtained from the JDI supervision scale. The perceived level of laissez-faire supervision was uncorrelated with satisfaction. The absolute magnitudes of the correlations for the insight-oriented, feelings-oriented, and laissez-faire styles were greater than the correlation for didactic-consultative supervision. The correlations between supervisory style and satisfaction with supervision seem consistent with the data on preferences and the actual–preferred discrepancies reported above.

Only one style of supervision was significantly correlated with clinical self-confidence, and the correlation shown was weak. (The relevant data are presented in Table 26–2.) Although the negative correlation between authoritative supervision and clinical self-confidence did reach significance ($p < .05$), the level of authoritative supervision accounts for less than 4 percent of the variance in clinical self-confidence. The correlations between the actual–preferred discrepancy scores for supervisory style and clinical self-confidence were even smaller.

TABLE 26–2. Association Among Supervisory Behaviors, Satisfaction, and Self-Confidence

Behavior	Satisfaction with Supervision	Clinical Self-Confidence	Clinical Self-Confidence— Novices Only[†]
Didactic consultative	.31**	.04	.43
	(150)	(143)	
Laissez-faire	−.48**	.03	−.26
	(151)	(144)	
Authoritative	.03	−.18*	.10
	(150)	(144)	
Insight-oriented	.51**	−.04	.28
	(151)	(144)	
Feelings-oriented	.53**	−.10	.04
	(149)	(143)	

NOTE: Numbers in parentheses refer to the number of respondents on the basis of which the mean score was computed. Numbers differ because of missing data; *$p < .05$; **$p < .001$.
† Novices were defined as staff with less than one year's experience in mental health work; $n = 11$.

Correlations between supervisory style and clinical self-confidence are larger for the novice staff. Because of the small size of the novice group ($N = 11$), however, none of the correlations reaches statistical significance at the .05 level. However, three of the correlations exceed $\pm$ .25, and the positive correlation between level of didactic-consultative emphasis in supervision and clinical self-confidence is substantial ($r = .43$). The relationships between feelings-oriented and authoritative supervision and clinical self-confidence remain small for the novice staff. Thus, the data on supervision and clinical self-confidence in novice clinicians are ambiguous.

The results suggest that for the typical staff member of a community mental health center involved in this study certain styles of clinical supervision are preferred over others and are reliably associated with a general level of satisfaction with supervision. The staff seem to prefer more active and available supervision. Didactic-consultative, insight-oriented, and feelings-oriented supervision are all seen as desirable. However, staff perceive a greater emphasis on didactic-consultative supervision than on the insight-oriented or feelings-oriented approaches. In addition, the latter two approaches are more strongly correlated with satisfaction scores. Nevertheless, staff would prefer greater emphasis on all three approaches than they actually receive.

Although there are reasons for believing that professionally oriented supervision is associated with increased clinical self-confidence in all staff, this study found no evidence for such a relationship. One possible explanation is that the self-report measures of supervisory style did not encompass those aspects of supervision that influence self-confidence. Another possibility is that the single-item, self-report measure of clinical self-confidence is not sensitive to real differences in the competence or effectiveness of staff members. Perhaps as certain styles of supervision encourage greater professional development in staff, the staff respond by setting higher goals for themselves so that reported self-confidence remains unchanged even though the staff are performing at higher levels.

When responses from only novice staff were examined, the correlations between supervisory style and clinical self-confidence increased. The small size of this group, however, makes it impossible to determine how stable and generalizable these relations are. However, subsequent studies with larger samples might show that supervisory style is associated with clinical self-confidence only for inexperienced staff.

The results tend to confirm previous research and add a new perspective to the study of supervision in mental health agencies. The staff in this sample did not like laissez-faire or authoritative supervision. Staff seem to prefer an active, available supervisor who provides advice when necessary, encourages self-directed thinking and problem-solving, and helps staff members assess the role of their personal feelings in clinical work. Also, the staff ratings of current supervision suggest that it is meaningful to distinguish among didactic-consultative, insight-oriented, and feelings-oriented approaches. The extent to which these three approaches to learning and professional development is emphasized may vary considerably with the supervisor. Also, individual staff may differ in their preferences. One staff member might prefer the didactic-consultative emphasis, another might prefer a predominantly insight-oriented approach, and other staff may prefer a mixture.

The staff as a group seem to prefer didactic-consultative, insight-oriented, and feelings-oriented supervision about equally, but they are less satisfied with the actually received amount of emphasis given to insight-oriented and feelings-oriented supervision. They seem to be saying that sometimes they wish their supervisors would encourage and help them to think through problems on their own and to examine how their personal feelings may be influencing their work. At other times, staff wish to be told the way to approach a problem. The ideal supervisor would thus appear to be one who knows when to ask questions and when to give advice without always doing just one or the other.

The one type of supervisory style that may not be meaningful to staff is authoritative supervision. This dimension was not correlated with job satisfaction, and there was practically no mean discrepancy between the actual and preferred levels for this group.

Given the apparent importance of supervision for the mental health professional, the dimensions of clinical supervision developed and used in this study could be useful tools for enhancing staff morale. Supervisors could periodically ask their supervisees to complete a survey asking for ratings of the actual and preferred levels of the five styles of supervision investigated in the present study. Such a survey would allow versatile supervisors to provide a blend of supervisory styles for each staff member and would also increase the supervisee's sense of involvement in shaping the character of supervision, thereby enhancing the satisfaction of both supervisor and supervisee. Hegarty reported an experiment in which this "survey-feedback" procedure was used in an industrial setting.[12] He found that following feedback of survey results to supervisors, levels of reported satisfaction with supervision among workers increased. Thus, measures of clinical supervisory styles, such as those used in this study, may have real value for improving the nature of supervision.

NOTES

1. William E. Henry, John H. Sims, and S. Lee Spray, *The Fifth Profession* (San Francisco: Jossey-Bass, 1971), pp. 150–156.
2. Cary Cherniss and Edward Egnatios, "Is There a Job Satisfaction Problem

in Community Mental Health?" *Community Mental Health Journal,* in press.

3. Alfred Kadushin, "Supervisor-Supervisee: A Survey," *Social Work,* 19 (May 1974), pp. 288–297 [Chapter 22 above]; W. Richard Scott, "Reactions to Supervision in a Heteronomous Professional Organization," *Administration Science Quarterly* 10 (June 1965), pp. 65–81 [Chapter 23 above]; Douglas T. Hall and Benjamin Schneider, *Organizational Climates and Careers: The Work Lives of Priests* (New York: Seminar Press, 1973), pp. 137–139.
4. Rensis Likert, *New Patterns of Management* (New York: McGraw-Hill, 1961), pp. 17–20; Douglas McGregor, *The Human Side of Enterprise* (New York: McGraw-Hill, 1960), pp. 82–85.
5. John A. Olmstead, *Organizational Factors in the Performance of Social and Rehabilitation Workers* (Fort Benning, Ga.: Human Resources Research Organization, 1970), pp. 33–40; Kadushin, op. cit., p. 291.
6. Kadushin, op. cit., p. 291.
7. Ibid.
8. Ezra Stotland and Alfred L. Kobler, *Life and Death of a Mental Hospital* (Seattle: University of Washington Press, 1965), pp. 73–82; Jerome D. Frank, "The Demoralized Mind," *Psychology Today,* 6 (November 1973), pp. 22–31.
9. Kadushin, op. cit., p. 291.
10. Patricia Crain Smith, Lorne M. Kendall, and Charles L. Hulin, *The Measurement of Satisfaction in Work and Retirement* (Chicago: Rand McNally, 1969), pp. 37–50.
11. William J. Dixon and Frank J. Massey, *Introduction to Statistical Analysis* (New York: McGraw-Hill, 1969), pp. 217–218.
12. William H. Hegarty, "Using Subordinate Ratings to Elicit Behavioral Changes in Supervisors," *Journal of Applied Psychology,* 59 (December 1974), pp. 764–766.

PART VI

Future Trends

INTRODUCTION

THERE IS NO DOUBT that, given the current nature of and projected trends in social work practice, supervision will continue to be seen as important in advancing effectiveness and efficiency. Despite the vast social changes that have occurred in the past decade regarding authority, individual rights, and individual freedoms, there have been only minor changes in how supervision is practiced. As Mandell points out (Chapter 27), the questioning of authority and the structure of supervision most likely reflects the questioning of authority at the societal level in terms of what has been labeled the equality revolution. Although there is increased interest in the private practice of social work, there does not appear to be a major shift toward large-scale independent, autonomous practice. Supervision will continue to be an essential component of social work, since practice will be carried out predominantly in organizational settings; where private practice does exist, regulation through licensing is emerging, and most licensing laws mandate some form of basic supervision.

The recent trend is the general introduction of new theoretical orientations about supervision into social work practice. It has been demonstrated that the application of psychoanalytic theory to social work practice was reflected in the conceptualization of supervision during the first half of this century. During the past two decades, there has been increased application of sociological theory to social work practice, and this theory has also found its way into theorizing about supervision. Kadushin draws on the interactional framework of Goffman; Scott uses the ideas of Weber, Parsons, and Etzioni; Munson discusses supervision from the perspective of Merton's role-set and interaction; and Mandell applies the work of Simmel. Clearly there has been a shift from psychological orientations to sociological models, and the articles in this section suggest that this trend will continue.

Mandell sees social agencies adopting changes similar to those of other complex organizations in response to pressures for more flexibility originating in the larger society. Broad-scale social changes, characterized as the equality revolution, have found their way into attitudes regarding supervision, and Simmel's ideas on subordination and superordination are used to develop an ideal model of supervision. Expansion

308

of autonomy is advocated through use of supervisory forms, identified as consultation and democratic peer-group relationships. The discussion of organizational structuring of subordination and superordination and the use of reciprocal influence can be related to the dual model of administration and consultation presented in the article by Munson.

Young emphasizes group supervision and clinical exposure in the context of broader changes in the profession: an emerging philosophy of consumerism, increased regulation of practice, and changes in the structuring and delivery of social work education. She articulates the shift in practice theory from the psychological to the sociological model and applies this unit of analysis to supervision. In this context, group supervision is described as a natural model, since the group pre-exists within the organization. Differences in individual and group supervision are explained from a perspective of accountability, and methods of translating the functioning work group into a productive supervisory group are covered.

Munson's article is based on the premise that authority has always been and remains an issue in supervision. An interactional framework is used to describe a dual model of supervision that separates the concepts of administrative supervision and clinical consultation. The model differentiates and defines authority in supervision and the advisory aspect of consultation. The model is advocated as being consistent with emerging events within the profession: (1) regulation of practice through licensing, (2) increased models of specialization in practice, and (3) changes in the structure of social work education. Munson's dual model confronts many of the issues raised by other writers in this collection and offers a way to deal structurally and interactionally with many of them.

The article by Finch is the only one in this volume that does not deal directly with supervision, and it is included in this last section because the issues raised are relevant to the profession as a whole and to supervision specifically. Problems associated with supervision cannot be separated from the larger questions that the profession faces. For Finch, the success of professionals in organizations depends on acquiring a set of beliefs and values that aid in deciding what is true, what questions to ask, and what is right and wrong. It is his belief that when professionalism and bureaucracy are mixed, the result is conflict. This conflict is mediated by the individual through a process of accommodation, and one form of accommodation is to engage in creative individualism. Inexperienced workers are portrayed as more idealistic, whereas experienced workers are more conformist, but the question that remains unanswered is whether this difference can be attributed to organizational constraints or to knowledge gained from experience. Increased specialization in practice is reviewed and related to structural restrictions and opportunities that can expand or contract autonomy. Specialization resulting in management roles for social workers could at worst decrease autonomy permanently over the long run, and at best produce temporary confusion in job functioning. Regardless, these issues are what lie ahead for the profession and must be addressed.

The concluding article by Feldman brings together many of the ideas that have been explored throughout this book. She uses a brief historical focus to highlight current demands, and emphasizes supervision in practice as it relates to establishing a relationship, formulating assessments, and communicating. The training components of supervision—helping the worker develop listening skills and empathy and promoting growth-producing strategies—are depicted and explained as a slow and complicated process. We are warned about the danger of losing sight of the client's goals and other common, but major, pitfalls in psychologizing workers.

27

The "Equality" Revolution and Supervision

Betty Mandell

THE ORGANIZATIONAL STRUCTURES of social work agencies reflect the dominant ideologies and structures of the larger society. Thus when the industrial revolution gave rise to hierarchical bureaucratic institutions, the organization of social agencies duplicated these structures. Individual supervision was assumed to be the most efficient way of training and socializing new personnel and assuring the stable continuation of organizational patterns. As agencies became more highly professionalized, the quality of this supervision was of paramount importance. Thus the most frequently offered lure to social workers in personnel ads of ten years ago was probably "competent supervision."

Apparently that is not enough today. Frequently used adjectives in a recent personnel bulletin are: dynamic, progressive, innovative, exciting, stimulating, flexible, challenging, and vibrant. Staff are sought who are capable of independent work, have initiative and stimulating ideas, are willing to experiment, can exercise creative leadership, want to progress and assume responsibility, and "in effect, be able to do his thing." [1] The kinds of supervision offered include peer group consultation, cooperative supervision, consultation, in-service training programs, and general supervision.

Following are excerpts from ads in the same bulletin:

"Do you like new approaches? Freedom to experiment? . . . " [2]

"Aren't you getting just a little tired of the rather narrow area in which you are functioning? The red tape that sometimes becomes more important than the people who need your help? The lack of opportunity to try some of your own ideas? The emphasis will be on service, not

Reprinted with permission of the Council on Social Work Education. From *Journal of Education for Social Work*, Vol. 9 (Winter 1973), pp. 43–54.

bureaucracy. This may be your chance to use your total capabilities. . . . " [3]

"Take immediate advantage of . . . stimulating opportunities for experimentation and diversification! A chance for independent work combined with whatever supervision and consultation are necessary, according to your background." [4]

Thus social agencies are, tentatively, adopting some of the organizational changes of some large corporations, and responding to pressures of the larger society. I shall discuss the following aspects of this process: (1) Supervision as preparation for changing the "whole personality," which grew out of an individualistic psychodynamic theory; (2) The training given for this therapeutic approach and how it shapes professional norms and values; (3) Social systems theory; (4) Professional identity and status factors in the helping profession; (5) Dysfunctional aspects of traditional supervision; (6) New trends in corporation managerial techniques as a response to cybernetic technology; and (7) Growing social discontent, which presses for more equalitarian social structures. These are not the only factors affecting the function and structure of supervision, nor have they necessarily occurred in the order discussed here. They are inter-related and perhaps inseparable, but they have contributed to a growing restiveness within all of the helping professions that press for change.

The work of Georg Simmel on subordination and superordination will be used in considering "ideal" forms of supervision. Finally, I shall consider two forms of supervision geared toward greater professional autonomy: consultation and democratic peer relationships.

TREATMENT AND SUPERVISION OF THE "WHOLE PERSONALITY"

Teaching methods in industry aimed to increase production and efficiency of workers. Social agencies, less task centered than businesses and industry, were more preoccupied with "the whole personality." In the early days of the Charity Organization Society when there was great preoccupation with the difference between "deserving" and "undeserving" poor, the treatment goals of social workers included instilling virtue, obedience, and industry into the marginal people of society. After World War I, when Freudian psychology captured the imagination of psychiatrists and social workers, psychiatric social workers delved into deeper recesses of the clients' psyches. Treatment agencies viewed the personality of the social worker as one of the tools of treating the client's personality. Thus it was logical that supervision should also concern itself with the "whole personality" of the learner, and seek to change or adapt the social worker's personality to the needs of treatment. Psychoanalytic supervision, carrying this philosophy the farthest, required an intensive personal psychoanalysis of the trainee. Although agencies which were offering intensive psychotherapy did not usually require social workers to undergo psychoanalysis, they considered it valuable. Supervision of psychoanalytic trainees included close inspection of their most intimate thoughts and actions. A trainee's resistance to this probing was often assumed to represent a problem of "counter-transference," and the usual prescription was to intensify the probing. Blitzsten and Fleming [5] advise conferring with the supervisee's analyst, if the supervisee does not voluntarily discuss his problem. If the supervisee objects, he should be told that absolute honesty is a requirement of a therapist. (This hardly seems calculated to develop a relationship of trust in which honesty can develop.)

To a less intense degree, social work supervision followed the psychiatric model, especially in psychoanalytically oriented casework treatment agencies. Since this model concentrates on intra-psychic rather than socio-economic phenomena, it was followed less in more task-oriented agencies such as public assistance agencies. In addition, poorly funded public assistance agencies could not afford the luxury of intra-psychic speculations.

TRAINING FOR PSYCHOTHERAPY AND CASEWORK

As Herbert Walberg [6] has pointed out, neither Freud nor any prominent psychoanalyst has made a sustained effort to apply dynamic theories to broad problems of teaching and learning. However, the psychiatrically oriented professions have generally modeled their teaching methods on Freud's clinical prescriptions. There is no certain proof that this is the most effective method of teaching. In fact, "In the absence of verified knowledge of the effectiveness of supervisory practices, all aspects of supervision remain open to question." [7]

Both the curriculum and the organizational structure of graduate training help to shape the treatment style and professional identity of graduates. Arthur and Birnbaum [8] document this through study of psychiatrists and psychologists in a residential treatment center. Respondents were asked to describe a pleasant incident and an unpleasant incident which they had with a child patient. Their responses revealed important differences between the two disciplines which seemed related to their training. Psychiatrists who undergo a rigorous program of study externally mapped out for them have had to fit into the hospital's hierarchical authority structure early in their training. Their medical training is pragmatic, action-oriented, not given to "the academic never-never-land of endless speculation." [9] Such traditions as the "death conference" which institutionalize the facing of catastrophes, "help provide the young physician with prefabricated defenses—a necessary objectivity in the face of unavoidable mistakes and inevitable tragedies. . . . " [10]

In contrast to medical education, graduate training in clinical psychology at the university is relatively loosely structured and the students have more autonomy. Requirements are comparatively flexible. "There is a good deal of theorizing and speculation about treatment but considerable hesitancy about taking action and enormous uncertainty regarding outcome." [11]

The researchers found that psychiatrists derived considerable narcissistic gain from the admiration and respect of others. It was important to them that other staff members and their child patients all recognize their authority and competence. "Although they were clearly protecting their image in the eyes of others, there was still a calmness, self-assurance, and self-confidence, even a brashness in their actions as therapist at the head of the team." [12] They were more action-oriented than psychologists, and used non-verbal communication more than psychologists did. They were more subject to shame than to guilt.

Psychologists on the other hand, were more introspective, more subject to guilt over perceived failure, less concerned with what others thought, had fantasies of therapeutic omnipotence, identified more with the patient as a rescued object, emphasized verbal communication rather than other forms of expressive behavior.

While psychologists more frequently reproached themselves, psychiatrists were more likely to become angry at the child or to withdraw.

Since social workers were not included in this study, one can only speculate about how their training affects their treatment style. Except for recent changes in some schools, the curriculum has been externally set, inflexible, and not generally geared to encourage the student to question or experiment. Field work supervision is intensive, and is usually done by one person through the study of process recording. One student complains that "the present . . . approach reflect[s] a greater capacity for educating students to become students than it does for educating them to become professionals." [13]

In both psychiatry and social work—and in psychology to a lesser extent—there is an increasing theoretical focus on the inter-relationships of social systems rather than exclusive preoccupation on the individual. More sociological theory is being incorporated into social work curricula. Family therapy, community organization, milieu therapy, and community psychiatry are receiving growing support. These group-oriented modalities often require a shift in relationships between agency staff members, frequently in the direction of greater equalitarianism. The socio-therapeutically oriented therapists advocate democratic participation in the conditions of one's work not only by staff, but by the recipients of service as well.

The socio-therapeutic philosophy views mental illness in social and interpersonal terms, and believes that treatment requires free and open communication between staff and patients. They do not prescribe a specific treatment for an illness, but use a large number of therapeutic resources. Interprofessional distinctions become blurred, and development of new staff roles is encouraged.[14] Strauss et al. demonstrated that psychiatrists with a socio-therapeutic orientation wanted to mobilize all available manpower resources for the treatment of mental illness, and were less preoccupied with questions of relative authority during the treatment process. They were less likely to believe that a medical degree was a necessary prerequisite for the practice of psychotherapy.[15]

PROFESSIONAL IDENTITY AND STATUS

A shift from hierarchical organization to equalitarianism in staff relationships involves a reassessment of one's professional identity. This affects psychiatrists, psychologists, and social workers when they work in the same agency. When one profession increases its power in a group, another must of necessity give up some power. The Strauss study points out that social workers and psychologists formed the ideological backbones of the more democratically organized teams.[16]

"It was social workers and psychologists—who wanted to break through the constraints of an auxiliary role and achieve full-fledged equality in the psychiatric arena—who blossomed. Those whose aspirations did not involve breaking with tradition faced real difficulties in making places for themselves."[17] The radically different organization of work forced the participants to invent new ways of working—and of working together. "Participation in these teams confirmed some in their dimly understood choice of careers: For others, it actually provided critical turning points in professional identity, leading to different types of careers."[18]

Social workers have traditionally worked in organizations rather than independently. This has helped to reduce their autonomy and encouraged "identification with organizational models that reflect the organizations value system."[19] Social workers' lack of full autonomy has been commented on by psychiatrists, psychologists, sociologists and the Census Bureau. In 1950 the Census Bureau debated whether to include social work as a profession, since social workers were apparently never responsible and accountable for their own acts.[20] Etzioni labels social work, along with nursing, as a "semi-profession," partly because of its lack of full autonomy.[21] Wallerstein and Ekstein say that the other clinical professions often see social workers as permanently dependent on their supervisors. Their dependence and their use of an extensive system of process recording "seem overritualistic, . . . an overdoing that cuts down on spontaneity and on effectiveness. . . . They seem to do too much of the work that psychologists and psychiatrists do too little of.[22]

In a quest for more autonomy, increasing numbers of social workers are "voting with their feet" by leaving bureaucratic agencies to enter private practice, or are considering it. In a study of Iowa social workers who were members of NASW,[23] 63 out of 124 respondents said they had thought of entering the private practice of social casework. The largest response given as a reason for this related to the gaining of independence. These responses included the desire for: "independence from agency policies, procedures and regulations; independence to try new techniques and methods; independence to break dependency ties to the agency; independence to arrange more flexible working hours and conditions; independence from agency because social workers are competent enough to function without agency sanction. The desire for additional income and prestige were reported with less frequency."[24]

Rather than viewing this desire for greater autonomy as "a problem with authority" (as many supervisors are apt to do), Etzioni regards it as a healthy growth. "The desire expressed by professionally oriented caseworkers to be allowed to make their own decisions and to work in an autonomous fashion rather than under close supervision is one seemingly shared by all types of professionals, and is certainly consistent with the generally accepted view of what a professional person is."[25]

The identity with the agency is important to social workers, and affects their treatment of clients (who seek the services of an agency, not an individual). "At times this has led to a sort of professional anonymity for the worker, he may submerge himself . . . in the agency, and offer the agency's service rather than his own. This is indeed a weak facet of an identity concept in that the social aspect, the connection with the agency, the clinic, or the hospital may be overemphasized at the expense of the private aspect, the core of individual therapeutic help."[26]

Strauss et al. suggest that psychiatrists may be less threatened by social workers than by psychologists because social workers function effectively in a subordinate role and willingly rely on psychiatrists for guidance and supervision.[27] Probably this heavy reliance reduces the social workers' spontaneity and readiness to experiment.

The desire for professional autonomy has resulted in discontent with individual supervision in a hierarchical bureaucracy. In social work, "supervisees have been howling for decades."[28]

Judging from the amount of professional literature on the subject, social work has seemed more preoccupied with supervision than either psychiatry or psychology. Yet psychiatrists have not been happy with it either. Martin Grotjahn, writing of his dissatisfaction with supervision, says, "When I asked others what they remembered about their own experience at being supervised, several of my senior colleagues who are known for their original research said, in effect, 'I always saw to it that I went to a supervisor who would interfere with me as little as possible.' "[29]

The dearth of articles on supervision in psychology journals indicates that psychologists are less preoccupied with their status vis-à-vis psychiatrists. Their main complaint about supervision seems to arise when psychiatric institutions assume that psychiatrists are most competent to supervise psychologists. Strauss et al. "suggest, that, by virtue of their more extended professional training, the psychologists lay stronger claims to professional autonomy and recognition. In what has been shaping up as a potentially prolonged interprofessional conflict between psychiatry and psychology, psychiatrists of both orientations (somatic and psychological) find some common cause." [30]

DYSFUNCTIONAL ASPECTS OF TRADITIONAL SUPERVISION

Perhaps the most frequently mentioned problem with hierarchical supervision is that it encourages dependence, and conversely discourages innovative and experimental action. Schein and Benis say, " . . . [G]iving the immediate superior practically complete authority over the career development of subordinates . . . is likely to have the effect of preoccupying subordinates with 'how to please their boss' rather than 'how to develop themselves.' Similarly, certain control systems which supply superiors with detailed information about a person's performance in the organization tend to lead to dependence and/or insecurity, neither of which stimulates change or growth." [31]

The desire to please one's superior, with its consequent dependence, often leads to dissembling and "gamesmanship" rather than a relationship of mutual trust. Kadushin describes a variety of games supervisees play.[32] They involve either appeasement, attack, or withdrawal—all designed to defend oneself against loss of face or loss of career advancement. The two supervisors' games mentioned involve attack in order to save face. Since the power is on the side of the supervisors, their games are more likely to involve attack.

The real trouble is that the games are not confined to the supervisor-supervisee relationship, but can do harm to the client. Polsky documents the vicious ranking that takes place among residents of a treatment center for delinquents, as a result of authoritarian hierarchical control.[33] The children lowest in the pecking order are sent to mental hospitals in disproportionate numbers. Strauss et al. give examples of how nurses' feelings toward a supervising doctor can affect the way the nurses handle patients: "The doctors who don't pay very much attention to what the nurses need and want by way of support from them, find their patients shunted around a bit more." And: "When a patient of his [a doctor the nurses don't like] is transferred off the unit, we try not to get her back." [34]

In individual therapy, the problems center around either pleasing or rebelling against the supervisor—which means that the supervisee is not using his energies primarily to understand and help the client. Prall and Stennis [35] give some examples: pushing the client to talk, out of fear of not having enough material for the supervisor; applying supervisory suggestions out of context; and generalizing inappropriately. Ackerman [36] gives others: submerging one's individuality and over-identifying with the supervisor (leading one to act out with the patient the projected image of the omnipotent and omniscient analyst); acting out a feeling of competitiveness with the supervisor; mimicking the supervisor's therapeutic conduct.

Ackerman lists some emotional difficulties supervisees experience, including: fear of failure; a need to appease the patient; fear of loss of the patient and a consequent loss of face for the student; fear of the supervisor's criticism and a too strong preoccupation with his authority.

NEW TRENDS IN CORPORATION MANAGERIAL TECHNIQUES

In the business world, the new theories of work relationships, especially the "Y" theory espoused by McGregor in 1960,[37] emphasize co-operative work relationships in a "team" approach. Management and line staff are recognized as being interdependent, and lose their specialized functions. Discussion groups include many levels of the hierarchy, making authority lines less important. This non-linear approach is widely used in Research and Development work, "in which normal 'echelon' hierarchies are not compatible with the creative personalities of certain kinds of scientists for morale reasons." [38]

This theory assumes that the knowledge explosion can make technical knowledge quickly obsolete and that "the unpredictable needs of tomorrow require broad education—those who conform to today's management type may be all wrong in tomorrow's organization." [39] Bureaucracy is assumed to be on the way out and more flexible people are needed for "new social systems better suited to 20th century demands." [40] Sensitivity training or "T-Groups" are used to prepare people for these new social systems, and most follow-up studies agree "that real shifts in such behavior as listening to others, sensitivity to others' needs, flexibility, work relations, and decision making takes place in a positive direction." [41]

The question of how this change is to come about is one of the knottiest problems with the Y theory of management according to Oppenheimer. Some theorists argue that the management elite must decide when the staff is ready for it. Yet others point out the contradiction in a theory that espouses involvement of line staff in making their own decisions, yet leaves the most important decisions to management. These theorists point out that it is precisely when people are ready for freedom that they are likely to take it, regardless of whether management is ready to grant it. The question remains as to how real the freedom is when it can be given or taken away by management.

SOCIAL DISCONTENT, PRESSING FOR EQUALITARIANISM

Traditional hierarchical authority is being questioned in many segments of society. The authority of the Pope, and even of God, has been undermined. It is no wonder that the authority of supervisors is being questioned. Herbert Gans says that the social protest of the 1960s now takes the form of the 'Equality' revolution.[42] For the poor, this concerns economic equality. The more affluent who are not as preoccupied with money expect their jobs to offer personal satisfactions, and upper-middle-class people gravitate to the jobs and careers that provide more equality and autonomy. As economic security increases in America, so do the demands of non-economic satisfactions; "as a result, aspirations for more equality, democracy and autonomy are rising all over America. . . . Social workers want more autonomy in aiding their clients. . . . The huge increase in graduate school enrollments suggests that many college students want the personal freedom available in an academic career; their decreasing interest in business careers indicates that they may be rejecting the autocracy and lack of autonomy found in many large corporations. . . . The right of the individual to determine his job is the hallmark of the professional, and eventually many workers will seek the privileges of professionalism whether or not they are professional in terms of skills." [43]

With a clear view of the history of revolutions, Gans adds that, since more equality for some means a reduction in privilege for others, "those who have the privilege and the power will not give them up without a struggle and will fight the demand for more equality with all the economic and political resources they can muster." [44] Anyone who has locked horns with a supervisor bent on exercising power can testify to the truth of this.

SUBORDINATION AND SUPERORDINATION

In the late 19th century, Georg Simmel wrestled with the problem of superordination and subordination. He talked of the development from "subordination under society" (needing traditional authoritative intermediaries to transmit the truth) to "subordination under objectivity." [45]

It seems as if man could not easily bear looking the object in the eye; as if he were equal neither to the rigidity of its lawfulness nor to the freedom which the object, in contrast to all coercion from men, gives him. By comparison, to bow to the authority of the many or their representatives, to traditional opinion, to socially accepted notions, is something intermediate. Traditional opinion, after all, is more modifiable than is the law of the object; in it, man can feel some psychological mediation; it transmits, as it were, something which is already digested psychologically. At the same time, it gives us a hold, a relief from responsibility—the compensation for the lack of that autonomy which we derive from the purely intrinsic relationship between ego and object. [46]

Simmel says that this kind of objectivity is psychologically and historically a later social development than the reliance upon intermediaries.

It is hard in psychotherapy, as in all relationships, to experience

the subjective pain that is often felt in honest confrontations of other people. . . . To give voice to our empathic understanding calls for unadorned, forthright statements. . . . A patient has little with which to shore himself up as he moves along the tortuous and trying road to health that counts for more than the integrity and sincerity of the therapist. . . . Indeed, we might well wonder if the psychotherapeutic situation does not owe much of its special efficacy to the vast freedom offered to two human beings to establish a straightforward tie with one another without the strain and warping of social propriety, etc. [47]

Perhaps traditional supervision (which is the instrument used to mediate traditional ways of viewing people) has as often hindered therapists from "looking directly at the object"—with all the freedom and responsibility this implies—as it has helped.

Simmel cites Proudhon (a 19th century French anarchist) as one who wanted to eliminate super-subordination by dissolving all dominating social structures, and founding all order and cohesion upon the direct interaction of free, coordinate individuals. Simmel believes that super-subordination has organizational value for the best use of technical knowledge, but is too often oppressive, one-sided, and unjust. He suggests that the ideal organization would be one where superordination and subordination are reciprocal "in which A is superordinate to B in one respect or at one time, but in which, in another respect or at another time, B is superordinate to A." [48] An example "might be the production association of workers for an enterprise for which they elect a master and a foreman. While they are subordinate to him in regard to the technique of the enterprise, they yet are his superordinates with respect to its general direction and results." [49] Further safeguards against misuse of power could be changing leaders frequently either through election or a rule of succession (which he says all outspoken democracies do); brief office terms or the prohibition of reelection or both. "In this fashion, the ideal of everybody having his turn is realized as far as possible. Simultaneous superordination and subordination is one of the most powerful forms of interaction. In its correct distribution over numerous fields, it can constitute a very strong bond between individuals, merely by the close interaction entailed by it." [50]

ALTERNATIVE MODELS OF SUPERVISION

There is little documented evidence of a large scale thrust toward changing the structure of supervision. Occasional articles have appeared which have argued the advantages of more autonomy,[51] peer group supervision,[52] time-limited supervision,[53] greater use of consultation.[54] Stevens and Hutchinson describe one agency's experience with substituting consultation for supervision.[55]

The rate of pay was divorced from the job classification so that supervisors did not necessarily receive more pay. This was based on the belief that the most vital work was done by the practitioners. This reorganization of values may be a prerequisite to changing the system. In addition, self-evaluations were done voluntarily and divorced from an administrative evaluation. No formal evaluations were made except for a recommendation when staff members left the agency.

The staff of this agency was allowed to seek consultation from whomever they chose, "making legitimate what already occurs in most agencies, often with misunderstanding and guilt." [56] When this is not made legitimate, it "can be a two-way destructive force." [57] The caseworker feels disloyal, and the supervisor feels she has failed.

The format of consultation varied greatly, from informal conversations spontaneously arranged to group conferences, joint work projects, and a staff development program. After seven years of using this system, the agency reported higher staff morale, no staff resignations for other jobs, greater motivation to learn, no petty jealousies and cliques. Staff members discovered previously unrealized capacities; timidities were overcome; uncertainties voluntarily brought forth. Staff were freer to experiment, less defensive about mistakes, made far reaching changes in the program when they were ready for them, rather than having them forced by the administration. They developed an attitude of cooperative sharing of professional goals, rather than competitiveness.[58]

In reading this and Strauss' description of democratic work relationships, one is struck by the increase in spontaneity and self-confidence; the discovery of new talents in oneself; the sense of release from anxiety; and even a newly discovered joy in living that surges forth when people can put their energies into self-discovery and creativity rather than placating authority.

Where consultation replaces supervision, power arrangements in the agency have to change. Achieved status would have to replace ascribed status. Becoming a supervisor would not be the way to prove one's competence in action, regardless of one's title. However, it would free both the supervisee and the supervisor from the need to play games, since neither would be trapped in the relationship. Consultation is "a voluntary coordinate relationship. . . . It cannot take place in a mandatory situation involving a superior and a subordinate. . . . It is a process of making knowledge, experience, and professional attitudes and values available to others, and their responsibility to use and implement as they choose or not. It is not an administrative relationship that requires adherence, utilization or accountability." [59]

Gilmore believes that both the treatment-oriented clinical model and the authoritative image seem to be barriers to successful consultation. Consultation is not concerned with the total personality. It is task oriented and work centered. It implies a mutuality of responsibility, with special knowledge and competence on both sides but perhaps in different areas. "The consultant may suggest *good* solutions to the problem, but only the consultee is in the position to assess what are the *workable* solutions. . . . " [60]

"There has to be a minimal amount of both know-what and know-how for a consultee to be a partner in the consultative process. This is why research consultants often observe that they more frequently function as teacher-trainees or as technical experts." [61] Etzioni's research indicates that less trained staff are more likely to want detailed technical supervision which can be obtained on the job, while trained professionals generally want training from people "well versed in social and psychological theories. They want their superiors to know the theoretical fundamentals to the discipline, which are not readily obtainable from on-the-job experience." [62] Etzioni believes that if these expectations were fulfilled, "it would go a long way toward reconciling the potential conflict in an arrangement prescribing routine supervision for professional employees." [63]

CONCLUSION

Although learning theory is still rough and relatively unsophisticated, it has validated some principles. One of these, which the helping professions would do well to bear in mind, is that " . . . [A] certain type of student, characterized as independent flexible, or in high need for achievement, likes and does well in classroom situations which give students opportunity for self-direction." [64] If this is true for students, is is probably also true for professionals. Greater creativity in social work will require greater self-direction for social workers.

If traditional forms of treatment and traditional forms of supervision were producing good results, one might ignore the complaints of supervisees—tell them it is for their own good—and continue with the status quo. But research findings have cast doubt on effectiveness of the helping professions. As these professions forge new tools to work with burgeoning social and individual problems, they will also need to forge new tools to train the workers to meet these problems.

POSTSCRIPT

This article was written before the current economic recession, which is causing a change in personnel relationships in both business and service agencies. Instead of a manpower shortage in social work, we are facing a shortage of jobs on some levels and in some sections of the country, as well as a cut-back in government funds for social services. The wage-price freeze, instituted in response to inflation and a declining rate of profit, has frozen wages more rigorously than profits. Corporations are "cutting out the fat," and some of what is defined as fat includes research and development, and human relations ventures such as T-groups and sensitivity training. While there is no precise parallel between corporations and service agencies, some of the same economic factors are at work. In colleges and universities, for example, there are cut-backs in faculty and staff; tenure is being questioned by some administrators; salary increases are frozen; part-time help is being substituted in some places for full-time salaried faculty; teaching loads and class size are increased in some places. One university president said, "Faculty will have to understand that they are employees." In such a climate of employee-employer polarization, some faculty are talking less about professionalization and more about unionization. Most social workers have not achieved (e.g. faculty senates and policy making committees), so that administrator-worker relationships in social agencies may not in fact change drastically in response to financial restrictions. However, to the extent that social workers have achieved more autonomous functioning and greater collaboration in administration, this may change to a more adversary relationship if personnel cut-backs and the social work equivalent of the speed-up become more widespread. Conditions of work, including supervisory relationships, may increasingly become bargaining issues handled by unions.

NOTES

1. *Personnel Information,* New York: National Association of Social Workers, March, 1969, p. 33.
2. *Ibid.,* p. 15.
3. *Op. cit.,* p. 16.
4. *Op. cit.,* p. 23.
5. N. Lionel Blitzsten and Joan Fleming, "What is a Supervisory Analysis?" *Bulletin of the Menninger Clinic,* July, 1953, p. 122.
6. Herbert J. Walberg, "Can Educational Research Contribute to the Practice of Teaching?" *Journal of Education for Social Work,* Vol. 4, No. 2 (Fall, 1968), pp. 77–85.
7. Nancy K. Carroll and Wayne D. Duehn, "The Trouble with Supervision," letter to the editor, *Social Work,* October, 1968, p. 3.
8. Bettie Arthur and Judith L. Birnbaum, "Professional Identity as a Determinant of the Response to Emotionally Disturbed Children," *Psychiatry,* May, 1968, pp. 138–149.
9. *Ibid.,* p. 140.
10. *Op. cit.,* p. 140.
11. *Op. cit.,* p. 140.
12. *Op. cit.,* p. 144.
13. Othello W. Poulard, "Orientation to the Student Role: Today's Student in the School of Social Work," *Social Work Education Reporter,* December, 1968, p. 54.
14. Anselm Strauss et al., *Psychiatric Ideologies and Institutions,* (New York: The Free Press, 1964), p. 57.
15. *Ibid.,* p. 84.
16. *Op. cit.,* p. 154.
17. *Op. cit.,* p. 157.
18. *Op. cit.,* p. 158.
19. Edgar H. Schein and Warren G. Bennis, *Personal and Organizational*

Change Through Group Methods (New York: John Wiley and Sons, 1967), p. 282.

20. Ruth Newton Stevens and Fred A. Hutchinson, "A New Concept of Supervision Is Tested," *Social Work*, July, 1956, p. 51.

21. Amitai Etzioni, *The Semi-Professions and Their Organizations*, (New York: The Free Press, 1969).

22. Robert S. Wallerstein and Rudolf Ekstein, *The Teaching and Learning of Psychotherapy* (New York: Basic Books, 1958), pp. 74–75.

23. Richard C. Throndset, "Attitudes of Iowa Social Workers Toward the Private Practice of Social Casework," Unpublished thesis for the MSW University of Iowa, June, 1966, p. 44.

24. *Ibid.*, p. 48.

25. Etzioni, *op. cit.*, p. 94.

26. Wallerstein and Ekstein, *op. cit.*, p. 75.

27. Strauss, *op. cit.*, p. 83.

28. Carroll and Duehn, *op. cit.*, p. 3.

29. Martin Grotjahn, "Problems and Techniques of Supervision," *Psychiatry*, February, 1955, p. 9.

30. Strauss, *op. cit.*, p. 84.

31. Schein and Bennis, *op. cit.*, p. 282.

32. Alfred Kadushin, "Games People Play in Supervision," *Social Work*, July, 1968 [Chapter 17 above].

33. Howard Polsky, *Cottage Six*, (New York: Russell Sage, 1962).

34. Strauss, *op. cit.*, p. 292.

35. Robert C. Prall and William Stennis, "Common Pitfalls in Psychotherapy with Children," *Pennsylvania Psychiatric Quarterly*, Summer, 1964, pp. 3–11.

36. Nathan W. Ackerman, "Selected Problems in Supervised Analysis," *Psychiatry*, August, 1953, pp. 283–290.

37. Douglas McGregor, *The Human Side of Enterprise* (New York: McGraw-Hill, 1960).

38. Martin Oppenheimer, "The 'Y' Theory: Enlightened Management Confronts Alienation," *New Politics* (Winter, 1967), p. 44.

39. *Ibid.*, p. 38.

40. Warren Bennis, "Changing Organizations," *Journal of Applied Behavioral Science*, July–September, 1966, pp. 247–263.

41. Oppenheimer, *op. cit.*, p. 42.

42. Herbert Gans, "The 'Equality' Revolution," *New York Times Magazine*, November 3, 1968, p. 36.

43. *Ibid.*, pp. 70–71.

44. *Op. cit.*, p. 73.

45. Georg Simmel, *The Sociology of Georg Simmel*, tr. and ed. by Kurt H. Wolff (New York: Free Press, 1964), p. 258.

46. *Ibid.*, p. 259.

47. Irving H. Frank, "Training and Supervision in Psychotherapy; A Non-traditional Viewpoint," Unpublished mimeo., undated, p. 16.

48. Simmel, *op. cit.*, p. 285.

49. *Ibid.*, p. 285.

50. *Op. cit.*, p. 285.

51. Stevens and Hutchinson, *op. cit.*, pp. 50–55.

52. Judwiga Judd et al., "Group Supervision: A Vehicle for Professional Development," *Social Work*, January, 1962; Ruth Fizdale, "Peer Group Supervision," *Social Casework*, October, 1958 [Chapter 12 above].

53. John Wax, "Time-Limited Supervision," *Social Work*, July, 1963 [Chapter 11 above].

54. Arthur L. Leader, "A New Program of Case Consultation," *Social Casework*, February, 1964.

55. Stevens and Hutchinson, *op. cit.*, pp. 50–55.

56. *Ibid.*, p. 52.

57. *Op. cit.*, p. 52.

58. *Op. cit.*, p. 54.

59. Mary Holmes Gilmore, "Consultation as a Social Work Activity," Unpublished mimeo., January 8, 1963, p. 14.

60. *Ibid.*, p. 20.

61. *Op. cit.*, p. 22.

62. Etzioni, *op. cit.*, p. 95.

63. *Ibid.*, p. 95.

64. W. J. McKeachie, "Research on Teaching at the College and University Level," *Handbook of Research on Teaching*, edited by N. L. Gage (Chicago: Rand-McNally, 1963), pp. 1118–1172. As cited in Walberg, *op. cit.*, p. 83.

28

Supervision:
Challenges for the Future

Ruth H. Young

SUPERVISION AND CHANGE

WE ARE IN AN AGE OF CONSUMERISM. Students and practitioners not only are developing their own philosophies about being consumers of social work education or any other kind of education but also are endeavoring to work out where the client should be able to have an impact on the services he receives and where the social worker should have an impact on the way his job is structured, the supervision he receives, and his relationship with the administration of the agency. We are in the middle of a changing set of role relationships that are related to the entire social scene around us.

The Academy of Certified Social Workers now has an examination for competence which makes ACSW a certification measure with substance. This examination is based on the central concept of the "self-directed" worker—"the autonomous social worker." Over twenty states now license social workers on the basis of examination oriented to self-directed practice. Those developments have implications for supervision that will be discussed in this paper.

Other trends that will affect the profession and the practice of supervision are the changes taking place in social work education. There has been belated but recent recognition of undergraduate education for social work by the Council on Social Work Education. The standards for accreditation of undergraduate programs include the requirement that students be prepared for entry into direct service positions, and the

An earlier version of this paper was presented at Mid-Winter Supervisors' Institute, Family Service Association of America, Philadelphia, Pa., March 1971. Reprinted by permission of the author.

programs must include field experience and methods courses. As this level of education expands, how and what should be its effect on the graduate schools? How and what should be its effect on differential expectations of the BA level practitioner and the MSW graduate? Some have hazarded a guess that within the next ten years all direct service positions at the entry level will be filled only by the BA graduate, and the MSW will be the supervisor and administrator.

Besides changes in patterns and expectations, graduate teaching itself is changing. One of the hallmarks of a professional, according to much of the literature on this subject, is the willingness of the person who has been admitted to practice as a professional to share his performance with his peers, to open his professional self to peer judgment and discussion. Most other professionals' practice has been "more public" than has been the case in social work. The traditional social work supervision structure has had great value but has tended to take away from the concept of sharing with one's colleagues and peers. In many schools today practice is more open, as methods courses use not only the students' material and the written dictation in a case presentation but also audio- and video-taped interviews and role playing as teaching tools. The use of the various media builds on the expectation that the professional will open his performance to view and will participate in its evaluation along with colleagues. A practitioner will have a different perception of his work if in all his learning, especially in the area of use of self, he is heard and seen on tape not only by himself but also by his peers. Exposure of one's work in this way is painful at times and often uncomfortable, but it does more closely approximate what our fellow professionals expect in the development of an autonomous worker. It also contributes to more capacity and ability to participate in team service delivery.

How does supervision fit into developing concepts of advocacy, client participation, service definition, and fiscal accountability? What are some of today's most persistent criticisms of our traditions in this area? What are some ideas as to possible techniques we might develop and use? Increasing numbers of workers are going into private practice, even among recent graduates. Many cite dissatisfaction with supervision as the primary reason for entering private practice. Regardless of the controversy about private practice, we need to address the implications of increased private practice for the profession.

Another criticism of supervision has been described as the "Socratic game." [1] This is supervision that gives the illusion of collaboration. The Socratic game is a series of questions for which the supervisor presumes to know the answers, leading the supervisee by the nose; both people are talking but only one is working. Supervision is not a process in which a person who *knows more* teaches someone who *knows less*, but one in which someone who is accountable on a higher level of authority *works with* someone accountable on a lower level of authority. To stop the Socratic game, supervisory practice has to be recorded, evaluated, and shared with someone else.

HISTORICAL IMPACTS

Barber in "The Sociology of the Professions" says that one of the chief characteristics of professional behavior is a "high-degree" of self-control of behavior. Some of this comes from knowledge that has been developed and some from internalized values and regulative codes of ethics and voluntary associations for the maintenance of standards.[2] Lubove in *The Professional Altruist* argues that our theory of supervision resulted from an organizational pressure for efficiency through assurance that the worker's performance did not fall below agency standards. Between 1920 and 1930, "a self-conscious awareness of supervision as a kind of casework with psychiatric content emerged—a helping process applied to the worker instead of the client. Just as the caseworker labored to remove the mental or emotional blocks which obstructed the client's social adjustment, the supervisor endeavored to eradicate or reshape personal attitudes and habits which detracted from the worker's professional effectiveness."[3] He goes on to describe the supervisory role as "a channel of communication between the executive and service staffs, between the shapers of agency policy and those who applied it. Agency efficiency depended, presumably upon . . . adroitness in coordinating casework practice with the ideals and policies of the administration."[4] This image of supervision conflicts with the changing modes of today's practice as well as with the kinds of individuals who are electing social work as a career. Some of the reaction to this model is seen as a preoccupation with professionalization over the years. Today's new graduates are not without some of the antiprofessionalism that characterized some of the war on poverty and is often used to support the "new careers" concept.

Additionally, all of us have developed a certain resistance to the results of bureaucratization of our society. Some of a professional's resistance to the supervisory process is perhaps justified in view of what can happen in the larger systems. It may also be the basic genesis of the development of the field of hospital administration, for example, because of the impossibility of working out a satisfactory organizational relationship between the MD and the health care system in a hospital. Social work has been an agency-directed profession, and to some extent employee-bound in orientation. This rather long tradition, based on a need for community sanction and efforts to deliver services in a rational way, is antithetical to the proposed ACSW self-directed worker concept and to Barber's ideal of a professional responsible to exercise self-control over his practice.

The literature is replete with studies of bureaucratic behavior which indicate that the higher the prestige of the professional group, the less members submit to control over their behavior except in administrative matters. Concomitant with this is a finding that in studies of social workers the more professionally oriented workers were more likely to express low loyalty to the agency. Many of these strains have affected the way we see supervision today.

STRUCTURE AND AUTHORITY

Pettes raises the question: "Can help appropriately be given to a professional Social Worker?" [5] Frances Scherz emphatically states that it is the social worker *only* who has responsibility for and is accountable for his own quality of performance, and the worker must assume responsibility for his own continued professional development.[6] Both authors deal with the familiar question of the administrative versus educative aspects of the supervisory job, but with different emphases stemming from their basic positions. Charlotte Towle describes supervision as an administrative process with an educational purpose.[7]

The role of supervisor does involve both the aspects of administration and teaching, but it primarily relates to the task of getting the service to the client. Crucial to any understanding of the role is the difficult realization that when one moves into supervision, problem-solving intervention cannot be done through the worker by the supervisor. Pettes can be answered by saying, "yes—help can be given to an MSW or professionally trained worker, but it must be task-focused. There must be recognition that normal anxiety accompanies all learning and this will diminish with development of knowledge and skill. If it does not, then the supervisor is in a therapeutic situation that is not the proper role for a supervisor. It is the worker's responsibility to change—not the supervisor's to treat." Perhaps the prime skill is to enable the worker and supervisor to have a reflective discussion that is not a treatment session. Some of the resistance to supervision today by new graduates is to this perception of "treatment." There is some reality in their concern. Towle commented that the profession has erred in being unable to establish learning norms. We have assumed both in schools and on the job that problematic functioning is necessarily evidence of neurotic difficulty in learning, and we have been slow to identify the uneducable.

To achieve all of the above stated goals—teaching, administration, and enabling—we have customarily used the one-to-one supervisory conference. Are there other ways to accomplish the same ends? Has the one-to-one conference behind closed doors contributed to some of the problems mentioned earlier? How can we enlarge the supervisory armamentarium of intervention strategies, teaching, accountability, and enabling of staff to get the job done? If we are as sensitive to the changing social scene as our professional commitment should enable us to be, how can supervisors become involved differently with their staffs so that they are not seen as having a monopoly on decision making? There is a relationship between involvement and the achievement of therapeutic goals. Shared responsibility for decision making and determination of service delivery goals may further enhance what we as professionals have done in the past in developing practitioners.

Supervision in the past has implied a considerable amount of dependency between the supervisor and worker. This is attested to partially by the fact that the older, advanced senior workers pride themselves on having reached the moment of no more supervision. In other words, supervision has been looked upon as a checking-up process, supposedly reflecting on the worker's capability to conduct work with clients without needing to be checked on. This is a distortion of what supervision was intended to be; yet there is a basis in reality for this view. This reality-based distortion needs clarification. It runs completely counter to the competence concept embraced in the ACSW examination. As long as one works with people, one must have an opportunity to seek and obtain consultation or even supervision without the current reflection that it makes one less professional to seek such assistance. As practice is now being defined, and as it moves away from designating the user of service as an individual pathologically unable to function to a definition of the user as a citizen for whom either the social or personal system may not be working at the moment, we have to conceptualize supervision with a view of the user of supervision as someone sharing a responsibility and a common professional identity.

Much can be done in restructuring the one-to-one type of supervisory relationship. The whole concept of setting up the learning contract between two individuals could be examined. The initial goals can be mapped out and ways of achieving them discussed. Any new practitioner arrives at the agency either hindered or aided by the field instruction experience. He has had at least four to six opportunities at grading periods and points of evaluation that involved discussing his learning needs with a competent professional. He should be able to engage directly in determining what he must do to consolidate gains and move ahead toward greater self-direction in practice. The supervisor has the opportunity to discuss with him perceived learning needs in terms of the job to be done.

USE OF GROUPS

Many students will graduate from schools of social work in which they have had considerable experience in a variety of group interactions in connection with field work. Most schools have moved more and more in the direction of securing funding for student units directed by full-time faculty members. These units engage in a variety of learning experiences together—orientation, training, staff meetings, case discussion, problem and issue discussions, and use of the group as a major tool for supervision and teaching. This use of groups in supervision has been slow to develop. There has been a growing recognition of the potential of the group as helpful in the change process. In group supervision, the major supervisory tasks (teaching, administration, enabling) are carried on in the group, with its support. The responsibilities for teaching and content become those of all the group members, not only the supervisor. The group offers its members opportunities to achieve goals that may be more difficult to achieve alone. Generally, groups offer satisfaction and security.

> The small group offers a natural setting in which problem solving can be carried out. For the social worker the quest is for a professional identity in common with other staff and with the help of a supervisor—teacher. Together they share responsibility for this quest, each according to his function and what he has to offer.[8]

The supervisor has the major goal of enabling the group to develop working relationships among the members that expedite the learning. The supervisor must show the same sensitivity and individualizing ability as he would in individual supervision. Simply because a group of people meet together does not mean that the individual is relatively unimportant and the group is the unit of overriding interest. Quite the contrary: The group exists in order to give each *individual* member an opportunity to put in or take out whatever he can contribute or use and to become a more effective individual in relation to his clients. Hence it follows that meeting with workers in a group is not a shortcut to success but is merely a different way of promoting adequate agency standards of performance. Neither the one-to-one nor the group situation is necessarily the only or best way of supervision, automatically superior in nature and product. The methods are different and tend to achieve the goals by somewhat different means. It is entirely possible that at one time the one, at another time the other, method would have greater relevance. Any group situation in which supervision takes place presumes first of all that the individuals who make up the group are willing to help, expose their own work, and contribute their thoughts, ideas, fears, and successes in a frank, open, and relaxed way. This is a difficult goal to achieve.

Several reasons can be supplied as to why the group situation can be a most efficient and useful tool in helping workers become aware of their performance. The main thesis here is that there are overriding advantages in using groups for certain kinds of supervisory activities and that these advantages can probably be attained by no other method.

ADVANTAGES OF GROUPS

The advantages to be obtained from group supervision are the very ones upon which the operation of most social agencies depends in a major way. As it is now and probably will continue to be, social work functions are performed most of the time within social agency settings. Social agencies are groups. They are either small groups in the sense that the agency has relatively few staff members or they are very large groups. But if the latter obtains there tend to be small units within it, namely, departments, and smaller groups within larger groups. In each of these units one of the considerations of great concern is that it operate smoothly. By this is meant that all parts of the unit interlock, with members cooperating with each other in such a way that not only does each individual worker perform his work satisfactorily, but he contributes to the functioning of the unit or the group as a whole. In the long run it is impossible for a worker to function effectively alone.

As we look at the group or the agency there is a considerable amount of dependency of persons upon each other. The purpose of having supervision in groups is to take advantage of this dependence, with supervisor and workers *together* guiding it. This dependence is there whether one has supervision in group settings or not. If one can bring the group together and focus this dependence, deal with it, and talk about how one member depends upon the other, using the combined talents and faults of everyone to help each individual member as well as the whole group do a better job, then one has achieved or is likely to achieve a degree of cohesion, an identification of each individual with the group, that can never be achieved if we persist in a one-to-one relationship only. The one-to-one approach uses two-dimensional interaction between the worker and the supervisor. Supervision can be done in groups, not because in having to set up a group one can then get members to know each other, but because the group exists in the first place and harbors a degree of possibility and potential that one ought to take advantage of in order to make the operation more effective. Group supervision is a way of doing something with the group that cannot but help in the long run to rebound to the good and the welfare of all.[9]

If there is a group process in which everybody participates, we can decrease the emphasis on hierarchy. Hierarchy simply means that some people supervise other people, or that some are responsible or account-able to one placed on a higher level within the administrative structure of the agency. Within the group structure it is possible to motivate staff members not only to think in terms of how they can please their super-visor or manipulate their supervisor into pleasing them, but to use the group to help the entire membership of this group within the hierarchy feel a closer identification, not only with staff and supervisor but with the operation as a whole. This means that within the group everybody must have an opportunity to say what he thinks is pertinent to the opera-tion of the agency or the department. This should not be so merely because some people are supervisors and others are not.

What happens in group situations is that members become more voluntary and more spontaneous in their willingness to make contribu-tions to the group as a whole because they feel they have an important place in the group. Out of this emerges a feeling of involvement, con-cern, and commitment that is not nearly as likely to be achieved when supervisor and worker sit together in a room, with the worker constantly feeling he is being evaluated. In a group the individual worker has his peers with him, and by sharing ideas and comments peers can make contributions to each other that would never occur if the group did not exist. Peers are likely to "take" ideas and comments from each other which a supervisor would have a very difficult time making acceptable to a worker. This is also true when working with client groups; clients are able to deal with comments and ideas from each other that they would hesitate to accept from a worker. Workers in a group are able and willing to say a great deal to each other which a supervisor would have a hard time putting across.

This is what groups can do; this is what groups are for; and an en-lightened administration will make use of the rich potential for good that resides within the staff groups. The groups exist anyway. The ques-tion is only what are we going to do with them? Are we going to use the group as a whole and let every member within the group interact with every other member, thereby creating feelings of support, under-standing, and satisfaction as well as creating motivation and skill to do an even better job?

CONCLUSION

The argument has been made about group process and its benefits, and it is this kind of relatedness that today's practitioners are seeking. They are "antiestablishment" in many ways but believe at the same time in offering high-quality services. They see our history of hierarchical arrangements and the increasing bureaucratization of social welfare in general as preventing delivery of services. The group process is one way to positively establish competency-based practice and to insure more autonomy for the worker.

We cannot give up accountability as a principle. We can be accountable if we are willing to redefine roles and role relationships so that accountability is appropriately demanded of all. Staff appreciate a different perspective on accountability if they share more in their own destinies and the destiny of the agency. The supervisory process must make this possible.

NOTES

1. William Schwartz, *Service and Supervision* (New York: United Neighborhood Houses, 1968), p. 16.
2. Barnard Barber, "The Sociology of the Professions," *Daedalus* (Fall 1963), p. 79.
3. Roy Lubove, *The Professional Altruist* (New York: Atheneum, 1969), p. 168.
4. *Ibid.*, pp. 168–169.
5. Dorothy E. Pettes, *Supervision in Social Work: A Method of Student Training and Staff Development* (London: George Allen and Unwin, Ltd., 1967), p. 16.
6. Frances Scherz, "A Concept of Supervision Based on Definitions of Job Responsibility," *Social Casework* (October 1958), pp. 435–443 [Chapter 8 above].
7. Charlotte Towle, *The Learner in Education for the Professions* (Chicago: University of Chicago Press, 1954).
8. Paul A. Abels, "On the Nature of Supervision: The Medium Is the Group," *Child Welfare* (June 1970), p. 306 [Chapter 13 above, pp. 134–135].
9. Hans Falck, "Supervision Can Be Done in Groups," paper delivered at an Institute, Missouri Association for Social Welfare, 1964, p. 4.

29

Authority and Social Work Supervision: An Emerging Model

Carlton E. Munson

AUTHORITY, ORGANIZATIONS, AND SUPERVISION

SOCIAL WORKERS HAVE ALWAYS functioned predominantly within the confines of organizational necessities.[1] Supervision is the arena where much of the conflict of professional autonomy versus organizational authority is encountered and confronted. Mandell has pointed out that this conflict has increased within the profession in conjunction with the equality revolution that has taken place at the societal level,[2] and sees only limited opportunities for more autonomous social work practice. Epstein holds the same view but argues that limited qualified autonomous practice is possible if authority can be decentralized and teaching de-emphasized in supervision.[3] Levy has suggested that the question of authority can be partially resolved by applying a code of ethics to supervision.[4] Kadushin has related problems in authority to interactional games played by supervisees to avoid risk and loss of control,[5] and Hawthorne has applied the same framework to supervisors.[6] Munson has related authority to supervision by analyzing interactional roles of supervisors and supervisees.[7] Most of these writers describe the process that occurs; but there has not been much progress in substantially reducing authority conflicts, and only limited theoretical and practical models have been developed to resolve the issues. The dual model of supervision and consultation described in this article is an attempt to decentralize authority in organizational settings and to maximize professional autonomy.

The dilemma of modern man as a creature of organizations and the nature of authority and autonomy have been articulated by Whyte:

> Every decision . . . on the problem of the individual versus authority is something of a dilemma. . . . We do need to know how to co-operate

with The Organization but, more than ever, so do we need to know how to resist it. . . . Organization has been made by man; it can be changed by man.[8]

Scott Briar has summarized the issue of authority and autonomy in practice through supervision, that faces the social work profession:

> Ninety percent or more of all caseworkers practice in bureaucratic organizations, and the demands of such organizations have a tendency to encroach upon professional autonomy. Every attempt by the agency to routinize some condition or aspect of professional practice amounts to a restriction of professional discretion, and for that reason probably should be resisted, in most instances by practitioners. . . . There are of course, realistic limits to the amount of autonomy and discretion an organization can grant to the practitioner, but no one knows just where that limit is, and we cannot know until we have tried to reach it.[9]

Hughes has epitomized the issue by asking, "There is . . . a problem of authority; what orders does one accept from an employer, especially one . . . whose interests may not always be those of the professional and his clients?"[10] The problem of control in modern professions and organizations leads to a number of questions especially appropriate to social work. Supervision has traditionally been summarized functionally as administration, teaching, and helping.[11] If this is the case, then what are the limits of control in these functions? What are the best means of carrying out these functions structurally? The major issue explored here is the question of authority and structure in social work supervision. Recent developments in this area are discussed, as are suggestions for analyzing supervision by using an interactional theoretical framework,[12] and a dual model of administrative supervision and clinical consultation is explored from this perspective.

AUTHORITY AND STRUCTURE OF SUPERVISION

The recent trend in the literature is to confront the issue of authority by suggesting alternative methods of structuring supervision. Most proponents of group supervision in social work argue that this structure is superior in most respects, including use of authority, to traditional one-to-one supervision. Kaslow holds that group supervision fosters autonomy and independence,[13] and Epstein believes it is superior when used in problem solving, dissolving hierarchical power and status, and promoting incentive for innovation and responsibility.[14] A great deal can be accomplished through applying individual and group supervision differentially according to experience, education, and preference of workers. However, this structure alone does not seem to be sufficient to cause optimal congruence among the worker, the supervisor, and the organization. Analysis of the extent and nature of interaction in supervision regardless of the structure used is helpful in sorting out issues and conflicts. How the supervisor interacts with the supervisees has been demonstrated to be the crucial variable. This fact has been demonstrated in psychiatric studies of supervision, which are substantially more controlled empirically than are those in social work. Balsam and Garber found that the personal style of the supervisor was important to outcome.[15] Grossman and Karmiol varied the supervisor's involvement in the supervisee's practice, finding that where supervisors had no direct involvement the supervisees functioned more autonomously; [16] Goin and associates found that inclusion of a faculty observer in the treatment was important to therapeutic outcome.[17] Stein and associates, in studying the diagnostic phase of intervention, discovered more diagnostic congruence when the supervisor participated in the evaluation than when the supervisee presented the case to the supervisor.[18]

The interactional framework can also be applied to the structure of supervision in terms of how the supervisor will exercise authority in individual and group supervision. A supervisor can exert a great deal of control in individual as well as group supervision although it does appear that control is more difficult to exercise in the latter. Regardless of the model, authority can be dealt with directly by establishing interactional ground rules and deciding at the outset what the roles of the supervisor and worker will be. Interactional questions that deal directly with authority are as follows: Who sets the agenda? Who establishes the frequency, time, and length of the sessions? Will emphasis be placed on case discussion, worker growth, or both? Will the supervisor present case material? Who will make what decisions? Who establishes the structure of presentations? Who establishes the content of presentations? These questions can be applied to either individual or group supervision and have less to do with how the supervisory process is structured in general and more to do with authority and interaction.

Based on two recent studies, interactional questions about presentation of case material and sharing of clinical material deserve more attention than they have been granted in the past and can be important to practice. Burgoyne and associates, in a study of eighty-nine patients treated by residents, found that there was an inequity in the cases presented in supervision, significantly differing from others in being younger, better educated, having higher incomes, better liked by the residents, and being given longer term treatment.[19] Dressler and associates found residents showed more warmth toward patients with low suicide risk and limited overall psychopathology, whereas they felt anxious toward patients with high suicidal risk and significant pathology. The authors suggest that using supervision interaction to modify these attitudes will improve the equity of service.[20]

These studies involved psychiatric residents, and no comparable studies of social work students or practitioners exist; but if they did, it is held the results would not differ since social workers often work with the same patients and their families. These studies demonstrate the importance supervision can have for adequate service purely on clinical grounds and involve interactions that should be shared free of administrative constraints and evaluation. Stiles has related such issues to the "implicit contract" that should be a part of the supervision process,[21] and it is my view that it is time to make such questions a part of the explicit supervisory contract.

THE DUAL MODEL

How interaction can be used to interrelate authority and the structure of supervision can be illustrated by a dual system of administrative supervision and case consultation.[22] Interactionally, supervision implies exercising authority, whereas consultation implies giving advice and recommendations without control. However, both the worker and the supervisor must be clear on the limits of their power and right to act in given situations. Comments by workers suggest that simply to relabel supervision "consultation" to make the process more palatable can lead to conflict, gradual isolation, and lack of interaction when the worker learns that in many instances he does not have the freedom to act contrary to the supervisor's views. For this reason it is best, where possible, to completely separate the two functions, to have one staff member designated the administrative supervisor and another staff member the clinical consultant. Where this type of separation has been used all the participants usually undergo an initial period of confusion and some misunderstanding of roles. Workers are not sure who to consult and the supervisor and consultant are not sure when approached with a problem whether it falls within their responsibility. Some questions clearly fall within one area or the other, but many do not, and the supervisor and consultant must begin to sort out what is administration, what is practice, and where the two areas are interrelated. The guiding principle in the dual model is that administrative supervision and clinical consultation must coalesce at the point a problem or conflict is perceived in practice as interfering with the job or task to be done. Initially a great deal of interaction must take place among the consultant, supervisor, and practitioners. As the appropriate lines of interaction are established, the frequency of contact decreases. Where the model has been used, the participants have developed high regard for the system once the difficulties of the initial period have been resolved. They do not agree with the argument that it is more time-consuming, more costly, and requires more manpower than more traditional models.

The model allows for variation in the structure of supervision. Individual or group supervision can be used in any combination that fits the organization's structure or workers' preferences. Generally, the one-to-one structure is used for administrative supervision, and group conferences are used for clinical consultation. One problem that can develop from this arrangement is that the administrative supervisor can develop a sense of isolation and a feeling that the clinical group has become an adversary coalition. This situation can be avoided if the administrative supervisor periodically meets with the clinical group and frequent contacts are held between the supervisor and consultant to promote clarity about expectations, but each must make clear to workers what information will be shared about them during such meetings. Clarity about sharing information between the supervisor and consultant when the practitioner's performance is evaluated is especially important.

There are several sound reasons for using a dual model. First, a precise distinction can be made among the administrative, teaching, and helping functions. Frequently, the last two involve psychological issues related to the relationship between practitioner and client, whereas administrative policies and issues involve sociological and organizational questions. Many conflicts in supervision in the past have been the result of failure to make a distinction in these areas, leading to complaints from workers that they are being "caseworked" and "psychologized" by their supervisors. Rosenbaum and Miller and associates, in separate studies of psychiatric supervision, argue that mixing the role of teaching and evaluation in clinical settings increases anxiety in the supervisee,[23] and the person responsible for clinical guidance should not be placed in an administrative role.[24] Fizdale suggests that mixing the two roles in social work impedes autonomous functioning.[25]

Second, the dual model distinguishes between client-centered questions and agency-centered issues. In settings where high-risk client groups such as battered wives [26] and child abusers are serviced, policy questions—such as workers having unlisted phone numbers, being on call beyond agency hours, making home visits, etc.—can be explored and resolved on the basis of whose priorities are most essential. Use of the dual model of supervision crystallizes such issues so that rights and responsibilities of clients, practitioners, supervisors, and agencies are made apparent.

Third, there is a temporal quality to administration and teaching/helping functions that should be taken into account. Often administrative functions can be dealt with in a brief period and on a terminal basis, whereas teaching and helping can be long, ongoing processes. By separating these functions, time can be more effectively used, teaching and helping can be more integrative, and content appropriate to one area cannot interfere with or be used to subvert the other.

RECENT DEVELOPMENTS
AND SUPERVISION

Recent developments in the social work profession suggest that the issues of authority, structure, teaching, and interaction in supervision need to be explored further and more clearly defined, and the dual model of supervision/consultation is consistent with the changes that are occurring.

First, the National Association of Social Workers (NASW) is working to bring about uniform licensing laws throughout the United States.[27] The current trend is to regulate social workers at several levels of education and practice. Each level of regulation generally carries a requirement for supervision with gradations of autonomy.[28] In this effort to upgrade the level of competence in practice, the profession must be clear about what kind and how much supervision to apply at a given level. Legislators are asking difficult questions about who is to be regulated and how, and social workers need empirical data and precise models to support contentions regarding the effectiveness and organization of regulation. In addition, legal regulation will require organizations to conform to externally imposed requirements for supervision, and agencies will need guidelines in implementing these sanctions. The profession should set standards of supervision to protect workers against possible arbitrary agency policies in meeting the requirements of regulated practice.[29] Such standards should be established by the profession through national organizations rather than through the vague current practice of expecting workers to negotiate supervision when seeking a position. The use of the dual model can be helpful in this regard in that a strong clinical consultant can be a valuable resource when the practitioner is in conflict with administrative policies, and vice versa. In this model the problems can be more easily viewed as organizational and practical rather than focusing on the functioning of the individual practitioner.

Second, in a related effort, NASW is currently recommending restructuring of social work practice along lines of specialization based on level of practice and methodological function.[30] If this model is implemented, the profession will need to develop specific definitions of consultation, supervision, in-service training, program development, and program coordination.[31] The issue of specialization is closely tied to supervision, which is demonstrated by the recommendation of one group, the Council on Social Work in Schools, that if social work would develop good professional supervision and a probation or learning period, there would be no need for specialization.[32] Both the trend toward regulation of and specialization in practice will increase the importance of the role of supervision.

Third, two task forces [33] sponsored by the Council on Social Work Education (CSWE) have made recommendations now under study, which if implemented could have major impact on how supervision is perceived and conducted in agencies. The Task Force on Structure and Quality in Social Work Education dealt with the emerging conceptualizations of various levels of practice in the context of "generalist" and "specialist" areas of competence.[34] The Task Force has made recommendations regarding the structure and content of AA, BSW, MSW, DSW, and PhD programs, and these recommendations have been placed in a "societal context":

> . . . social workers must be helped and prepared to accept individual professional responsibility for their practice. In the expectation that much of this practice will take place in bureaucratic multidisciplinary structures, social workers must be prepared to function . . . with more professional independence.[35]

Although this contention is valid, some form of supervision, or more likely genuine consultation, must be available as a support system for workers to prevent a sense of isolation. Autonomy is essential, but support is important. Authority is necessary in administrative supervision, but not to the point of giving rise to resentment. A dual supervision/consultation model will balance autonomy and support.

The Task Force on Social Work Practice and Education raised the question of learning-oriented support in pointing out that "social workers must be prepared for lifelong learning and agencies be prepared for their contributions to this continued learning." [36] Social workers in practice recognize this need for lifelong learning at a higher level than do supervisors. As agency representatives, supervisors frequently are not prepared or are unwilling to work to provide such opportunities. The desire for and recognition of the importance of such learning is especially acute among experienced workers. The Task Force raises specific questions about this issue:

> Where does "lifelong" learning take place? What is the role of supervision and of what importance are the changes in the styles of supervision? Who is responsible for this learning? While there is needed a clarification as to where and how practice offers learning opportunities . . . there is as well a need for clarification of the expectations one can have for a person who is a professional practitioner. At this time, there appear to be inadequate and ambiguous definitions of what one can expect from professional practitioners.[37]

To confront these issues the profession must launch a broader study of where learning takes place, who is responsible for it, and what the expectations of practitioners will be. The dual model advocated here can help focus these issues. Coordination of clinical consultation to identify what learning needs are and administrative supervision to develop and implement educational plans can give added force to such efforts.

Fourth, using a dual model is consistent with the trend in graduate schools of social work to make a distinction between clinical practice and administration by offering specializations in practice and management and administration. Graduates of these programs have little understanding outside their specialty. For example, a graduate of a management program can relate to a graduate of administration, but has little basis for understanding matters and issues of practice. As graduates of management specializations move into administrative positions in clinically oriented agencies, some system of balancing input is needed. Where views on both administration and practice can be presented on an equal basis, genuine progress in decentralization of authority will have been achieved—which is consistent with the idea of democratic involvement of workers in developing agency policy, an issue identified in the literature as early as the 1920s.[38] The ideas of balance of input and democratic involvement are central to the dual model of supervision.

Fifth, Scherz concluded almost twenty years ago that "the job of casework supervisor is, in essence, an administrative job."[39] More recently Turem has argued that "administration is defined as the process of management,"[40] and that "management . . . requires an underlying knowledge base for determining what does or does not 'work,' what is or is not 'efficient.'"[41] Social work supervision has been viewed historically as a vehicle of accountability and efficiency, but the emphasis appears to have been on *how* to be accountable and efficient rather than on what accountability and efficiency *are*. A shift in emphasis and more administrative and clinical coordination in supervision could help the profession clarify both broad issues about practice and specific ones relating to supervision. This change in emphasis would be in keeping with the trends within the profession and Morris's prediction that

> in the 1980s . . . on the MSW and Ph.D. levels there will be increased attention to the management side of administering . . . services and to complexities of team leadership, especially when such leadership includes administrative responsibilities.[42]

CONCLUSION

The trends toward regulation of practice through licensing, developing specializations based on level of practice, increasing emphasis on accountability, and reconceptualizing and restructuring education for practice seem to constitute the major areas for exploring supervision during the next several decades.* The profession needs to encourage and support new models of supervision and consultation to keep pace with these changes. The idea of separating administrative and practice functions in supervision is not new, but providing for such functions through separate staff member roles is.[43] Mary Richmond alluded to such separation,[44] and the Report of the Milford Conference identifies the dual function of supervision as promoting standards of service and professional development of staff.[45] Fizdale has used a model which possesses many of the characteristics of the dual model to completely replace the traditional form of supervision.[46] Earlier writings by Berl,[47] Scherz,[48] and Austin [49] all indirectly suggest a framework for a dual model in attempting to distinguish educative and administrative functions in supervision. Much of the literature defines the functions of supervision without developing models to organize and implement these functions, although some agencies and schools of social work are moving toward the dual model. The limited application thus far has produced positive results, and the model deserves further application, consideration, and research.

NOTES

1. Bernard Barber, "Some Problems in the Sociology of the Professions," *Daedalus* (Fall 1963), pp. 678–682.
2. Betty Mandell, "The 'Equality' Revolution and Supervision," *Journal of Education for Social Work* 9 (Winter 1973), pp. 43–54 [Chapter 27 above].
3. Laura Epstein, "Is Autonomous Practice Possible?" *Social Work* 18 (March 1973), pp. 5–12 [Chapter 14 above].
4. Charles Levy, "The Ethics of Supervision," *Social Work* 18 (March 1973), pp. 14–21 [Chapter 20 above].
5. Alfred Kadushin, "Games People Play in Supervision," *Social Work* 13 (July 1968), pp. 23–32 [Chapter 17 above].
6. Lillian Hawthorne, "Games Supervisors Play," *Social Work* 20 (May 1975), pp. 179–183 [Chapter 18 above].
7. Carlton E. Munson, "Professional Autonomy and Social Work Supervision," *Journal of Education for Social Work* 12 (Fall 1976), pp. 95–102 [Chapter 21 above].

* There are several other developments within the profession that could have impact on supervision within the context of the areas explored in this research, but these areas are not clearly defined, developed, or documented to allow adequate exploration or valid comment here. They are (1) unionization and collective bargaining by workers, (2) involvement of social workers in Professional Standards Review Organizations (PSRO) in some settings, and (3) the increased use of untrained and paraprofessional workers in some agencies.

8. William H. Whyte, *The Organization Man* (New York: Simon and Schuster, 1956), pp. 3–14.

9. Scott Briar, "The Current Crisis in Social Casework," in Robert W. Klenk and Robert M. Ryan, eds., *The Practice of Social Work* (Belmont, Calif., Wadsworth Publishing Company, 1970), p. 96.

10. Everett C. Hughes, "Professions," *Daedalus* (Fall 1963), p. 665.

11. Dorothy Pettes, *Supervision in Social Work: A Method of Student Training and Staff Development* (London: George Allen and Unwin Ltd., 1967), p. 15.

12. For a discussion of the interactional model, see Munson, *op. cit.*

13. Florence Kaslow, *Issues in Human Services* (San Francisco: Jossey-Bass, 1972), p. 119.

14. Epstein, *op. cit.*, p. 10.

15. Alan Balsam and Norton Garber, "Characteristics of Psychotherapy Supervision," *Journal of Medical Education* 45 (October 1970), pp. 789–797.

16. William Grossman and Edward Karmiol, "Group Psychotherapy Supervision and Its Effects on Resident Training," *American Journal of Psychiatry* 130 (August 1973), pp. 920–921.

17. M. K. Goin *et al.*, "Teaching Dynamic Psychotherapy by Observation," *American Journal of Psychotherapy* 30 (January 1976), pp. 112–120.

18. S. P. Stein *et al.*, "Supervision of the Initial Interview: A Study of Two Methods," *Archives of General Psychiatry* 32 (February 1975), pp. 265–268.

19. R. W. Burgoyne *et al.*, "Who Gets Supervised? An Extension of Patient Selection Inequity," *American Journal of Psychiatry* 133 (November 1976), pp. 1313–1315.

20. D. M. Dressler *et al.*, "Clinical Attitudes Toward the Suicide Attempter," *Journal of Nervous and Mental Disease* 160 (February 1975), pp. 146–155.

21. Evelyn Stiles, "Supervision in Perspective," *Social Casework* 44 (January 1963), p. 24 [Chapter 9 above, p. 91].

22. For a detailed description of this model, see Dean J. Champion, *The Sociology of Organizations* (New York: McGraw-Hill Book Company, 1975), pp. 166–167.

23. Milton Rosenbaum, "Problems in Supervision of Psychiatric Residents in Psychotherapy," *Archives of Neurology and Psychiatry* 69 (1953), pp. 43–48.

24. Arthur A. Miller, *et al.*, "Teaching and Evaluation of Diagnostic Skills," *Archives of General Psychiatry* 24 (March 1971), pp. 255–259.

25. Ruth Fizdale, "Peer-Group Supervision," *Social Casework* 39 (October 1958), pp. 443–450 [Chapter 12 above].

26. For a specific example of this issue, see Celia Medina and Maria R. Reyes, "Dilemmas of Chicana Counselors," *Social Work* 21 (November 1976), p. 516.

27. "Legal Regulations of Social Work Practice Policies for a Continuing Effort," *NASW News* 20 (March 1975), p. 5.

28. *Ibid.*, p. 1.

29. For an actual incident of this issue related to supervision, see Jane K. Thompson, "Fighting Discrimination: Up Against the Ivied Wall," *Social Work* 21 (November 1976), p. 509.

30. Bo Thiemann and Mark Battle, "Developing a System of Social Work Specialization," National Association of Social Workers, 1975 (mimeographed).

31. *Ibid.*, Appendix A, p. 8.

32. *Ibid.*, p. 17.

33. Task Force on Structure and Quality in Social Work Education and Task Force on Social Work Practice in Education.

34. Lillian Ripple, *Report to the Task Force on Structure and Quality in Social Work Education* (New York: Council on Social Work Education, 1974), pp. 24–29.

35. *Ibid.*, p. 67.

36. Ralph Dolgoff, *Report to the Task Force on Social Work Practice and Education* (New York: Council on Social Work Education, 1974), p. 11.

37. *Ibid.*, p. 11.

38. Report of the Milford Conference, *Social Casework: Generic and Specific* (New York: American Association of Social Workers, 1929; reprint ed., Washington, D.C.: National Association of Social Workers Classic Series, 1974), pp. 51–55 [Chapter 4 above].

39. Frances Scherz, "A Concept of Supervision Based on Definitions of Job Responsibility," *Social Casework* 39 (October 1958), p. 435 [Chapter 8 above, p. 70].

40. Jerry S. Turem, "The Call for a Management Stance," *Social Work* 19 (September 1974), p. 616.

41. *Ibid.*, p. 616.

42. Robert Morris, "The Place of Social Work in the Human Services," *Social Work* 19 (September 1974), p. 531.

43. For example, see Edward E. Schwartz and William C. Sample, *The Midway Office: An Experiment in the Organization of Work Groups* (New York: National Association of Social Workers, 1972).

44. Mary Richmond, *Social Diagnosis* (New York: Free Press, 1965), pp. 347–352 [Chapter 2 above].

45. Report of the Milford Conference, *op. cit.*, p. 55.

46. Fizdale, *op. cit.*, pp. 443–450.

47. Fred Berl, "An Attempt to Construct a Conceptual Framework for Supervision," *Social Casework* 41 (July 1960), pp. 339–346 [Chapter 10 above].

48. Scherz, *op. cit.*

49. Lucille Austin, "The Changing Role of the Supervisor," *Smith College Studies in Social Work* 31 (June 1961), pp. 179–195.

30

Social Workers Versus
Bureaucracy

Wilbur A. Finch, Jr.

SOCIAL WORK IS often described as an organizational profession because most of its activities are carried out within formal agency settings. Thus, the vast majority of social workers carry at least three distinguishable roles: the role of practitioner or "helper," the role of professional working in a formal agency, and the role of bureaucrat who must negotiate the stresses and capitalize on the opportunities of organizational life.[1] Because most social workers cannot avoid contact with formal, bureaucratic organizations, one can assume that they have some perspective on the nature of such organizations and the ways in which workers may achieve personal and professional goals while working within their context. The success of professionals in organizations may ultimately depend on their acquiring a set of beliefs and values that helps them decide what is true, what questions need to be asked, and what is right or wrong in any given situation.[2]

The question of whether the pursuit of professionalism inevitably involves a conflict with bureaucracy has been of major interest to social work authors. While the demands of professionalism and the demands of work in a bureaucracy may be compatible in many ways, major sources of conflict exist that are usually related to the service ideal of professionals and their desire for autonomy in working with clients.[3] This article will review the potential sources of conflict for the social worker as these have been identified in the literature and will offer in light of recent changes in the field a redefinition of the problem of professionalism versus bureaucratization.

PRACTICE AND BUREAUCRACY

Basic to the argument that professionalism and bureaucratization are incompatible is the dilemma of professional autonomy versus bureaucratic control. A number of social work authors believe a certain tension exists between the organization's need for the professional's expertise on the one hand and its requirement of employee loyalty that may, on the other hand, inhibit the worker's identification with the profession. Green argues that ". . . when responsible to both a profession and a bureaucracy, the individual finds himself confronted by two sets of mutually incompatible demands." [4] For example, limits placed on professional activity by an organization may become viewed by the worker as impediments to the effective delivery of services. Similarly, the increased specialization of bureaucratic organizations may constrain the professional's ability to address client needs in their totality. Wasserman has posed a question that is therefore of basic concern to the social work practitioner: "How (and in what ways) does the bureaucratic structure support or constrain the worker's professional activities?" [5]

However, the controversy over professionalism versus bureaucratization has tended to obscure the accommodations that can be reached between professionals and the organizations in which they work. In order to effect accommodations, social workers may have to temper their feelings of professional and organizational identification, which can vary between the extremes of "high" and "low." By working from these two extremes, four possible categories can be examined.

Cell A, as indicated in Table 30–1, represents the orientation of the worker whose professional as well as bureaucratic identification is high. One would expect compatibility to prevail between professionals having such an orientation and the organizations in which they work. Cell B represents an orientation in which identification with the organization is high but professional identification low. Workers having such an orientation might experience minimal conflict only with their agencies, although at the cost of isolation from their professional peers. When the worker's bureaucratic identification is low, as represented by Cells C and D, one would expect the development of intensified conflict between worker and organization.

Most studies of professionals in formal organizations emphasize that workers often go to polar extremes in their orientations. For example, professionals who adopt a bureaucratic identification give primacy to agency policies and procedures. This situation is represented by Cell B. Other workers who adopt a professional orientation give primacy to professional values, norms, and expectations. This orientation is represented by

Cell C. However, the adoption of an orientation that is not extreme is an alternative available to the worker in an organization.

OTHER ORIENTATIONS

In studying patterns of orientation among professionally educated caseworkers in voluntary agencies, Billingsley has identified two subpatterns between the extremes of bureaucratic and professional orientations.[6] Because they conform to expectations that prevail both in their agencies and in the profession, he labels as "conformists" a group of social workers who evince a relatively high commitment to both agency policies and professional standards. Billingsley ranks this group highly in terms of their overall effectiveness within their agencies. The orientation of such a group is represented in Table 30–1 by Cell A. Another group of workers termed "innovators" by Billingsley express a relatively low commitment to both agency policies and professional standards. Their feelings of commitment are represented by Cell D in Table 30–1.

These findings raise an interesting question: Why are "conformists" significantly more prevalent on the staffs of family agencies and "innovators" more prevalent in protective service agencies? Billingsley believes this staffing pattern prevails because family agencies operate in terms of the professional education of their workers with more consistency than do protective service agencies.

As a means of coping with conflict between professional standards and organizational demands, Green believes that the individual consciously or unconsciously develops a pattern of accommodation.[7] His typology of accommodation therefore focuses on the internal dynamics of the individual rather than on the individual's behavior as a direct response to a bureaucratic environment. For example, the social worker who overidentifies with clients to the detriment of agency standards of performance and other organizational requirements is described as a "victim." Although such an accommodation does not fit neatly into the cell

T A B L E 30–1. Cell Representation of Worker Identification with Bureaucracy or Profession

BUREAUCRATIC IDENTIFICATION	PROFESSIONAL IDENTIFICATION	
	High	Low
High	Cell A	Cell B
Low	Cell C	Cell D

analysis shown in Table 30–1, because the "victim's" identification represents a distortion of professional norms and values, it may be included within Cell C for the purposes of this discussion.

Another pattern of accommodation is, according to Green, seen in the "immature professional," who has not successfully integrated professional principals into a coherent frame of reference. This individual accommodates by clinging to organizational procedures, thus fulfilling his need for structure and certainty. Such an accommodation may be considered an adaptation of that represented by Cell B. The orientation of Green's "social work reformer," who holds humanitarian sentiments above both organizational and professional requirements, may be included within Cell D.

Green's typology is useful in examining possible adjustments that can be made within the social worker who is practicing in an organizational setting. Nevertheless, attempts to categorize worker orientations leave important questions unanswered: Under what circumstances can an individual worker maintain a high identification with both his profession and his organization? For that matter, is high worker identification with both profession and organization desirable or even possible? Some social work authors are not certain that benefits are to be gained when the worker identifies highly with both his profession and the organization in which he is employed or that this kind of identification can in fact be sustained. They imply that such an orientation can be maintained only at the cost of a reduced commitment to professional values, norms, and expectations as feelings of employee loyalty dominate the worker's professional concerns.

Billingsley, for example, argues that "conformists," when forced ". . . to choose . . . between professional standards and agency policies, . . . choose the latter more frequently. . . ."[8] As mentioned previously, however, he also rates such workers highly in terms of overall effectiveness, which leaves uncertain what conclusions might be drawn here about the relationship between effectiveness on the job and high professional identification. Pruger has also commented on the worker's identification with the organization:

> A strong identification between helper and organization, however desirable, inevitably confuses the necessary distinction between them. When the environment is congenial, a special kind of commitment or strength is required to maintain an independence of mind.[9]

In contrast, Green has emphasized that the social worker's task is to function as best he can with a minimum of conflict within both the system of professional requirements and that of organizational demands. This requires the worker to integrate professional and organizational roles to some extent and to modify the demands of either or both.[10] The stance described by Green is not unlike what Schein has termed "creative individualism," meaning acceptance by the worker of only the organization's pivotal values and norms while mediating between professional and organizational standards.[11] Effecting such an accommodation enables the worker to avoid more extreme responses, such as rebellion or conformity. Because most social welfare organizations attach different importance to particular norms and values, one can hypothesize that potential conflict is reduced when "pivotal" norms and values are consistent with the professional beliefs of the individual.

Although many of those writing on the professionalism-versus-bureaucratization conflict have implicitly or explicitly taken sides—Wasserman, for example, has pointed his accusing finger at the organization, and Green has pointed his at the individual—their answers to the central question of the conflict remain incomplete. No one has clearly determined whether bureaucratic structures support or constrain the worker's professional activities nor have the ways in which they may do so been defined. Until this determination is made, potential conflict within different organizational structures cannot be predicted or anticipated. More important, conflict therefore cannot be reduced by changing the organizational structures in which it is commonly experienced by workers.

EXAMINING THE CONFLICT

The conflict between the professional and the organization has thus been a recurring theme in social work literature. Is there evidence that this conflict does in fact exist? Certainly, studies have documented the discontent of social welfare employees, but such conflict is often not limited to professional staff. A study conducted by the author found that social service employees interviewed were generally dissatisfied with their jobs. The study concluded that positions held within an organizational background were not factors determining how employees perceived their jobs and work environment.[12] The author of another study pursues this point:

> However, social workers who are not professionally trained, i.e., do not possess an MSW, also find themselves caught up in the same conflicting situations that face the MSW. They, too, often must choose between client need and agency policy and practice, between agency policy and community expectations, between agency policy and the standards of the social work profession; though they are not members of the profession, per se, many non-MSW social workers strongly identify with the profession and the values and norms therein.[13]

It becomes more difficult to define conflict between professional autonomy and bureaucratic control as a strictly professional problem if it is experienced by all social service employees in bureaucratic settings and not just by those who are professionally educated. A different question may be asked at this point: What are the organizational, personal, and professional characteristics associated with organization-worker conflict?

While studying workers in public welfare, Blau focused on the orientation of caseworkers toward their clients and addressed the question of how the organization and social context of an agency influence worker orientation.[14] The attitudes of new workers toward clients is seen in his study as strongly positive, if somewhat sentimental and idealistic. These workers are highly vocal in their complaints about the organization, and compliance with rules and procedures is viewed by them as a hindrance to the delivery of services. The compliance of "old timers" is perceived by the new worker as rigidity. However, in the process of working with clients, situations that may cause them to change their idealistic orientation confront these new workers. For example, some clients lie to them, and others do not want their help. Blau observes that new workers actually provide clients with fewer services because they lack knowledge of agency procedures and rules and, therefore, focus more exclusively on determining whether clients have met eligibility requirements.

Paradoxically, then, Blau found that experience increases the worker's ability to serve clients but decreases his interest in doing so, at least during the initial three years of employment. In contrast, adjustment in older employees who continue beyond their initial three years of employment does not lead to greater rigidity or a lack of interest in helping clients but to a greater emphasis on providing services and a different, less emotional, client involvement.

If experience and length of service affect the way in which workers function in organizational settings, the source of conflict between the individual and the organization may not be solely professional in nature. Conflict experienced by a worker may be caused in part by personal concerns, stemming from the difficulty workers often have addressing client problems they have not solved for themselves.[15] If the source of dissonance between the individual and the organization is in part personal rather than professional, much of the conflict experienced by workers may result, for example, from their often having to use utilitarian, normative, and coercive measures while working with clients. Use of these measures may pose unique personal and moral problems for the practitioner.[16]

The professional has traditionally been viewed as flexible and creative, the bureaucracy as rigid, insensitive to the needs of clients, and unresponsive to their requests. However, one must remember that the behavior of professionals is largely determined by their expectations and perspectives, which in turn are derived from their education and work experience.[17] Social worker expectations, those beliefs about certain causes in the work environment bringing about certain effects, may grow increasingly incongruent as the nature, organization, and structure of professional practice change in social welfare agencies.[18] How does social work education currently influence the expectations of workers holding baccalaureate and master's degrees? Are expectations of worker autonomy being encouraged in social work students? Fostering belief in the possibility of autonomy within organizations may ultimately increase the dissonance between the worker and the organization. Similarly, students encouraged to perceive professional practice solely in terms of worker-client interactions may lack the organizational skills that they will increasingly need to support their helping activities.

PRESENT TRENDS

More and more often, organizational needs are being viewed as best served when workers of different education and training perform specialized functions.[19] In this situation different benefits are expected to accrue from the utilization of each kind of worker, and different criteria are used in measuring individual success. If technology is understood as the methods by which available resources are used to achieve a desired end, then selecting an individual worker to provide a particular service actually represents selecting a technology to address a particular area of client needs. A study conducted by the author concluded that this technology finds expression in certain critical interactions between worker and client and, depending on the individual worker involved, can determine (1) the particular client problem that will be addressed, (2) the way in which client problems may be defined, and (3) the particular problem-solving methods that will be used.[20] Workers of different education and training function differently, and the particular workers employed by an organization can determine the kinds of problems that it will be able to resolve.

When working within a system of specialization, the latitude allowed professionals in exercising discretionary judgment with clients will depend on whether their work can be completed alone: specialization means that workers with different skills perform complementary functions.[21] Segregating tasks and roles has traditionally permitted social welfare organizations to differentiate their control procedures among different kinds of personnel, thereby assuring that professionals and other employees were fulfilling their respective job functions.[22] Such differentiation can be sustained with relative ease among largely homogeneous groups of employees, but problems of unclear and debatable boundaries between job roles increase as the number of different kinds of workers grows. Boundaries may be further confused as definitions of social work's

special competencies, rather than remaining set and referential, continue
to evolve.

Brown has argued that "effective organization is a function of the work
to be done and the resources and techniques available for doing it." [23]
Unless based on a clear understanding of the dynamic relationship between work performed within an organization and the organizational
structure itself, managerial decisions can dramatically alter this relationship in totally unexpected ways. In many public agencies, a growing use
of specialization has enabled new, frequently complex, and sometimes
rapidly changing programs to be undertaken without a consequent dis-
ruption in overall organizational functioning. In such instances, only a
relatively small group of employees learn and administer new programs.
However, in spite of solving a number of problems effectively, specialization often represents what is in fact a short-term solution. Its introduction
within an organization may cause long-term difficulties, especially when
the increasing communication and coordination costs inevitably resulting
from its use have not been anticipated. The author's findings elsewhere
pursued this point in the following way:

> The specialization of social services in this organization means that or-
> ganizational response to client needs increasingly occurs in terms of fixed
> roles and specified sets of behaviors. Although the relationships between
> these various roles permit some degree of interaction through formalized
> channels, such interaction appears to be increasingly controlled and
> limited. . . . Such practices appear to encourage a kind of parochialism
> of thought in the collection of information which relates only to the
> particular program and justifies its continuation, but offers little guid-
> ance for total agency response to the client. Frequent changes in worker
> assignments and the placing of specialized units in different physical
> locations further discourage interspecialization communication, except
> for the most persistent.[24]

As is evident, bureaucratic practices can encourage professionals to
assume more limited and specialized responsibility for clients. If a social
worker's assigned job activities do not involve the performance of complementary functions, the combined effect of services that might otherwise be achieved through the organization's helping processes are often
lost to clients. The client is instead left with the impression of an ad hoc
reactive approach to problem-solving, and experiences services as hap-
hazard rather than as coherent attempts at help.[25] When bureaucratic
specialization exists, furthermore, interaction between worker and client
often rests on untested assumptions regarding activities performed by
other workers who are seeing the client. In such a situation possible service gains may be lost in various ways. Perhaps a worker, unaware of
what other workers are doing, may fail to support client efforts at
problem-solving that are within the domain of another worker's specializa-

tion. It also becomes more likely that several workers will encourage the client in separate endeavors individually within his capability but cumulatively more than he can handle.

Hall has suggested that the number and quality of social services provided by an agency are not simply a function of the number of professionals employed there. The way in which the agency's work is organized and structured can be equally important in determining the services performed.[26] As specialization and the differential use of manpower increasingly appear within social work practice, many organizational and professional traditions may prove inadequate to the changing demands placed on service delivery by organizational complexity. Specialization requires that work be organized into categories, and this structuring of services predetermines how the organization and client are to interact. As social welfare organizations become more specialized, their inability to meet client needs falling outside of established work categories will be open to increasing criticism.

As specialization and the differential use of manpower increase, the structure and procedures needed to coordinate individual activities must be determined. Thompson suggests that in general organizations must face a new set of circumstances before adapting their structures to meet them, and social welfare agencies may well represent an example of this.[27] Hidden in present manpower patterns are both assumptions and costs that agencies eventually will have to weigh. For example, the greater the variety of workers and specializations involved with a particular client, the greater will become the need for a division of labor maximizing the use of individual worker skill. Similarly, the more workers are involved with a particular client, the more costly communication processes required for coordinated delivery of services will become. Finally, as both the organization's workers and structure become more compartmentalized, the greater will become its need for coordination among operations and services.[28]

FURTHER DEVELOPMENTS

Growing trends toward differential use of manpower and increased specialization bring the importance of the organization, as opposed to the individual professional, into focus: only an organization will be able to undertake the varied forms of intervention increasingly needed to deal with client problems.[29] Trends such as these indicate that, except for a small number of social workers in private practice, the possibility of worker autonomy appears to be less a reality today than in the past. Continued concern with the issue of professional autonomy versus bureaucratic control may offer little help to future social workers who will perform professional functions primarily within a bureaucratic setting. Professional definitions of practice will increasingly preclude the possibility of autonomy; the organization and structure of social services will increasingly determine the number and quality of services provided to clients. Management functions such as control, coordination, direction, and planning will become predominant concerns for the profession in years ahead.

Several years ago, Meyer predicted that a new round of specialization would initiate a period of uncertainty in which the profession would have difficulty in clarifying job roles and functions.[30] This may be reflected in the recent decision of the Joint Board Committee of the Council on Social Work Education and the National Association of Social Workers to plan for a joint project to clarify the concepts of "core" and "specialization" in social work education.[31] Behind this action lies the belief that a core of social work education should be received at the BSW level and that specialization should begin with the MSW. It would not surprise the author if management eventually emerges as a major specialization at the MSW level.

If the social worker is to be subjected to bureaucratic controls, it is likely that the form and nature of these controls will be of growing concern to professionals. If anything, bureaucracy probably enfeebles the worker's service ideal more than it threatens his autonomy: organizational demands may increasingly preclude work routines such as prolonged intake procedures, which, although relatively time-consuming, are often viewed by workers as important in effectively meeting client needs.[32] Toren assumes that social workers will accept some degree of control exerted over their professional activities, and the same assumption can be made of the many different kinds of employees now comprising the social service manpower pool.[33] Professional concern may then focus on whether control is exercised by people who are knowledgeable and sympathetic. In the meantime, many social workers in organizational settings will remain discontent, clinging to their misconception of the organization as a thing of independent existence and will that interferes with their autonomy, rather than recognizing it as a group of interacting individuals who are similar to themselves.

The growing recognition within the field of the effects of organizational structure on service delivery has led to deliberate attempts at modifying organizational patterns and thereby eliminating the problems that clients encounter. Vinter has argued that the social worker "is a sophisticated and accomplished 'organization man'" and that his education, which combines both theory and actual practice, should do much to prepare him for his organizational roles.[34] However, the educational experiences currently available to students may not be accurate representations of the organizational world they will encounter as professionals. Gartner has commented on social work training in this way:

> To the extent that the practice situation is juggled to meet training needs —by reducing the caseload or making it more selective—then practice loses some of the reality which is its uniqueness.[35]

Social workers surveyed by the author felt that their professional education had not adequately trained them to utilize their skills effectively within the organizational settings in which they now worked.[36] Subsequent observation of their work behavior revealed that these workers failed to perceive the influence of the work environment on worker behavior and to recognize its structure as potentially damaging rather than supportive in relation to service goals. This evidence suggests that many social workers are not ready to recognize the effects of organizational structure on service delivery or to search for alternative structures.

CONCLUSION

It is likely that the strains between social workers and organizations will increase as long as the beliefs that workers hold about cause and effect in their work environments do not fit changing realities in social welfare agencies. The success of social workers in organizational settings will increasingly hinge on their ability to recognize the ways in which organizational structure affects the delivery of services. The effective worker will be skillful at modifying the organization's patterns to remove impediments to practice.

Although adept in the role of practitioner or "helper," social workers too often lack skills needed to fill organizational roles in ways supportive of their service ideal, which allow them to pursue personal and professional goals within the organization. Filling an organizational role in a way that is personally satisfying may well require a more sophisticated and accomplished knowledge of organizational dynamics than many social workers presently possess.

NOTES

1. Robert Pruger, "The Good Bureaucrat," *Social Work*, 18 (July 1973), pp. 26–27.
2. Carl F. Stover, "Changing Patterns in the Philosophy of Management," *Public Administration Review*, 18 (Winter 1958), p. 22.

3. *See,* for example, Peter Blau and W. Richard Scott, *Formal Organizations* (San Francisco: Chandler Publishing Co., 1962), pp. 59–63.

4. A. D. Green, "The Professional Worker in the Bureaucracy," *Social Service Review,* 40 (March 1966), p. 71.

5. Harry Wasserman, "The Professional Social Worker in a Bureaucracy," *Social Work,* 16 (January 1971), p. 89 [Chapter 19 above, p. 206].

6. Andrew Billingsley, "Bureaucratic and Professional Orientation Patterns in Social Casework," *Social Service Review,* 38 (December 1964), pp. 404–407.

7. Green, op cit., pp. 74–76.

8. Billingsley, op. cit., p. 406.

9. Pruger, op. cit., p. 31.

10. Green, op. cit., p. 77 and p. 80.

11. Edgar H. Schein, "Organizational Socialization and the Profession of Management," *Industrial Management Review,* 9 (1969), p. 6.

12. Wilbur A. Finch, Jr., "Education and Jobs: A Study of the Performance of Social Service Tasks in Public Welfare," p. 83. Unpublished DSW dissertation, School of Social Welfare, University of California at Berkeley, 1975.

13. Neil A. Cohen, "The Public Welfare Department's Separation into Social Service and Income Maintenance Divisions: Its Impact on Role Conflict Perceptions and Job Orientations Among Non-MSW Welfare Workers," p. 32. Unpublished Ph.D. dissertation, School of Applied Social Sciences, Case Western Reserve University, 1973.

14. Peter M. Blau, "Orientation Toward Clients in a Public Welfare Agency," in Blau, ed., *On The Nature of Organizations* (New York: John Wiley & Sons, 1974), pp. 170–186.

15. Lydia Rapoport, "In Defense of Social Work: An Examination of Stress in the Profession," *Social Service Review,* 34 (March 1960), pp. 62–74.

16. Nina Toren, "Semi-Professionalism and Social Work: A Theoretical Perspective," in Amitai Etzioni, ed., *The Semi-Professions and Their Organizations: Teachers, Nurses, Social Workers* (New York: Free Press, 1969), p. 166.

17. Eliot Freidson, "Dominant Professions, Bureaucracy, and Client Services," in William R. Rosengran and Mark Lefton, eds., *Organizations and Clients* (Columbus, Ohio: Charles E. Merrill Publishing Co., 1970), p. 74.

18. Lyman W. Porter, Edward E. Lawler III, and J. Richard Hackman, *Behavior in Organizations* (New York: McGraw-Hill Book Co., 1975), p. 52.

19. Sidney A. Fine and Wretha W. Wiley, *An Introduction to Functional Job Analysis* (Kalamazoo, Mich.: W. E. Upjohn Institute for Employment Research, 1971), p. 37.

20. Finch, op. cit., pp. 175–176.

21. Fred H. Goldner and R. R. Ritti, "Professionalization as Career Immobility," in Oscar Grusky and George A. Miller, eds., *The Sociology of Organization* (New York: Free Press, 1970), p. 466.

22. Robert D. Vinter, "Analysis of Treatment Organizations," in Yeheskel

Hasenfeld and Richard A. English, eds., *Human Service Organizations* (Ann Arbor: University of Michigan Press, 1974), p. 43.

23. Wilfred Brown, *Explorations in Management* (New York: John Wiley & Sons, 1960), p. 18.

24. Finch, op. cit., p. 145.

25. Ibid., p. 146.

26. Oswald Hall, "Organization of Manpower in Some Helping Professions," in Edward E. Schwartz, ed., *Manpower in Social Welfare: Research Perspectives* (New York: National Association of Social Workers, 1966), p. 59.

27. James D. Thompson, *Organizations in Action* (New York: McGraw-Hill Book Co., 1967), pp. 119–120.

28. Finch, op. cit., p. 181.

29. Henry J. Meyer, "Sociological Comments," in Charles Grosser, William E. Henry, and James G. Kelly, eds., *Nonprofessionals in the Human Services* (San Francisco: Jossey-Bass, 1969), p. 55.

30. Ibid., p. 56.

31. *NASW News*, 20 (September 1975), p. 10.

32. Harold Wilensky, "The Professionalization of Everyone?" in Oscar Grusky and George A. Miller, eds., *The Sociology of Organizations* (New York: Free Press, 1970), p. 491.

33. Toren, op. cit., p. 183.

34. Robert D. Vinter, "The Social Structure of Service," in Alfred J. Kahn, ed., *Issues in American Social Work* (New York: Columbia University Press, 1959), p. 242.

35. Alan Gartner, "Four Professions: How Different, How Alike," *Social Work*, 20 (September 1975), p. 357.

36. Finch, op. cit., p. 80.

31

The Supervisory Process: An Experience in Teaching and Learning

Yonata Feldman

MARY ELLEN CHASE, AN OUTSTANDING TEACHER at Smith College, identified a cardinal principle of teaching in her book, *A Goodly Fellowship.* "One must one's self be consumed with interest in the subject one is called upon to teach" (1939, 8). My interest in the supervisory process derives in part from my sense of its place in the history of social work itself. My interest in the subject also derives from some things I have learned as the result of my efforts to teach through supervision.

There has always existed a certain disposition to meet the needs of the unfortunate. People have readily appreciated distress such as occasioned by hunger, illness and lack of shelter or clothing. "There but for the grace of God, go I!" And it has always been easy to release our feelings by putting a penny in the outstretched hands of the beggar, and to be happy that we have been spared such a fate. The quantity of giving does not change its underlying sentiment. In people's bequests we oftentimes find reflected the need of the giver, rather than the need of the recipient.

In the United States, a radical change in the orientation of helping efforts took place with the emergence of the Charity Organization Society movement in the 19th century. Social work developed as part of a deliberate effort to shift the focus from the sentimental need of the giver to the need of the recipient. The history of social work traces a journey of discovery on which we embarked as we sought to discover and address the true needs of the recipients of help.

Central to the Charity Organization movement was the conception

From *Smith College Studies in Social Work* 47 (March 1977), pp. 154–160. Reprinted by permission of the author and Smith College School for Social Work.

that help, such as indiscriminate almsgiving, could have deleterious consequences for the recipient. As a safeguard, financial assistance was extended only after a rigorous investigation. The movement also embodied a recognition that a client's presenting request and his need might differ. The financial help offered by early voluntary agencies was coupled with help offered by "friendly visitors," volunteers who were assigned to families to provide personal support and to influence behavior in socially desirable directions.

It was through the experiences of volunteers, and the paid agents who functioned as their supervisors, that we began to discover what was involved in relating helpfully to the needs of the client. Kadushin (1976) traces the origin of professional education to the work of these supervisors, which expressed the view that good intentions and sympathy were not enough to enable a helper to learn about and understand the client's real needs. The problems encountered by the volunteers were of such complexity as to require a more sustained effort and preparation than was possible for most volunteers. Consequently, from the ranks of volunteers, the initial staff of friendly visitors was recruited and became the first social workers.

With the emergence of a career line, provisions for the formal education of social workers evolved. Training was initially offered by college departments of sociology and economics, as social work was considered applied sociology. However, people close to the work realized that the problems social workers were called upon to deal with needed a more specialized education. The training functions, pioneered by agencies, were gradually relocated to universities with the establishment of the initial schools of social work.

Today, we can look at some of the profound ideas expressed by our predecessors in the Charity Organization Societies; derivatives of these ideas are part of our present day understanding of practice. These ideas include the conception that the helper is obligated to understand as fully as possible the needs of an applicant, and to offer help that will enhance growth rather than promote his dependency. While initially the rigorous investigation was directed to establish the justification for a client's request for financial help, and was based on direct questioning as well as provisions for checking the truth of the clients' statements through such devices as the Social Service Exchange, help was also seen as occurring in the context of a relationship.

With our present day knowledge we know that a casework relationship precedes a rigorous investigation. We also know that the casework relationship is established by the client, not by the worker, and that this relationship is not always a friendly one. We also know that it is this casework relationship that permits us to obtain information about the client, which he himself has forgotten, but which is important for us to know before we grant the client his request. I am referring to unconscious constructive or destructive drives that all people have. Our investigation has to make certain that granting the request will be for the client's benefit, not his destruction.

A casework relationship serves as a major vehicle for the client's communication with the worker. A person applies to an agency for help when he has depleted his own resources. Because of the client's helplessness, the social worker, even by just listening to his request, elicits from him a feeling that she is all powerful and will help. Psychologically, there is thus recreated a situation of early childhood—of the helpless infant and all powerful mother. The casework relationship then conveys a psychological history of the client, a history which is revealed in the ways that he repeats himself, brings in irrelevant material, and jumps from subject to subject. This is the way the client, unbeknown to himself, and in a symbolic way, tells the worker about events forgotten—unmet childish needs and frustrated wishes. And it is for this reason that the supervisor will have to teach the worker to decode the language of the unconscious.

The investigation will then have two different methods of inquiry. The worker, by asking questions, must be able to assess the client's reality situation and be able to find out how the client himself sees the situation. But the worker must apply another method in order to investigate the unconscious factors which influence the client's present-day life, factors that he himself is not aware of. This method consists of permitting the client free spontaneous expression while the worker listens quietly without interrupting, until the full meaning of the client's unconscious message emerges. By using this method of inquiry, the help the worker renders can be based not only on the request but the total need of the client.

Here arises a most important problem in supervision. Though the worker may have the best intentions of listening without interrupting, she may find herself unable to do so, except inadvertently.

When the supervisor analyzes a worker's process recorded material, she might observe that at times the worker has responded verbally correctly to a client's symbolically expressed emotional need and that this was constructive to the client. In the conference the supervisor may find that the worker did not know what the client was telling her; neither did she know why she responded the way she did. When the client's message and the worker's intervention is decoded by the supervisor, the worker will not only learn a lesson about the symbolic meaning of material, but the experience will give the worker the thrill of a new discovery. What really happens is that the client's need found an echo in the worker—she felt empathy and was able to perceive emotionally her client's need and respond constructively—without herself being aware of it. I am mentioning this for the simple reason that often supervisors are happy to see the worker's proper responses and do not think it necessary to analyze what happened between worker and client, presuming that the worker knew what she was doing, and not realizing that analyzing with workers their intuitively correct responses is the best way of teaching.

Most often the supervisor will find that the worker has interrupted her client with a statement or a question when the client was ready to express strong primitive feelings of rage or inappropriate love, which the worker could not tolerate. The supervisor will know that the interruptions are the worker's defense against these feelings. The supervisor will then have to study every individual worker's pattern of operation and find a way to enable the worker to tolerate primitive feelings—to be aware of them—to permit her client to express them and be able to control her own emotional reaction to such feelings for the benefit of her client.

Are we then to come to the conclusion that the worker who interrupts her client has a personality problem? Though some workers might have one, we cannot make such a deduction because all professionals who engage in psychological work with people have to be trained to be able to listen. This is so because the emotions expressed, which the worker interrupts, are dangerous. These, after all, are emotions which we all have had, but have been able to deal with through proper parental guidance; part of these feelings we successfully repressed, part neutralized and part sublimated. But our clients have not been able to go through the normal processes of maturation and their strong sexual or aggressive feelings can overwhelm the worker.

I read once in a newspaper about an experiment where a man was able by crossbreeding to breed a horse backward and get a wild horse. Supervision and training in social work have to go through the same process. The worker should be helped to develop empathy—so as to feel as the client feels, but be in full control of her reactions. Through empathy the social worker can fully understand, not only theoretically, but emotionally how his client felt at various developmental stages—and can know what attitude to take in order to foster his maturation.

In the past, there existed an opinion that social workers should not get emotionally involved with their clients. As we are human, we do get involved, and this can be useful if we become aware of our feelings. Psychotic and borderline clients often induce strong feelings in workers. The worker should know that the feelings the client evokes are the feelings which the client had toward his parents or which his parents had toward him.

To teach the social worker to be able to listen to the client, to be able to decode his message and develop empathy, will by necessity be a slow process. Both experience and our present-day knowledge of the protective nature of defense mechanisms justify a conservative view about the rate of learning in this area. Mary Richmond describes the case of a woman who was helped by the friendly visitor:

> We remember her distinctly as quite ordinary. Then imagine our surprise (4 years later) that a certain dignity and earnestness, akin to that of the visitor, had crept into this woman's life, and found expression in her face and bearing. Such transfiguration cannot take place in a few weeks or months. They are of slow growth, but they are the best rewards of friendship. [1916, 181–182]

The training of social workers too is a slow and complicated process.

In the process of training, the supervisor's main interest and aim is to enable the worker to become a skilled professional. In order to do this the supervisor must create an atmosphere in which the worker feels free to experiment and make mistakes. The base of discussing a case should always be process recorded material based on notes taken right after the interview. Such recording, intended to recapture as much as possible of what took place in the interview, enables the worker to report important facts, the value of which she is not always aware.

I find that if a worker has a strong conviction about how to respond to her client, it might be well to permit her to go ahead. Even when the supervisor knows that an approach will slow up the casework process, it may be worthwhile for the worker to learn this from her own experience. The permission to use her own ideas sets a worker free to use her intuitive capacities.

However, a worker's experimenting on her own is not enough. Often a supervisor must suggest to a worker concrete moves to widen her horizon of possibilities, and sometimes give a concrete suggestion in order to bring out an emotional response from the client that will open the worker's capacity for empathy. For example, the supervisor in a child guidance agency observed that worker B identified with the children and was blind to the needs of the mothers. The supervisor's first encounter with worker B was when she refused to accompany the mother of her child-client to see the school principal. The supervisor suggested she go with the mother, as this mother was afraid to face the school principal alone. Miss B's response to the supervisor was hostile: she came to the agency to learn Modern Techniques, not to make home visits and encourage dependency needs. The supervisor accepted the worker's decision. Next, the supervisor noticed that in another case, Miss B saw her seven-year-old client every week, but the mother only rarely, and there were many broken appointments. When Miss B was asked for an explanation, she said that the mother was very resistive. The supervisor then asked Miss B whether she would like to try a modern technique to resolve resistance. She was willing. The supervisor then suggested to Miss B that she should discuss with the mother the broken appointments but instead of blaming the mother, blame herself and tell the mother that she was "a bad social worker." When Miss B reported her interview with this mother she had been deeply moved. The mother began to sob in response to Miss B's statement. The mother said she was ill and missed an appointment. Miss B never phoned to find out why she did not come. The mother felt Miss B did not care whether she lived or died. She told Miss B of a bleak childhood, without care or love. In supervision, Miss B said that her client was right, she did neglect her. When the client missed an appointment, she was glad, as she could use the time for other things. Miss B realized that her own subjective feelings had kept her from seeing the mother as a neglected, needy child.

The second difficult problem which confronts the supervisor is when the worker begins to lose confidence in herself because her client shows dissatisfaction with the help he is receiving. The client may complain that he is not getting better but worse—that the worker is too passive— that he thinks he is just wasting his time, and so on and so on. These attacks can continue and grow in strength, and they are very difficult for the worker to take. Social workers, as a rule, are easily convinced that they are doing a poor job. The supervisor must then explain to the worker that the client's ability to express hostility and rage toward the worker is very therapeutic for the client. The client is not expressing his feelings of anger because the worker lacks skill, but he is expressing the infantile childish rage that he had toward his mother, which he had repressed and which is the cause of his present problem. It is like pus in an infection—it must come out before healthy tissue can grow. But the impact of the client's complaints and hostile attitude can overpower the worker. Here the worker needs the supervisor's help more than ever, to show her that often while the client has been attacking the worker there has actually been much improvement in his life.

I have seen too many cases, when supervisory help was lacking, closed with the worker reporting failure when actually the client was on the road to fundamental changes for the better.

Here is where Mary Richmond's idea about the rewards of friendship parts from modern casework. We cannot expect gratitude from our clients, even in successful treatment. Often the clients ascribe insight and success to themselves, not to the worker. This is how it should be. We should be glad that through our treatment, the client has gained confidence in himself and can give himself credit for achievement.

Social work is a special profession, shaped by a serious and sustained effort to understand and appreciate the needs of the client, and to relate responsibly and helpfully to those needs. There is a very large number of the poor and near poor who apply to agencies and clinics, suffering from serious emotional problems in addition to social and health problems. Our clients usually have no resources for private treatment, and I question whether the present-day private treatment models could meet the needs of this group. In reality, it is the social worker who is called upon to treat the resistive client, who does not know he has a problem, does not want help, and is forced to come to an agency by courts, schools, hospitals. The needs of these challenging clients have impelled our long and sustained pursuit of practice competence, and made necessary the elaboration of supervisory support for the learning of practice. It is for these reasons that I find myself consumed with interest in the supervisory process, which has long provided me with experience both in teaching and learning.

REFERENCES

Chase, Mary Ellen. 1939. *A goodly fellowship*. New York: Macmillan Co., 8.

Kadushin, Alfred. 1976. *Supervision in social work*. New York: Columbia University Press, 4–5.

Richmond, Mary. 1916. *Friendly visiting among the poor: a handbook for charity workers*. New York: Macmillan Co., 180–81.

Bibliography

ABBOTT, E. *Social Welfare and Professional Education.* Chicago: University of Chicago Press, 1942.

ABELS, P. "On the Nature of Supervision: The Medium is the Group." *Child Welfare* 49 (June 1970): 304–311.

ABRAHAMSON, A. "Group Methods in Field Work Teaching." *Social Casework* 35 (February 1954): 68–71.

———. *Group Methods in Supervision and Staff Development.* New York: Harper and Row, 1959.

ABRAMOWITZ, S. I., AND ABRAMOWITZ, C. V. "Sex Role Psychodynamics in Psychotherapy Supervision." *American Journal of Psychotherapy* 30 (October 1976): 583–592.

ALLEN, J. D. "Peer Group Supervision in Family Therapy." *Child Welfare* 55 (March 1976): 183–189.

ANCHOR, K. N., *et al.* "Supervisors Perceptions of the Relationship Between Therapist Self-Disclosure and Clinical Effectiveness." *Journal of Clinical Psychology* 32 (January 1976): 158.

ANDERSON, J. "Bureaucratic Rules—Bearers of Organizational Authority." *Educational Administrative Quarterly* 2 (Winter 1966): 5–34.

APAKA, T., *et al.* "Establishing Group Supervision in a Hospital Social Work Department." *Social Work* 12 (October 1967): 54–60.

APPLEBY, J. J., *et al.* "A Group Method of Supervision." *Social Work* 3 (July 1958): 18–22.

APTEKAR, H. H. "The Significance of Dependence and Independence in Supervision." *Social Casework* 35 (June 1954): 238–245.

———. "Supervision and the Development of Professional Responsibility: An Application of Systems Thought." *Jewish Social Work Forum* 3 (Fall 1965).

ARLOW, J. "The Supervisory Situation." *Journal of American Psychoanalysis* 11 (1963): 576–594.

ARNDT, H. "Effective Supervision in a Public Welfare Setting." *Public Welfare* 31 (1973): 50–54.

———. "Principles of Supervision in Public Assistance Agencies." *Social Casework* 36 (July 1955): 307–313.

AUSTIN, L. "Supervision of the Experienced Caseworker." *The Family* 22 (1942): 314–320.

———. "Basic Principles of Supervision." *Social Casework* 33 (December 1952): 411–419.

———. "An Evaluation of Supervision." *Social Casework* 37 (October 1956): 375–382.

———. "Supervision in Social Work." In Kurtz, R. A. (ed.), *Social Work Yearbook*. New York: National Association of Social Workers, 1957, pp. 569–573.

———. "The Changing Role of the Supervisor." *Smith College Studies in Social Work* 31 (June 1961): 179–195.

BALSAM, A., AND GARBER, N. "Characteristics of Psychotherapy Supervision." *Journal of Medical Education* 45 (1970): 789–797.

BARBER, B. "Some Problems in the Sociology of Professions." *Daedalus* 92 (Fall 1963): 669–688.

BARNAT, M. "Student Reactions to the First Supervisory Year—Relationship and Resolutions." *Journal of Education for Social Work* 9 (Fall 1973): 3–8.

BAUM, O. E., AND HERRING, C. "The Pregnant Psychotherapist in Training—Some Preliminary Findings and Impressions." *American Journal of Psychiatry* 132 (April 1975): 419–422.

BEDFORD, C. "Analysis of the Problem of Case Supervision." *The Family* 10 (February 1930): 307–312.

BELINKOFF, C. "Supervision of the First Year Worker." *The Family* 11 (October 1940): 175–180.

BELL, G. *Organization and Human Behavior—A Book of Readings*. Englewood Cliffs, N.J.: Prentice-Hall, 1967.

BELL, J. I. *Staff Development and Practice Supervision*. Social and Rehabilitation Service, Department of Health, Education and Welfare. Washington, D.C.: Government Printing Office, 1968.

BENEDEK, E. P., *et al.* "Problems for Women in Psychiatric Residency." *American Journal of Psychiatry* 134 (November 1977): 1244–1248.

BERENGARTEN, S. "Identifying Learning Patterns of Individual Students—An Exploratory Study." *Social Service Review* 31 (December 1957): 407–417.

BERG, R. "Developing a Broadened View of the Educational Contribution of Field Practice." *Journal of Social Work Process* 17 (1969): 55–68.

BERKOWITZ, S. "The Administrative Process in Casework Supervision." *Social Casework* 33 (December 1952): 419–423.

BERL, F. "An Attempt to Construct a Conceptual Framework for Supervision." *Social Casework* 41 (July 1960): 339–346.

———. "The Content and Method of Supervisory Teaching." *Social Casework* 44 (November 1963): 516–522.

BILLINGSLEY, A. "Bureaucratic and Professional Orientation Patterns in Social Casework." *Social Service Review* 38 (December 1964): 400–407.

BLACKEY, E. *Group Leadership in Staff Training.* Washington, D.C.: Department of Health, Education and Welfare, 1957.

BLAU, P. *Bureaucracy in Modern Society.* Random House Studies in Sociology. New York: Random House, 1956.

BLETHEN, E. "Supervision of Students in Casework with Delinquents." *The Family* 21 (March 1940): 26–30.

BLITZSTEN, N. L., AND FLEMING, J. "What Is a Supervisory Analysis?" *Bulletin of the Menninger Clinic* (July 1953).

BLOCH, S., *et al.* "The Use of a Written Summary in Group Psychotherapy Supervision." *American Journal of Psychiatry* 132 (October 1975): 1055–1057.

BLOOM, L., AND HERMAN, C. "A Problem of Relationship in Supervision." *Social Casework* 39 (July 1958): 402–406.

Board of Directors, Associated Charities. *Ways and Means Used by Ward VII Conference of Associated Charities.* Boston: Associated Charities, 1895.

BOGGS, B. "Advance Preparation of Caseworkers for the Supervision of Graduate Students." *Journal of Social Work Process* 12 (1961): 57–72.

BOGUE, M., AND MAGDALEN, P. "Two Experiments in Training for Supervisory Personnel in New Jersey." *The Family* 16 (February 1936): 295–301.

BONN, E., AND SCHIFF, S. "Clinical Supervision of Psychiatric Residents." *Bulletin of the Menninger Clinic* 27 (1963): 15–23.

BRACKETT, J. R. *Supervision and Education in Charity.* New York: Macmillan Co., 1903.

BRAGER, G. "A First Conference with an Inexperienced Group Leader." In Trecher, H. B. (ed.), *Group Work—Foundations and Frontiers.* New York: Association Press, 1955.

BRIAR, S., AND MILLER, H. *Problems and Issues in Social Casework.* New York: Columbia University Press, 1971.

BRINKERHOFF, M., AND KUNZ, P. *Complex Organizations and Their Environments.* Dubuque, Iowa: Wm. C. Brown Co., 1972.

BROWN, E. *Social Work as a Profession.* New York: Russell Sage Foundation, 1936.

BRUNO, F. *Trends in Social Work Practice, 1874–1956.* New York: Columbia University Press, 1957.

BUCHER, R., *et al.* "Implications of Prior Socialization for Residency Programs in Psychiatry." *Archives of General Psychiatry* 20 (1969): 395–402.

BURGOYNE, R. W., *et al.* "Who Gets Supervised: An Extension of Patient Selection Inequity." *American Journal of Psychiatry* 133 (November 1976): 1313–1315.

BURNS, M. "Supervision in Social Work." In Lurie, H. (ed.), *Encyclopedia of*

Social Work. New York: National Association of Social Workers, 1965, pp. 785–790.

CABOT, R. *Social Service and the Art of Healing.* New York: Moffatt, Yard and Co., 1915. Reprint ed., National Association of Social Workers Classic Series. Washington, D.C.: National Association of Social Workers, 1973.

CARROLL, N. K., AND DUEHN, W. D. "The Trouble with Supervision." *Social Work* 13 (October 1968): 3.

CARTER, I. "The Routine of Supervision in Emergency Relief." *The Family* 16 (June 1935): 112–114.

CHAMPION, D. *The Sociology of Organizations.* New York: McGraw-Hill, 1975.

CHERNISS, C., AND EGNATIOS, E. "Styles of Clinical Supervision in Community Mental Health." *Journal of Consulting Clinical Psychology* 45 (December 1977): 1195–1196.

———. "Clinical Supervision in Community Mental Health." *Social Work* 23 (May 1978): 219–223.

CHICHESTER, E. "Group Meetings as an Aid to Student Supervision." *Social Casework* 36 (June 1955): 264–269.

———, et al. "Field Work Criteria for Second Year Casework Students." *Social Casework* 31 (June 1950): 229–237.

COHEN, R. J., AND DEBETZ, B. "Responsive Supervision of the Psychiatric Resident and Clinical Psychology Intern." *American Journal of Psychoanalysis* 37 (Spring 1977): 51–64.

COHEN, Y. "Staff Supervision in Probation." *Federal Probation* 40 (September 1976): 17–23.

CONNOLLY, J., AND BIRD, J. "Video-Tape in Teaching and Examining Clinical Skills: A Short Case Format." *Medical Education* 11 (July 1977): 271–275.

Council on Social Work Education. *Potentials and Problems in the Changing School Agency Relationships in Social Work Education.* New York: Council on Social Work Education, 1967.

COWAN, B., et al. "Group Supervision as a Teaching-Learning Modality in Social Work." *Social Worker Travaileur* 40 (1972): 256–261.

CRAIG, M. "Field Supervision—An Adaptation of Social Work Skills." *Social Casework* 30 (May 1949): 200–203.

CRAMER, M. "Fieldwork Preparation for Entrance into Mental Retardation Practice." *Journal of Education for Social Work* 13 (Winter 1977): 37–43.

DALY, D. "Supervision of the Newly Employed Experienced Worker." *The Family* 27 (June 1946): 146–150.

DANA, B. S., AND SIKKEMA, M. "Field Instruction—Fact and Fantasy." In *Proceedings, Twelfth Annual Program Meeting, Council on Social Work Education.* New York: Council on Social Work Education, 1964, pp. 90–101.

DAVIS, G. "The Executive Process in the Administration of the Social Casework Agency." *The Family* 25 (February 1945): 375–377.

DAWSON, J. B. "The Case Supervisor in a Family Agency." *The Family* 6 (February 1926): 293–295.

DAY, R. C., AND HAMBLIN, R. L. "Some Effects of Close and Punitive Styles of Supervision." In Bell, G. D. (ed.), *Organizations and Human Behavior— A Book of Readings*. Englewood Cliffs, N. J.: Prentice-Hall, 1967, pp. 172–182.

DEBELL, D. "A Critical Digest of the Literature on Psychoanalytic Supervision." *Journal of the American Psychoanalytic Association* 11 (1963): 546–575.

DE LA TORRE, J. "Use and Misuse of Cliches in Clinical Supervision." *Archives of General Psychiatry* 31 (September 1974): 302–306.

DEVIS, D. "Teaching and Administrative Functions in Supervision." *Social Work* 1 (April 1965): 83–89.

DIMOCK, H., AND TRECKER, H. *The Supervision of Group Work and Recreation*. New York: Association Press, 1949.

DOLGOFF, R. *Report to the Task Force on Social Work Practice and Education*. New York: Council on Social Work Education, 1974.

DORN, R. M. "The Pleasures and Dangers of Educating and Being Educated— Supervision." *Reiss-Davis Clinic Bulletin* 3 (1966): 105–112.

DORNBUSCH, S. M., AND SCOTT, W. R. *Evaluation and the Exercise of Authority*. San Francisco: Jossey-Bass, 1975.

DRUCKER, P. F. *Management—Tasks, Responsibilities, Practices*. New York: Harper and Row, 1973.

DUNCAN, M. G. "An Experiment in Applying New Methods in Field Work." *Social Casework* 44 (April 1963): 179–184.

D'ZURMA, T. L. "The Functions of Individual Supervision." In Hoffman, F. H. (ed.), *The Teaching of Psychotherapy*. Boston: Little, Brown and Co., 1964.

EBAUGH, F. "Graduate Teaching of Psychiatry Through Individual Supervision." *American Journal of Psychiatry* 107 (1950): 274–278.

EISENBERG, S. "Supervision as an Agency Need." *Social Casework* 37 (May 1956): 233–237.

———. *Supervision in the Changing Field of Social Work*. Philadelphia: University of Pennsylvania Press, 1956.

EISNER, C. "Group Process in Staff Development in Public Assistance Agencies." *The Family* 27 (April 1946): 71–77.

———. "Specifics of Training New Workers in Public Assistance Agencies." *Social Casework* 28 (December 1947): 382–388.

EKSTEIN, R. "A Historical Survey on the Teaching of Psychoanalytic Technique." *Journal of the American Psychoanalytic Association* 8 (1960): 500–513.

EMSCH, M. "The Social Content of Supervision." *International Journal of Psychoanalysis* 36 (1955): 298–306.

ENGEL, G. "Professional Autonomy and Bureaucratic Organization." *Administrative Science Quarterly* 15 (1970): 12–31.

EPSTEIN, L. "Is Autonomous Practice Possible?" *Social Work* 18 (March 1973): 5–12.

ESCOLI, P., AND WOOD, H. "Perception in Residency Training—Methods and Problems." *American Journal of Psychiatry* 124 (1967): 187–193.

ETZIONI, A. *Comparative Analysis of Complex Organizations.* New York: Free Press, 1961.

FEDER, L. "The Group Conference as a Method of Supervision." *The Family* 13 (March 1932): 24–28.

FELDMAN, Y. "The Teaching Aspect of Casework Supervision." *Social Casework* 31 (April 1950): 156–161.

———. "The Supervisory Process: An Experience in Teaching and Learning." *Smith College Studies in Social Work* 47 (March 1977): 154–160.

———, et al. "One Aspect of Casework Training Through Supervision." *Social Casework* 34 (April 1953): 150–156.

FINCH, W. "Social Workers Versus Bureaucracy." *Social Work* 21 (September 1976): 370–375.

FIZDALE, R. "Peer-Group Supervision." *Social Casework* 39 (October 1958): 443–450.

FLEMING, J. "Teaching the Basic Skills of Psychotherapy." *Archives of General Psychiatry* 16 (1967): 416–426.

———, AND BENEDEX, T. *Psychoanalytic Supervision—A Method of Clinical Teaching.* New York: Grune and Stratton, 1966.

———, AND HAMBURG, D. "An Analysis of Methods for Teaching Psychotherapy with Description of a New Approach." *Archives of Neurology and Psychiatry* 79 (1958): 179–200.

FOECKLER, M. "Orientation to Field Instruction in Light of Current Needs of Social Work Education." *Social Work Education Reporter* 16 (September 1968): 34–46.

———, AND DEULSCHBERGER, P. "Growth-Oriented Supervision." *Public Welfare* 28 (1970): 297–299.

FOLLETT, M. "The Teacher-Student Relation." *Administrative Science Quarterly* 15 (1970): 137–148.

FOX, R. "Supervision by Contract." *Social Casework* 55 (April 1974): 247–251.

FRANKS, V. *The Autonomous Social Worker.* An Occasional Paper, No. 1. Madison: University of Wisconsin Press, 1967.

GALE, M. S. "Resident Perception of Psychotherapy Supervision." *Comprehensive Psychiatry* 17 (January-February 1976): 191–194.

GARETZ, F. K., et al. "The Disturbed and the Disturbing Psychiatric Resident." *Archives of General Psychiatry* 33 (April 1976): 446–450.

GARRETT, A. "Learning Through Supervision." *Smith College Studies in Social Work* 24 (February 1954).

GASKILL, H., AND NORTON, J. "Observations on Psychiatric Residency Training." *Archives of General Psychiatry* 18 (1968): 7–15.

GETZEL, G., et al. "Supervising in Groups as a Model for Today." *Social Casework* 52 (March 1971): 154–163.

GOIN, M. K., AND KLINE, F. "Countertransference—A Neglected Subject in

Clinical Supervision." *American Journal of Psychiatry* 133 (January 1976): 41–44.

———. "Supervision Observed." *Journal of Nervous and Mental Disease* 158 (3): 208–213.

———, *et al.* "Teaching Dynamic Psychotherapy by Observation." *American Journal of Psychotherapy* 30 (January 1976): 112–120.

GREENBERG, I., AND MARNEL, SARAH S. "Field Supervision—A Basic Tool in Administration." *Social Casework* 29 (February 1948): 70–74.

GREGG, D. E., *et al.* "Individual Supervision—A Method of Teaching Psychiatric Concepts in Nursing Education." *Perspectives on Psychiatric Care* 14 (July–September 1976): 115–129.

GRONEWALD, D. "Supervision Practices in the Federal Probation System." *Federal Probation* 28 (September 1964): 19–25.

GROSS, M. J. "Parallel Process in Supervision and Psychotherapy." *Bulletin of the Menninger Clinic* 40 (January 1976): 1–104.

GROSSMAN, W. K., AND KARMOIL, E. "Group Psychotherapy Supervision and Its Effects on Resident Training." *American Journal of Psychiatry* 130 (August 1973): 920–921.

GROTJAHN, M. "The Role of Identification in Psychiatric and Psychoanalytic Training." *Psychiatry* 12 (1949): 141–151.

———. "Problems and Techniques of Supervision." *Psychiatry* 18 (February 1955): 9–15.

GUTHEIL, T. G. "Ideology as Resistance: A Supervisory Challenge." *Psychiatric Quarterly* 49 (Summer 1977): 88–96.

———, AND GRUNEBAUM, H. U. "The Teaching of Clinical Administration: Opportunities and Problems of Role Ambiguity." *Psychiatric Quarterly* 49 (Winter 1977): 259–272.

HAGA, W. "Professionalism and Role Making in a Service Organization—A Longitudinal Investigation." *American Sociological Review* 39 (February 1974): 122–133.

HALE, M. "The Parameters of Agency-School Social Work Education Planning." *Journal of Education for Social Work* 2 (Spring 1968): 32–40.

———. "Innovations in Field Learning and Teaching." In Jones, B. L. (ed.), *Current Patterns in Field Instruction in Graduate Social Work Education.* New York: Council on Social Work Education, 1969, pp. 21–30.

HALL, D., AND LAWLER, E. "Job Characteristics and Pressures and the Organizational Integration of Professionals." *Administrative Science Quarterly* 15 (1970): 271–281.

HALLOWITZ, D. "The Supervisor as Practitioner." *Social Casework* 43 (June 1962): 287–292.

HAMILTON, G. "Self-Awareness in Professional Education." *Social Casework* 35 (November 1954): 371–379.

HAMILTON, J. "Some Aspects of Learning Supervision, and Identity Formation in the Psychiatric Residency." *Psychiatric Quarterly* 45 (1971): 410–422.

HARDCASTLE, D. A. "The Indigenous Nonprofessional in the Social Service Bureaucracy—A Critical Examination." *Social Work* 16 (April 1971): 56–63.

HARDESTY, A. "Teaching Job Organization to New Workers in a Public Agency." *The Family* 26 (1945): 227–233.

HARE, R., AND FRANKENA, A. "Peer Group Supervision." *American Journal of Orthopsychiatry* 42 (1972): 527–529.

HAWTHORNE, L. "Games Supervisors Play." *Social Work* 20 (May 1975): 179–183.

HESTER, L., *et al.* "The Supervisor-Supervisee Relationship in Psychotherapy Training from the Perspective of Interpersonal Attraction." *Comprehensive Psychiatry* 17 (September–October 1976): 671–681.

HESTER, M. "Educational Process in Supervision." *Social Casework* 32 (June 1951): 242–251.

HILL, R. "A Field Work By-Product." *The Family* 1 (February 1921): 22–23.

HOBART, A. "What the Visitor Expects from Supervision." *The Family* 12 (March 1931): 17–19.

HOFFMAN, F. (ed.). *The Teaching of Psychotherapy.* Boston: Little, Brown and Co., 1964.

HOLLIS, F. "Emotional Growth of the Worker Through Supervision." In *Proceedings of the National Conference of Social Work: 1936.* Chicago: University of Chicago Press, 1936.

HOLT, R. R. "Personality Growth in Psychiatric Residents." *Archives of Neurology and Psychiatry* 81 (1959): 203–215.

HOMANS, G. "Social Relations in a Bureaucracy." In Schuler, E. (ed.), *Readings in Sociology.* New York: Thomas Y. Crowell, 1971, pp. 210–221.

HORA, T. "Contributions to the Phenomenology of the Supervisory Process." *American Journal of Psychotherapy* 11 (1957): 769–773.

HOUWINK, E. "The Endowment of the Supervisor." *The Family* 25 (April 1944): 57–60.

HUGHES, E. "Professions." *Daedalus* 92 (Fall 1963): 655–668.

HUTCHINSON, D. "Supervision in Social Casework." *The Family* 16 (April 1935): 44–47.

HUTCHINSON, S., AND TALLEY, N. "The Group Supervisory Conference." *Journal of Nursing Education* 13 (November 1974): 13–17.

IGEL, A. "Training and Supervision in a Public Agency." *The Family* 17 (June 1936): 107–111.

IRVING, H. "A Social Science Approach to a Problem in Field Instruction— The Analysis of a Three-Part Role-Set." *Journal of Education for Social Work* 5 (Spring 1969): 49–56.

ISAACSON, R., *et al.* "Correlation of Teacher Personality Variables and Student Rating." *Journal of Educational Psychology* 51 (1960): 21–25.

———. "Dimensions of Student Evaluations of Teaching." *Journal of Educational Psychology* 55 (1964): 344–351.

ITZIN, F. "The Use of Tape Recording in Field Work." *Social Casework* 41 (April 1960): 197–202.

JACOBSON, F., *et al.* "Status Overestimation, Objective Status and Job Satisfaction Among Professionals." *American Sociological Review* 23 (February 1958): 75–82.

JOHNSON, V., AND WINDAU, M. "The Supervisor-Worker Relationship as an Element in Training." *The Family* 15 (October 1934): 184–187.

JONES, B. (ed.). *Current Patterns in Field Instruction in Graduate Social Work Education.* New York: Council on Social Work Education, 1969.

JUDD, J., *et al.* "Group Supervision—A Vehicle for Professional Development." *Social Work* 7 (January 1962): 96–102.

KADUSHIN, A. "Interview Observation as a Teaching Device." *Social Casework* 37 (July 1956): 334–341.

———. "Games People Play in Supervision." *Social Work* 13 (July 1968): 23–32.

———. "Supervisor–Supervisee: A Survey." *Social Work* 19 (May 1974): 288–297.

———. *Supervision in Social Work.* New York: Columbia University Press, 1976.

KANDLER, II., *et al.* "Prediction of Performance of Psychiatric Residents—A Three-Year Follow-Up Study." *American Journal of Psychiatry* 132 (December 1975): 1286–1290.

KARLSRUHER, A. E. "The Influence of Supervision and Facilitative Conditions on the Psychotherapeutic Effectiveness of Nonprofessional and Professional Therapists." *American Journal of Community Psychology* 4 (June 1976): 145–154.

KASLOW, F. *Issues in Human Services.* San Francisco: Jossey-Bass, 1972.

KAUFFMAN, M. "Supervision of Case Work Staffs." *The Family* 19 (October 1938): 196–200.

KENDALL, K. "Selected Issues in Field Instruction in Education for Social Work." *Social Service Review* 33 (March 1959): 1–9.

KENNEDY, M., AND KEITNER, L. "What Is Supervision: The Need for a Redefinition." *Social Worker* 38 (February 1970): 50–52.

KEPECS, J. G. "Teaching Psychotherapy by Use of Brief Transcripts." *American Journal of Psychotherapy* 31 (July 1977): 383–393.

KNEZNEK, E. *Supervision: For Public Welfare Supervisors.* Chicago: American Public Welfare Association, 1966.

KNOTT, B. H. "Symbolic Interaction and Social Work Education." *Journal of Education for Social Work* 9 (Fall 1973): 24–30.

KOGAN, W., *et al.* "Personality Changes in Psychiatric Residents During Training." *Journal of Psychology* 62 (1966): 229–240.

KOHN, R. "Differential Use of the Observed Interview in Student Training." *Social Work Education Reporter* 3 (1971): 45.

KOSBERG, J. I., *et al.* "Comparison of Supervisors' Attitudes in a Home for the Aged." *Gerontologist* (October 1972): 241–245.

KUBIE, L. "Research into the Process of Supervision in Psychoanalysis." *Psychoanalytic Quarterly* 27 (1958): 226–236.

LAV, A. Y., AND OFFORD, D. R. "A Study of Student Attitudes Toward a Psychiatric Clerkship." *Journal of Medical Education* 51 (November 1976): 919–928.

LAZAR, N. D. "Some Problems in Faculty Selection of Patients for Supervised Psychoanalysis." *Psychoanalytic Quarterly* 45 (July 1976): 416–429.

LEADER, A. "New Directions in Supervision." *Social Casework* 38 (November 1957): 462–468.

———. "Supervision and Consultation Through Observed Interviewing." *Social Casework* 49 (1968): 288–293.

LEHMAN, A., AND GINSBERG, S. "In-Service Training in Military Social Work." *The Family* 27 (April 1946): 58–64.

LEVEY, B. "The Intake Interview from the Standpoint of Supervision." *The Family* 20 (January 1940): 289–295.

LEVINE, N. "Educational Components of Supervision in a Family Agency." *Social Casework* 31 (June 1950): 245–250.

LEVINSON, F. "Psychological Components of Supervision in a Family Agency." *Social Casework* 31 (June 1950): 237–245.

LEVY, C. S. "In Defense of Supervision." *Journal of Jewish Communal Service* 37 (Winter 1960): 194–201.

———. "The Ethics of Supervision." *Social Work* 18 (March 1973): 14–21.

LEWIS, M., *et al. An Experimental Design for First Year Field Instruction.* Tulane Studies in Social Welfare. New Orleans: Tulane University Press, 1962.

LEWIS, V. "Charity Organization Society." In Morris, R., *et al.* (eds.), *Encyclopedia of Social Work,* sixteenth issue, vol. 1. New York: National Association of Social Workers, 1972, pp. 94–99.

LEYENDECKER, G. "A Critique of Current Trends in Supervision." In *Casework Papers: National Conference on Social Welfare, 1959.* New York: Family Service Association of America, 1959.

LIDE, P. "A Supervisory Record." *Social Casework* 29 (January 1948): 27–33.

LINDENBERG, R. "Changing Traditional Patterns of Supervision." *Social Work* 2 (April 1957): 42–46.

LINDENBERG, S. *Supervision in Social Group Work.* New York: Association Press, 1939.

LOEBER, R., AND WEISMAN, R. G. "Contingencies of Therapist and Trainer Performance—A Review." *Psychology Bulletin* 82 (September 1975): 660–688.

LOWRY, F. "A Philosophy of Supervision in Social Casework." In *Proceedings of the National Conference of Social Work: 1936.* Chicago: University of Chicago Press, 1936.

————. (ed.). *Readings in Social Case Work—1920–1938*. New York: Columbia University Press, 1939.

McCabe, A. "The Supervisor's Part in Teaching Casework." *The Family* 21 (June 1940): 141–149.

McCaffery, M. "Criteria for Student Progress in Field Work." *Social Casework* 28 (January 1947): 9–17.

McFadden, E. J. "Helping the Inexperienced Worker in the Public Child Welfare Agency." *Child Welfare* 54 (May 1975): 319–330.

McGee, T. F. "The Triadic Approach to Supervision in Group Psychotherapy." *International Journal of Group Psychotherapy* 24 (October 1974): 471–476.

MacKay, E. "Organization and Supervision of Field Work from the Viewpoint of the Social Agency." *The Family* 5 (February 1925): 253–256.

Mandell, B. "The Equality Revolution and Supervision." *Journal of Education for Social Work* 9 (Winter 1973): 43–54.

Mangrum, C. "The Function of Coercive Casework in Corrections." *Federal Probation* 35 (March 1971): 26–29.

Manis, F. *Field Practice in Social Work Education*. Calif.: The Sultana Press, 1974.

Marcus, P. M., and Marcus, D. "Control in Modern Organizations." In Brinkerhoff, M. B., and Kunz, P. P. (eds.), *Complex Organizations and Their Environments*. Dubuque, Iowa: Wm. C. Brown Co., 1972, pp. 234–243.

Martin, R. M., and Prosen, H. "Psychotherapy Supervision and Life Tasks— The Young Therapist and the Middle-Aged Patient." *Bulletin of the Menninger Clinic* 40 (March 1976): 125–133.

Mattinson, J. *The Reflection Process in Casework Supervision*. Washington, D.C.: National Association of Social Workers, 1975.

Mayers, F. "Differential Use of Group Teaching in First Year Field Work." *Social Service Review* 44 (March 1970): 63–75.

Meltzer, R. "School and Agency Cooperation in Using Videotape in Social Work Education." *Journal of Education for Social Work* 13 (Winter 1977): 90–95.

Merklin, L., and Little, R. "Beginning Psychiatry Training Syndrome." *American Journal of Psychiatry* 124 (1967): 193–197.

Meron, D. "Training of Psychiatrists." *Comprehensive Psychiatry* 6 (1965): 227–235.

Meyer, C. H., and Baker, M. R. "Integrating Practice Demands in Social Work Education." *Social Casework* 49 (October 1968): 481–488.

Meyerson, A. T., *et al.* "Evaluation of a Psychiatric Clerkship by Videotape." *American Journal of Psychiatry* 134 (August 1977): 883–886.

Meyerson, E. "Educational Linkages Between Undergraduate Education in Social Welfare and Professional Social Work Education." *Journal of Education for Social Work* 5 (Fall 1969): 31–37.

MILLER, A., et al. "Teaching and Evaluation of Diagnostic Skills." *Archives of General Psychiatry* 24 (1971): 255–259.

MILLER, G. "Professionals in Bureaucracy—Alienation Among Industrial Scientists and Engineers." *American Sociological Review* 16 (October 1967): 755–768.

MILLER, I. "Distinctive Characteristics of Supervision in Group Work." *Social Work* 5 (January 1960): 69–76.

———. "Supervision in Social Work." In Morris, R., et al. (eds.), *Encyclopedia of Social Work*, Sixteenth Issue, Vol. 1. New York: National Association of Social Workers, 1971.

MINER, G. "Techniques of Mutual Evaluation." *Social Casework* (December 1948): 400–403.

MOORE, S. "Group Supervision: Forerunner or Trend Reflector, Part I—Trends and Duties in Group Supervision." *Social Worker* 38 (November 1970): 16–20.

———. "Group Supervision: Forerunner or Trend Reflector, Part II—Advantages and Disadvantages." *Social Worker* 39 (February 1971): 3–7.

MORRILL, E. "Field Supervision in a Public Agency." *The Family* 21 (May 1940): 71–74.

MUNSON, C. "Symbolic Interaction and Social Work Supervision." In Hickey, P., et al., *Proceedings—Sociological Research Symposium*. Richmond: Virginia Commonwealth University Press, 1976, pp. 374–379.

———. "Professional Autonomy and Social Work Supervision." *Journal of Education for Social Work* 12 (Fall 1976): 95–102.

MUSLIN, H. L., et al. (eds.). *Evaluative Methods in Psychiatric Education*. Washington, D.C.: American Psychiatric Association, 1974.

NADELSON, C., AND NOTMAN, M. "Psychotherapy Supervision: The Problem of Conflicting Values." *American Journal of Psychotherapy* 31 (April 1977): 275–283.

NASON, J. D. "On Teaching Psychotherapy in a Community Mental Health Center." *American Journal of Psychiatry* 134 (December 1977): 1419–1421.

National Conference of Social Work. *Administration, Supervision and Consultation Papers from the 1954 Social Welfare Forum*. New York: NCSW, 1955.

NELSEN, J. C. "Teaching Content of Early Fieldwork Conferences." *Social Casework* 55 (March 1974): 147–153.

———. "Relationship Communication in Early Fieldwork Conferences." *Social Casework* 55 (April 1974): 237–243.

NEUSTAEDTER, E. "The Field Supervisor as Educator." *Social Casework* 29 (December 1948): 375–382.

ORCHARD, B. "The Use of Authority in Supervision." *Public Welfare* 23 (January 1965): 32–40.

ORNSTEIN, P. "Sorcerer's Apprentice—The Initial Phase of Training and Education in Psychiatry." *Comprehensive Psychiatry* 9 (1968): 293–315.

PAIGE, C. "Supervising Casework in a District Office." *The Family* 7 (February 1927): 307–310.

PERLMUTTER, M., AND GUMPERT, G. "Field Instruction and Group Process: An Experiment in the Use of Television." *Social Work Education Reporter* 15 (September 1967): 26–29.

PETERS, M. O. "Supervising the Experienced Worker." *Social Casework* 30 (May 1949): 188–195.

PETTES, D. *Supervision in Social Work—A Method of Student Training and Staff Development.* London: George Allen and Unwin Ltd., 1967.

PINNEY, E., AND WEIDENBACHER, R. "The Outcome of Group Psychotherapy in a Group Used for Teaching." *Psychiatric Quarterly* 44 (1970): 271–250.

POHEK, M. V. "Report on Developments in Teaching and Teaching Methodology." *Social Work Education Reporter* 16 (June 1968): 20–21.

POOR, J. "Field Work Training of a Visually Handicapped Student." *The Family* 26 (February 1946): 368–371.

POSER, E. "The Effects of Therapists' Training on Group Therapeutic Outcome." *Journal of Consulting and Clinical Psychology* 30 (1966): 283–289.

POULARD, O. W. "Orientation to the Student Role—Today's Student in the School of Social Work." *Social Work Education Reporter* 16 (December 1968): 53.

"Professional Training for Social Casework." *The Family* 2 (October 1921): 134–136.

PRUGER, R. "The Good Bureaucrat." *Social Work* 18 (July 1973): 26–32.

PUMPHREY, R., AND PUMPHREY, M. *The Heritage of American Social Work.* New York: Columbia University Press, 1961.

RABKIN, L. Y. "Survivor Themes in the Supervision of Psychotherapy." *American Journal of Psychotherapy* 30 (October 1976): 593–600.

REEVE, M. "An Illustration of the Learning Process in Supervision." *The Family* 18 (June 1937): 131–133.

Report of the Milford Conference. *Social Casework: Generic and Specific.* New York: American Association of Social Workers, 1929. Reprint ed., Washington, D.C.: National Association of Social Workers Classic Series, 1974.

REYNOLDS, B. C. "The Art of Supervision." *The Family* 17 (June 1936): 103–107.

———. *Learning and Teaching in the Practice of Social Work.* New York: Russell and Russell, 1965.

RICE, D., AND FEY, W. "Student Satisfaction with Small Group Teaching of Psychiatry." *Archives of General Psychiatry* 23 (1970): 174–179.

RICH, M. "Supervision." *The Family* 10 (April 1929): 35–45.

RICHMOND, M. *Social Diagnosis.* 1917. Reprint. New York: Free Press, 1965.

RICKERT, V. C., AND TURNER, J. E. "Through the Looking Glass: Supervision in Family Therapy." *Social Casework* 59 (March 1978): 131–137.

ROBINSON, V. "The Organization of Field Work in a Professional Setting." *The Family* 1 (October 1920): 1–7.

———. *Supervision in Social Casework*. Chapel Hill: University of North Carolina Press, 1936.

———. *Dynamics of Supervision Under Functional Controls*. Philadelphia: University of Pennsylvania Press, 1949.

ROSE, S. "Students View Their Supervision—A Scale Analysis." *Social Work* 10 (April 1965): 90–96.

Rosenbaum, M. "Problems in Supervision of Psychiatric Residents in Psychotherapy." *Archives of Neurology and Psychiatry* 69 (1953): 43–48.

ROSENBLATT, A., AND MAYER, J. "Objectionable Supervisory Styles—Students' Views." *Social Work* 20 (May 1975): 184–189.

ROSKIN, G., AND RABINER, C. J. "Psychotherapists Passivity—A Major Training Problem." *International Journal of Psychoanalytic Psychotherapy* 5 (1976): 319–331.

ROTHMAN, J. "Development of a Profession—Field Instruction Correlates." *Social Service Review* 51 (June 1977): 289–310.

———, AND JONES, W. *A New Look at Field Instruction*. New York: Council on Social Work Education, 1971.

SAFIRSTEIN, S. "Institutional Transference." *Psychiatric Quarterly* 41 (1967): 566–577.

ST. GEORGE, HENRY C. "An Examination of Field Work Models at Adelphi University School of Social Work." *Journal of Education for Social Work* 11 (Fall 1975): 62–68.

ST. JOHN, D. "Goal-Directed Supervision of Social Work Students in Field Placement." *Journal of Education for Social Work* 11 (Fall 1975): 89–94.

SALES, E., AND NAVARRE, E. "Individual and Group Supervision in Field Instruction—A Research Report." University of Michigan School of Social Work, 1970.

SALSBERRY, P. C. "Supervision." *The Family* 10 (February 1930): 291–297.

SARNAT, R. G. "Supervision of the Experienced Student." *Social Casework* 23 (1952): 147–152.

SCHEIN, E., AND HALL, D. "The Student Image of the Teacher." *Journal of Applied Behavioral Science* 3 (1967): 305–337.

SCHER, M., AND NEHREN, J. "A Student Experience that Taught Faculty and Hospital Staff." *Nursing Outlook* 14 (1966): 26–29.

———, et al. "Complexities of the Clinical Psychiatric Teaching Institution." *Psychiatry* 34 (1971): 419–424.

SCHERZ, F. "A Concept of Supervision Based on Definitions of Job Responsibility." *Social Casework* 39 (October 1958): 435–443.

SCHLESSINGER, N. "Supervision of Psychotherapy—A Critical Review of the Literature." *Archives of General Psychiatry* 15 (1966): 129–134.

SCHOUR, E. "Helping Social Workers to Handle Work Stress." *Social Casework* 34 (December 1953): 423–428.

SCHUBERT, M. *Field Instruction in Social Casework: A Report of an Experi-*

ment. Social Service Monographs. Chicago: University of Chicago Press, 1963.

————. "Curriculum Policy Dilemmas in Field Instruction." *Journal of Education for Social Work* 1 (Fall 1965): 27–34.

SCHULHOFER, E. "Agency Experience for the Preprofessional Student." *Social Casework* (May 1949): 197–200.

SCHWARTZ, E. E., AND SAMPLE, W. C. *The Midway Office—An Experiment in the Organization of Work Groups.* New York: National Association of Social Workers, 1972.

SCOTT, W. "Reactions to Supervision in a Heteronomous Organization." *Administrative Science Quarterly* 10 (June 1965): 65–81.

SEARLES, H. F. "The Informational Value of Supervisor's Emotional Experiences." *Psychiatry* 18 (1955): 135–146.

SEMRAD, E. V. "Effects of First-Year Resident Identity Crisis on Training." *Frontiers of Hospital Psychiatry* (March 1969): 6.

SHANNON, R. "Developing a Framework for Field Work Instruction in a Public Assistance Agency." *Social Casework* 43 (July 1962): 355–360.

SHERMAN, S. "Teaching Casework Through Participant Observation." *Social Casework* 44 (December 1968): 595–601.

SHOWALTER, J. E., AND PRUETT, K. "The Supervision Process for Individual Child Psychotherapy." *Journal of the American Academy of Child Psychiatry* 14 (Autumn 1975): 708–718.

SIMON, B. K. "Design of Learning Experiences in Field Instruction." *Social Service Review* 40 (December 1966): 397–409.

SOMERS, M., AND GITLIN, P. "Innovations in Field Instruction in Social Group Work." *Journal of Education for Social Work* 2 (Spring 1966): 52–58.

SPENCER, S. "Case Work in a Public Assistance Agency." *The Family* 22 (February 1942): 336–342.

SPIEGEL, D., AND GRUNEBAUM, H. "Training Versus Treating the Psychiatric Resident." *American Journal of Psychotherapy* 31 (October 1977): 618–625.

STEVENS, R. N., AND HUTCHINSON, F. A. "A New Concept of Supervision is Tested." *Social Work* 1 (July 1956): 50–55.

STILES, E. "Supervision in Perspective." *Social Casework* 44 (January 1963): 19–25.

STINCHCOMBE, A. "Bureaucrats and Craft Administration of Production—A Comparative Study." *Administrative Science Quarterly* 4 (September 1965): 167–187.

SUESS, J. "Self-Confrontation of Videotaped Psychotherapy as a Teaching Device for Psychiatric Students." *Journal of Medical Education* 45 (1970): 271–282.

SUMNER, D. "An Experiment with Field Work in Generic Social Work." *Social Casework* 37 (June 1956): 288–294.

SWELL, L. "Role Playing in the Context of Learning Theory in Casework Teaching." *Journal of Education for Social Work* 4 (Spring 1968): 70–76.

SYTZ, F. "Teaching Recording." *Social Casework* 30 (December 1949): 399–405.

TAFT, J. "The Concepts of the Growth Process Underlying Social Work Practice." *Social Casework* 31 (October 1950): 311–318.

TANNAR, V. "Student Problems in Field Work in a Public Assistance Agency." *The Family* 25 (January 1945): 345–350.

TAUBER, L. F. "Choice Point Analysis-Formulation, Strategy, Intervention, and Result in Group Process Therapy and Supervision." *International Journal of Group Psychotherapy* 28 (April 1978): 163–184.

TAYLOR, R., *et al.* "The Self-Education of Psychiatric Residents." *American Journal of Psychiatry* 128 (1972): 106–111.

TAYNOR, J., *et al.* "A Brief Program to Upgrade the Skills of Community Caregivers." *Community Mental Health Journal* 12 (Spring 1976): 13–19.

THIEMANN, B., AND BATTLE, M. *Developing a System of Social Work Specialization.* Washington, D.C.: National Association of Social Workers, 1975.

THOMAS, G. R. "Intraorganizational Influences on Supervisory Functions—Some Practice Implications for Professional Social Workers." *Arete* 2 (Fall 1973): 169–184.

THOMAS, M. "Supervisors, Faculty, and Students Exchange Ideas." *The Family* 19 (May 1938): 89–90.

TISCHLER, G. L. "The Beginning Resident and Supervision." *Archives of General Psychiatry* 19 (October 1968): 418–422.

TITCHENER, J., *et al.* "Observing Psychotherapy—An Experience in Faculty-Resident Relations." *Comprehensive Psychiatry* 9 (1968): 392–399.

TOWLE, C. *The Learner in Education for the Professions as Seen in Education for Social Work.* Chicago: University of Chicago Press, 1954.

———. "Role of Supervision in the Union of Cause and Function in Social Work." *Social Service Review* 36 (December 1962): 396–411.

———. "The Place of Help in Supervision." *Social Service Review* 37 (December 1963): 403–415.

TSUNEKO, A., *et al.* "Establishing Group Supervision in a Hospital Social Work Department." *Social Work* 12 (October 1967): 54–60.

TUFTS, J. *Education and Training for Social Work.* New York: Russell Sage Foundation, 1923.

VAUGHAN, M., AND MARKS, J. N. "Teaching Interviewing Skills to Medical Students—a Comparison of Two Methods." *Medical Education* 10 (May 1976): 170–175.

VELDMAN, D., AND PECK, R. "Student Teacher Characteristics from the Pupil's Viewpoint." *Journal of Educational Psychology* 54 (1963): 346–355.

VITNER, R. "Analysis of Treatment Organizations." *Social Work* 8 (July 1963): 5–15.

VOLKAN, V., AND HAWKINS, D. "The Learning Group." *American Journal of Psychiatry* 128 (1972): 111–117.

WADDINGTON, M. "The Student Unit—Some Problems and Psychological Implications." *Social Casework* (March 1949): 113–117.

WALKER, H. "The Aide in Action—Problems of Treatment and Supervision." *The Family* 14 (December 1933): 281–300.

WANDO, J. S. "Supervision by Objectives—A Management Content Base for Trainers." Paper presented at Council on Social Work Education Annual Program Meeting, Atlanta, Ga., 1974.

WASSERMAN, H. "Early Careers of Professional Social Workers in a Public Welfare Agency." *Social Work* 15 (July 1970): 93–101.

———. "The Professional Social Worker in a Bureaucracy." *Social Work* 16 (January 1971): 89–95.

WATSON, K. "Differential Supervision." *Social Work* 18 (November 1973): 80–88.

WAX, J. "The Pros and Cons of Group Supervision." *Social Casework* 40 (June 1959): 307–313.

———. "Time-Limited Supervision." *Social Work* 8 (July 1963): 37–43.

WEDEL, K. R., AND PRESS, A. "Expectations for Field Learning—An Initial Assessment." *Journal of Social Welfare* 4 (Spring 1977): 5–14.

WEINBERG, G. "Dynamics and Content of Group Supervision." *Child Welfare* 39 (June 1960): 1–6.

WEISS, S. S., AND FLEMING, J. "Evaluation of Progress in Supervision." *Psychoanalytic Quarterly* 44 (1975): 191–205.

WENZEL, K. *Curriculum Guides for Undergraduate Field Instruction.* New York: Council on Social Work Education, 1972.

———. *Undergraduate Field Instruction Programs: Current Issues and Predictions.* New York: Council on Social Work Education, 1972.

WEST, L. "Future of Psychiatric Education." *American Journal of Psychiatry* 130 (1973): 521–528.

WHATCOTT, W. "Bureaucratic Focus and Service Delivery." *Social Work* 19 (July 1974): 432–437.

WIDEN, P. "Organizational Structure for Casework Supervision." *Social Work* 7 (October 1962): 78–85.

WIJNBERG, M. H., AND SCHWARTZ, M. C. "Models of Student Supervision— The Apprentice, Growth and Role Systems Models." *Journal of Education for Social Work* 13 (Fall 1977): 107–113.

WILENSKY, H. L., AND LEBEAUX, C. N. *Industrial Society and Social Welfare.* New York: Free Press, 1965.

WILLIAMSON, M. *Supervision—New Patterns and Processes.* New York: Association Press, 1961.

WILSON, G., AND RYLAND, G. *Social Group Work Practice.* Boston: Houghton Mifflin Co., 1949.

WOLKON, G. H., *et al.* "Personality Changes and Compatibility in the Psychiatric Resident–Supervisor Relationship." *Journal of Medical Education* 53 (January 1978): 59–63.

YEARND, J. "Credo of a Supervisor." *The Family* (February 1937): 342–344.

YOUNG, M. "Supervision—a Worm's Eye View." *The Family* 11 (April 1930): 44–47.

YOUNG, R. "Supervision: Challenges for the Future." Paper presented at Mid-Winter Supervisors' Institute, Family Service Association of America, Philadelphia, Pa., March 1971.

ZETZEL, E. "The Dynamic Basis of Supervision." *Social Casework* 34 (1953): 143–149.

Index